Women Nobel Peace Prize Winners

ALSO BY ANITA PRICE DAVIS

North Carolina During the Great Depression:
A Documentary Portrait of a Decade
(McFarland, 2003)

Women Nobel Peace Prize Winners

ANITA PRICE DAVIS
and MARLA J. SELVIDGE

Foreword by Regina Birchem

McFarland & Company, Inc., Publishers
Jefferson, North Carolina, and London

All photographs of Nobel Peace Prize winners are © The Nobel Foundation.
Used with permission.

LIBRARY OF CONGRESS CATALOGUING-IN-PUBLICATION DATA

Davis, Anita Price.
Women Nobel Peace Prize winners / Anita Price Davis and
Marla J. Selvidge ; foreword by Regina Birchem.
p.   cm.
Includes bibliographical references and index.

ISBN-13: 978-0-7864-2399-6
softcover : 50# alkaline paper ∞

1. Pacifists—Biography.   2. Nobel Prizes—History.
3. Women and peace—History.   4. Peace—Awards—History.
I. Selvidge, Marla J., 1948–   II. Title.
JZ5540.D38 2006   303.6'6079—dc22   2005036351

British Library cataloguing data are available

On the cover: *Background:* ©2006 PhotoSpin; *center:* Emily Greene Balch;
clockwise from top: Bertha Sophie Felicita von Suttner,
Wangari Muta Maathai, Aung San Suu Kyi,
Rigoberta Menchú Tum, Mother Teresa (Agnes G. Bohjaxhiu)

Manufactured in the United States of America

McFarland & Company, Inc., Publishers
Box 611, Jefferson, North Carolina 28640
www.mcfarlandpub.com

To the first peacemakers in our lives, our mothers:

Nell Daves Price Burns
and
Mary M. Gilreath Selvidge

Acknowledgments

Many thanks from Anita Price Davis to Annika Ekdah, Public Relations Manager of the Nobel Foundation in Stockholm; Annika has been an indispensable consultant and participant in the project. Regina Birchem, International President of Women's International League for Peace and Freedom, has given us her valuable time in reading the manuscript and her expertise in writing the foreword. We are extremely grateful. Anita also wishes to thank Shannon Wardlow, Mark Collier, Becky Poole and Wade Woodward for their friendship and reference help with the project. The faculty, staff and administration—particularly Katharine Slemenda and Thomas R. McDaniel—of Converse College never fail to encourage and provide support for research and writing. As always, Anita acknowledges her church and her family—Buren (her husband of 43 years), Robbie and Stacey (her loving attorney son and beautiful attorney daughter-in law), and little grandson Evan (three years old)—who listen, love and look past the flaws in their very human family member. Anita gives special thanks to Marla—her colleague, friend and co-writer—as they begin their twenty-first year of confidences, collaboration and camaraderie.

Marla J. Selvidge would like to thank Heather Lillard, her student assistant at the Center for Religious Studies, and the interlibrary loan wizard Vanessa Chappell at Central Missouri State University for their wonderful efforts in discovering and obtaining resources used in writing this book. Most importantly, she would like to thank her companion and husband, Thomas C. Hemling, Ph.D., who gave up vacations and weekends so that she could do this project. And lastly, many thanks to Anita Price Davis, a jewel of a friend, who kept this project alive!

Table of Contents

Foreword
by Regina Birchem

It is 100 years since the Nobel Prize for Peace was first presented to a woman—Bertha von Suttner, who was responsible for planting the idea of a peace prize in the mind of Alfred Nobel. In 2004 the award was given, for the first time, to an African woman, Wangari Muta Maathai, known for planting trees in Kenya and for her distinction of linking peace among human beings with a peaceful and harmonious relationship with nature.

The authors of *Women Nobel Peace Prize Winners* skillfully reveal for us the personal lives, and the courage expressed in diverse and inspiring ways, of the 12 women who over the past century have received the Nobel Peace Prize. Of the hundreds of peace prizes awarded annually, the Nobel is the highest honor. It calls attention globally to the longing and necessity for human beings to find the path of peaceful and just co-existence. It honors those who put aside fear, discouragement, personal risks and dangers to commit their lives to achieving that goal. One is tempted to remark, also, that among all the Nobel peace laureates, the 12 women Nobel laureates are notably consistent in struggling with integrity toward that goal.

As we learn from both recorded history and oral traditions, women in many cultures have found ways to work together to resolve conflicts. Many continue to risk their lives for peace and for an end to war. They organize in their communities, across national boundaries, across political, religious and ethnic barriers. Their humiliation and violation by rape and disfigurement are often used as a weapon of war.

Dr. Maathai said in her Nobel acceptance speech (December 10, 2004), "Although this prize comes to me, it acknowledges the work of countless individuals and groups across the globe. They work quietly and often without recognition to protect the environment, promote democracy, defend human rights and ensure equality between men and women. By doing so, they plant seeds of peace."

To meet and know some of these women has been a remarkable experience of my life. This was first as a young woman living in an intentional community (in which everything is shared in common). And, later in life, as a member of Women's International League for Peace and Freedom (WILPF), an organization spanning borders, uniting women of peaceful and warring nations, removing the barriers to permanent and lasting peace. It was founded—or its vision born—nine months after the outbreak of World War I, during a time when the world was "hypnotized in blood" (Generations of Courage, 2004, WILPF-US Section).

The origin of WILPF is intimately connected with the lives of two Nobel Prize winners described in this book: Jane Addams and Emily Greene Balch. They were social reformers and pioneers and members of the distinguished and large international union of suffragists in the early 1900s. When the war broke out in Europe with deadly fury, they saw that it was threatening to destroy all they had tried to achieve in bettering the life of the poor, especially immigrants, and securing women's right to vote.

Dr. Aletta Jacobs (1854–1919), one of the first women university students and the first woman physician in the Netherlands, called for a Congress of Women in The Hague to find a way to end the hostilities. There had been peace congresses in the past. For example, those Bertha von Suttner was instrumental in organizing one in Vienna. This was the first time women from neutral and warring nations came together. More than 1100 attended and sometimes as many as 2000 crowded in the largest room available at The Hague—which happened to be at the zoo. It was not called a "peace congress" but an International Congress of Women.

Representatives of more than 150 organizations and women from 12 countries gathered. In spite of the difficulty of many languages and divergent views, the women were united against the war. They voted to adopt 20 resolutions, such as:

> We women, in International Congress assembled, protest against the madness and horror of war, involving as it does a reckless sacrifice of human life and the destruction of so much that humanity has labored through the centuries to build up.
> This International Congress of Women ... urges the governments of the world to put an end to this bloodshed, and to begin peace negotiations. It demands that the peace which follows shall be permanent and therefore based on principles of justice.

The women also demanded equal political and social rights.

> Since the combined influence of women of all countries is one of the strongest forces in the prevention of war ... this Congress ... demands their political enfranchisement.

Women's suffrage did not bring an end to war. The organization founded at this International Congress of Women, WILPF, continued through World War II, the wars in Vietnam and Korea, and the so-called low intensity wars in Asia and Latin America. Today the organization unites with many other groups to oppose the Iraq war and violent conflicts elsewhere, whether declared as war or not. Establishing the conditions for a permanent peace is linked to economic justice, racial justice and gender equity, with a healthy and respectful co-existence with nature.

Jane Addams and Emily Greene Balch were awarded the Nobel Peace Prize for their international work as WILPF members to promote and build peace. Alva Myrdal, Nobel recipient in 1982, is said to have been a lifelong member of WILPF's Swedish Section.

Though their awards were not given for work with WILPF, Nobel Peace Prize winner (1962) Linus Pauling, whose pacifism was inspired by his wife Ava, was a WILPF member and sponsor, as was Martin Luther King, who won the award in 1964. According to Pauling, "My wife had been interested in social, political and economic problems ever since she was a teenage girl.... I'm sure that if I had not married her, I would not have had this aspect of my career—working for world peace. It was her influence on me and her continued support that caused me to continue. In fact, I have said that during the McCarthy period when many people gave up, especially scientists, I continued because I had to retain the respect of my wife" (Linus Pauling Interview: Conversations with History, 1983. Institute of International Studies, Berkeley).

Sean MacBride, Nobel Peace Prize recipient in 1974 and 1977 Lenin Prize winner (also 1961–75 President of Amnesty International and Secretary General of the International Commission of Jurists, 1963–70), claimed to be the oldest living WILPF member before his death in 1988. He always identified with WILPF. His mother was president of the Irish Section between the wars, and because he was a toddler, "dragged him" to WILPF meetings and demonstrations.

Others among the women peace prize laureates championed causes which WILPF also supported. For example, Jody Williams has worked for a treaty to ban land mines, and Wangari Maathai addressed the impact of military activities on the environment and sustainable development at the Earth Summit in 1992. Our concerns coincide in advocating for a free and democratic Burma and for the safety and freedom of Aung San Suu Kyi. WILPF sections throughout the world have supported non-violent initiatives in Ireland, exposed the violence against indigenous peoples in Guatemala and Latin America, and provided sanctuary for refugees.

Regina Birchem, International President of the Women's International League of Peace and Freedom

The authors of *Women Nobel Peace Prize Winners* beautifully describe the lives of 12 women who did not expect to become famous by their work for peace and justice. Emily Greene Balch was surprised that many people even knew about her.

All these women worked with others; none worked in isolation. All met derision, threats, deprivation, discouragement, and opposition of some kind during their lives. It is very sobering to recall that even today, at the time of writing this book, Aung San Suu Kyi is still under house arrest.

Women take great risks to remove the barriers to peace. In Colombia under threats from government and armed military factions, their work for peace and protection of the displaced families is considered a reason for death threats. In Palestine and Israel, women defy the occupation and the divisive checkpoints and walls. In Sri Lanka, Nepal, Burundi and Sierra Leone, WILPF members work in solidarity with others and refuse to accept ethnic, religious and political barriers between groups. They work amidst extreme poverty, with few resources, and are often not taken seriously or included in negotiations.

Emily Greene Balch closed her Nobel lecture, "Toward Human Unity or Beyond Nationalism," with the words:

> As the world community develops in peace, it will open up great untapped reservoirs in human nature. Like a spring released from pressure would be the response of a generation of young men and women growing up in an atmosphere of friendliness and security, in a world demanding of their service, offering them comradeship, calling to all adventurous and forward-reaching natures.
>
> We are not asked to subscribe to any utopia or to believe in a perfect world just around the corner. We are asked to be patient with necessarily slow and groping advance on the road forward, and to be ready for each step ahead as it becomes practicable. We are asked to equip ourselves with courage, hope, readiness for hard work, and to cherish large and generous ideals.

Preface

"Death will be no more;
mourning and crying and pain will be no more...."
[Rev. 21:4 NRSV]

What is peace? The obvious answer is "a cessation of fighting." The killing stops. People plant their gardens with hope in their hearts and begin to engage in healthy, productive lives. Security reigns. Peace, then, implies tranquility in the land, fraternity among nations, the reduction of standing armies, and a feeling of calm and repose among citizens.

War, however, may be enduring and peace may be elusive. The psychological effects of wars leave their marks on battered family members, incapacitated survivors, and disillusioned young men and women whose lives have been shattered by the gun. Death can devastate a family economically. The very soldiers who fought so valiantly for their country may end up on the "soup line" because jobs are not waiting for them when they return home. Mairead Corrigan and Betty Williams, Nobel Peace Prize recipients in 1976, can testify to the personal and corporeal side effects of violence that psychologically and economically crippled Northern Ireland for decades.

The Norwegian Nobel Committee selected its first Nobel Peace Prize Winner in 1901 and—except for times of war—it has presented the award annually. In its wisdom, the committee has awarded peace prizes to 12 women in the last 100 years.

These 12 women recognized that human beings are often the victims of exploitation by neighbors, governments, religions, enemies, families, employers (or Big Business), terrorists, dictators, kings and queens, and others who seek to take advantage. Such exploitation is a never-ending war against humanity itself. It is a modern form of enslavement.

When human beings use other human beings unfairly, they declare war on another's livelihood, health, and even life expectancy. There is also the obvious physical destruction that takes place. The effects of such war can last for generations.

Alva Myrdal, a 1982 recipient of the Peace Prize, understood that the only way to begin ending massive physical destruction was to destroy armaments, nuclear armaments. Emily Greene Balch, winner of the 1946 Prize, stood with thousands of other women who worked for peace, The Women's International League for Peace and Freedom. The name of the organization says it all: War is slavery and peace is freedom.

Jody Williams, Nobel Laureate of 1999, heading the International Campaign to Ban Landmines, demonstrated that war can affect people for years after the cessation of the

organized fighting. Princess Diana, another advocate of banning and destroying landmines, reported that 800 people died each month from the terrible injuries that landmines
cause and that another 1200 suffer devastating injuries. Estimates are that as many as 30
million landmines may still be in Afghanistan. Even though major conflicts have ended,
every time a farmer digs up a mine or a child steps on one, a life or body part can be lost.

War costs money. Governments expend exponential sums on wars that devastate cultures and their foundations. Education, health, and the physical infrastructures of countries at war suffer damage—which is sometimes irrevocable. Sustaining arms and an army
also takes away from funds that could be used to improve living and working conditions
of the unfortunate. Both Jane Addams, 1931 recipient, and Mother Teresa, 1979 Nobel
Peace Prize winner, spent their entire lives wrestling with the problems of the poor.

Aung San Suu Kyi (1991) believes that striving for peace is a way of striving for per-
fection. It is a religious struggle for her. She recognizes that we are all part of the family
of the earth and we must take responsibility for our brothers and sisters. As she put it,
"To live the full life, one must have the courage to bear the responsibility of the needs of
others." When one recognizes the needs and rights of others, then equity and democracy
must be the foundation of a society.

Both Wangari Matthai (2004) and Shirin Ebadi (2003) have risked their lives to fos-
ter democracy in their own countries. Imperialism, a motivator behind colonial wars and
the domination of African countries, had left Kenya ecologically devastated. Educating
people about reclaiming the land was Matthai's peaceful and successful method of address-
ing the ecological issue while also helping Kenyans to reclaim their own lives and freedom. Ebadi, in the face of death threats, tirelessly works for equality in Iran by helping
to re-examine the new regime's legal code that discriminates against a huge segment of
her society.

Most of us hope for peace. We close our eyes and wish that the effects of the wars
did not penetrate our lives. The three great monotheistic religious traditions of Judaism,
Christianity and Islam tell stories about a hope for a future life of peace. The Book of
Revelation, one of the most violent books in the Bible, ends with a cessation of fighting
and the absence of tears: "Death will be no more; mourning and crying and pain will be
no more..." (Rev. 21:4 NRSV).

Alfred Nobel
and the Peace Prize

"Promote the fraternity of nations, the abolition of armies, and the formation and increase of Peace Congresses."

Alfred Bernard Nobel

He collapsed at the desk. In those last moments, when he cried out for help, no one understood him because he spoke in Swedish. Some servants found him and carried him to a comfortable bedroom where an Italian physician quickly determined that the elderly man had suffered a cerebral hemorrhage—a stroke; parts of his brain were destroyed (Halasz, 210). On December 10, 1896, three days after his stroke, he died (Sechrist, x).

Who was this man who died? Was he a beggar? Was he a hired man like the servants who found him? Did he receive a pauper's burial?

The man was Alfred Bernard Nobel (October 21, 1833–December 10, 1896), one of the richest men in the world. Nobel's final death struggle—like his life—contained many contradictions. He was a multi-millionaire; yet with all his money, Alfred Nobel was without the comfort of a single close friend or relative in his last hours. He hated noise and yet he made his fame through inventing materials that produced thunderous explosions (Evlanoff, *Alfred Nobel*, 182).

Ironically, Alfred Nobel had read his obituary about seven years before he died. In April 1888, his brother Ludvig (Ludwig) Nobel (1831–88) had died; a French reporter confused the two brothers and declared in the paper that Alfred Nobel was dead (Bankston, 7; Halasz, 3; Binns, 10).

Seeing the write-up, of course, surprised Alfred. The content, however, saddened Alfred and brought about his self-evaluation. The obituary mentioned that Alfred Nobel had invented dynamite and blasting gelatin; the writer referred to Nobel as "the merchant of death." Alfred had always hoped that his explosives would serve useful purposes for the world and that the land mines, dynamite, and other weapons of destruction made from them would deter warfare and bring about peace. Now he began to consider how his actual obituary might read (Evlanoff, *Alfred Nobel*, 5). Nobel hoped that he might leave a legacy that would reveal the truth about him and make known his hopes and dreams (Halasz, 4).

Composing a biography of Alfred Nobel or even a complete, accurate obituary would be a daunting task for any writer. There are several reasons for this: Written information about Nobel is limited, Nobel wrote no complete autobiography, he kept no diary, and the language barriers of Nobel's many countries of residence make it difficult for most people to gather enough information to give a complete picture of the private man.

Henricksson notes that the Nobels did not seem interested in the history of their family and left few notes to help researchers. Alfred Nobel adopted the same attitude towards the interest of posterity. He was most reserved about himself, and "data about his life and work have had to be drawn chiefly from technical archives which are now preserved in the Nobel Foundation" (Henricksson, 35).

Nobel had written very modestly to his long-time friend Bertha Kinsky von Suttner: "What shall I tell you of myself—a shipwreck of youth, of joy, of hope? An empty heart whose inventory is only a white or gray page" (Halasz, 182).

Even his brother Ludwig had difficulty composing a biographical write-up about his brother Alfred. Nobel responded to one request by saying: "Owing to pressure of business I am just now compelled to put off pressing duties and conclusion of contracts for weeks, sometimes even for months. In these circumstances it is quite impossible for me to write biographies..." (Henricksson, 35).

Nobel continued, "Why do you want to torment me with biographical essays? No one reads essays except those about actors and murderers, and preferably the latter..." (Halasz, 179; Henricksson, 35).

Ludwig continued to ask Alfred to comply with his request. Alfred at last wrote:

A.N.: His miserable existence should have been terminated at birth by a humane doctor as he drew his first howling breath. Principal virtues: keeping his nails clean and never being a burden on anyone. Principal faults: that he has no family, is bad tempered and has poor digestion. One and only wish: not to be buried alive. Greatest sin: that he does not worship Mammon. Important event in his life: none. Is that not enough and more than enough? And what is there in our time that could properly deserve the title "important event"? [Halasz, 179; Henricksson, 35].

In 1893, when Alfred learned that he would receive an honorary Doctor of Philosophy degree, he did compose a meager life summary. After mentioning his birth and his work (devoting "himself particularly to applied chemistry and ... explosives"), he noted that he had been a part of the Royal Society of London, the Society of "Ingenieurs Civils in Paris" (since 1884), the Royal Swedish Academy of Science (since 1880), a knight of the Order of the Polar Star, and an officer of the Legion of Honor. He mentioned his "sole publication" was a paper in the English language, which brought an award of a silver medal. The biographer Henricksson mentioned that because of "the reticence which [Nobel] maintained regarding himself, a biography can only be fragmentary. Of extensive periods of his life nothing is known" (Henricksson, 36).

Like written information on the man, even likenesses of Alfred Nobel are few. When his nephew asked Alfred to sit for Makoffsky, a Russian painter, Alfred responded: "as soon as God the Father ... makes my carcass thirty years younger, so that it is worthy the oil and canvas, I shall sit ... and present posterity with a futile representation of my interesting, beautiful and remarkable hog-bristle beard..." (Halasz, 180).

Alfred was 63 when he died. He had lived longer than his brother Ludwig, who died at age 57 and whose obituary erroneously listed Alfred's name (Bankston, 7; Binns 101–02). The death of Ludwig at an age younger than Alfred's was another irony. When Alfred had been born to Caroline Andriette Ahlsell (called "Caroline," according to Evlanoff, *Alfred Nobel*, on page 14, and called "Andriette," according to Bankston on page 14) and Immanuel Nobel on October 21, 1833, in Stockholm, Sweden, Alfred's parents had feared for his life. He was a weak child, and they worried about his being in the cold, drafty house. The year before his birth, their home had caught fire and it was only through the "quick, courageous action" of his mother that the family members survived (Evlanoff, *Alfred Nobel*, 14). In addition to this misfortune, a barge carrying Alfred's father's materials had sunk and a project had gone wrong. The family had had to declare bankruptcy in 1817, and the current dwelling at the time of Alfred's birth was not the best environment for a sickly child (Evlanoff, *Alfred Nobel*, 14; Binns, 7–8, 102).

Alfred had come at a time when the family was less than able economically to care for another person (Halasz, 7). His father Immanuel, however, did not despair. He continued to work on his landmines and to develop a safe explosive to use to cut a canal at Suez, to improve road building, to improve mining, and to make life better and safer (Halasz, 8, 9). He designed rubber bags for the military; these containers would carry a mattress and life-saving devices. He managed to create his way out of a bad situation. It took Immanuel 17 years to pay off his indebtedness, but by 1834—the year after Alfred was born—Immanuel was able to pay "every farthing of it" (Evlanoff, *Alfred Nobel*, 14).

It is not surprising that Immanuel Nobel was interested in inventions. His ancestor was Olof Rudbeck, "the best-known technical genius of Sweden's seventeenth-century era as a Great Power in Northern Europe" (Frangsmyr, 5). The inventiveness of Immanuel was evident from the time he was a child. At the age of six he developed an "incendiary glass to use to light his father's pipe." When he was placed into a dark room for punishment, he devised inventions to pass the time (Evlanoff, *Alfred Nobel*, 13).

Immanuel moved to St. Petersburg, Russia, to try to improve the family's lifestyle. He opened a factory that specialized in mines, machine tools, and gun carriages; because the factory was successful, Immanuel was able to send for his wife and three sons (Bankston, 14). Another boy—Oscar Emil (October 1843–September 3, 1864)—would be born there, along with another child who died and another who was stillborn. According to Evlanoff in *Alfred Nobel*, Immanuel and Caroline would have eight children, but only three would reach the age of 21 (13).

At the age of 18, Alfred wrote a poem about his difficult childhood.

> My cradle looked a deathbed, and for years
> a mother watched with ever anxious care,
> so little chance, to save the flickering light,
> We find him now a boy. His weakness still
> makes him a stranger in the little world,
> wherein he moves. When fellow boys are playing
> he joins them not, a pensive looker-on
> [Binns, 13; Evlanoff, *Alfred Nobel*, 9;
> Halasz, 11–12].

Ironically, Alfred's lifespan exceeded that of his brother and many other people of the time (Bankston, 14).

Most of Alfred's studies were at home with his tutors and his brothers (Binns, 15; Halasz, 18). Despite having only two years of schooling outside his home (Sechrist, viii, says one year, and Feuerlicht, 13, says one year), Alfred—with the help of his tutors—became proficient in five languages: Swedish, Russian, English, French, and German (Bankston, 15; Halasz, 20). Because of his ability to communicate, because of his father's desire for Alfred to learn a trade, and perhaps because Immanuel Nobel hoped to glean information that might help the family business, Alfred's father sent his 16-year-old son to many countries to study (Meyer, *In Search of Peace*, 11). He spent 1850 to 1852 abroad (Levinovits, 6). The teenager went to England, France, New York, and Germany. He did visit Italy for a holiday, but most of his travels were strictly for business and education (Bankston, 17–19).

When he was just a teenager, he had a Russian gypsy woman read his palm. Although he professed that he did not believe in such palm readings, he seemed never able to forget her words. "'You will cross the widest oceans ... dwell in many lands. You will have such riches that you cannot count the pieces of gold you will own. But love will break your heart, and when you die ... you will be left alone without a gentle hand to stroke your brow, or a word of love to comfort you" (Evlanoff, *Alfred Nobel*, 185).

Unfortunately, there are no journals and diaries to document Alfred's travels. Nobel learned at this time—if not even earlier—about nitroglycerin. Frangsmyr remarks that "Strangely enough, this has not been pointed out by many scholars, who have dated the crucial moment 10 years later" (Frangsmyr, 6).

Alfred did write a poem later in his life about his disappointment as he viewed the Atlantic.

> I left in early youth my home for distant lands
> beyond the sea, but strange to say, even when the Ocean

spread its grandeur 'round, it struck me not as new—my
mind had pictured Oceans far more wide
[Bankston, 17; Halasz, 24].

Despite the ill health that remained a part of his entire life, Alfred always managed to work hard. He admitted he was never happier than when he was working (Binns, 7–8). The devotion to work seems to have run in the family. Even when Ludwig was sick and buyers tried to pay him for his oil business, he rejected their offer by saying, "You want me to convert my money into stock certificates and to buy shears for clipping coupons. But what I need is not only money—I need work!" (Evlanoff, *Alfred Nobel*, 53).

Alfred did find time to court a young girl. This was perhaps Alfred's first serious romance; this first infatuation was for a girl named Alexandra who lived in Russia and turned him down when he proposed (Evlanoff, *Alfred Nobel*, 62; Halasz, 28–29).

Alfred also became serious about a young woman in Paris. He wrote that he and the beautiful, pale, blonde-haired girl "...met again, and again and again." Alfred was devastated when she died of tuberculosis (Binns, 18). He wrote of his feelings about her death.

> ... my love is with the dead
> Nor was I there to soothe her last hours
> But came to gape upon a putrid corpse.
> ... From that hour
> I have not shared the pleasures of the crowd
> Nor moved in Beauty's eye compassion's tear
> [Evlanoff, *Alfred Nobel*, 62].

Alfred may have had two other infatuations in his life: Sophie Hess and Bertha Kinsky von Chinic und Tettau von Suttner. Even with Alfred's power and wealth, none of his relationships led to marriage. Alfred even tried to buy love. He later regretted this action and "found its nectar poisoned with its dregs," as a poem of his stated (Halasz, 25). Perhaps the person who loved him most was his mother. He wrote

> I had all that upon my bubble;
> Then it burst and left
> A drop of water
> [Halasz, 28].

A letter to his brother Ludwig may reveal one of the tangible reasons that future biographers sometimes attached a label of "lonely" to the entire life of Alfred Nobel. Another basis for this impression might be a letter to his sister-in-law (Henricksson, 52): "...I drift about without rudder or compass, a wreck on the sea of life; I have no memories to cheer me, no pleasant illusions of the future to comfort me ... I have no family to furnish the only kind of survival that concerns us; no friends for the wholesome development of my affection..." (Halasz, 180).

Evlanoff identifies a quote that Erik Bergengren found in a letter from Nobel: "I, like others, and perhaps more than others, feel the heavy weight of loneliness and for many a long year I have been seeking someone whose heart could find its way to mine" (Evlanoff, *Alfred Nobel*, 96).

Some of Nobel's biographers, however, caution against giving too much weight to "sentimental depictions of a lonely millionaire who—despite his wealth—was unhappy or at least deeply melancholic, emotionally attached to his mother, and with a few heart-rending love stories behind him" (Frangsmyr, 5). Frangsmyr admits that perhaps this picture is not altogether false, but such biographical "accounts are not so instructive. Romantic tales constitute a special genre, to which I shall not attempt to contribute" (Frangsmyr, 5).

Henricksson notes, "Nobel was one of the most complete optimists that have ever lived; an enthusiast who believed it possible that science could make men happy, and that everlasting peace would in the end supersede the barbarity of war" (Henricksson, 53).

Another irony in his life was that Alfred Nobel spent most of his adulthood working with his family on developing uses for the explosive nitroglycerin, a weapon of destruction (Binns, 29). The Italian chemist Ascanio Sobrero had found in 1847 that sulfuric acid, nitric acid, and glycerin produced an oily substance that was explosive and unstable; Sobrero had invented nitroglycerin (Bankston, 23–31; Evlanoff, *Alfred Nobel*, 30). The Nobels spent much of their adult lives studying this and other explosives.

During the Crimean War (which began in 1854), Russia called on the Nobels to help with their defense. The Nobels started to manufacture equipment and machines for obsolete vessels that the country was attempting to convert to steam-driven warships at the request of Nicholas I and the government. In 1855, however, Nicholas I died (Halasz, 33–35). With the end of the Crimean War in 1856, there was no longer a great need for war materials (Frangsmyr, 7).

When Alexander II came to rule, he informed the Nobels that the government had canceled all contracts to domestic enterprises and had contracted with foreign industry. When the government denied Immanuel's appeal to the government for indemnity, Immanuel had to declare bankruptcy again (Halasz, 36–37).

Alfred's chemistry teacher Niolaj Zinin gave some demonstrations with nitroglycerin to Alfred in 1855. Alfred was intrigued with the mixture. Although he had begun experimenting with nitroglycerin during the Crimean War, it would be more than a decade before a safe way to use it would be available (Halasz, 63).

In October 1863, Alfred Nobel received his patent for a new explosive. He called his explosive "blasting oil" (Frangsmyr, 7). He used first a lead tube (later a glass tube) and gunpowder in a cap with a fuse attached; when he lit the fuse, the gunpowder exploded and "blasted" the nitroglycerin (Bankston, 23–31; Evlanoff, *Alfred Nobel*, 42; Halasz, 45–46; 84; Frangsmyr, 7). According to Frangsmyr, Nobel wrote, "I am the first to have brought these subjects from the area of science to that of industry." He was also able to secure a loan from a French bank to help with his nitroglycerin experiments (Frangsmyr, 7).

On September 3, 1864, Emil Nobel and three workers (Meyer [p.13] and Bankston [p.44] say four) were experimenting with nitroglycerin in the building behind Immanuel's home; Immanuel and Caroline were having breakfast when an explosion rocked their home and frightened the populace of their neighborhood. Immanuel blamed himself for the disaster that killed Emil and the three workers (Halasz, 55–58). About a month later, on October 6, Immanuel suffered a stroke and a blood clot paralyzed him. Caroline nursed her husband, who was incapable of the slightest movement (Halasz, 63).

Nobel found that by mixing the nitro with a clay-like substance called kieselguhr earth, the nitroglycerin would not explode until he was ready (Bankston, 23–31; Evlanoff, *Alfred Nobel*, 42; Halasz, 45–46; 84). Kieselguhr earth was a diatomaceous material (diatomite) formed by fossils being pressed together over millions of years. Alfred called his new invention of nitroglycerin and kieselguhr "dynamite" (Halasz, 84). In 1867, Alfred Nobel received patents from Britain, the United States (Binns, page 51, says 1868), and Sweden (Frangsmyr, 9) for his "paste" that only a blasting cap could cause to explode.

It was ironic that it was Alfred Nobel who invented dynamite from the nitroglycerin because his older brothers and his father had worked with explosives longer than he. Yet it was Alfred who secured a British patent for the explosive dynamite in 1867 and the American patent in 1868 (Binns, 101; Henricksson gives the date as 1865 on page 38). The explosive nitroglycerin caused many accidents—including the forementioned death of Emil Nobel. Alfred was able to say truthfully, however, that "whilst nitro-glycerin with a small sale gave rise to many accidents, dynamite in spite of a large trade has caused none" (Binns, 51).

In 1868, the Swedish Academy of Science presented jointly to Alfred and Immanuel Nobel the Letterstedt Prize. The gold medal was "for outstanding original work in the realm of art, literature and science, or for important discoveries of practical value for mankind" (Halasz, 9). Frangsmyr suggests that one "can hear an echo of this wording in Nobel's will, where he stated the criteria for awarding his own prizes" (Frangsmyr, 9). Alfred resented the fact that his father kept the prize in his home (Halasz, 85).

On the eighth anniversary of Emil's death, September 3, 1872, Immanuel died. Evlanoff speculated that "emotion caused by these reminiscences may have brought on the fatal heart attack" (Evlanoff, *Alfred Nobel*, 37). Caroline asked Alfred not to offend the memory of Immanuel by taking the medal before she herself died. Alfred allowed the medal to remain in her home (Halasz, 86).

Caroline remained in good health. Her son Alfred never forgot to honor his mother with money and with love. Her letters to Alfred often acknowledged his correspondence and gifts.

> [Y]our [Christmas] telegram and then the dear letter I had so longed for; they both came from my dear son, who in his indefatigable goodness never forgets at a festival to add to the joys of the young and old. ... There is plenty here for me, all of which I owe to the industrious work of my dear Alfred ... [Halasz, 106; Sohlman, 5–6].

When Caroline Nobel died on December 7, 1889, Alfred asked for her portrait, some items he had given her, and the Letterstedt Prize, which Caroline had kept in a case since before the death of Immanuel (Halasz 85–86, 125, 211, 214).

By 1876, Alfred Nobel (in Paris) realized that he needed help with his accounts and correspondence. He needed also someone who could speak several languages. He decided to place an advertisement in the papers (Bankston, 36–37). The ad stated:

> A very wealthy, cultured, elderly gentleman living in Paris, desires to find a lady also of mature years, familiar with languages, as secretary and manager of his household [von Suttner, *Memoirs, Volume I*, 204; Halasz, 111].

Bertha Sofia Felitas Kinsky, who was 33 years old, answered the ad immediately. After a few more letters, he hired her! When she arrived in Paris, Bertha found that the elderly gentleman was not so elderly after all. He was only 44 and was the famous Alfred Nobel, the chemist who had patented dynamite (Bankston 36–37).

Bertha said that Alfred asked her if she was "fancy free." She told Alfred that she had come to Paris to forget Arthur von Suttner, whom she loved but whose family disapproved of her because she was seven years older than he and because she was not wealthy (Halasz, 117).

Alfred responded:

> "You have acted bravely; but be completely courageous, break off the correspondence also—then let a little time pass ... a new life, new impressions—and you will both forget—he perhaps even sooner than you!" [von Suttner, *Memoirs, Volume I*, 209; Meyer, *Dynamite and Peace*, 140].

The next day, Alfred had to leave town on business (Bankston 36–37). A week later, Bertha received two dispatches, one from Sweden and another from Vienna. Nobel had written from Sweden saying, "Arrived safely. Shall be back in Paris in week." Bertha's former sweetheart Arthur von Suttner had written the second telegram from Vienna. His telegram read, "I cannot live without thee!"

Bertha made a quick decision. She sold her last valuable possession (a diamond cross), paid her hotel bill, wrote to Nobel, and rushed back to Vienna to marry Arthur von Suttner. She continued her correspondence with Alfred for the rest of his life, however, and she and Arthur were even able to visit with Alfred upon several occasions. It was she who would help him to develop the idea for the Nobel Peace Prize and who would later become a recipient of the prestigious award.

Nobel, however, was "heartbroken and vulnerable" after Bertha's departure in 1876 (Bankston, 37, 44). Later that same year, Alfred entered a florist's shop to purchase flowers for his hostess for a business luncheon. There he met Sofie Hess, and they began an 18-year relationship (Halasz, 131; Bankston, 44). (Other biographers give different lengths to the relationship: 15 years, according to Bankston, 37; ten years, according to Evlanoff, *Alfred Nobel*, 153; and 18 years, according to Evlanoff, *Alfred Nobel*, 197.) His 216 letters to her (in the Nobel Institute) were a secret for many years (Halasz, 280). He often used a nickname for her ("The Troll") in his cash accounts (Evlanoff, *Alfred Nobel*, 145). Though they never married, Sophie was fond of calling herself "Madame Nobel of Nice" (Halasz, 206). The letters that Sophie saved indicate affection ("I send you a thousand hearty regards and best wishes" [Halasz, 151; Evlanoff, *Alfred Nobel*, 119]), the reprimands ("Sometimes one cannot find a reasonable sentence on half a page [from you]" [Halasz, 162]) and the exorbitant purchases made by Sophie and paid for by Alfred ("You want a villa in Ischl. Good. We buy it, and then? ... You will nag me to buy a villa in Reichenau, Villach, Gorz or Murzzuschlag—or God knows where..." [Halasz, 171]), and they mention Sophie's child with another (Bankston, 37). Nobel's letters comment on the child: "Your child is quite pretty. She must get a good education. I don't know your relation to the child's father ... it is not my business" (Halasz, 231). In 1895, Nobel wrote to Sophie to ask: "Is it true that the cavalry wants to marry you? If so, he would not only be doing the right thing but acting wisely as well" (Halasz, 231; Evlanoff, *Alfred Nobel*, 171). Nobel seemed aware that the relationship was not permanent when he wrote, "Everyone my age has the need to have someone around him to live for and to love. It was up to you to be that person, but you have done everything imaginable to make it impossible" (Evlanoff, *Alfred Nobel*, 149).

Sophie brought a suit against Alfred's estate after his death. Publicizing the scandal might have alienated the Swedish and Norwegian institutions that awarded the Nobel Prizes, belittled Alfred Nobel, and brought other repercussions. The settlement required that Sophie continue to receive her annual annuity; that Sophie turn over the letters, envelopes, and portrait of Nobel; and that she refrain from besmirching his memory. If Sophie did not comply with the stipulations, the result would be the cancellation of her annuities (Halasz, 279–80).

Other biographers have suggested that Alfred also enjoyed the companionship of the widow Juliette Adam (Evlanoff, *Alfred Nobel*, 80). Evlanoff, however, indicated that there was no romance between the two. Alfred might have frequented her salon because she was "clever, good-looking, educated, and possessed, in a large measure, that quality which French call *charme*." Another reason for his visits might have been because her salon made a convenient observation post for him (Evlanoff, *Nobel-Prize Donor*, 95; Evlanoff, *Alfred Nobel*, 80).

In a letter of October 1887, Alfred complained about his health to a friend:

For the last nine days I have been ill and have had to stay indoors with no other company than a paid footman; no one inquires about me. It seems to me that this time I am much worse and my physician believes it, for the pain (angina pectoris) is so persistent. It does not let up at all. And besides, my heart has become as heavy as lead. When at the age of fifty-four, one is left alone in the world, and a paid servant is the only person who has so far showed one the most kindness, then come heavy thoughts, heavier than most people can imagine. I can see in my valet's eyes how much he pities me [Halasz, 210].

Later he commented, "Weariness and illness gnaw at me, and often before I fall asleep I think how sad my end one day will be with only an old servant near my bed who keeps wondering, perhaps, whether I have remembered him in my will" (Halasz, 214).

Nobel's health worsened. In 1889 he wrote that he had "great things to think about, at least one great thing—the passing from light to darkness, from life into the eternal unknown, or, as Spencer calls it, the unknowable" (Henricksson, 56). Nobel went on to quote a line from the English poet Campbell: "Coming events cast their shadows before. It is especially the case with that event which puts a full stop to further events" (Henricksson, 56).

Nobel continued to correspond periodically with Bertha and Arthur. He warned her in a 1891 letter that "what you need is not money but a program. Mere resolutions will not secure peace."

In 1892 he hired Aristarkhi Bey, a Turkish ambassador, to help with a study of peace problems. In the winter of the same year, Alfred suggested to Bertha that he would like to allot part of his wealth to the founding of a prize. He envisioned awarding the prize every five years and for six times only. "[I]f we have failed in thirty years to reform the present system we shall inevitably fall back into barbarism. This prize would be awarded to the [one] ... who had done the most to advance the idea of general peace in Europe" (Meyer, *Dynamite and Peace*, 204). He suggested that the best solution for peace would be an organization that would allow all the governments to bind together and defend any attacked country. This seemed to be the cornerstone idea 30 years later for the League of Nations (Meyer, *Dynamite and Peace*, 204–05).

Aristarkhi Bey did not meet Alfred's expectations, however. When Aristarkhi suggested that they publish a periodical, Nobel reminded him that Bertha was already producing one and that those who read such a magazine were already proponents of peace (Evlanoff, *Nobel-Prize Donor*, 106–07).

After one year, Alfred dismissed Aristarkhi Bey with a letter. One section of the document stated, "I have faithfully carried out our year's experiment, but I see that you have failed to advance the cause even by one step" (Evlanoff, *Nobel-Prize Donor*, 107). When Aristarkhi tried to appeal, Alfred refused to enter into arbitration with Aristarkhi on the matter (Evlanoff, *Nobel-Prize Donor*, 109).

Arthur and Bertha von Suttner invited Alfred to the Peace Congress in Bern in 1892. Alfred did not commit himself to attending. Imagine their surprise when he arrived at their lodging in Switzerland. He cautioned them that he wanted to listen, but he wanted to remain "incognito, so to speak" (Meyer, *Dynamite and Peace*, 196–201). He urged Bertha von Suttner, "Inform me; convince me, and I will do something great for the movement" (Meyer, *Dynamite and Peace*, 199). Their serious talks continued over the next few days as they attended meetings, shared meals, and completed sightseeing visits.

In 1893 he wrote: "Two specialists, both idiots—ascribe my pains—one to rheumatic gout and the other to goutish rheumatism; this is nothing but jargon which does not explain to me why my heart beats like a horse" (Evlanoff, *Alfred Nobel*, 183). In 1894 he wrote that he was "almost in a worse way than before, as I have had the rheumatic devils paying a visit to the heart muscles or thereabouts ... and feel that at any moment eternity may be welcoming me with open arms" (Henricksson, 56).

Halasz editorializes that Alfred had "a terror of death and especially the terror of facing death alone." Halasz also speculates that Nobel "longed desperately for the presence of someone attached to him through ties of blood or of love..." (Halasz, 210).

Certainly the late 1880s and early 1890s posed many problems for Alfred Nobel. He found business associates were embezzling his funds and a government ruling that he could make no more explosives in France caused him to move his laboratories elsewhere (Halasz, 220–28). In April 1890, Nobel wrote to his nephew Emanuel about the situation.

> At the beginning of March Barbe and Freycinet began to dispute in parliament. Barbe behaved rather stupidly, and incurred a merited reprimand. But the unfortunate consequence is that the Government has ... prohibited me from manufacturing even the smallest amount of explosive, or possessing any kind of weapon for my shooting tests. This is pure chicanery; but as they threaten to put me in a fortress, which would have had the disadvantage of still further spoiling my digestion, I cannot resist or defy the prohibition.
> The delightful thing is that the War Minister, some days before he prohibited me from manufacturing explosives, himself asked me in writing to make him some samples.... It is not at all easy to move my laboratory abroad, quite apart from the considerable expense involved [Sohlman, 2–3].

Nobel wrote to Emanuel again on October 12, 1892, about this period of troubles.

> My position here [in Paris] is no longer what it once was; I am at daggers' points with all the co-directors I had to get rid of. The result is that I have had to acquire and keep a majority of the stock, which means 20,000 shares at 450 to 500 francs. Even if a few friends help me, it is nevertheless a tremendous parcel which I must be prepared to carry ... we are dealing with a pack of crooked lawyers and bloodsuckers [Halasz, 228].

Unfortunately, his troubles continued. Two English scientists, Sir James Dewar and Sir Fredrick Abel, claimed the invention of cordite and obtained patents in England and in several other countries on a modified form of nitroglycerine powder and nitro-cellulose (listed specifically in Nobel's patent). The two scientists who had worked with Nobel transferred their English patent rights to the British government (Henricksson, 41; Evlanoff, *Alfred Nobel*, 187). English government factories began turning out cordite, and Nobel brought a "friendly suit" to find out if they had infringed on his copyright. In 1894, Nobel had to pay $120,000 for the court costs, but he was "wounded" most by the fact that "a high court in Britain was insensible to a moral wrong and, in effect, rewarded it" (Halasz, 249). "Alfred Nobel bitterly resented the verdict, a fact which in all likelihood seriously affected his health. The pecuniary loss was ... subordinate [to] ... the feeling of having suffered an injustice and what he felt to be a disgraceful lack of appreciation for his achievements..." (Henricksson, 42).

Because Nobel very seldom sold his patents for a fixed sum, he insisted on a share in any enterprise employing his ideas. Alfred was aware that many inventors died in poverty; some sold all their rights to their own products for a "one-time" sum. Patent infringements, lawsuits, and legal battles were nothing new to Alfred Nobel; to a man who had 355 patents, some controversy was inevitable, but this struggle was particularly draining because his health was already failing (Evlanoff, *Alfred Nobel*, 179, 43).

Nitroglycerin, the same substance that brought destruction, was the prescribed medicine to use for Nobel's heart disease—hardening of the aorta—and to prolong his life. In a letter from Paris, where he had gone to consult with a famous heart specialist, Nobel noted, "[It] seems an irony of fate that they should be prescribing nitroglycerin internally for me! They call it trinktin, to avoid terrifying the chemists and the public" (Halasz, 253; Henricksson, 56–57; Meyer, *Dynamite and Peace*, 243).

On his return to his villa "Mon Nid" in San Remo, Italy (Evlanoff, *Alfred Nobel*, 191) ("Mio Nido" according to Sohlman, 3) and about two weeks before his death, Alfred wrote to Bertha von Suttner, responded to her question about his health, and identified another irony in his life: "'Feeling well?'—No, unhappily for me, I am not, and I am even consulting doctors, which is contrary not only to my custom, but also to my principle. I, who have a heart, figuratively speaking, have one organically, and I am conscious of it" (Halasz, 271). Equally ironic was the fact that even though Alfred Nobel was a rich man, no amounts of his nitroglycerin or of his wealth could extend his life when the end came for him.

Alfred came to San Remo in 1896 because of difficulties with the French government over his explosives (Meyer, *In Search of Peace*, 17). He was actually journeying to his death. When Alfred's good friend Dr. Nathan Söderblom, pastor of the Swedish church in Paris and a future Nobel Peace Prize winner, joined him in San Remo, it was not to visit but to conduct Alfred's short funeral service. Söderblom's sermon did not stress the wealth of Nobel; rather, it emphasized Nobel's life of loneliness and poor health—factors which all of Nobel's power and wealth could not change. Söderblom praised Nobel's warmhearted nature—a disposition that Nobel displayed to the end, yet his congenial disposition did not give Alfred the comfort of the presence of others at his death.

Alfred Nobel had a high appreciation of spiritual values. He feared that war might lead the masses to self-destruction and spiritual numbness. He saw his instruments of war as a way to ensure peace (Bankston, 7–8). "My factories may make an end to war sooner than your congresses.... The day when two Army corps can annihilate each other in one second, all civilized nations, it is hoped, will recoil from war and discharge their troops" (Bankston, 8). Before his death, however, Nobel would admit the error of instruments of war as a way to ensure peace. Instead, he professed that only knowledge could change people from warring creatures to those who would work for peace (Evlanoff, *Alfred Nobel*, 219). He remarked to an assistant that the explosives they were working on were "rather fiendish things" (Feuerlicht, 15). His love of peace, however, had became apparent when he was just a youth. He had written that he would "avoid disputes like the plague, even with people who give me every reason" (Evlanoff, *Alfred Nobel*, 218).

Nobel was a baptized, confirmed Lutheran in childhood. At times in his life he claimed to be an agnostic. As a mature adult, however, Nobel consistently and liberally supported the Swedish Church in Paris. Nobel was not miserly with his wealth as others might be. To Nobel, religion without deeds was not religion. Nathan Söderblom, pastor of the Swedish church in Paris, future Archbishop of Sweden, and future Nobel Peace Prize winner, once asked for a donation from Nobel. Nobel doubled the amount Söderblom requested; he attached a note saying that he realized "that insufficient help is practically the same as no help at all..." (Sohlman, 9–10). In later years, a friend and biographer, Prof. Henrik Schuck, described Nobel's God as one "of peace and all-embracing love for mankind," not "a cruel unjust ruler who was to blame for all religious wars and all persecution of other faiths" (Bergengren, 157–58).

Alfred Nobel frequently received requests for financial help. Nobel wrote:

Not a day passes without the mail bringing me at least two dozen such requests for help averaging about twenty thousand crowns. This amounts to at least seven million crown a year; enough to demoralize even J. Gould, Vanderbilt and Rothschild. I have long since come to the conclusion that it would have been preferable to have acquired a reputation for meanness than to have that of being ready to help. It always hurts me when I have to refuse and this happens so often that it takes up a large part of my rather limited time [Halasz, 147–48; Henricksson, 53].

The requests for financial aid continued. Alfred's friend Liedbeck, an engineer, was beginning to grow deaf and was shunning contact with others. Alfred wrote, "During the last few years the demands on my purse have been so heavy that I have been ... forced, in each of the last two years, to supplement it with a million francs [about $170,000 at the time] taken from my capital. One can go on like this for a time but not forever" (Halasz, 148).

Later, when Alfred contributed to the monument of "a great man," he accompanied his donation with a note: "My natural inclination is less to honor the dead, who feel nothing and must be indifferent to marble monuments, than to help the living" (Halasz, 148).

Perhaps this observation was an indication that Alfred was thinking of what he wanted to do and how he wanted to be remembered after his death. Frangsmyr, however, indicates that it was earlier (around 1864) that another personality trait became evident. About that time, Nobel became an entrepreneur and—in the opinion of Frangsmyr—he was "unbeatable" in that role (Frangsmyr, 8).

In 1875 he invented a blasting gelatin (nitroglycerin combined with gun cotton) that he called "rubber dynamite" (Opfell, viii). This invention could be used under water and was the forerunner of TNT. In 1887 (Opfell, on page viii, says 1888) he would invent still another weapon: a smokeless explosive for the military. He called this new invention *ballistite* and increased his income even more (Bankston, 23–35; Halasz, 109–110, 203, 207).

Evlanoff noted that Nobel's daily correspondence was often as many as 50 (Evlanoff, *Alfred Nobel*, 179) but was usually about 30 letters (Henricksson, 53) in "careful, flowing hand, and in whichever language befitted his correspondent." More of these were answers to "'begging letters' [rather] than responses to business queries, or his personal correspondence" (Evlanoff, *Alfred Nobel*, 179).

Söderblom was one of Nobel's best friends. Nobel's influence, in fact, resulted in Söderblom's dedication to peace. Yet this good friend was not there when Nobel needed him before his death on December 10, 1896.

A telegram arrived in San Remo. The cable announced that Stockholm bank officials, upon learning of the death of Alfred Nobel, had opened his last will and testament. The urgency of the contents necessitated a telegram to San Remo; the wire quoted Alfred Nobel's wishes for his remains immediately after his death: "It is my express will and injunction that my veins shall be opened after my death, and that when this has been done, and competent doctors have noted definite signs of death, my body shall be cremated" (Halasz, 273).

Nobel's memorial service was in the church in Stockholm two weeks after his death. His burial was in the church cemetery beside his parents and his brother. In death, as in life, the important place of his immediate family was evident to others.

As a last contradiction, Nobel's name after death will be forever associated with peace although he built his life around nitroglycerin, dynamite, and gunpowder—items of destruction. It was he, Alfred Bernard Nobel, who established the Nobel Peace Prize with earnings from the invention of dynamite and explosives, often used for destruction, not specifically for peace. Meyer describes this contradiction as "outrageous" (Meyer, *In Search of Peace*, 23).

The Nobel Peace Prize may not have been Nobel's original idea; it may have been the brainchild of Bertha von Suttner, the woman who had served as a secretary to Nobel for less than a month. For 25 years she wrote letters and was finally able to convince the wealthy Nobel to do something for peace in a troubled world (Meyer, *In Search of Peace*, 18).

However, Evlanoff said that Bertha's contention that she aroused his interest in pacifism and the Nobel Peace Prize was incorrect. According to Evlanoff, peace had always occupied Alfred Nobel's mind (Evlanoff, *Alfred Nobel*, 154).

His last will, which was hardly more than a page, was not a first draft. Alfred had re-written it several times and had finally signed it on November 27, 1895, at the Swedish-Norwegian Club in Paris (Frangsmyr, 11–12). Nobel ordered the investment of his ten million dollar estate and interest from the investments should go to prizes for those who had done the greatest services to the world (Bankston, 39). The chief executor of Nobel's will was Sohlman, the Swedish chemist that Nobel had hired in 1893 and one of his biographers (Bergengren, 121).

The fact that Nobel left his wealth to others should not have surprised anyone who really knew him. He had written earlier, "I am a misanthrope and yet utterly benevolent, have more than one screw loose yet am a super-idealist who digests philosophy more efficiently than food" (Frangsmyr, 11).

The last version of his wills, kept in a Stockholm bank, bequeathed his fortune to those people and groups who had benefited humanity through science (physics, chemistry, physiology or medicine, and the economic sciences), literature, and peace. The purpose of the designation "to benefit humanity" was to encourage world peace and progress (Frangsmyr, 11–12).

The will specified that a five-person committee designated by the parliament of Norway would choose the recipient of the Nobel Peace Prize. Swedish committees, however, selected the winners of his other prizes. Why he specified different countries for his five awards is unclear even though the two countries were united when Nobel was writing his will. The distinction seems even more puzzling when one considers that Nobel's native country was Sweden—not Norway (Levinovitz, 164–65; Halasz, 274–75).

Nobel's will provided: "[O]ne share to the person who shall have the most or best promoted the fraternity of nations and the abolition ... of standing armies and the formation and increase of Peace Congresses.... [The Nobel Prize for Peace] shall be awarded ... by a committee of five persons.... I declare it to be my express desire that, in the awarding of prizes, no consideration whatever be paid to the nationality of the candidates, that is to say, that the most deserving be awarded the prize, whether he or she be a Scandinavian or not..." (Halasz, 278; Meyer, *In Search of Peace*, 21; Opfell, viii–ix; Evlanoff, *Alfred Nobel*, 193).

Nobel was indeed a wealthy man. When he asked a servant who was getting married what she desired, she said that she wanted "as much as Monsieur Nobel himself earns in one day." He wrote her a check for 40,000 francs—over $100,000 (Bankston, 39).

Despite his financial ability to have employed a well-trained lawyer, Nobel wrote his own last will and testament. Interestingly, Nobel, who had such a vast knowledge of law, developed a document that some contested. For one thing, he failed to designate an heir (Halasz, 276). For another, the Swedish nationalists objected to the "international flavor" (Bankston, 41). In fact, Meyer described naming the Norwegian Parliament (Storthing) as the selector of the peace prize winner when Sweden and Norway had not been on friendly terms as "outrageous." Another point of contention within the family was his exclusion of his nephew Hjalmar Nobel from the will (Meyer, *In Search of Peace*, 23). Hjalmar was the eldest son of Alfred's elder brother Robert. Many referred to his disregard of custom and his exclusion of family, friends, and Swedish institutions as a "crackbrained international scheme." Because Nobel had residences in France, in Italy, and in Sweden, even the country in which to probate the will was a problem (Meyer, *In Search of Peace*, 23).

His other nephew Emanuel, the eldest son of Alfred's brother Ludwig, did not contest the will. In fact, Emanuel, then the manager of the Nobel Brother Naphtha Company, worked hard to soothe the feelings within the family and to plan a dignified burial service (Nobel Foundation, 37).

The King of Sweden even fought awarding the Peace Prize in Norway. It was December 31, 1900, before the implementation of the will because of legal complexities (Bankston, 41) and because of the difficulties of listing and evaluating in eight countries all his assets (Meyer, *In Search of Peace*, 25; Opfell, xi).

Bertha von Suttner, Nobel's friend and a person who encouraged him to establish the Nobel Peace Prize, did not receive the first Peace Prize awarded on December 10, 1901, the anniversary of Nobel's death. Rather the award went to another. Between 1901 and 1903 there were 332 nominations for the Nobel Peace Prize (Evlanoff, *Alfred Nobel*, 195).

Her time came soon enough, however. In 1905, Bertha von Suttner became the fifth person and the first woman to receive this prestigious award. Ironically, Bertha's husband of more than 30 years died on December 10, 1901, exactly six years after Nobel, on the same date that she had been denied the Nobel Peace Prize, and on the day that she received the award.

The Nobel Peace Prize, of all the prizes that Nobel established, had the highest average age for its recipients. In the first years of the award, the prize often went to persons who had carried out pioneer peace work; many of these people had reached a fairly advanced age by the time the committee began its search. Today, however, there is no optimum age for workers for peace. People can carry out this work as easily at 30 as they can at 70. Some of the winners who received their reward at an advanced age include Emily Balch, 79, and Alva Myrdal, 80. Others have been much younger: Mairead Corrigan was 33, and Betty Williams was 34. Some of the winners have been institutions, some women, and some men (Nobel Foundation, 489).

Criticisms of the award have included the fact that those whose work showed promise often did not win the award. Nobel had hoped that the prize money might enable a person with great potential, as a result of the money, to occupy a position of total independence and "be able to devote their whole energies to their work." Nobel had wanted "to encourage great minds to continued activity in the service of humanity." Sometimes this has happened; other times the Nobel Peace Prize has been more of a crowning achievement (Meyer, *Dynamite and Peace*, 280–81).

The nominators—specifically the prescribed members of the parliament of Norway, the governments of other nations, members of the Interparliamentary Union, advisers to the Nobel Institute, and university professors of history, law and political science—have often had difficulty with the meaning of Nobel's phrase "the previous year." Often one cannot prove "service to mankind" for several years (Meyer, *Dynamite and Peace*, 280–81).

Nobel had stated: "I would not leave anything to a man of action, as he would be tempted to give up work. On the other hand I would like to help dreamers, as they find it difficult to get on in life." Critics have asked, "How can one separate *dreamers* from persons of *action*?" (Meyer, *Dynamite and Peace*, 280–81).

Need is not a criterion for receiving the prize. Indeed, some recipients have not been needy individuals. Those without monetary needs have often used the money to help others, accomplish a goal, or complete something in line with the desires of Nobel (Meyer, *Dynamite and Peace*, 282).

Winners of the Nobel Peace Prize have continued to receive the prize with pride each year on December 10, the anniversary of Nobel's death. The Nobel Peace Prize has only increased in prestige and influence through the years. The honor outweighs the monetary value for most recipients (Meyer, *Dynamite and Peace*, 282–283).

The Storting president announces the Nobel Peace Prize winner(s). The Swedish prince normally presents the medals and the monetary gift (Meyer, *Dynamite and Peace*, 279).

Press representatives go to Sweden and Norway and report the ceremonies around the world (Meyer, *Dynamite and Peace*, 282–83). The name of Alfred Nobel, though connected to science, connects with the Nobel Prizes in the minds of most people throughout the world. Therefore he "makes his continuing contribution to the advancement of mankind, and in doing so, the shadow of the man lengthens" (Meyer, *Dynamite and Peace*, 285). The Nobel Peace Prize has helped keep the cause of peace in the public eye (Meyer, *Dynamite and Peace*, 286).

Through the Nobel Peace Prize, Alfred Nobel's dreams of peace remain alive. The prize is an annual event except in times of war. "The Nobel Prize is one of the highest honors a man or woman can receive. The most important is the one that is given for peace...." More than a century after Nobel's death, the world still remembers the inventor of dynamite best as a generous man who left his entire fortune to encourage world peace and progress (Meyer, *In Search of Peace*, 20).

Geir Lundestad, Director of the Norwegian Nobel Institute in Oslo and Secretary of the Norwegian Nobel Committee from 1990, notes that none of the 300-plus peace prizes in the world is as highly respected and well-known as the Nobel Peace Prize. He quotes *The Oxford Dictionary of Twentieth Century World History* as defining the Nobel Peace Prize as "the world's most prestigious prize awarded for the 'preservation of peace'" (Lundestad, 163).

Lundestad expresses his opinions as to why the Nobel Peace Prize holds its prestige: "The fact that it belongs to a family of prizes, i.e. the Nobel family, where all the family members benefit from the relationship; the growing political independence of the Norwegian Nobel Committee; the monetary value of the prize, particularly in the early and in the most recent years of its history" (Lundestad, 163).

Tore Browaldh, Deputy Chair of the Nobel Foundation, declared at the Stockholm ceremonies in 1982 that Nobel's Peace Prize is the symbol of the work to prevent the extinction our species (Abrams, 3). There is no rule that there has to be a recipient of the Nobel Peace Prize each year. During wartime, there is no award. Since 1901, there have been 18 years when there has been no recipient. There have been 12 women recipients of the Nobel Peace Prize; two of the women—Mairead Corrigan and Betty Williams—won the award in the same year, 1976. The countries that the 12 women winners represented varied considerably: Austria, the United States (three), Ireland (two), India (two), Sweden, Burma, Guatemala, and Kenya.

The Nobel Peace Prize is an important legacy of Alfred Nobel, who believed with others that "the man or woman who helps bring peace to the world gives mankind its greatest gift" (Feuerlicht, 17). Alfred Nobel helped to honor those people and groups that have sought to bring about peace. Nobel was a man of peace.

Bibliography

Abrams, Irwin. *The Nobel Peace Prize and the Laureates: An Illustrated Biographical History, 1901–1987*. Boston: G. K. Hall, 1989.

Bankston, John. *Alfred Nobel and the Story of the Nobel Prize*. Bear, DE: Mitchell Lane, 2004.

Bergengren, Erik. *Alfred Nobel: The Man and His Work*. London: Thomas Nelson, 1962.

Binns, Tristan Boyer. *Alfred Nobel: Inventive Thinker*. New York: Franklin Watts, 2004.

Evlanoff, Michael. *Nobel-Prize Donor*. Philadelphia: Blakiston, 1943.

_____, and Marjorie Fluor. *Alfred Nobel: The Loneliest Millionaire*. Los Angeles: The Ward Ritchie Press, 1969.

Feuerlicht, Roberta Strauss. *In Search of Peace*. New York: Julian Messner, 1970.

Frangsmyr, Tore. "Life and Philosophy of Alfred Nobel: Memorial Address at the Royal Swedish Academy of Science, March 26, 1996" cited by Agneta Wallin Levinovits and Nils Ringertz. *The Nobel Prize: The First 100 Years*. London: Imperial College Press and River Edge, NJ: World Scientific, n.d.

Halasz, Nicholas. *Nobel: A Biography of Alfred Nobel*. New York: Orion Press, 1959.

Henricksson, Fritz. *The Nobel Prizes and Their Founder Alfred Nobel*. Stockholm: Alb Bonniers Boktryckeri, 1938.

Levinovits, Agneta Wallin, and Ringertz, Nils. *The Nobel Prize: The First 100 Years*. London: Imperial College Press and River Edge, NJ: World Scientific, n.d.

Lundestad, Geir. "The Nobel Peace Prize" cited by Agneta Wallin Levinovits and Nils Ringertz. *The Nobel Prize: The First 100 Years*. London: Imperial College Press and River Edge, NJ: World Scientific, n.d.

Meyer, Edith Patterson. *Dynamite and Peace*. Boston: Little Brown, 1958.

_____. *In Search of Peace*. Nashville: Abingdon Press, 1978.

Nobel Foundation (editor), and W. Odelberg (coordinating editor). New York: American Elsevfier, 1950.

Opfell, Olga S. *The Lady Laureates: Women Who Have Won the Nobel Prize*. Second Edition. Metuchen, NJ: Scarecrow, 1986.

Sechrist, Elizabeth Hough, and Janette Woolsey. *It's Time for Brotherhood*. Philadelphia: Macrae Smith, 1962.

Sohlman, Ragnar, and Henrik Schuck. *Nobel: Dynamite and Peace*. New York: Cosmopolitan, 1929.

von Suttner, Bertha. *Memoirs of Bertha von Suttner: The Records of an Eventful Life in Two Volumes*. New York: Garland, 1972.

Bertha von Suttner
(1905)
"The Peace Fury"
(June 9, 1843–June 21, 1914)

Bertha Sophie Felicita von Suttner, Nobel Peace Laureate 1905.

"Lay down your arms! Tell this to many, many people!" These were among the last words uttered by Bertha von Suttner, the first woman Nobel Peace Prize winner. Bertha's friends were not surprised to learn that she had spent her last moments as she had spent her last 50 years: urging peace.

Neither were they surprised to learn that Bertha's last words were "Lay down your arms!" Bertha had used these same words to title her book and to call for an end to war in her many speeches. It seemed fitting that these very words should be on her mind until the last (Meyer, *In Search of Peace*, 49).

In her youth, however, Bertha Felicita Sophie Kinsky had not concentrated on war. She was born on June 9, 1843, in Austria. Her birth came shortly after the death of her father, Count Franz Joseph Kinsky von Chinic and Tettau; Feldmarschalleutnant (Field Marshal) Kinsky died in the service of the imperial army (Kempf, 7). Bertha's heritage was very important to her. When she wrote her autobiography *Memoirs* in her adult years, she began with a statement about her birth. She verified her ancestry with a copy of her certificate of baptism "in accordance with the use of the Catholic Christian Church by the then parish priest, the Reverend Father Thomas Bazan" (Suttner, *Memoirs, Volume I*, 6–23).

War did not mar Bertha's childhood. Her earliest years were happy ones. One of her earliest memories was when she was three years old and her mother, Sophia Wilhelmine Kinsky, Countess of Chinic and Tettau, was going to a dance. Bertha pleasantly remembered how elegantly her mother was dressed. When Bertha asked to accompany her, her mother said that she could go to a feather ball. Bertha later found out that the "feather ball" was actually a feather bed (Suttner, *Memoirs, Volume I*, 6–23).

Another memory—not quite so happy—was the spanking that Bertha (at age three) got for throwing a temper tantrum and for refusing to change her clothes. A happier remembrance for Bertha was her first love: at ten she fell in love with Franz Joseph I, the Emperor of Austria (Suttner, *Memoirs, Volume I*, 6–23).

Bertha's happy, peaceful early years were quite different from most childhoods. Bertha's unusual lifestyle resulted from her mother's traveling from one place to another. Convinced that she had a gift of prophecy, Bertha's mother—the Honorable Lady Sophia Wilhelmine von Kinsky—traveled about to "test" this gift. The Countess Kinsky often conducted her "experiments" in gambling casinos. In the beginning, she merely attempted to guess the cards and the numbers; she tried placing imaginary bets. She kept detailed records on the results of these trials. When she seemed to be "winning," she finally decided to try the experiments in actuality.

Because Bertha was underage and could not join her mother in the gambling establishments, the young girl spent a lot of her time studying alone in hotel rooms. She did not mind being alone, however; she learned to value her privacy and to use her time wisely. She often spent three or four hours per day writing; she began this pursuit at age eight. In the hotel rooms she also read Hegel, Kant, and Shakespeare. She used the time to advance her education (Suttner, *Memoirs, Volume I*, 6–23).

Things changed somewhat for Bertha when she became 12. She gained a companion. Sophia's sister, Lotti, had a daughter, Elvira, about the same age as Bertha. The two girls began to spend a lot of time together while their mothers visited gambling casinos.

Elvira and Bertha often passed the time with a secret game that they had invented. The game was "Puff." With this word, the two could carry themselves from a garden, a room, or even a carriage to a fantasy world of their own. That one secret word could change them—in their imaginations—into men or women, boys or girls in any era that they might choose. With the word "Paff!," they could stop the game. The word "Puff," however, renewed the fun again.

Once when they were involved in a game of "Puff," Elvira was pretending to be a very sick man. Their mothers, who were sewing and visiting in a corner of the same room, were unaware of the secret game.

"We must ask the doctor about your cough, Elvira," her mother said. "I don't like the sound of it one bit!"

Bertha immediately said "Paff!" to stop the game. The two girls giggled and laughed for a very long time (Suttner, *Memoirs, Volume I*, 24, 25).

Many times in the days to come, Bertha must have wished she could shout "Paff!" to stop the horrors of war. She must have often wished she could shout "Puff!" and cause negotiation to begin. Bertha would become famous internationally for her work to bring peace to the world.

In addition to having lost her father in battle, there was perhaps another reason that young Bertha despised war. Her brother—who was much older than she—was also in service. He was sent home in 1854 because he "spit blood." War remained repugnant—though distant—to Bertha (Suttner, *Memoirs, Volume I*, 55–75).

Bertha's mother and aunt continued to keep regular accounts of their experiments at making "pretend" bets. The result of these trials seemed to indicate uniformly a large amount of winnings. With this "evidence" of success, in 1856 the four left for Wiesbaden. The mothers were going to try their clairvoyance in a real situation. They would be in a setting where the people would not recognize them, and they would use real money. The two women decided at the conclusion of the experiments, however, that real gambling paralyzed their predictive skills.

Bertha and her mother moved to Vienna. Now Bertha saw Elvira only once or twice a week so both girls had more time for their studies. Elvira wrote poetry while Bertha doubled her time on the piano and on languages.

Bertha fell in love with Fredrich von Hadeln—and so did Elvira. To prove her loyalty to Elvira, Bertha "gave up" Fredrich. In her diary she wrote. "My friendship shall not only be sworn, it shall be proved too. I step back, I renounce—be Fredrich van Hadeln yours." Later in the journal she wrote, "On the 8th of July you have proved your friendship." The next summer he ignored them both (Suttner, *Memoirs, Volume I*, 55).

In 1859, the four went back to Wiesbaden. The result of this visit was—simply put—more gambling losses. The four would spend more time in Vienna in the days to come.

Bertha began to practice her writing skills in an unusual way. Without telling even her mother or Elvira, Bertha composed an advertisement to place in the Vienna *Presse*, the local paper. Her family immediately read the ad and talked about it. The ad was from "a brother and sister." When Elvira insisted upon responding, her mother forbade it. Bertha's mother also said that her daughter must not do anything like responding. Bertha continued to maintain her silence about what she knew (Suttner, *Memoirs, Volume I*, 75–77).

When Bertha checked at the post office a few days later, she had 60–70 letters—one of which was from Elvira. The four were amused with the responses. Although some were "imbecile," others were "interesting" and "witty" (Suttner, *Memoirs, Volume I*, 77).

One of the letters was from "Doris in See"; that letter caught the attention of Elvira. She responded to the letter and signed her reply "Kurt im Walde." Their correspondence continued for a whole year. The letters from Doris to Kurt and Kurt to Doris were filled with poems, devotion, and whole essays.

At last Elvira decided that the deception could not continue. "Doris" believed she had been writing to a young man—not Elvira. Elvira wrote a letter of confession and eagerly awaited an answer to her epistle. At last the reply came. Elvira exclaimed: "'Glorious!'" Her best friend, her poet, her correspondent, her thinker was actually Joseph Tiefenbacher, an ensign on a ship of the Austrian fleet. They soon married (Suttner, *Memoirs, Volume I*, 75–78).

Bertha's mother continued her "experiments" in the casinos. Bertha practiced her voice lessons and read in the hotels while her mother was away. She said that she always led two lives: her own and the one in the book she was currently reading. Bertha could borrow six books at a time from the circulating library, and she availed herself of the opportunity.

Bertha also began to flirt with some romantic interests. Her first engagement was to the richest man in Vienna but, deciding he was too old, she broke the engagement (Suttner, *Memoirs, Volume I*, 84).

While Bertha and her mother were visiting in Homburg, Bertha made some important friends from an intriguing place. Mingrelia was then a part of Russian Georgia. The Princess of Mingrelia—Ekaterina Dadiana, formerly the princess of the Caucasian Country—was also in Homburg. The Princess asked some of the young ladies in the area to visit with her. Bertha accepted the invitation and met both the Princess of Mingrelia and her daughter Princess Salome. Bertha and Princess Salome were close in age, and Bertha began to visit the family often, especially while the Countess Wilhelmine Kinsky "worked." Soon Bertha became almost like another daughter to the Princess of Mingrelia. Bertha called the Princess of Mingrelia by the nickname "Dedopali," which means "Mother of Mothers" (Suttner, *Memoirs, Volume I*, 84–102).

Dedopali shared many exciting parts of her life with Bertha. When her husband had died, she had taken up government in her husband's place. Bertha heard a story of how the Princess of Mingrelia had once actually gone to battle: "[H]ard pressed by the Turks, [the Princess of Mingrelia—Dedopali] went against the enemy at the head of her horsemen. But it had been impossible for her to hold her ground, and she had to accept the protection of Russia, a protection that was practically annexation." Bertha had mixed emotions about this story (Suttner, *Memoirs, Volume I*, 102–03).

Visitors to the quarters of Princess Ekaterina Dadiana varied. Tsar Alexander II visited one day. The great singer Adelina Patti also came and sang for them. Prince Heraclius, the son of the last King of Georgia, left his palace in Tiflis and his castle in the mountains and spent some time there. William I, who was 73 at the time, asked her for a picture. A rich suitor from Austria asked Bertha to marry him (Suttner, *Memoirs, Volume I*, 103).

Bertha became engaged to Gustav von Heine-Geldera, an older man with power and money. When he kissed her romantically, however, she broke off the engagement because she really did not love him. She had learned that material things can be bought, but that true love, honor, and glory were *not* items that one can purchase (Hamann, 8–9).

In 1872, when Bertha was 29, she met Prince Adolf Wittgenstein. She sang, and he played; she played, and he sang; they sang together. Within a month the pair planned to go to America under assumed names to appear in concerts. The two had no expectation of wealth, but they believed that they could make money singing. Prince Wittgenstein asked for her hand, but it was not to be.

Prince Willgenstein died. In the paper was an item: "A cable dispatch received by the family of Fürst Wittgenstein, at Castle Wittgenstein, reports that Prince Adolf Willgenstein, who was on his way to America, suddenly died on board and was buried at sea." He had been traveling first class and had a contract for an American concert in his pocket (Suttner, *Memoirs, Volume I*, 104–81).

Bertha in her *Memoirs* quotes correspondence from Adolf's twin brother:

His heart has ceased to beat! Poor Adolf died, as we learn through the office of the Imperial Chancery, suddenly, on the 30th of October, in consequence of some physical injury apparently caused by terrible seasickness; his dear body was buried at sea [Suttner, *Memoirs, Volume I*, 181].

Bertha herself wrote of his death and burial at sea:

... On the silent heart of the man who there disappeared in the waters—an artist, a prince, a good-hearted man—was laid the photograph of his betrothed, and the billows of the ocean murmured a sobbing wedding song to the dead and my picture [Suttner, *Memoirs, Volume I*, 187].

Bertha's friend Alfred Fried did not want her to include information about these early years and the men in *Memoirs*. Fried feared that the information would hurt the movement for peace. Bertha insisted that the stories were truth, and she determined to be always honest. She would not omit the information (Hamann, 14–16).

Soon Bertha and her mother left Homburg and Dedopali; Princess Salome returned to Russia and married a nephew of Emperor Napoleon III. Their friendship, however, would bring them together again in the years ahead.

Bertha was almost 30, single, educated, well-traveled, and ready to begin her own life. First, she looked for employment. Although Bertha was a trained singer, she suffered from stage fright and lacked the talent to perform professionally. At a time in history when women of high social rank did not work outside the home, many people must have thought it very strange for a 29-year-old, single countess to be seeking employment! Her job qualifications seemed limited (Suttner, *Memoirs, Volume I*, 181–204).

Bertha soon found, however, a suitable position for which she was well-qualified. In January 1873 she accepted a job as an instructor and companion to the four daughters of the Baron and Baroness Karl von Suttner. Bertha developed a close, loving relationship with the four girls—and with their older brother Arthur Gundaccar von Suttner, when he arrived home from school. Arthur and Bertha sang together and took long walks. They produced a play. From the beginning, he called her "Fairy." It was only later that he called her by her real name. Arthur and Bertha fell in love, but there was an age difference: Arthur was 23, Bertha 30. Bertha talked with the Baroness, who made it very plain that she would never approve of her son's marrying an older woman (Suttner, *Memoirs, Volume I*, 181–204).

Bertha decided to leave Vienna as soon as she could find work. A newspaper advertisement seemed to offer the perfect position. A "wealthy, cultured, elderly gentleman" living in Paris had placed the advertisement. The advertiser was seeking a mature woman proficient in several languages to manage his household and to serve as secretary. Bertha responded immediately—and he hired her (Suttner, *Memoirs, Volume I*, 204; Wintterle, 26).

Bertha went to Paris to forget Arthur. When she arrived, however, she found that the "elderly" gentleman was not so elderly after all. He was the 44-year-old Alfred Nobel, the famous chemist who had patented dynamite in 1867.

She and Alfred spent some time discussing their lives. When Nobel asked "if her heart were free" (Bergengren, 198), Bertha told him of leaving Vienna to forget Arthur. In her *Memoirs*, Volume I, she shares the advice that Nobel gave her: "'You have acted bravely; but be completely courageous, break off the correspondence also—then let a little time pass ... a new life, new impressions—and you will both forget—he perhaps even soon than you!'" (Suttner, *Memoirs, Volume I*, 209).

Shortly thereafter, Nobel left on business. One week later, Bertha received two telegrams. Her responses to these cables were to affect the rest of her life.

One telegram was from Sweden, and the other was from Vienna. Nobel wrote from Sweden : "Arrived safely. Shall be back in Paris in week." Arthur wrote from Vienna. His telegram read, "I cannot live without thee!" (Suttner, *Memoirs, Volume I*, 210; Suttner, *Memoirs, Volume II*, 221).

Bertha, the newly employed secretary and manager of Nobel's household, made a quick decision. She sold her last valuable possession (a diamond cross), paid her hotel bill, wrote to Nobel, took the leftover money, and rushed back to Vienna to be with Arthur von Suttner. Upon arriving at the hotel in Vienna, Bertha sent her love, Arthur, a note in a disguised handwriting. The note asked him to meet a woman from Paris who had a message from Bertha. Arthur came immediately! The two lovers were delighted to be together and decided to remain together always—even if their parents did not approve (Suttner, *Memoirs, Volume I*, 211–12).

Arthur published the notice of their impending marriage in the papers, secured witnesses, and made all the arrangements for the wedding trip. On June 12, 1876, Arthur and Bertha married secretly in a remote parish church (Suttner, *Memoirs, Volume I*, 220). Bertha wrote that she was married in the parish church of Gumpoldskirchen; Hamann states, however, that the couple actually married in St Giles in Gumpendorf (Hamann, 27).

She was 33, and he was 26; after the ceremony, she referred to him as "My Own"; he now called her "Dearos" for "Dearest." The newlyweds left for a quiet honeymoon in Russia, where Bertha hoped to visit Dedopali, her "mother of mothers" (Suttner, *Memoirs, Volume I*, 220).

The loving pair found that life in Asia was nothing like their life in Europe. Their first night in Asia, the two chose to sleep all night in the chairs in their hotel room because bugs infested the beds. The following morning they found that all the guests in the hotel had to draw their own water and that they used the same tin wash basin, which lodgers carried from one room to another as needed. There was one towel for all the boarders (Suttner, *Memoirs, Volume I*, 220).

Nevertheless, the new couple decided to remain abroad. Bertha's humor shows through when she wrote, "Our wedding excursion to the Caucasus lasted 9 years. A long honeymoon!" To commemorate their new life, Arthur gave her a new nickname: "Boulotte" (Suttner, *Memoirs, Volume I*, 227).

Jobs were very scarce in Kutais in Russian Georgia, where the newlyweds decided to live. Because Arthur could speak both English and French, he was able to find part-time work as a bilingual secretary. The hours were few, and his salary was small. Bertha gave music lessons, but sometimes her students did not pay. The couple was often hungry and poor, but being together brought them happiness (Suttner, *Memoirs, Volume I*, 228). Bertha did not write much of those nine years of hardship. She did comment, however, that the worse things grew, the closer they became (Hamann, 34).

The newlyweds finally heard from their mothers. The Countess von Suttner sent them "a worthy letter of reproach and repudiation and never another word." Although Bertha's mother had not initially approved of the "erratic elopement," within a few days "she had taken My Own into her heart, and her blessing accompanied us" (Suttner, *Memoirs, Volume I*, 228).

Arthur tried earning money in a variety of ways: He worked for a wallpaper factory and for a construction company. He drew designs for wallpaper and developed plans for homes (Hamann, 38–39).

The couple was far from home, but they were not without friends; Dedopali lived near them. Even though Dedopali had been well off at one time, she now had no money to give them, but she did help by sending them a paying student! The couple was now able to purchase a kerosene stove and cook their meals. With an increase in the number of pupils, they made two important purchases: a curtain for the window and a shade for their lamp.

Arthur began to write, for pay, of the beautiful area where they lived. Bertha, in her autobiography, stated that the "magnificence of a beautiful landscape, the sublimity of the sea, and the glory of a glittering firmament inspired in him ... a religious awe" (Suttner, *Memoirs, Volume I*, 249).

Life outside their home was not so tranquil. Russia and Turkey were on the verge of war. Letters from Vienna urged Arthur and Bertha to leave before it was too late. Bertha and Arthur, however, chose to remain in Russian Georgia. On April 24, 1877, Russia and Turkey declared war. Bertha and Arthur decided to join a volunteer medical company.

The couple traveled to a hospital to offer their services. When Bertha saw the wards and halls filled with the wounded and dying, she was horrified and became terribly nauseated. While Arthur tried to complete the necessary paperwork for enlisting in the medical service, Bertha fought down her revulsion at the sights she saw. When the Suttners learned that couples in the medical company could not remain together, they decided to return to their Kutais home. Arthur now had no job, and no one had money to pay Bertha for her lessons. They were destitute (Suttner, *Memoirs, Volume I*, 228–76).

Each day the couple saw the return of the wounded and learned of others who had been killed in battle. The war brought disease to the city. Arthur wrote of the misery of those who fought and of those who remained at home. The *Presse*, a Vienna newspaper, bought his writings eagerly. The small stipends that Arthur earned kept them alive. They managed to live through the horrors of war.

In private, Bertha, too, started to write. She began her first article by discussing things that people considered important: jobs, hobbies, precious objects, accomplishments. At the end, however, the article stated that life and love were the most important things. "Love," said the article, "and you will live." She titled the work "The Most Important Thing."

Bertha, very nervous about using her real name on the piece, signed it "B. Oulot." This pen name came from the nickname "Boulotte" that Arthur had given her for their new life abroad; Bertha used the initial and "last name" because she thought a publisher might be more likely to publish an article written by a man. Her article sold! It appeared in print at Christmas time 1878. With her payment, Bertha bought Arthur a shirt, a tie, an inkwell, a portfolio (into which she put a copy of her article) and a Christmas tree. Arthur was delighted! From then on, they wrote together. Arthur sat at one side of the desk, and she sat at the other (Suttner, *Memoirs, Volume I*, 228–76).

After Bertha's publication of an anti-war article (September 1891), she received another letter from Alfred Nobel. He said that he was delighted "to see that your eloquent pleading against the horror of horrors, war, has found its way into the French press." He asked also, "And your pen? Whither is it wandering now?" (Sohlman, 224–25; Suttner, *Memoirs, Volume I*, 387).

One thing that Bertha sometimes thought about was the way she had left Nobel so suddenly. She felt guilty about this. Alfred and Bertha continued to correspond occasionally, however, and the time would soon come when they would work together again.

Nine years after leaving Vienna, Bertha and Arthur returned to Europe. Much had changed since their marriage. Dedopali had died in 1882; in 1884, Bertha's mother had died and left them many debts to repay (Hamann, 43). Arthur and Bertha, however, were still very much in love.

The couple visited Nobel in Paris soon after their arrival. Nobel was very complimentary about Bertha's writings. Always honest, however, he noted that her articles were short. He suggested that she might concentrate on novels and books.

Bertha began to write *The Machine Age* as soon as she returned to her hotel room. This book was to show the change from production methods that were thousands of years old to the production methods of modern industry. As she did with the first article, Bertha used an alias. Bertha designed this book for those in scientific circles. She also continued to believe that the likelihood of its publication would be greater if it did not carry a woman's name (Suttner, *Memoirs, Volume I*, 278–94).

While Bertha was working on *The Machine Age*, she was also forming in her mind an idea for a new book that she knew would be controversial. The purpose of the book would be to urge peace and to show the horrors of war. Bertha said, "I wanted to be of service to the Peace League, and how could I better do so than by trying to write a book which should propagate its ideas?" Bertha determined to include in the book "not what I thought but what I felt, felt passionately..." (Suttner, *Memoirs, Volume I*, 290–94).

Bertha later said that only a woman could write the book she had in mind; only a female could speak of war the way the heroine in the book would do. Although Bertha was carefully researching the book and basing it on fact, she decided to write the information as a novel because she believed that more people would read fiction.

Bertha titled the book *Die Waffen Nieder*, which in English means "Lay Down Your Arms" or "Throw Down Your Weapons." War was popular at the time, however; many publishers rejected her work. One company wrote to her that its readers might take offense at the book's contents and at its title. Others wrote that "there was no need for this kind of antiwar message during peacetime with no war in sight." Nationalism was high, and war threatened; an arms buildup "in more sophisticated armament did not bode well for a continuation of peace..." (Braker, 82). Many people at that time actually seemed to want war and to oppose peace! Many of Bertha's contemporaries even considered her "a utopian, or worse, a fool" (Hamann, ix).

At last Bertha decided to try a publishing company she had used before, but still she met some resistance. Her previous editor told her finally that his company would publish her book if she would remove everything the publisher found offensive. Bertha refused! The publisher then asked that she change the title. Again she refused! The publisher at last decided to go ahead and publish the book, but he was not enthusiastic. The book sold rapidly. The public seemed to like the idea of peace! (Suttner, *Memoirs, Volume I*, 294–301).

Bertha's *Lay Down Your Arms* contained many graphic passages about "rotting corpses," "ravaging pain," "unspeakable pain," "Hungry dogs [which] lick the blood from the wounds [of the injured soldiers]...." The vivid descriptions and her condemnation of churches that bless weapons and call for war created discussion among the readers (Suttner, *Lay Down Your Arms*). The books continued to sell well for years. Bertha saw these reprints as proof that the book met a need of the heart and the time (Hamann, 74).

Alfred Nobel read the book and wrote to her immediately:

> I have just finished reading your admirable masterpiece. We are told that there are two thousand languages—1999 too many!—but certainly there is not one into which your delightful work should not be translated, read and studied.
>
> How long did it take you to write this marvel? You shall tell me when I next have the honor and happiness of pressing your hand—that Amazonian hand which so valiantly makes war on war.
>
> Nevertheless you make a mistake to cry, "Lay Down Your Arms!" because you yourself make use of them, and because yours—the charm of your style and the grandeur of your ideas— carry and will carry much farther than the Lebels, Nordenfelts, the De Banges, and all the other implements of hell [Suttner, *Memoirs, Volume I*, 299; Halasz, 234].

Russian writer Leo Tolstoy recognized the potential of Bertha's book *Lay Down Your Arms*:

> The abolition of slavery was preceded by the famous book of a woman, Mrs. Beecher Stowe; God grant that the abolition of war may follow yours. I do not believe that arbitration is a means of abolishing wars.... Nevertheless, all efforts dictated by a sincere love for humanity will bear fruit [Suttner, *Memoirs, Volume I*, 343; Halasz, 234–235].

Bertha von Suttner had become "the first female peace worker of real stature, and through her novel *Die Waffen Nieder* [1889] she gave the movement an effective slogan" (Odelberg, 498). Both Hamann and Alfred Fried noted that Bertha had to reach the age of 46 before she identified peace as her life's purpose (Hamann, 80).

Bertha became increasingly involved with peace efforts; she was particularly enthusiastic about an international congress to advance world peace. She and Arthur attended the First Peace Congress, held in Paris in 1889. Bertha worried that Austria had no peace organization with representatives to send to international meetings; "The thought gave me no rest" (Suttner, *Memoirs, Volume I*, 335).

Bertha and Arthur found another cause in 1890. They began to work to found a movement to counteract the anti–Semitic movement that seemed to be sweeping the world. Arthur took the initiative in writing and pushing for support of the cause. Bertha supported him completely and made sure that others knew the work was largely his. She refused to take credit for the progress that she believed that Arthur was making. As always, however, the two lacked the finances to do all the things they wanted to do to further their cause (Hamann, 115–119).

She became involved in another task: to try to form a peace organization in Austria before the meeting of the Second Peace Congress in Rome the following year. Her strategy was to write an article to inform the people of the First Peace Congress and to point out the need for an Austrian Peace Association. She was successful! The Austrian Peace Association tried to enlist Bertha as the chair. Bertha, however, admitted being "too inexperienced to perform the duties of the office...." The organization, which soon had 2000 members, appointed Bertha as a delegate to the Congress to meet in Rome in 1890 (Suttner, *Memoirs, Volume I*, 335).

Bertha was delighted with this outcome. She unhesitatingly expressed her pleasure in her appointment. She was going to the "Peace Congress in Rome as the delegate of a society which I myself had called into existence" (Suttner, *Memoirs, Volume I*, 357).

The first event on the agenda was the meeting of the Interparliamentary Council; 14 different parliaments assembled. As an official delegate, Bertha held a special seat and had to deliver a public address. Although she had experienced severe stage fright in the past, when she had attempted to sing before an audience, she gave no thought to fear when she spoke before this group. She decided that fear before a performance happens only when the performers are concerned with how well they personally are able to please. At the Peace Congress, Bertha concentrated on what she had to say; she forgot her appearance. She had conquered a fear that had been a problem in the past—and she had made history! She was the first woman to speak publicly—and speak very well—in the capitol of Rome! Bertha admits that she "was rather proud of it." A newspaper item, however, reported, "one of the sisterhood had quacked on this spot" (Suttner, *Memoirs, Volume I*, 364–66).

Bertha continued with her peace efforts. She helped plan a peace congress in Berne, Switzerland. She aided the Berne Bureau by permitting an Italian translation of *Lay Down Your Arms*—on the condition that the Treasury of the Bern Bureau would receive the profits. On January 1, 1891, she and A. H. Fried began to publish a "review" named after the novel *Lay Down Your Arms* (Suttner, *Memoirs, Volume I*, 364–66).

Bertha, without modesty, wrote:

> Through my participation in the Congress at Rome, through my editorial labors on the peace review, through correspondence with sympathizers in all parts of the world, through the duties connected with the Vienna Union, I was now wholly absorbed in the [peace] movement. The next object of my desire—and in this also I was incited and supported by A. H. Fried— was to see a peace society established in Berlin likewise [Suttner, *Memoirs, Volume I*, 389–390].

Bertha believed that there was progress towards her goal of a peace society in Berlin when she received an invitation from the Berlin Press Society to give a public reading of some chapters from *Lay Down Your Arms*; the reading would be on "behalf of the endowment fund of the society." Bertha learned from Fried "that a very special honor was in store for me, namely a banquet." Fried hoped that her presence would help establish a peace organization in Berlin. Even though Berlin had an Interparliamentary Council, Bertha wrote that "this must now be followed by a private peace society which might send its representatives to that year's Peace Congress at Berne" (Suttner, *Memoirs, Volume I*, 389–91).

After the banquet, the editor-in-chief of the *Berliner Tageblatt* wrote:

> [T]he festival that was planned in honor of a single person may be considered as a link in the chain of phenomena by means of which the enlightened spirits of the century are seeking to build up the higher (*kulturellen*) interests of humanity [Suttner, *Memoirs, Volume I*, 394].

Not all Berlin newspapers wrote as approvingly of the event, however. One made reference to a "so-often-cited saying of Moltke, 'Perpetual peace is a dream and not even a beautiful one!'" (Suttner, *Memoirs, Volume I*, 394).

In the future, Bjørnstjerne Bjørnson would deliver the Nobel Peace Prize introduction speech for Bertha von Suttner. He would mention her "real influence on the growth of the peace movement and how in one of the most militaristic countries of Europe she had continued to cry, 'Down with arms'" (Abrams, *Heroines*, 4–5). The Norwegian foreign minister Jorgen Gunnarsson Lovland and his wife gave Bertha a banquet after her Nobel address on April 18, 1906; he noted that von Suttner had attacked war with her plea, "Lay down your arms," and he predicted, "This call will be your eternal honor" (Haberman, 81).

Bertha became even more engrossed with her peace efforts. She made plans to attend the Fourth International Peace Congress and the Fourth World's Peace Congress, both scheduled for Bern, Switzerland, in August 1892. She invited Alfred Nobel to attend but received no reply. While she was resting on a veranda in her hotel on Lake Zurich in Bern during the conference, a waiter announced that she had a visitor. It was Alfred Nobel! How surprised she must have been to find her millionaire, former employer waiting for her! They immediately began to talk, and she brought him up to date on the proceedings of the International Peace Conference; he was very interested in attending. He, however, had a special request: He asked that she not reveal his identity to the others who were present. Bertha was not surprised to see his enthusiasm. "There is no lightning without an atmosphere electrically charged" (Halasz, 238–39; Meyer, *Dynamite*, 199).

Nobel invited the von Suttners to visit with him in Zurich, Switzerland, when the meeting was over. This would be their last visit with Nobel. At this meeting, Nobel promised Bertha that if she could convince him of the importance of the peace movement and keep him posted on it, he might help financially. Bertha accepted the challenge! She believed that Alfred Nobel had the influence and the financial power to do much for the cause of peace (Suttner, 438; Meyer, *Dynamite*, 199).

On their trip around a lake in Zurich in Nobel's bright aluminum motorboat, Bertha noted the villas along the shoreline; Nobel said, "Yes, the silkworms have spun all of that." Bertha retorted shortly, "Perhaps dynamite factories are even more profitable than silk mills and definitely less innocent" (Halasz, 241). Alfred responded:

> Perhaps my factories will put an end to war even sooner than your congresses. On the day when two army camps may mutually annihilate each other in a second, all civilized nations will probably recoil with horror and disband their troops [Halasz, 241; Suttner, *Memoirs, Volume I*, 437].

In her *Memoirs*, Bertha declared, "On our departure I had to reiterate my promise to keep Alfred Nobel regularly informed about the progress of the peace movement" (Suttner, *Memoirs, Volume I*, 438).

Theodore Herzl, who argued strongly against anti–Semitism and who founded Zionism, had written in his diary, "A man who would discover a terrible explosive would do more for peace than a thousand of its mild apostles" (Halasz, 241). Bertha wanted assurance of Nobel's help and continued to write frequently to Nobel about her work to advance world peace. Nobel responded in one of his letters:

> It is to be admitted that anything is better than war; the frontiers as they are would therefore be accepted and a declaration would be made that any aggressor would have to meet a coalition of the whole of Europe. That would not amount to disarmament, and I do not even know that disarmament would be really advisable.
> ... But peace guaranteed by the power of collective armies, which would impose respect upon any disturbing elements, would soon release the tension; and from year to year we would see the strength of standing armies in the various countries being reduced cautiously but surely, as there would be no further reason for maintaining such armies in any but a country inhabited by assassins and their victims [Halasz, 244].

A few months later, Nobel wrote and told Bertha that he intended to give part of his fortune as an annual prize for the person who had done the most to promote peace. The time when his fortune was ready to be divided would not be far away. He wrote her on November 5, 1896, from Paris; he indicated that he was "sick and bedridden" (Hamann, 197). On November 21, Nobel's last letter to Bertha again indicated his poor health. "Feeling well—no unhappily for me, I am not, and I am even consulting doctors, which is contrary not only to my custom, but also to my principles" (Meyer, *Dynamite*, 243). Nobel, on the same date, commented on the peace movement:

> I am enchanted to see that the peace movement is gaining ground. That is due to the civilizing of the masses, and especially to those who fight prejudice and ignorance, among whom you hold exalted rank. These are your titles of nobility [Halasz, 271].

Less than three weeks later—on December 10, 1896—Nobel died, and a 20-year friendship ended.

"Peace Bertha," as her friends now called her, was eager to find out Nobel's provisions for peace. When she had read his will, she called it "magnificent" and "a masterpiece of immeasurable significance" (Meyer, *In Search of Peace*, 45). The Peace Prize brought the total number of Nobel Prizes to five rather than the four he had planned before she began her persuasion.

"Peace Fury," as her *enemies* called Bertha, continued to work for peace. One of the highlights of her life was the Peace Conference held at The Hague in the Netherlands from May 18 to June 28, 1899 (Schraff, 15).

On the beginning day of The Hague Peace Conference, Bertha declared the official opening of the event. She confirmed the formal designation of May 18 "Peace Day" (Hamann, 154).

Bertha von Suttner was the only woman delegate among the 96 persons from 26 countries in attendance. This was a very important event in Bertha's life. She and Arthur attended every event in the ten-week conference (Schraff, 15).

One of the important events to follow The Hague Peace Conference was the coining of the term *pacifism*. Proponents of the peace movement had been using various words to describe their work and followers. After the conference, the participants discarded the terms *friends of peace, followers of peace, socialism, federalism*, and related terms. At Bertha's suggestion, peace proponents began to employ the term *pacifism* (Hamann, 155).

After The Hague Peace Conference, Bertha became very sick. Her *Hague Diary* was a tremendous failure. Not only was it a financial failure, but the lack of public interest in the proceedings and in peace in general was a deep disappointment to Bertha. There were other problems after the event (Hamann, 158). Bertha, however, was not one to lament for a long time about something she could not change (Hamann, 235).

All her life Bertha had been reasonably healthy, but now she felt the physical and emotional stress of illness. The treatment prescribed by her doctor was—of all things—bicycling! The heavy-set, 56-year-old woman mounted a bicycle for the first time in her life! The delightful pastime of children became a duty for Bertha. She viewed the prescription as comical, yet tempting! "It had always been my keen desire to enjoy this skimming away on the thin-legged iron steed, and I had regretted that I was born too early to experience this delight. Now it was imposed on me as a duty to my health" (Suttner, *Memoirs, Volume II*, 341).

Bertha's husband helped her mount the bicycle 20 times, and each time she fell off! Arthur laughingly asked her if it would not be better for her to use a tricycle, but she was determined to regain her health. After a time—she would not confess how long—she learned to ride. She lost weight, felt better, and said that her veins seemed filled again with youth! (Suttner, *Memoirs, Volume II*, 341).

On December 10, 1901, the Norwegian Parliament (through Alfred Nobel) awarded the first Nobel Peace Prize. Although Bertha was a nominee for the prize, she did not receive it. The award went instead to Jean Henri Dunant, one of the founders of the Red Cross. Bertha complained that the Swiss philanthropist had tried to "humanize" war and not end it. She noted that "Sir George rode forth to kill the dragon, not to trim its claws" (Schraff, 16–17; Meyer, *In Search of Peace*, 4). Bertha, however, was very positive about Dunant in a letter to Nobel; she compared The Hague Peace Conference of 1894 to the priceless Geneva conference that Dunant had helped to achieve (Hamann, 134).

The next year on this date, Arthur von Suttner died. Bertha was grief-stricken. Two important people in her life now shared the same death date. In his will, Arthur reminded Bertha of his love and told her to continue working for peace (Suttner, *Memoirs II*, 397–98):

And now, My Own, one single word to thee: Thanks! Thou hast made me happy; thou has helped me to win from life its loveliest aspects, to get delight from it. Not a second of discontent has ever come between us, and for this I thank thy great understanding, thy great heart, thy great love! [Suttner, *Memoirs II*, 398].

Arthur told her to continue working for peace.

Thou must work on in our plans, for the sake of the good cause keep up the work until thou also at last shall reach the end of the brief journey of life. Courage then! No hesitation! In what we are trying to do we are at one, and therefore must thou try still to accomplish much [Suttner, *Memoirs II*, 398].

Bertha did try to accomplish much! In the fall of 1904 she attended a Boston peace conference. America reached out its arms to "Peace Bertha." It was the first time she had ever crossed the Atlantic (Schraff, 16; Meyer, *In Search of Peace*, 47).

She found out in the fall of 1905 that she would be the next recipient of the Nobel Peace Prize. On December 10, 1905, the Fifth Nobel Peace Prize Recipient was a woman: Bertha Kinsky von Suttner. She could not accept the prize until April 18, 1906, because she was touring in Germany and did not feel that she could cut short her work there. With financial difficulties still troubling her, Bertha put the money in the bank; she intended to use it for an annual income of 12,000 crowns, then double or triple the salary of a university professor. She began, however, to receive requests for money from family and strangers, and the money began to fly through her fingers (Hamann, 212).

Bertha's speech, titled "The Development of the Peace Movement," gave much credit to Alfred Nobel. She remarked that he had convinced himself that the peace movement was no longer merely pious theory but was now accessible; she stated that his will proved his convictions (Hamann, 213).

In 1907 she attended the Second Hague Peace Conference. Her speaking invitations came from throughout the world (Schraff, 17).

Bertha did not rest on her past accomplishments; she continued to spread her influence. Even Andrew Carnegie began to make some financial contributions to the cause of peace. In 1910 he made President William Howard Taft an honorary president of the board of trustees of his fund for peace; Carnegie had just endowed the fund with $10,000,000. Carnegie also supplied $10,000,000 that he earmarked for the "Pan American Office." Bertha praised Carnegie's actions highly (Hamann, 220–21). She was also able to secure funds from some others, like Prince Albert of Monaco (Hamann, 234).

In 1912, at the age of 69 and not in the best of health, Bertha made a seven-month lecture tour of the United States and found a devout follower. Eve Thompson, daughter of a physics professor at the University of California in Berkeley, began to accompany Bertha as she worked; Eve even assisted her to the podium when she made a speech (Schaff, 17; Hamann, xiv). Bertha described the tour in this way: "I'm not on a joy ride; I'm making a last crusade for a cause" (Hamann, xiv). The Carnegie Endowment for Peace allotted her a monthly stipend that helped "end her lifelong strategy with intermittent poverty" (Schraff, 17).

In August 1913, although in very poor health, Bertha spoke at the International Peace Congress at The Hague. The Congress honored her as "the generalissimo" of the peace movement.

Soon thereafter, Bertha collapsed while lecturing at a public meeting for peace. Her doctor diagnosed a tumor in her abdomen and recommended surgery, but Bertha would not consent. On her sickbed, with Eve to nurse her, she compiled her last book. She titled it *From the Workshop of Pacifism* (Pauli, 203–06).

Carl-Theodore Dreyer (film screenplay writer), Dane Holge-Madsen (director) and other from Nordisk Films arrived at Bertha von Suttner's home on April 20, 1914. They wished to film her at her desk and to use the images in the introduction to the anti-war film *Lay Down Your Arms*. The plan was to show the resulting film in the upcoming World Peace Congress in Vienna. As a result of the war's outbreak, however, there was no festive showing of the film. The inmates at Sing Sing Prison viewed the film with enthusiasm in 1915, and its reviews in the media were excellent, according to Kelly. The film is still on file in the Denmark Film Archives. There were showings in Denmark in 1960, in Paris in the 1960s, at the Pordenone Silent Film Festival in 1986, and in London in 1989. The only person who has provided many details about the film was Brigitte Hamann, a German journalist who produced a biography of Bertha von Suttner after "using the largely unexploited Suttner-Fried papers" (Hamann, xix). There are some differences between the book and the film; the film includes no information—on uniforms, on buildings, on trains, or in the words—that identifies the countries in the film, but the book identified the countries (Kelly, 97–113).

On June 21, 1914, just past her seventy-first birthday, Baroness von Suttner died "like a tired person in the evening" (Hamann, xvi). Before her death she called out in delirium: "Lay down your arms." Her very last words were, "I'm going to Durazzo." The Balkan conflicts over possession of Durazzo had caused Bertha much heartache. Durazzo belonged to Albania, and the threat of war over the ownership shook Bertha more than the disease in her body, her physician said.

More than a century later the evidence of her life and work still exist:

- The Nobel Peace Prize she inspired;
- The records of the Austrian Peace Society she helped to form;
- The minutes of the Peace Congresses, which she helped organize in Berlin and Berne;
- The many books and articles she authored;
- Her name listed as a recipient of the coveted Nobel Peace Prize;
- Her likeness on the Austrian 100-crown bank note in recognition of her achievements;
- Her *Memoirs*;
- Her correspondence with Alfred Nobel;
- Her model of dedication to a cause.

Across the world, people still remember her book *Lay Down Your Arms*. Peace organizations held commemorative events in 1989 to celebrate the publication of the work. In

Italy, West Germany and the German Democratic Republic, for example, authors—especially women—and pacifists met to discuss questions related to peace, feminism, literature, and the writer herself. A new edition of *Lay Down Your Arms* was published when it hit the 100-year mark. Articles and new biographies began to appear (Abrams, "Bertha von Suttner," 64–65).

In 1936, Abrams, who held the Harvard Sheldon Fellowship, wrote his doctoral dissertation on the European Peace Movement; he wrote *Bertha von Suttner and the Nobel Peace Prize* some 20 years later. He and others "note how far the image of Suttner has come from the unkind caricatures of her own day" (Abrams, 64–67). Abrams and Bjørnstjerne Bjørnson note that although Bertha was a laughing matter at first, "her words received a hearing because they were uttered by a person of noble character and because they proclaimed humanity's greatest cause" (Abrams, *Heroines of Peace*; Bjørnson, "Introduction to Nobel Peace Prize 2005").

Abrams concludes: "The evidence seemed clear that had it not been for her, there would not be such a prize." He mentioned Ursula Jorfald, a feminist and peace activist from Norway, who believed that Bertha von Suttner was instrumental in Nobel's decision to set up the Nobel Peace Prize and who attacked the prevalent view in Scandinavia that she did not influence Nobel in his action (Abrams, "Bertha von Suttner," 64–67).

Opfell, however, points out that some friends of Nobel disagree with the claims of the Austrian aristocrat that she had convinced Nobel to write the Nobel Peace Prize into his will. These friends noted that Shelley had inspired Nobel, and that Nobel had been interested in peace for a long time before Bertha and he met. These friends argued further that Suttner and Nobel had seldom met and had exchanged correspondence only a few times; in the 20 years of Suttner's and Nobel's friendship, they had exchanged only 30 letters and only 15 had concerned peace (Opfell, 1–3).

Brigitte Hamann in her biography *Bertha von Suttner* used many unpublished papers and the papers in Geneva. Abrams touts Hamann's work as "the first comprehensive Suttner biography" and asserts that Hamann presents a picture of Bertha as a human; he believes that Hamann's "achievement is to tell a very human story, bringing the baroness to vivid life in her pages, writing sympathetically, but giving a balanced picture, with faults and all. Hamann is a polished writer and this is a very moving account.... Hamann gives only Suttner's rather naive interpretation of how [the first Hague Peace Conference] all began" (Abrams, "Bertha von Suttner," 68–70).

Abrams is, however, skeptical of Hamann's interpretation of why Nobel chose Norwegians as the presenters of the Nobel Peace Prize. Even though he says that "Hamann writes as though she knows just why ... [n]obody else knows" (Abrams, "Bertha von Suttner," 68–70).

Abrams notes Bertha's personal problems, her financial concerns, and the baroness's awareness of having sacrificed literary greatness for the cause of peace. Abrams even observes Bertha's fear that toward the end Arthur was "becoming infatuated with his young niece" and that "Arthur's love for her was cooling" (Abrams, "Bertha von Suttner," 68–71).

Hamann suggests that when Bertha started her peace work, the income from her writing decreased and that her activity for peace *cost* money but did not *produce* any. The couple's financial concerns increased. To help with expenses, Bertha had to write fiction and serial stories, but she still kept up with her pacifist concerns. She, therefore, had to write in haste on subjects in which she had no real interest. "Every new novel cost her agony" (Hamann, 165).

Aside from the financial worries there were far more serious personal problems. These were connected with Arthur, for whom marriage to such a successful woman was not easy. The difference in age became a problem, too. Bertha was nearing fifty, Arthur had just turned forty [Hamann, 168–69].

The real problem ... was the pretty, vivacious niece, Marie Louise Suttner. She was fourteen when she came to Harmannsdorf [the von Suttner home] after the death of her father, and from the very first day on, she attached herself to her beloved "Onkeles" Arthur.... [N]one of her admirers were good enough for her: she preferred to stay in Harmannsdorf. Her relationship with her uncle became closer and Bertha's family relationships harder. Only too frequently, quarrels broke out between them, and Arthur was always in the middle....

Living together became torture. [Arthur and Marie Louise] went for a walk every day from ten to twelve. Bertha stayed at her desk, tormented by jealousy.... There were also occasions when Arthur and Marie Louise had things to do in Vienna at the same time ... and Bertha remained in Harmannsdorf—desperate and sleepless ... [Hamann, 169–70].

Marie Louise authored a book describing her love for Arthur, who was constrained in an unhappy marriage. Bertha also wrote in her diary about finding "compromising" correspondence between the two. Hamann noted that Bertha's diary had many, many pages filled with "her pain." Bertha wrote that the only thing that could make her feel happy would be if she and Arthur could live together as a couple again. Bertha even wrote that she had "not been necessary for Arthur's happiness for a long time—perhaps the opposite"; she had told Arthur that she would like to die and that he could find an account of her sorrows in her diary. Even though Bertha indicated that Arthur had written that the relationship was platonic, she noted that he had "completely forgotten the book, the book." Later she wrote that she should "get away from this *shattered* family life" (Hamann, 171–73).

Hamann discovered that entries from June 1901 to July 1902 are missing from the diaries so that one assumes "the very worst things ... are kept secret. But that which remains is bad enough. Quarrels and money matters continued in 1902. Arthur's illness got worse.... In October the couple went to Abbazia, in the hope that Arthur would find relief.... Bertha insisted on accompanying him alone—that is, without Marie Louise—and tried to get her husband back on her side again.... But Arthur was restless. He wrote to his niece in secret and wanted to go home.... Marie Louise asked for permission to sleep in the room next to his and to take over caring for him, which Bertha allowed" (Hamann, 174–75). After his death, "Marie Louise was desperate and was thinking of suicide" (Hamann, 177). Hamann notes that in Bertha's April 11, 1903, diary entry, she took consolation in the fact that "despite everything: his love for me was faithful to the end. Boulotte, he called out while he was dying—and not Marie Louise. That should be a consolation and a satisfaction to me" (Hamann, 182).

Hamann notes that Bertha did make up with Marie Louise. Bertha remembered that Arthur loved Marie Louise and that Marie Louise loved Arthur. Bertha considered the fact that only his niece grieved his passing as much as she had done; she concluded, therefore, that Marie Louise should be valuable to her also. In 1905, Marie Louise became engaged to Baron Haebler; on their wedding day, his former wife and their three children appeared and threatened a scandal. Thereafter, the Haeblers lived abroad (Hamann, 184–185).

Braker suggests that Bertha's life with Arthur and with his family helped her learn more about compromise, tolerance, and mutual benefit—all of which were beneficial to the peace movement (Braker, 78).

Abrams credits Suttner and her works with "having laid the spiritual foundations of the international organizations of the twentieth century" (Abrams, "Bertha von Suttner," 68–71). Braker, too, refers to the positive impact of *Lay Down Your Arms*. In her opinion, the work "was the impetus for the Austrian and German Peace Societies" and became "a watchword for the European peace movement before World War I." She wrote that the book was the most widely read fictional exposition of an anti-war message in the quarter century before 1914. Through the internationally best-selling novel—with its "radical criticism" and "cautious solutions"—Suttner received her initiation into public life and pacifism. Like Stowe's *Uncle Tom's Cabin*, *Lay Down Your Arms* was a combination of didacticism and entertainment and did not achieve "literary recognition, nor did either seem to strive for it…." The main concern of both books was reform (Braker, 74, 82). Suttner wrote from inner conviction and took a "non-sectarian moral stance" that had roots in a "humanistic belief in the ethical perfectibility of humankind." Even though her main theme was anti-war, she also attacked anti–Semitism, criticized "the rigid authority of the Catholic Church, and … [pleaded] for greater human rights and freedom" (Braker, 79).

Like Hamann, Braker suggests that Suttner's activism and profit—not artistic reputation—may have drawn Suttner into writing. In fact, Braker suggests that Suttner was an activist, not a recluse; the more time that she devoted to activism, the more she turned to journalism. Her organizational efforts in her writing and the communication of a message to her readers were of high importance to Bertha. She condemned the role of the churches and of education in encouraging enthusiasm toward the military and strongly advocated the role of women in politics; her novel did not advocate future reward as adequate compensation for present sacrifice. Her platforms were not as radical as those of some of the other activists of the time, but to her the messages remained urgent. Her main taskmaster continued to be financial motives, which she never escaped. Even after the couple returned to the Suttner family estate, writing became merely a "question of staving off the family's financial ruin" (Braker, 78–81).

Truly "Peace Bertha" worked and lived for what she proclaimed. Even after her death, people acknowledged the wisdom of the "woman everybody thought had nothing to say to the world except for her four words…" (Hamann, x). If she could speak to us today, her message would be unchanged: "Lay down your arms!"

Bibliography

Abrams, Irwin. "Bertha von Suttner." *Peace and Change*, January 1991, XVI, 64–74.
_____. "Heroines of Peace: The Nine Nobel Women." Available online at http://nobelprize.org/peace/articles/heroines.
Bergengren, Erik. *Alfred Nobel*. London: Thomas Nelson and Sons, 1960.
Bjørnstjerne Bjørnson. "Introduction to Nobel Peace Prize 1905." Available online at http://www.nobel.se/peace/laureates/1905/speeches.html.
Braker, Regina. "Bertha von Suttner as Author." *Peace and Change*, January 1991, XVI, 74–97.
Evlanoff, Michael. *Nobel-Prize Donor*. Philadelphia: The Blakiston Company, 1943.
Haberman, Frederick W. *Nobel Lectures, Peace 1901–1925*. Amsterdam: American Elsevier, 1972.
Halasz, Nicholas. *Nobel: A Biography of Alfred Nobel*. New York: Orion Press, 1959.
Hamann, Brigitte. *Bertha von Suttner: A Life for Peace*. (Trans. Ann Dubsky. Syracuse: Syracuse University Press, 1996.
Kelly, Andrew. "Film as Antiwar Propaganda" *Peace and Change*. January 1991, Volume XVI, 97–113.
Kempf, Beatrix. *Women for Peace*. Park Ridge, New Jersey: Noyes Press, 1973.
Meyer, Edith Patterson. *Dynamite and Peace*. Boston: Little Brown, 1958.

_____. *In Search of Peace: The Winners of the Nobel Peace Prize, 1901–1975.* Nashville: Abingdon Press, 1978.

Odelberg, Wilhelm. *Nobel: The Man and His Prizes.* New York: American Elsevier, 1972.

Opfell, Olga S. *The Lady Laureates: Women Who Have Won the Nobel Prize.* Metuchen, New Jersey: Scarecrow, 1986.

Pauli, Hertha. *Cry of the Heart: The Story of Bertha von Suttner.* Trans. Richard and Clarion Winston. New York: Ives Washburn, 1957.

Schraff, Anne. *Women of Peace.* Hillside, New Jersey: Enslow, 1994.

Suttner, Bertha von. *Memoirs of Bertha von Suttner: The Records of an Eventful Life, Volumes I and II.* New York: Garland, 1972. (Reprinted from 1909.)

_____, Blanche Cook, Sandi Cooper, and Charles Chatfield, eds. *Lay Down Your Arms: The Autobiography of Martha von Tilling.* Authorized translation by T. Holmes. New York: Longmans, Green and Company, 1914.

Wintterle, John. *Portraits of Nobel Laureates in Peace.* New York: Abelard-Schuman, 1971.

Jane Addams
(1931)
"The Most Dangerous Woman in America"
(September 6, 1860–May 21, 1935)

Jane Addams, Nobel Peace Laureate 1931.

"The most dangerous woman in America!" This warning in the 1920s from *Scabbard and Blade*, a military journal of the honor students of the R. O. T. C., generates visions of an undercover spy or an underground traitor sharing vital information with the enemy (Villard, 536–37).

The Commander of the Illinois American Legion even called her home "the rallying point of every radical and communist movement in the country" (Kittredge, 95). Those who read these words likely imagined a seemingly deserted structure with national traitors and enemy workers stealthily coming and going in the dead of night.

The New York State Legislature produced in 1920 a four-volume report on "radical activities." Titled the Lusk Report, the information included Jane Addams' name because of her peace efforts and her attempts at reform. The frequent inclusion of her name in the report caused many to brand her a Communist (Wheeler, 112).

The Daughters of the American Revolution (DAR) produced in the same decade a book titled *The Common Enemy*. Included in the book were people and organizations that were "doubtful speakers" (Kittredge, 95). The DAR stated that these people and representatives of the organizations "because of publicly expressed views ... out of harmony with our [the DAR's] avowed purposes" should not serve as speakers (Kittredge, 95). Included in the DAR list was the same woman vilified by *Scabbard and Blade* (Villard, 530).

The individual whom the DAR condemned, whom the *Scabbard and Blade* attacked, and whom certain groups of the American Legion criticized was not the person one might imagine. Instead she was a frail, 60-year-old woman. She had worked with dedication for America's wartime Food Administration at the request of Herbert Hoover, had helped Americans to produce and distribute foods in wartime, had advocated during World War I a quick and negotiated end to hostilities, and had worked after the war for medical aid and food for innocent war victims (Kittredge, 95–96). The woman who was the victim of these vicious attacks would later receive the Nobel Peace Prize. Her name was Jane Addams.

Carrie Chapman Catt, the woman suffragette, "made a gallant defense [of Laura Jane Addams] as a pacifist in an able document, 'An Open Letter to the D. A. R.,' published in the *Woman Citizen* in July 1927" (Addams, *Second Twenty*, 182). Catt said openly and without fear that Jane Addams "is one of the greatest women this republic of ours has produced. She has given her life to serve others. She knows no selfish thought. You slap her on the right cheek; she only turns the left.... She is the kind of Christian who might have been thrown to the lions and would have gone cheerfully" (Kittredge, 96).

Jane's legal name was Laura Jane Addams, but her nickname as a child had been "Jenny." Jane, whose adult nickname was "J. A.," had quickly found out that working for peace and helping others could be unpopular. Instead of advocating annihilation of the enemy, she had encouraged pursuing a quick, negotiated peace—not always a commonly accepted solution to the hostilities (Kittredge, 89).

At first J. A. could not understand why pacifism should be confused with Bolshevism, but she later understood. Many citizens who were fearful of enemy actions equated pacifism with reducing the armed forces; the end result would be that, when/if the Bolshevists arrived, they would encounter no resistance. Because of their way of thinking, they considered her a "dangerous woman" and castigated her in the *Scabbard and Blade* (Addams, *Second Twenty Years*, 162).

Jane had difficulty understanding the stereotyping and attack by the DAR. They had elected her to membership in 1895 (Linn, 214) and had taken her into their ranks as an honorary member in 1900. Jane remarked, "I supposed at that time that it had been for life, but it was apparently only for good behavior, for I am quite sure that during the war I was considered unfit for membership" (Addams, *Second Twenty Years*, 180–81). Her biographer and nephew James Weber Linn remarked that his aunt guardian never viewed the animosity of the DAR with anything but amusement (Linn, 350). Kittredge, on the other hand, noted that Jane Addams was "emotionally wounded by the constant assaults on her character. Aware of her pain, her friends often reminded her that the accusations came from America's 'lunatic fringe,' not the bulk of its people" (Kittredge, 96).

Jane found also that many businesses advocated the child labor that she opposed and that this was a reason for their insults. They called her "a Trojan horse concealing Bolshevists, Communists, Socialists, and all that traitorous and destructive brood" (Addams, *Second Twenty Years*, 158).

Addams dismissed the attacks by mildly commenting, "The nation forgot that nothing is so dangerous as to prohibit social changes, nothing so unnatural ... as to forbid its growth and development." (Addams, *Second Twenty Years*, 154) Jane observed that this fear of change spread to most areas—particularly politics (Addams, *Second Twenty Years*, 155).

Jane herself, however, had never feared change. One of her earliest memories was a dream of changing her world. On a trip in 1867, seven-year-old "Jenny" and her father John Huy Addams were visiting a mill in a neighboring Illinois town. Because the structure was in the poorest residential section of town, Jane saw her "first sight of the poverty which implies squalor and felt the curious distinction between the ruddy poverty of the country and that which even a small city presents in its shabbiest streets" (Addams, *Twenty Years*, 3). In this part of town that Jane had never visited before, she saw dirty, ragged, hungry-looking children trying to play in the littered, unpaved streets. Shabby houses without yards and often even without panes in the windows seemed to fill every available lot. Tired-looking women were coming out of their houses to throw dirty water, garbage, and even human waste into the ditches beside the street; the smells were sickening. The noise level was uncomfortable. Little "Jenny" had never seen such poverty and unhappiness. She always remembered asking her father "why people lived in such horrid little houses so close together" (Addams, *Twenty Years*, 3). All her life she remembered that she lifted her face to her father and "declared with much firmness that when I grew up I should, of course, have a large house, but it would not be built among the other large houses, but right in the midst of horrid little houses like these" (Addams, *Twenty Years*, 3–5).

Jane would keep her promise! She and her Hull House became a model of help and support for over 50 years. Her peaceful influence, demonstrated in Chicago, would reach around the world. As a Nobel Peace Prize winner, she would become an international figure.

International success had not come easily for Jane. She had many obstacles to overcome from her birth. First of all, Jane was born "a delicate little girl ... with the further disability of a curved spine" (Addams, *Twenty Years*, 6). One of her biographers—the nephew over whom she gained custody after his mother (Jane's sister Mary) died—attributed the spinal problem to abscesses (Linn, 24). Other writers stated that at an early age Jane had had tuberculosis of the spine (Polikoff, 7–8; Wheeler, 4). Whatever the cause of her crooked spine, her neck did not properly support her head, her back curved, her head tilted to one side, and her walk was a pigeon-toed gait.

A second hurdle presented itself when Jane was only two. Jane's 46-year-old mother

Sarah Weber Addams collapsed while serving as a midwife to a neighbor. Sarah's own child (her ninth) was born dead, and Sarah herself died a week later. Little Jane (only two years and four months old at the time) remembers distinctly banging at the door of her mother's room and demanding entrance. She recalls clearly hearing her mother say, "Let her in. She is only a baby herself" (Linn, 22). Sarah and John Huy Addams had been married when he was 22 and she was 27; she was an intelligent young woman who was the sister-in-law of the miller to whom John was an apprentice (Wheeler, 1–2).

Jane was left in the care of her father, three older sisters (Mary, Martha, and Alice), an older brother (James Weber), and the hired woman (Polly Bear) (Addams, *Twenty Years*, 10). With all the attention and material possessions lavished upon Jane by these well-meaning adults, many people suspected that the little girl would grow up to be pampered and interested in only herself and those things that directly affected her.

These people misjudged Jane, the influence of her father, and the role of the church in Jane's life! Jane's father, John Huy Addams, came from a family of Pennsylvania Quakers. John made his living as an Illinois banker, mill owner, and real estate broker (Addams, *Twenty Years*, 17). He also served on the Senate from 1854 until 1870, when he declined to run again. (Kittredge, 22). One of his best friends was Abraham Lincoln, whom he always called "Mr. Lincoln" (Addams, *Twenty Years*, 32–33; Kittredge, 22; Linn, 4). The public respected his integrity (Addams, *Twenty Years*, 32–33).

Four-year-old Jenny found her father in tears in the spring of 1865. John told Jane that his friend Abe Lincoln was dead. He then took his little daughter on his lap and explained what had happened to President Lincoln. Little Jane had come in contact with death again (Kittredge, 24). Throughout her life, Jane would recall: "The two flags [that greeted her when she returned home that day], my father's tears, and his impressive statement that the greatest man in the world had died" (Addams, *Twenty Years*, 23). Occasionally over the years Mr. Addams would take out a thin stack of letters from this admired man: Mr. Lincoln. He would sometimes share the letters with his daughter. The letters often began: "My dear Double-D'ed Addams" (Addams, *Twenty Years*, 31).

When Jane was about five, she had to cope again with death: that of a beloved sister. Sixteen-year-old Martha, who had helped care for Jane, died of typhoid. Martha had always watched over her little sister. Jane missed her terribly (Kittredge, 22). Later, when Jane was only 15, she was present when Polly Bear (an elderly family friend and former employee) died; the old woman called out to Sarah, Jane's mother who had been dead for many years. Jane never regretted being there for her friend's passing. She always believed that children should not be "denied the common human experience. They too wish to climb steep stairs and to eat their bread with tears" (Addams, *Twenty Years*, 31; Kittredge, 29; Hovde, 21).

In 1868 Anna Haldeman became John Addams' new wife. Anna brought her son George (who was Jane's age) with her (Kittredge, 21). George and Jane would become best friends. Anna's other son was 18-year-old Harry (Kittredge refers to him as "Henry"). A graduate of a European medical school, he would later marry Jane's older sister Alice and would even serve as Jane's doctor when she had very serious surgery in 1882 (Polikoff, 12; Wheeler, 6).

Closely associated with this memory of Jane's expanding family was another memory: that of visiting the Illinois capital and seeing Old Abe, the mascot of the Civil War's 8th Wisconsin Regiment. The eagle entered—and survived—each of the regiment's encounters. Jane often told the story of the outing that her father, George, Jane's stepmother, and she shared. (Mooney, 24–25). The 65-mile trip to the capital city took more than a day and was a good experience for the Addams family.

John Addams and his family attended church regularly. One Sunday when Jane was eight, Mr. Addams taught Jane a lesson in humility and concern for others that she would never forget. Jane was wearing a brand new cloak. This gift was the most elegant piece of clothing Jane had ever owned, and she was very proud as she started to leave the house with her father. Mr. Addams surprised her with his request (Addams, *Twenty Years*, 13–14; Kittredge, 26).

"Since your cloak is far prettier than anything the other little girls will have, they will feel bad. I would like you to wear your old cloak." Jane remembered this lesson in equality all her life (Addams, *Twenty Years*, 13–14; Kittredge, 26).

John Addams encouraged Jane to study and to learn. He gave her five cents for each volume of *Plutarch's Lives* that she read and 25 cents for each volume of Washington Irving's *Life of Washington* that she completed. Jane loved reading and studying (Kittredge, 28; Wheeler, 8). Jane noted that *Little Women* "never seems to grow old" and that Dickens "never wrote anything stupid" (Kittredge, 28).

Jane was an intelligent, hard-working young woman. At a time when most women were planning parties and weddings, Jane was striving to further her education. The goal she set for herself was to earn a college degree, an accomplishment that was not common for a nineteenth-century woman. She particularly wanted to attend Smith College; in Massachusetts this was one of the few colleges that would admit women into a degree program. Despite the fact that Jane passed the difficult entrance tests and met the requirements for matriculation, her father would not allow her to enroll there. He was a trustee at Rockford Seminary in Rockford, Illinois, and he insisted that 17-year-old Jane, like her sisters before her, attend that school.

Presbyterian and Congregational ministers had established Rockford [DeBenedett calls it *Rockville* on page 32] in 1846, ten years after Mount Holyoke. Rockford's nickname was the "Mount Holyoke of the West." Jane entered in September 1877 (Wheeler, 10–11). Jane had many friends at Rockford, but her special friends were Ellen Starr and Catherine ("Kittie") Waugh. Ellen Starr later transferred, but the two classmates would remain friends for life. Together they would later open Hull House, a settlement house in Chicago (Kittredge, 19, 32).

Life at Rockford was very disciplined. Students had to make their own fires and keep their own room (Addams, *Twenty Years*, 51). They arose at 6:30 A.M. and ate breakfast promptly at 7:00. A faculty member sat at each table. The students had to keep ledgers and account for all their expenses. They provided their own sheets, tableware, and napkins and shared in washing glasses, sorting mail, making pies and cakes, setting the tables, and even carrying the water (Wheeler, 11–12). Like the other girls, Jane had to walk around the grounds for one hour per day. Even with her spinal condition, Jane was able to perform this exercise daily—and preferred it to some other exercises (Linn, 49).

Frequent weekend occurrences were visits from the men at Beloit College in nearby Beloit, Wisconsin. George Haldeman, Jane's stepbrother, was a student at Beloit and an admirer of Jane's; he often came to visit her on Fridays (Mooney, 32–33). During the time that Jane was at Rockford, 16 of her classmates left to marry Beloit men. One of the Beloit men, Rollin Salisbury, asked Jane to marry him. She refused, and he never married (Kittredge, 33). Jane had no romantic interest in either George or Salisbury (Wheeler, 13).

Although Jane knew that a degree was not possible from Rockford Seminary, she and her friend Kittie persuaded their professors to prepare for them the advanced courses and requirements that would comprise a degree program at another college. Kittie and Jane completed with honors every assigned task. Jane was a particularly outstanding student; her grades ranged from 9.5 to 10, with a 10 being perfect (Kittredge, 34). She even found time to participate in the Illinois Intercollegiate oratorical contest with Kittie. Out of the ten teams participating, Kittie and Jane ranked number five—not a bad position considering that their competition included William Jennings Bryan, who was to become one the nation's best-known orators (Mooney, 33–34; Wheeler, 17).

Kittie and Jane decided to use the trip to Jacksonville to learn even more. They toured the school for the deaf and blind and observed the methods and facilities. Their friends at Rockford, however, were not expecting this detour from their representatives. They had woven flowers into garlands and crowns to welcome their returning heroines. By the time Jane and Kittie arrived, however, the flowers had wilted. Jane was a long time forgiving herself for disappointing them (Mooney, 34–35).

Jane and four of her classmates had been reading *Dreams* by Thomas De Quincey. He talked about experimenting with opium to produce fantastic dreams. Opium was not an illegal drug at the time. Jane and her friends tried it over a holiday interval until a teacher found out about their "research," confiscated the drug, and sent them to their rooms (Wheeler, 15). There is no evidence that the students used enough of the drug to experience the dreams.

At the end of the 1881 school year, Jane was first in her class as both the class president and the valedictorian (Linn, 63). She delivered the commencement address at Rockford (Mooney, 36).

Jane's first summer after her formal graduation was not the time of rest and relaxation for which she had hoped. Jane, her stepbrother George, her father, and her stepmother decided to take a trip to the copper country around Lake Superior. John Huy Addams was thinking of investing in some land there, and the family decided to combine business with pleasure. It was not to be.

Mr. Addams became violently ill on the trip. They took him back to Green Bay, Wisconsin, and he died within 36 hours. The diagnosis was "inflammation of the bowels" (a ruptured appendix). The family laid his 59-year-old body to rest in the cemetery at Cedarville, a quarter mile from his Illinois home (Linn, 65).

One expression of sympathy was particularly important to Jane. At John Huy Addams' death, an editor of a Chicago daily wrote about his friend John (Addams, *Twenty Years*, 32–33; Kittredge, 22; Linn, 4). The editor reported that there were some Illinois legislators who during the days of the Civil War and Reconstruction had never taken a bribe. The editor, however, proudly "wished to bear testimony that he personally had known but this one man who had never been offered a bribe because bad men were instinctively afraid of him" (Addams, *Twenty Years*, 32–33).

Three days after the service, Jane wrote to her friend Ellen Starr about her feelings. "The greatest sorrow that can ever come to me has passed, and I hope it is only a question of time until I get my moral purposes straightened" (Linn, 66).

Jane decided to go ahead with plans to become a doctor. She entered the Women's Medical College of Philadelphia in October 1881. Her studies there, however, did not bring a lot of pleasure to her life and her health continued to decline. James Weber Linn— her biographer, nephew, the son of her sister Mary, and her former charge—commented, "She would not have made a good doctor, any more than she would have made a good poet; neither the purely scientific nor the purely esthetic were ever her basic interests" (Linn, 34). By February she had discontinued her studies completely. (Wheeler, 22)

Jane's health did not improve. For treatment she entered S. Weir Mitchell's Hospital of Orthopedic and Nervous Diseases. She remained there—for a while—with complete rest and with no books, visitors, or papers before returning to Cedarville (Wheeler, 22).

When Rockford Seminary, which had gained the status of a college for women and was now able to confer degrees, called her back early in 1882, Jane was still "shaky with the fatigue of a long illness that spring" (Linn, 63–64). When she found that Rockford wanted to award her a degree at the 1882 commencement exercises for her earlier, completed work (Addams, *Twenty Years*, 63), "she stepped out proudly" (Linn, 64) Jane, as valedictorian and class president, came to the stage after the two graduates for 1882 received their Rockford College degrees. The college would list Jane Addams as its first graduate because she had completed a full college program in 1881 (Addams, *Twenty Years*, 63). This would be the first of 14 degrees Jane would receive (Linn, 64). Kittie Waugh, Jane's friend, received her degree just after Jane (Mooney, 32).

Jane's health worsened. She went to Mitchelville, Iowa, where Dr. Harry Haldeman, her stepbrother and brother-in-law, performed an operation to correct the curvature of her spine (Wheeler, 23). Afterwards she was "literally bound to a bed in my sister's [Alice's] house for six months" (Addams, *Twenty Years*, 65).

After the surgery and the six-month period were over, Dr. Haldeman fitted her with a leather, steel and whalebone brace to support her spine (Wheeler, 23). Her trials, however, were not complete. When she returned to Cedarville, she found that her older brother Weber had suffered a mental breakdown. Jane tried to help Weber's wife and family with the financial arrangements. In addition to helping his family, Jane also had to manage the farm, bonds, stocks and accounts she had inherited. The value of this inheritance would be equal to about half a million dollars today (Wheeler, 23).

Despite Jane's physical problems, her spiritual struggles, her concern for others, her many chores, her limited energy, and her "nervous exhaustion," she managed to read and to keep a journal. She later read over the writings she had made "in moments of deep depression when overwhelmed by a sense of failure" and recognized the severity of her illness. To hasten her mending and to remedy her "nervous exhaustion" and lack of energy, Dr. Haldeman prescribed "two years in Europe." Jane heeded his advice (Addams, *Twenty Years*, 66).

Jane and her stepmother Anna Haldeman Addams sailed on the *Servia* for the prescribed tour of Europe in August 1883 (Mooney, 42). Two college friends (Mary and "Puss" Ellwood) and Sarah Anderson (a friend and teacher from Rockford) accompanied them; also on board was the writer Henry James (Wheeler, 23–24). Jane was not completely well, but she was mending. Actually, her struggles to heal would continue for many years (Mooney, 42). Anna and Jane's tour of Europe lasted almost two years. They visited England, Holland, Italy, Germany, Austria, France, and Greece (Mooney, 44).

Jane's stepmother kept pushing for marriage between George and Jane, but Jane was not interested. Jane saw George as a brother, but he had romantic interests in Jane. When George suffered a nervous breakdown from which he never recovered, Anna Addams blamed Jane (Wheeler, 26).

Jane decided to take a second trip to Europe to help Ellen Starr collect art reproductions in Italy and Spain both for Rockford College and for the school where Ellen was currently teaching. Jane even offered to pay half of Ellen's expenses and those of Sarah

Anderson, with whom she had traveled before. Although Ellen left in the fall, Sarah and Jane did not leave until December. Jane suffered a bout of sciatic rheumatism in Italy and had to go to bed for weeks. Her studies continued, however, when she was able to begin her tour. It was in June of 1888 while she was in England that she visited Toynbee House, the first settlement house. Persons who wanted to help the underprivileged were actually "settling" or living in the slums with the poor; the locals called these houses "settlement houses" (Addams, *Twenty Years*, 87; Wheeler, 26–28).

Jane began to make concrete plans for the future. She would help the poor and under-privileged in the United States by establishing a settlement house like Toynbee and per-haps like the one Jane had envisioned as a child. Jane admitted, however, that she could not "tell just when the very simple plan that afterward developed into the Settlement began to form itself in my mind" (Addams, *Twenty Years*, 85).

The social, religious movement Jane saw in London influenced her. She decided to join a church so that her decision to help others would be a religious commitment. Jane believed that the religion she chose should be one that encouraged service as well as belief; she would not, however, impose her religion upon others. When she returned from her travels, the Presbyterian Church in Cedarville, Illinois, accepted her for baptism in the fall of 1888. Within 11 months, she became a member in full standing (Addams, *Twenty Years*, 78).

Jane and Ellen Gates Starr—her friend from Rockford—decided to make their home in one of the poorest districts of Chicago and moved there in January 1889. Immigrants from many foreign countries settled in this ghetto. Jane and Ellen wanted to share and help solve the problems of illness, death, disease, unemployment, illiteracy, hunger, divorce, child care, injustice, and violence. Jane and Ellen began a diligent search for a suitable settlement house (Addams, *Twenty Years*, 92–94).

One Sunday afternoon on her way to a Bohemian mission meeting, Jane saw a fine old house that looked perfect. Because it was Sunday and because she was in someone else's carriage, she had to postpone her inquiry until later. The very next day—and for sev-eral days thereafter—she returned to the area, but she was unable to locate the house. She gave up hope of finding it again (Addams, *Twenty Years*, 92).

Ellen and Jane began to search Chicago for a house in which to live. Three weeks later they were overjoyed to find unexpectedly the hospitable-looking home that Jane had first seen on her carriage three weeks before. Located on Halstead Street (Kent, 9), the fine old house had been built in 1856 and had "responded kindly to repairs." The bottom floor was being used for offices and store rooms for a factory behind it. Helen Culver, the current owner of the house and the cousin of original owner Charles J. Hull, allowed Jane and Ellen to sublet both the reception area on the main floor of the building and the entire second floor. After their initial move on September 18, 1889, the current owner gave them a free lease for the entire building starting the next spring (Addams, *Twenty Years*, 93–94).

Jane and Starr named their large building "Hull House" in honor of Charles J. Hull (Addams, *Twenty Years*, 93–94). They took great pride in moving into the new house. Jane wrote: "Probably no young matron ever placed her own things in her own house with more pleasure than that with which we first furnished Hull-House" (Addams, *Twenty Years*, 94) Mary Keyser, the housekeeper, rounded out their staff. Jane reported that Miss Keyser became essential to their work and that her "death five years later was most sincerely mourned by hundreds of our neighbors" (Addams, *Twenty Years*, 95).

The area was not a popular place to live. Jane found that people moved away as soon as they could afford to do so. Immigrants who were newly arrived and ignorant of their rights and duties moved into the vacated homes—originally built for one family but now occupied by several. Often the only water supply for the families was a faucet in the back-yard. Fire escapes were rare. Sweat shops flourished (Addams, *Twenty Years*, 99).

Jane had been at Hull House for only a few days when she realized that many young mothers were in particular need of help. In order to get to their jobs, they had been lock-ing their children in their homes. The first three crippled children she saw there had been injured while their mothers were away; one child had fallen out of the third-floor window, another had been severely burned, and the third had a curved spine from being tied to a table leg each day while its mother worked for three long years (Addams, *Twenty Years*, 167–68). Their work was cut out for them. They opened a day nursery—an innovative idea for that area of Chicago—to provide care for the many local children who needed quality adult supervision. Some children brought a penny to help pay for their care, but Jane and Ellen never turned away those who did not have payment (Addams, *Twenty Years*, 169). Jane observed that the locals recognized that they were willing to help in any way—no matter how "humble." She commented, "We were asked to wash the new-born babies, and to prepare the dead for burial, to nurse the sick, and 'to mind the children,'" (Addams, *Twenty Years*, 109). Whenever people needed her, she was there.

Around Christmas of that first year at Hull House, Jane identified another need for change. Jane and some Hull House workers planned a celebration party for the children in the area. When the youngsters came, however, they were too tired to enjoy the party and refused the candy served to them. These children had been working as many as 14 hours a day, seven days a week in a local candy factory. Their employers sometimes had not given them a lunch break but instead had told them just to eat the candy they were wrapping. The sight of the sweets sickened the little children. Jane and others at Hull House began to work peacefully but effectively to help establish child labor laws (Mooney, 96–98; Kent, 21). The Illinois legislature passed a law forbidding labor for children under 14 years of age; it also limited the conditions under which children could work. Florence Kelley and Jane Addams were instrumental in apprising others of the conditions of work for children. The laws and regulations were not popular with everyone, however; many of the businesses disliked the elimination of a cheap, easily controlled work force and, sad to say, some parents objected to eliminating another source of family income (Mooney, 101–102).

Jane always enjoyed telling about her first public stand for peace. After she came to Hull House, she noticed some young boys pretending to be soldiers and marching in for-mation with sticks as guns. Jane encouraged them to use shovels; she told them that they could clean the streets after their game. She noticed, however, that when she was not pres-ent, they took up their "arms" again. In 1898 she told the story in her address to the Acad-emy of Political and Social Sciences (Polikoff, 173).

Jane's work at Hull House led her to become politically active on another front. Young, single women who worked in the factories received poor treatment and low wages. Yet these women had to accept this abuse because they had no one to help them. Jane found an apartment house for these young women, furnished two apartments for them, paid the first month's rent, and helped them plan peaceful, effective strategies to change their unde-sirable working conditions. They called themselves "The Jane Club" (Mooney, 89–90; Wheeler, 48).

One example of workers' trying to stand up for their rights, however, impacted Jane directly. In July 1894, Jane's sister Mary—who had married a Presbyterian minister after her matriculation to Rockford—was dying and waiting for her family to arrive. The Pullman strike of 1894 was in full swing. Mary realized that employees in many public transportation companies were backing the Pullman Transportation Workers. Mary kept asking for family, and Jane kept explaining what was happening. Mary, even in very poor health, recognized the necessity for human rights (Addams, *Twenty Years*, 216–18; Mooney, 104–05).

The strike brought arguments and bloodshed. Jane could see both sides of the situation and wanted the two parties to try to settle the dispute and bring about conciliation (Hovde, 83). Jane's ability to see both sides of a problem disturbed her friends and co-workers. They wanted her to "take a firm stand" (Wheeler, 63).

The Pullman strike forced the promotion of arbitration and conciliation in the industry. Jane's *A Modern King Lear* was her contribution to the literature about the strike. After George M. Pullman reduced the wages of his workers five separate times, the workers had begun their strike and the American Railway Union engaged in a sympathetic boycott of Pullman cars. President Cleveland sent in federal troops and defeated both groups. Jane saw dispute as an example of the class distinction: Pullman was a benevolent parent who develops a town for the good of his employees and his own satisfaction; the dependent workers had an employer who seemed more intent on presenting a positive image than giving them the monetary compensation they needed and deserved for their work (Lasch, *The Social Thought of Jane Addams*, 105–06).

Addams compared Pullman to King Lear and the workers to Cordelia, Lear's daughter. Pullman believed that he was right and that he deserved loyalty and love; he felt self-pity because the workers were angry with him. Like Cordelia, the workers spoke without tenderness, memory, pity, or loyalty (Addams, *A Modern Lear*, included in Lasch, *The Social Thought of Jane Addams*, 107–23). Addams observed, "The entire strike demonstrated how often the outcome of far-reaching industrial disturbances is dependent upon the personal will of the employer or the temperament of the strike leader" (Addams, *Twenty Years*, 215). She viewed the strike as a social conflict between the unorganized worker and the employer.

A Modern Lear, which she read at the Chicago Woman's Club and the Twentieth Century Club in Boston, received many comments. Most listeners noted that the work would probably anger both groups: the strikers and George M. Pullman. She decided therefore not to attempt publication until much later—1912, in fact (Lasch, *The Social Thought of Jane Addams*, 105–06).

The area around Hull House (the Nineteenth Ward) had the third highest death rate in Chicago. One reason was the infrequent garbage collection. Rats and flies bred in the filth at the curbs. Children played in streets paved with rubbish because their homes had no yards. Jane found a peaceful but successful way to change this shocking condition (Mooney, 101–102). Jane and some of the Hull House residents investigated the system of garbage collection. In their ward alone they found 1,037 violations of sanitary laws. When the problem persisted, Jane submitted a bid to remove the garbage. The mayor threw out her bid on a technicality (Wheeler, 6–63), but in 1894 he appointed her as Sanitary Inspector. Jane was the first woman to hold that position in the Chicago area. It was the only paid position she ever held in her life; she earned $1000 a year (Elshtain, 168; Kent, 22; Wheeler, 65). Soon the ward near Hull House dropped from the third highest death rate to the seventh—a decided improvement (Mooney, 111).

During Jane's clean-up campaign, sanitation workers found a paved street under a five-inch layer of rubbish. Filth had hidden the pavement for so many years that the residents had forgotten the road existed. With Jane's personal supervision of the garbage collection each day, the illness and death rate in the ward began to drop. Her work to develop a clean play area for the children further reduced the spread of germs. With the title of Garbage Inspector, Jane brought a healthy change to Chicago (Mooney, 110).

Jane worked also with senior citizens. The elderly in the "poor house" were often despondent and lonely. Jane developed a special program by which they could visit at Hull House for a two-week vacation, enjoy some freedom to come and go as they wished, and relish some time in a local coffee house. This small favor created great happiness and generated stories that the vacationers told all winter in the more organized facility (Mooney, 87).

Marching bands, music clubs, printing rooms, libraries, and socials all became very much a part of Hull House. Her settlement house, "a living thing," received "in exchange for the music of isolated pieces the volume and strength of the chorus" (Addams, *Twenty Years*, 125). Jane wanted to bring art and music to the lives of the people in the Chicago area. Once when she overheard someone condemning the supplying of these pleasures to area residents who were hungry, she responded: "Art feeds hungry souls. People who go through life with no beauty for comfort are as underfed as those with an empty stomach" (Mooney, 137).

Jane's work was varied and intense. Even an elevator operator recognized her many responsibilities and concerns. Once when she arrived at the Chicago City Club for lunch, he asked, "Are you eating with garbage or social evil today?" Jane smiled and responded, "With garbage. Third floor, I believe" (Mooney, 144).

Jane herself contracted typhoid fever in 1895 and was very sick for a while. Mary Roset Smith, a friend of Jenny Dow who taught in the Hull House kindergarten, helped care for her. Her doctor prescribed a trip abroad to help her to rest and recover from the ravages of her illness. One of the highlights of Jane's trip was meeting and dining with the Russian author, reformer and philosopher Leo Tolstoy, who lived with the poor. She always remembered that he ate only black bread and porridge although he served his guests a better fare (Kittredge, 74–75).

People throughout the world began to recognize the name of Jane Addams and Hull House. Famous visitors regularly found their way to Jane's door. President Theodore Roosevelt, the premier of Canada and the president of American Telegraph and Telephone Company were among the distinguished visitors to Hull House. Jane also traveled the country giving speeches and telling the world about Hull House; she still managed Hull and oversaw the remodeling of the original structure (Wheeler, 68–70). Many persons contributed to the remodeling and helped to keep Hull House open.

One person whom Jane could never get to contribute to Hull House was her stepmother, Anna Haldeman Addams. Jane seemed to make matters worse when she suggested that if her father had lived, he would have made donations to the settlement (Wheeler, 70).

Several Hull House workers achieved national fame. For instance, Frances Perkins became the first female Secretary of Labor. Dr. Alice Hamilton accepted the position of Professor of Industrial Medicine at Harvard. Florence Kelley helped establish and became General Secretary of the National Consumers League. Julia Lathrop was instrumental in organizing the first juvenile court in the nation. Of course, Jane's name is still a household word.

In 1901, Jane again encountered death. Leon Czolgosz assassinated America's President William McKinley. The murder produced hysteria, and the police began to round up immigrants suspected of holding radical views. One of the families arrested and held without bail was that of Abraham Isaaks, who had attended lectures and discussions at Hull House. While Jane was unable to post bail, the mayor did allow her to visit Isaaks and to secure a lawyer. Shortly thereafter, the prison system freed Isaaks and his family. Jane received much unfavorable exposure but continued to do what she believed was right. A short time later she intervened again when the sister of a suspected assassin was arrested, area printing offices were ransacked, and tenements were searched. The lawyer she secured was Harold Ickes, who later became Franklin Delano Roosevelt's Secretary of the Interior (Wheeler, 70–72).

In 1905, Jane began serving in an additional capacity. She began a period of service with the Board of Education. She immediately found herself in a struggle between the superintendent—supported by most of the board—and the Teachers' Federation. She described her service by saying, "I certainly played a most inglorious part in this unnecessary conflict; I was chairman of the School Management committee during one year when a majority of the members seemed to me exasperatingly conservative, and during another year when they were frustratingly radical, and I was of course highly unsatisfactory to both" (Addams, *Twenty Years*, 335).

Jane stated that before the experience, she had believed "existing arrangements and the hoped for improvements must be mediated and reconciled to each other" (Addams, *Twenty Years*, 336); she found, however, that on this occasion, both sides looked on these efforts as "uncompromising and unworthy" (Addams, *Twenty Years*, 336). Even the general public seemed to regard attempts at discussion with ridicule—rightly or not. Addams expressed her "discouragement over this complicated difficulty of open discussion" (Addams, *Twenty Years*, 338).

Sadovnik and Semel note that in a letter to Graham Wallace (July 1, 1906), Jane regretted taking the appointment to the Board of Education. She found her first year "stormy and very unsatisfactory." She wondered if there was a way for education to become "more democratically self-governing" (Sadovnik and Semel, 158). She yearned for a curriculum not only to help immigrant students adjust to life in America but also to help them appreciate their culture (Palmer, 182).

Between 1902 and 1910, Jane entered into a period of intense writing. Addams based her book *Democracy and Social Ethics* (1902) on her earlier speeches and lectures; she formed these speeches and lectures into articles, some of which had already been published in *Atlantic Monthly* and the *American Journal of Sociology*. She believed that this book would help her reach an even wider audience. Although she noted in her writing that there were faults with the social system of the country, she did not attack the economic system. She stressed that there can be no social justice without enduring peace. Hers was a hopeful message (Hovde, 91, 120).

Democracy and Social Ethics received excellent reviews. On page 172 of *The Long Road of Woman's Memory*, the publisher quotes from *The Review of Reviews*: "Its pages are remarkably—we were about to say refreshingly—free from the customary academic limitations...." The publisher also notes a review from the *Philadelphia Ledger*: "Too much emphasis cannot be laid upon the efficiency and inspiration ... [contained] by these essays.... The book is startling, stimulating, and intelligent" (Addams, *The Long Road of Woman's Memory*, 172). William James remarked that Addams had said instinctively "the truth we others vainly seek" (Linn, 438).

In *Newer Ideals of Peace* (1907), Jane tried to advance alternatives to war. She advocated nourishing human life and cited the "peaceful" struggles of scientists from all countries working together to combat tuberculosis (Hovde, 101). She expressed desire that working people would not accept war (Wheeler, 92).

In *The Spirit of Youth and the City Streets* (1909) Jane related some of the case histories of the youth she knew. She identified particular dangers that beset young people in Chicago and shared some of the stories of "hobo" youth. Her book included also the delinquencies and hard times of these young people (Hovde, 53). Soon after its publication, she received the appointment of first woman president of the National Conference of Charities and Corrections (Wheeler, 76).

In 1909 Jane attended by special invitation a Washington conference on caring for dependent children. The speakers were waiting to step up on the stage. The flustered young man in charge began to check to see that the platform party was ready. "Are we all here? Yes, here is my Catholic speaker, my Jewish speaker, the Protestant, the colored man and the woman. Let's all go on." Jane remarked to Booker T. Washington, "You see, I am last; that is because I have no vote." He replied, "I am glad to know the reason. I have always before been the end of such a procession myself" (Addams, *A Second Twenty Years*, 18).

In 1910 her best-known book appeared in print. *Twenty Years at Hull House* became the first volume of her autobiography (Kent, 23). Jill Ker Conway saw this volume as a way to build support for her goals. Conway viewed Addams's writing in the volume as the "romantic style of women's narrative [and described] her key decisions as conversion experiences ... [she] presented herself as the embodiment of maternal instincts." Conway opinioned Addams as "a prisoner of the mystique created by her public's response to her intellect and moral character" (Conway, 506).

Jane had wanted to pursue a degree from Smith, but she had gone to Rockford instead. In 1910, Smith fulfilled Jane's earlier desire. Smith conferred on Jane Addams the LL.D. (Linn, 293). On the October day when she received this degree, she shared the stage with 95-year-old Julia Ward Howe, the author of "The Battle Hymn of the Republic." Jane was the first of these "two champions of American democracy" to receive her degree. When Howe's turn came, 2,000 young women, accompanied by the organ, began the chorus: "Mine eyes have seen the glory...." It was a memorable ceremony for everyone present (Wheeler, 78).

A New Conscience and an Ancient Evil appeared in print in 1911. Her friends encouraged her not to write or to publish this book because of its controversy. In the book she treated a taboo subject: prostitution. Jane argued that proper wages for women would help to put an end to prostitution; women would not resort to this way of making a living if they had other sources of income. Jane also wrote that eliminating such breeding grounds as dance halls, pool parlors, and bars would help bring control of the profession; she argued that giving women the vote would help to eliminate this ancient evil (Wheeler, 79–83).

On August 7, 1912, Jane attempted to solve social problems in a new ways: She endorsed a political candidate at the national level. Not only did Jane campaign for the re-election of Theodore Roosevelt as presidential candidate on the National Progressive Party ticket but she also made history on the night of his nomination by being the first woman to second the nomination of a presidential candidate. The audience recognized her brief speech with cheering, and the convention burst out singing, "The Battle Hymn of the Republic." The *Chicago Tribune* reported that her appearance was a "marker in the political history of the nation" (Hovde, 4). Her pithy, concise speech was, according to an editorial in the *Philadel-*

phia North American, "one of the greatest examples of pure oratory since Lincoln's address at Gettysburg.... She is one of the ten greatest citizens of this republic" (Hovde, 4).

Theodore Roosevelt had already served two terms as leader of the Republican Party and president of the United States. He could have served a third, but he left the country to vacation in Africa and Europe; the people elected William Howard Taft. Roosevelt could not win the Republican election upon his return to the country so he sought to establish a platform for a third party: the National Progressive Party (Hovde, 7–9).

Roosevelt met with Jane about this plan when he visited Chicago in 1911. She talked with him about the party's platform and encouraged the vote for women; he admitted that Jane was one of the best arguments for the vote for women. They discussed also the objectives of the National Child Labor Committee, the Women's Trade Union, and the American Association for Labor Legislation, all organizations that Jane supported. Whereas the Republican Party had expressed no interest in proposals for the prohibition of child labor for those under 16, a six-day work week, an eight-hour day, woman suffrage, and the abolition of sweatshops, the National Progressive Party showed interest.

Now throngs of people pushed and shoved to get a better view of the proceedings in the Chicago armory. By the time the event was over and Jane had returned home, she realized she had lost her hat. When the Union League Club found out about her loss, they presented her with a check for $50 to purchase a new one. She sent the check back with a note saying that the two-year-old hat had cost only $10 when it was new (Addams, *Twenty Years,* 44).

Jane had had to accept the Progressive Party Platform as a whole at the convention. The platform had included building two battleships a year, unless an international agreement limited the naval forces. Jane was opposed to war—and she knew well the cost of their construction and their maintenance. She later said, "I confess that I found it very difficult to swallow those two battleships" (Addams, "Jane Addams Stands," as cited by Resek, 329).

Although many people were proud to see women moving into politics, some considered her actions unbecoming to a woman. Nevertheless, Jane continued her work for social reform. Her next effort came in 1913 when she attended in Vienna the International Suffrage Alliance. This was a stepping stone to her later, significant work for peace—a passion in her life (Mooney, 148–49). When she returned to Hull House, she found that Roosevelt and his friends were no longer supporting the National Progressive Party; the party was disintegrating. Jane still had hopes for peace (Hovde, 98).

Peace, however, was not to be. War broke out in Europe in 1914.

On January 10, 1915, Jane, Carrie Chapman Catt, Lillian Wald and labor defender Crystal Eastman called together 26 representatives of women's groups. From this group came the Woman's Peace Party, the WPP; this was the first major, independent peace group for women (Brill, 65). The women advocated a voice for women in foreign policy and controls over the manufacture and sale of weapons; they vowed to educate children for peace and to eradicate the economic causes of war (Brill, 66).

The International Congress of Women at The Hague planned for 1915 would become instead the first meeting of the Women's League for Peace—with Jane as its head (Fisher, 3). On April 14, 1915, Jane, Emily Balch, and 40 other American women who wanted to bring about world peace began their revolutionary, controversial, dangerous voyage to attend the First Congress of Women. Their route would take them across underwater mine fields and through war zones on the old Holland-American steamship *Noordam* (Fisher, 3).

Many people opposed the voyage and the goals of the women. Even Jane was not sure what the outcome would be. She wrote to Emily Greene Balch, her friend who taught economics at Wellesley College and who later received the Nobel Peace Prize, that "the whole undertaking ... may easily fail—even do harm" (Hovde, 105). These words seemed to foreshadow Balch's fate: Wellesley did not renew her contract (Hovde, 105).

The reaction of Theodore Roosevelt was distaste. Only months before, Roosevelt had visited Jane in Chicago, and she had seconded his nomination as a presidential candidate. Now he was calling their strategy for peace "silly and base" (Hovde, 105). He tried to insult her by calling her "poor bleeding Jane" (Polikoff, 177). Roosevelt declared that the work was silly because it would be futile; it was base because they dared not stand up against wickedness (Hovde, 105).

In her book *Peace and Bread in Time of War* (1922, 1960), Addams does not exert time or energy in discussing his ridicule. She does indicate, however, that the responsibility for continuing the war does not rest entirely on the belligerent nations; the people of the world and neutral governments must assume some responsibility also—and that seemed to be a major goal of their meeting abroad (Addams, *Peace and War*, 21; Polikoff, 177).

Peace and Bread in Time of War contains some war-time experiences and reflections. She recounts some of the activities of women to prevent the bloodshed and to deal with its consequences during and after the war years. Elshtain describes *Peace and Bread in Time of War* as one of Addams's most powerful books (Elshtain, 205, 222).

At one point on the voyage, an English boat approached the *Noordam* and trained a machine gun on it. English sailors came aboard, searched the liner, and removed two German stowaways. Other vessels approached the *Noordam* and five of them lined up at its side for a while (Fisher, 3). Alice Hamilton, Emily Greene Balch, and Jane give a complete account of this harrowing encounter and of the meeting of the women in their book *The Women at The Hague.*

When the group was finally able to move forward and meet with the other delegates, they planned for annual conferences to pursue peace in the years to come; they produced 11 "planks" for peace (Mooney, 150). One of the planks was the funding of a court to resolve international disputes (Kent, 24). President Wilson would later use many of these planks in his peace plans. Another important outcome of the meetings of women at the congresses would be the founding of the Women's International League for Peace and Freedom.

In August 1915 Henry Ford became excited about the work for peace and funded a ship to sail and to promote the cause of tolerance and understanding (Mooney, 84, 151). Jane, who never pursued the limelight, felt that she should participate in the mission. The *Oskar II* was scheduled to sail on December 4. A bout of pneumonia, however, prevented her from sailing on the ship. While she was in the Presbyterian Hospital, President Woodrow Wilson sent her flowers and a note of sympathy (Linn, 317).

Jane and Carrie Chapman Catt gave the "call" to the convention of the Women's Peace Party in Washington. Only five weeks after her bout with pneumonia, Jane forced herself to attend the meeting. This relatively new organization had 3000 in attendance (Addams, *Peace and Bread*, 7). In her weakened condition, Jane seemed on the verge of collapse. Her friends took her to California for a rest. In April when she returned to Chicago, she became worse again. Dr. James B. Herrick diagnosed her condition as tuberculosis of the kidney, and surgeons removed one of her kidneys. Henry Ford once again contacted her and urged her to go to a peace conference in Stockholm; her doctors informed her, however, that she would die if she attempted the trip. Emily Balch, the Nobel Peace Prize recipient of 1946, went in her place (Linn, 317).

World War I brought Jane additional challenges. She, along with Emily Balch. Alice Hamilton, and more than 1000 other committed women throughout the world, continued to work for peace even after America's entry into the war. The Hague International Congress of Women had been a threat to Jane's physical well being and her prestige in Chicago, the United States, and the world. Many people thought that Jane should devote her energies to helping the war effort. That she had been advocating peace when her nation was at war caused many to condemn and despise her. She took comfort in the fact that President Wilson used some of the ideas that the women developed at The Hague in his Fourteen-Point Plan for Peace.

Jane described her feelings during this period: "It was at this time that I first learned to use for my own edification a statement of Booker T. Washington's: 'I will permit no man to make me hate him'" (Kittredge, 87). She did not permit the criticisms by others to keep her from talking about what she believed important: peace (Kittredge, 87). Jane noted that the "misunderstanding" brought her very close to self-pity, "perhaps the lowest pit into which human nature can sink." She also had to caution herself not to "travel from the mire of self-pity straight to the barren hills of self-righteousness" because she would hate herself "equally in both places" (Kittredge, 91). As always, Jane gave little thought to herself when lives were at stake. She continued to work for peace in every way that she could—despite much public opposition and despite continued medical problems.

In 1916 Addams saw in print another of her books: *The Long Road of Woman's Memory*, which became one of Jane's favorite. In the work she discusses such topics as women who challenged war, women in industry, and laws that do not allow women to retain their own wages (Addams, *The Long Road of Woman's Memory*, vii).

In 1919 Jane presided over the Second Women's Peace Congress in Zurich. She helped to form and became the first international president of the Women's International League of Peace and Freedom (WILPF); she retained this position until 1929 (Schraff, 32). The secretary-treasurer was Emily Balch (Opfell, 30). The creed of the WILPF reflected Addams's personal philosophy: "To unite women in all countries who are opposed to any kind of war, exploitation and oppression, and who work for universal disarmament..." (Opfell, 30).

Many of Jane's actions resulted in ill will from various groups and individuals. Her advocaton of peace organization during wartime caused the rancor of the DAR. Her active involvement in the Civil Liberties Union, an organization to help secure the rights of African Americans and all people, caused the disapproval of some other groups. She worked to let the world know about human needs after the war; she cared about all who were hungry and sick. Her concern for postwar Germany caused public opinion against her to increase. She was no longer a saint to the masses (Kent, 26). Upon her return from Germany—and even the neutral country of Switzerland—where she observed the child victims of war, she reported "moving skeletons," "listlessness," "emaciated bodies," (Addams, *Peace and Bread*, 169–70), "pallid gray faces, swollen bellies, matchstick legs, and shoulder blades like wings" (Polikoff, 189). The press charged her with "pro–Germanism" (Hovde, 117).

Jane continued to serve people personally and to write for the public. She chaired and led national and international women's organizations concerned with world peace. With her traveling companion Mary Smith, she traveled extensively because, according to

Polikoff, "she no longer felt her own country to be a hospitable place" (Polikoff, 193). She still managed Hull House successfully. During the campaign for the voting rights of women, Jane was there. She had to work long, hard hours with others to assist her. To do all these jobs seemed a task for a superhuman. Jane was able to do it all well, but those who knew her best said she always looked tired (Polikoff, 193).

There was one campaign, however, that Jane did not enter. She did not support the Equal Rights Amendment to the Constitution (ERA). Her explanation was that if Congress passed the ERA, the labor laws that she and others, like Dr. Florence Kelley and Alice Hamilton, had worked so hard to pass for the protection of women might become worthless (Wheeler, 117).

In 1923 Jane had another bout with illness. While she was in Japan, a doctor found a malignancy in her breast. Surgery followed. Her friend Alice Hamilton dropped everything and came to Japan to be with her during her recuperation period (Polikoff, 193).

Polikoff notes that Jane's brand of social work was old-fashioned to many. She did not achieve re-election in the National Federation of Settlements. Her role was, to her, a demotion: emeritus status. She remarked that some people regarded her ideas as a wreck, but she said that she could "still feel the rudder in my hand and I think I can still steer." Jane went on to state "that it takes more courage to abandon one's principles and habits of life than to keep on with them" (Polikoff, 192).

In January 1927 many of Jane's friends held a dinner to honor her. President Calvin Coolidge sent greetings to the party. New York Governor Al Smith telegraphed the group: "In honoring Jane Addams we honor the idealism of American womanhood" (Kent 27). More than 1500 people planned to attend the function. Her friends secured the Chicago Furniture Mart—the largest floor space in the city—for the event (Polikoff, 195). Jane did not pretend contentment with her achievements. She admitted some successes, but she also claimed much to do (Polikoff, 197). After her introduction she described herself as "'a very simple person; most of the time not right ... but—wanting to be.'" Linn said that Jane believed she was simple, but he saw her as unique (Linn, 437).

Conway saw a different picture of Jane Addams than that which Jane professed on that night. Conway theorized that the 1927 speech in which she described herself as "simple" and a person "who was often not sure of what she was doing" was merely a strategy Jane had used successfully for more than 40 years; Conway interpreted Addams's words as being merely a tactic to increase support for her controversial measures. Conway asserted that Jane assumed "the role of a woman who was more fitted to run a home than an organization, who was a passive player in her own history and who, should she achieve something of significance in the wide world, would not claim credit for it" (Polikoff, 196).

Jane created even more dissension at a national meeting of the Women's International League for Peace and Freedom. Lillian Cantor, who had earlier arranged a speaking tour for Addams in Pennsylvania, was just back from a European trip. She expressed concern about Hitler and what he was doing to others; Cantor wanted the WILPF to develop a resolution to condemn Hitler's actions. Jane, however, saw the resolution as an aggressive act that could promote war and openly expressed her opposition; the membership defeated the resolution. Three hundred members walked out of the meeting. Many canceled their membership. Jane mourned the fact that she was the reason for discord in the Women's International League for Peace and Freedom (Polikoff, 202).

By 1930 many of her angry critics had forgotten all of the insults and the anger they had directed toward Jane. They acknowledged her endless work to help others and to try to bring about world peace. They honored her in 1930 with a seventieth birthday dinner. After Jane's introduction, she remarked, "I do not know any such person as you have described here tonight" (Linn, 416). Jane used the occasion to speak about peace. "We don't expect to change human nature, we people of peace, but we do expect to change behavior." She was not overly optimistic. "Ours may not be an inspiring role.... It tests our endurance and our moral enterprise, and we must see that we keep on" (Linn, 416).

Mrs. Eleanor Roosevelt was among those who celebrated Jane's writings, work for international peace, service to others, and Hull House. Mrs. Roosevelt said, "It is for being yourself that I thank you tonight" (Linn, 414–415). She continued, "When the day comes when difficulties are faced and settled without resorting to the type of waste which war has always meant, we shall look ... upon the leadership you have given us, Miss Addams, and be grateful for having had you living with us" (Linn, 415).

In 1931 Jane received the Nobel Peace Prize. At the time that Jane and Dr. Nicholas Murray Butler received word that they would share the Nobel Peace Prize, Jane was very sick in a hospital bed. She could not travel abroad to accept her award. It was 1935 before Jane was able to celebrate her great honor with others. Accompanying the Nobel Peace Prize was a gift of $16,480; Jane awarded the money to a favorite organization, the Women's International League for Peace and Freedom (Linn, 392).

Professor Halvdan Koht, a member of the Nobel Committee and professor of history at the University of Oslo, gave the presentation speech for both Jane and Butler on December 10, 1931. (They were *both* absent.) Koht honored the war-time leadership of the International Congress of Women that met in 1915 at The Hague. He did not hesitate to comment on Addams's unpopular status during the 1920s. "She held fast to the ideal of peace even during the difficult hours when others [were drawn] ... into the conflict" (Koht, 3). He went on to remark on the fact that at times her views were not popular ones, but "she never gave in, and in the end she regained the place of honor she had had before in the hearts of her people" (Koht, 3).

Addams donated some of her other monetary awards to help the jobless in the Hull House neighborhood—and the need was there with the economic impact of the Great Depression (Wheeler, 122; Hovde, 18).

One of the successes she enjoyed reporting was that of matching some of the jobless to the perfect place of employment. She once found a circus trapeze performer a job of washing the upper windows at Hull House. The children especially liked to watch him "run along the sills and open and shut the windows" (Polikoff, 190).

Jane seemed always ready to admit her shortcomings. She loved to tell the story of how she saw a poor woman shivering in the cold and how she had removed her fur-lined cape and draped it around the poor woman's shoulders. Rather than end the story here, however, Jane liked to show her honesty and her humanness. She told how she later regretted that she gave away her beautiful coat!

Jane received many more awards and honors including an honorary degree from Smith College, the college she had longed to attend. She became "one of the six most outstanding present-day Americans, the other five being men." Swarthmore College gave a degree recognizing her work for peace. Rockford, her alma mater, presented her with an honorary doctoral degree.

She published *The Excellent Become the Permanent* in 1932; this book was a collection of eulogies. She believed that eulogies helped to maintain the links between the living and the dead. The people eulogized in the book are generally not well-known, but the reader grows to know them through her writings. The eulogies help to keep the person alive.

When Julia Lathrop, Jane's friend and co-worker, died in 1932, Jane decided to write a tribute; the biography became a history of the time and the events that the two women, their friends, and fellow workers shared. *My Friend Julia Lathrop* appeared in 1935. Jane recognized Julia's work with the Federal Children's Bureau and Hull House. Elshtain calls the volume a "loving biography"; Addams notes that both Julia and she opposed the death penalty (Elshtain, 16, 92, 93, 191, 222, 247). In the same year, she received the American Education Award (Edwards, 82). Throughout her life she lectured, traveled, and published her articles; she had a wide readership (Cahill, 1–3).

On the morning of May 15, 1935, Jane experienced severe pain in her left side. She did not call for help at that time, but Dr. James A. Britton came the next day. When Dr. Adam Curtis and Dr. Britton conferred on May 17, they believed that it was necessary to consult with a surgeon. The surgery on May 18 revealed knotted intestines and an inoperable cancerous condition that had probably exsisted since 1931 (Linn, 419–421).

On May 20, 1935, Dr. Britton asked her if she would like some water. Still humorously promoting abstinence, Jane smiled. "Always," she said. "Always water for me." She was not, however, able to drink it, and she never spoke again (Linn, 419–21).

Jane died on May 21, 1935. The Cedarville cemetery where her father, mother, brothers, and sisters were interred was the inevitable resting place for Jane Addams. James Weber Linn, her nephew and biographer, notes that his aunt was "not a combatant"; instead she was one who "sought peace without victory. [H]er sympathy was perceptive, her sacrifices were planned, her acts were deliberate, her love was reflective" (Linn, 428–429).

Linn was willing, however, to describe his aunt as a human being with flaws but one he loved. He noted that she "occasionally mixed impatience with her devotion. She took ... acceptance of her social philosophy for granted rather than with thankful amazement, and sometimes resented the fact that tolerance seems to the fanatic either stupid or a crime" (Linn, 432).

Jane was "in small things even impatient, to direct, yet eager to serve; open in attack sometimes ... saddened by life but never frightened by it..." (Linn, 438–439).

Linn told of his aunt's habit in later years of conversing while moving about the room. Once she had climbed on a chair to straighten an etching on the wall. The picture fell and broke Jane's arm. The next day in the hospital, a visitor was reprimanding her for her impulsiveness. Jane quickly replied, "If that picture had been hung right in the first place, this needn't have happened'" (Linn, 120).

Others "adored her, but they felt her sometimes to be a little withdrawn...." Although those who knew her best often called her "Saint Jane" behind her back, they called her "J.A." or "Sister Jane" to her face. (Linn, 433) In her early days at Hull House she was "always very sad, as if the sorrows of the neighborhood were pressing upon her, which indeed they were." Jane Addams may have "never married because she never had time" (Linn, 435).

Jane knew the torture of bodily pain and illness, "but she never knew the pangs of an offended or wounded spirit" (Linn, 437). Jane Addams had lost through death many of her friends: Julia Lathrop, Florence Kelley, and Mary Smith. After the death of Mary Smith, Jane expressed her sadness: "I suppose I could have willed my heart to stop beating ... but the thought of what she had been to me for so long kept me from being cowardly" (Linn, 408; Wheeler, 125). Jane's passing was another loss to the world. Women—and men—around the globe had felt Jane's leadership.

In his Nobel Peace Prize Presentation Speech in 1931, Halvdan Koht commented on the personal characteristics of Jane Addams. "She is not one to talk much, but her quiet, great-hearted personality inspires confidence and creates an atmosphere of goodwill which instinctively brings out the best in everyone" (Koht, 2).

The Dean of the Chicago Chapel gave advice to those who were present at the funeral. He said that those who wanted to see the monuments of Jane Addams needed merely to look. He indicated that her achievements were all around them (Opfell, 33).

Emily Balch (who would become the next female Nobel Prize winner) wrote her response to the death of Jane Addams on an undated scrap of paper. It could be the charge of this generation:

> I am thankful to have known ... Jane Addams ... Help me not to dwell on my loss. Help me to enjoy her still. To learn from her and be glad of her and do what is in me to do, as she did, living to the full of her great soul (Randall, 324).

In the spring of 1943—eight years after the death of Addams—Balch sent her description of knowing and working with Jane Addams to the Women's International League for Peace and Freedom and their close comrades.

> Of all my experiences the greatest and dearest was being privileged to know Jane Addams. It is as impossible to evoke her for those who did not have the happiness of knowing her as to evoke the fragrance of a ripe strawberry or of a water-lily for someone who has never smelled one. She was so utterly unlike anyone else that I have known ... (Randall, 325).

The columnist Walter Lippman summed up Jane Addams by saying, "...those who have known her say that she was not only good, but great" (Kent, 31). Jane's gravestone succinctly records for posterity her life: "Jane Addams of Hull House and the Women's International League for Peace and Freedom" (Wheeler, 1).

Bibliography

Addams, Jane. *Democracy and Social Ethics*. New York: Macmillan. 1913.
_____. "Jane Addams Stands at Armageddon." *McClure's*, XL (1913): 12–14, as cited by Carl Resek, ed. *The Progressives*. Boston: The Bobbs-Merrill Company, 1967.
_____. *The Long Road of Woman's Memory*. New York: Macmillan, 1916.
_____. *Peace and Bread in Time of War*. Boston: G. K. Hall, 1960. (First published in 1922.)
_____. *The Second Twenty Years*. New York: Macmillan, 1930.
_____. *Twenty Years at Hull-House*. New York: Macmillan, 1938. (First published in 1910.)
_____, Emily Greene Balch and Alice Hamilton. *Women at The Hague*. New York: Macmillan, 1915.
Brill, Marlene Targ. *Women for Peace*. Danbury, Connecticut: Franklin Watts, 1997.
Cahill, Susan. *Writing Women's Lives*. New York: HarperPerennial, 1994.
Conway, Jill Ker. *Written by Herself: Autobiographies of American Women*. New York: Vintage Books, 1992.
DeBenedetti, Charles. *Peace Heroes in Twentieth-Century America*. Bloomington: Indiana University Press, 1986.
Edwards, June. *Women in American Education, 1820–1955: The Female Force and Educational Reform*. Westport, Connecticut: Greenwood Press, 2002.
Elshtain, Jean Bethke. *Jane Addams and the Dream of American Democracy*. New York: Basic Books, 2002.
Fisher, Dorothy Canfield. "Emily Greene Balch." *Bryn Mawr Alumnae Bulletin*, Winter 1956, 3. In the papers of the Swarthmore College Peace Collection.

Hovde, Jane. *Makers of America: Jane Addams*. New York: Facts on File, 1989.

Kent, Deborah. *Cornerstones of Freedom: Jane Addams and Hull House*. Chicago: Childrens Press, 1992.

Kittredge, Mary. *American Women of Achievement: Jane Addams*. New York: Chelsea House, 1988.

Koht, Halvdan. "Presentation Speech for the Nobel Peace Prize of 1931." Available online at http://www.nobelprize.org/peace/laureates/1931/press.html.

Lasch, Christopher. *The Social Thought of Jane Addams*. Indianapolis: Bobbs-Merrill, 1965.

Linn, James Weber. *Jane Addams: A Biography*. Urbana and Chicago: University of Illinois Press, 2000.

Meyer, Edith Patterson. *In Search of Peace: The Winners of the Nobel Peace Prize*. Nashville: Abingdon Press, 1978.

Mooney, Elizabeth Comstock. *Jane Addams*. Chicago: Follett, 1968.

Opfell, Olga S. *The Lady Laureates: Women Who Have Won the Nobel Prize*. Metuchen, New Jersey: Scarecrow, 1986.

Palmer, Joy A. *Fifty Major Thinkers on Education*. New York and London: Routledge, 2001.

Polikoff, Barbara Garland. *With One Bold Act: The Story of Jane Addams*. Chicago: Boswell Books, 1999.

Randall, Mercedes M. *Improper Bostonian: Emily Greene Balch, Nobel Peace Laureate, 1946*. New York: Twain, 1964.

Sadovnik, Alan R., and Susan F. Semel. *Founding Mothers and Others: Women Educational Leaders During the Progressive Era*. New York: Palgrave, 2002.

Schraff, Anne. *Women of Peace: Nobel Peace Prize Winners*. Hillside, New Jersey: Enslow, 1994.

Villard, Oswald Garrison. "What the Blue Menace Means." *Harpers Magazine*, Volume 157. October 1928, 529–49.

Wheeler, Leslie A. *Jane Addams: Pioneer in Change*. Englewood Cliffs, New Jersey: Silver Burdett, 1990.

Emily Greene Balch
(1946)

Social Worker, Teacher, Pacifist, Practical Idealist

(January 4, 1867–January 9, 1961)

Emily Greene Balch, Nobel Peace Laureate 1946.

A casual observer of 75-year-old Emily Balch on May 7, 1942, would have glimpsed an elderly woman wearing rather outdated clothing and moving purposefully. As she walked erectly and proudly into the Hotel Adelphia in Philadelphia, she wore the trusty, black velvet jacket that a Geneva tailor had made for her years before; Emily still used the garment to try to transform her "Sunday dress" into the formal attire that she needed for special events—in this case, a public birthday celebration in her honor. The Women's International League for Peace and Freedom (W.I.L.P.F.) was sponsoring the gala for one of its hardest-working, most effective leaders.

As usual, Emily wore little jewelry. Her simple necklace was one of only two that she highly treasured. The worn little black bag she carried was a part of her "formal attire" that those who knew her had often seen. At the moment, this thin, stately woman was bareheaded. She did not wear the familiar hat that Mercedes Randall—her biographer and one of her youngest and closest friends—had known Emily sometimes to wear backwards in her haste to get dressed and to go about important business. Emily prided herself on what she did—not how she appeared. Her work was more important to her than her appearance (Randall, *Improper Bostonian*, 313–14).

Emily was not a very impressive individual from a distance, but she was special upon close inspection. Her eyes expressed her concern for others—even through her thick lenses. Although Emily was in her mid-seventies, she still moved with determination and speed; her posture reflected her dignity and her resolve to be about the business at hand. Those who knew her best admitted that she sometimes displayed a coolness toward those whom she did not like, but she could welcome those she treasured with what her friend Mercedes Randall described as warmth. Those who might differ with Emily Greene Balch, Mercedes confided, often saw her as "austere" (Randall, *Improper Bostonian*, 313). This day the outstanding "old" lady who had served others as social worker, writer, teacher, pacifist, and humanitarian was the honored birthday guest of many people across the nation at a $1.50-a-plate luncheon in the "City of Brotherly Love."

The gala occasion began with the reading aloud of cables and letters from people around the globe; the many messages from supporters and personal friends wished Emily many happy returns and thanked her for her contributions to international peace. Next came the speeches—nine to be exact. Most of the lecturers, however, focused on world affairs and—at the request of Emily—not on the honoree herself.

The long-awaited orator for the day, however, was Emily Balch herself. Emily called her address "Towards a Planetary Civilization." At the end of her speech, which focused on her dreams for the planet, she expressed her longings. First, she encouraged politics that gave little thought to power and prestige for the politicians. She encouraged a civilization focused "on human beings in their every day living, with its sufferings and their aspirations." Ideally, she dreamed of a time when "a warm personal desire to serve the common good" would permeate the planet (Balch, "Towards a Planetary Civilization").

When Emily finished her address, there was no applause and no ovation. Instead there was throughout the audience "a moment's pause, and a suspicious tightening of throats, as though the audience felt this might be Emily Balch's [last appearance]" (John H. Randall, Jr., 12).

The perceptive guest of honor was quick to sense the emotions of her guests. With her usual dry wit, she responded quickly: "[T]his is not my swan song. I intend to live quite a while longer. My grandfather [Dr. Francis Vergnies Noyes] used to say, 'An old woman is as tough as a boiled owl'" (John H. Randall, Jr., 12).

Emily's humor saved the day. She had again revealed her ability to laugh—and even to make herself the butt of the joke. The audience rose as one to its feet and applauded loudly when she again paused.

This ability not to take herself too seriously was one of her most endearing attributes, according to her philosopher friend John H. Randall, Jr., the husband of Mercedes Randall. He observed that her gentle, kindly, dry wit expressed "the human wisdom of generations of New England ancestors" (John H. Randall, Jr., 12).

Indeed, when Gunnar Jahn, Chair of the Nobel Committee, made the Nobel Peace Prize Presentation Speech in 1946 to honor Emily, he, too, would refer to her background and her personal traits. Jahn would note that Emily had come from an old New England family that had left a distinct, indelible mark on her. The stimulating, intellectual Boston surroundings in which Emily found herself had traditions traceable to the Puritans who had colonized the area. Jahn quickly noted, however, that although the Balch family had detached itself from the harshness of Puritanism, it had retained its emphasis on self-discipline, personal responsibility, and an idealism based on realism. As an adult, Emily would devote all her energies to work to create a better world; she would retain many of these characteristics that her family modeled and encouraged (Jahn, 1).

Jahn, world leaders, peace workers, and women everywhere would often use the words *tough, dedicated, tireless, kindly, gentle*, and *humorous* to depict accurately Emily Greene Balch. Many other words would also be necessary to give a full description of this woman who did indeed "live quite a while longer" after her seventy-fifth birthday celebration; four years later, she even became a Nobel Peace Prize winner.

Finding both the complete range of her works and the most appropriate words to describe Emily is an easy task for primary researchers because Emily had the habit of keeping almost everything. Mercedes Randall was the recipient of many of Emily's diaries, letters, writings, personal papers, and other information; other priceless primary materials are available in the Swarthmore Peace Collection. Mercedes described Emily's papers in this way:

> When Emily Balch turned over to me, several years before her death in 1961, all her private papers, letters, journals, and unpublished manuscripts, I was amazed at the quantity of the materials, the extent of her industry, and the range of her thinking. In addition to six published books, some 110 published articles and pamphlets, there were countless mimeographed articles and speeches, manuscripts in ink or pencil, and autobiographical fragments. There were random reflections on refreshingly unexpected subjects: "Little known vegetables," "On the business of standing," "Modes of consciousness," "On the pronoun *I*." On a small pad of paper she had jotted down a series of vignettes, evocations of remembered scenes and moods [Randall, "Emily Greene Balch," 1].

Mercedes confessed that upon beginning to read the intimate journals, letters, and personal materials, she felt as if she were eavesdropping upon her friend. The shared materials, however, enabled Mercedes "to enter 'the inner life' and mind of this reticent New Englander." Mercedes was quick to note that in all the materials, "there was not one damaging revelation, nothing that cried for deletion. I found only a fulfillment of what her Bryn Mawr professors had discerned in 1889 ... 'a woman of unusual ability, of extraordinary beauty of moral character'" (Randall, "Emily Greene Balch," 1)

Emily was born in 1867 into "an age of diaries." From the time Emily was nine until she was 94, Emily kept little leather journals "in an almost unbroken succession." These diaries are a treasure to historians and to her biographers. Emily, it seemed, wrote endlessly. Mercedes said,

She never threw away a written word. In later years she filed these papers away in manila envelopes slit on the long side, which she labeled "Scripta." She even kept scraps and jottings thriftily written on torn pieces of papers or leaves of ledgers; she kept random notes; notes for speeches; ideas on religion, economics, aesthetics; evocations of remembered scenes and moods; lists of books to be read (filed under "Legenda"); autobiographical fragments. Even in the busiest periods of her life when preoccupied with international affairs, she found time for these jottings, sometimes on refreshingly unexpected subjects [Randall, *Improper Bostonian: Emily Greene Balch*, 24–25].

Mercedes indicated that the holdings in the Swarthmore College Peace Collection complemented those that she owned. Through these materials (available on microfilm for those unable to visit Swarthmore in person), one can trace Emily's life and note how Boston and the Bostonians helped make Emily the peaceful, humble woman that she became.

The documentation of the life of Emily Greene Balch began the day she was born. Her mother, Ellen Marie ("Nelly") Noyes Balch, notes in her diary the arrival of 8.5-pound Emily on January 4, 1867. Nelly Balch named her third daughter "at once for Emily Greene [a bridesmaid of Ellen Marie ('Nelly') Noyes Balch]" (Diary of Ellen Marie Balch, January 4, 1867, Diaries of 1876–1955, Swarthmore College Peace Collection).

Emily's Aunt Catherine Porter Noyes also used a diary to note the event of Emily's birth. She described Little Emily as having "[n]ice dark hair and a tolerable face" (Randall, *Improper Bostonian: Emily Greene Balch*, 24).

Nelly Balch's diaries contained further entries that indicated the importance that she placed on her daughter Emily Balch and on her entire family. Her entries noted the weaning of Emily on January 3, 1968; Emily's falling from her carriage and hurting her head on January 15, 1870; the caring required when the Balch family contracted chicken pox, coughs, and colds ("We have all been sick and all are sick and we all are going to be sick with colds and colds and colds..." January 15, 1870); the weight of Emily (65 pounds on September 10, 1876; 59 pounds on July 2, 1877); and even the weight of Nelly Balch herself (203 pounds on October 3, 1874) (Diary of Ellen Marie "Nelly" Balch, Diaries of 1876–1955, Swarthmore College Peace Collection).

The Balch family consisted of the father (Francis Balch), "Nelly" Noyes Balch, Nelly's sister (Catherine Porter Noyes), the servants, a hired man (Herbert) and occasionally nurses whom the family needed to help with the children. The family continued to grow; there was a total of six girls (Annie, Elizabeth, Emily, Elly, Alice, and Marion [Maidie]) and one boy, Francis (or "Frankie").

It was in her home, from her family, that Emily learned appreciation of others and the value of peace and harmony. Emily's first memory was a tiff with Carrie (Caroline) Ticknor, her neighbor and childhood playmate. In the bits and pieces of papers in Emily's own handwriting and in the oral recollections she shared with others are accounts of the spat and how her family helped her solve the problem. This guidance from her family stayed with her always. It is even more poignant when one reads Emily's own words:

The summer I was four and a half, the family moved to an unattractive but larger house on Burroughs Street, near Jamaica Plain. The day of the moving we [Annie Balch, Elizabeth, and Emily Balch] noticed two pretty little girls across the street. Carrie Ticknor became my great pal.... Carrie was active and ambitious and we were rivals in tree climbing and other adventures. I once told·my mother that I did not like [Carrie] because she always wanted to be first. My mother looked at me and said, "Is it because you want to be first yourself?" This was my first act of conscious self-recognition [recollection shared with Mercedes Randall and others and published in *Improper Bostonian: Emily Greene Balch*, 39].

Caroline Ticknor later became the author of *Hawthorne and His Publisher* and *Dr. Holmes' Boston.* In the years to come, Emily would hear praise for her first friend and playmate from another good friend Edith de G. Heath. In Edith's undated letter to Emily, Edith asked,

Did you know that [Caroline] has shot like a meteor of great brilliancy into the literary coterie of the country? And has had enough newspaper puffs to make her hair curl? Jamaica Plain may yet be immortalized as the birthplace of this famous author [Letter to Emily Balch from Edith de G. Heath, n.d., Swarthmore College Peace Collection].

True to form, Emily saved the letter along with many other documents, including the diaries of her mother. Nelly Balch's diaries continued to indicate her concern with the health of her seven children. On December 6, 1873, she wrote that "Bessie and the baby have chicken pox and are pretty sick"; on December 8, she added that a third child, Elly, had developed chicken pox. On January 25, 1874, she wrote again that all seven of the children were sick with colds; on May 26, illness seemed to persist because "Emily, Bessie, Elly, and baby began a cough." On December 4, 1874, Nelly wrote. "Elly violently worse." The entry of December 10, indicates a grievous event: "Funeral service...." On July 12, 1875, seven months after the funeral, Nelly Balch wrote, "My poor little baby born too soon ... pretty little baby..." (Ellen Marie "Nelly" Balch Diaries, diaries of 1873–75, Entries of December 6, 1873–July 12, 1875, Swarthmore College Peace Collection).

Emily's family made sure that Emily received a good early education. She attended private schools and welcomed further instruction at home by her tutors, by her parents, and by her Aunt Catherine Noyes. Emily was able to read *Grimm Brothers' Fairy Tales* and *Alice in Wonderland* before she even entered the first grade; she had a gift for languages and tried to teach herself German before she was nine. Her father often read to the entire family; his selections included *Gulliver's Travels* and *Arabian Nights.*

Emily's memoirs tell of the time when she was about ten and very sick with scarlet fever. Although this illness could have been a very bitter episode in her life, Emily remembered the time fondly because her mother spent much uninterrupted time with her. Mrs. Balch read aloud the novels *Ivanhoe* and *The Talisman* to her child.

A whole new world opened to Emily when she was ten and received a prescription for glasses. Even though Emily had always loved nature, this nearsighted little girl was now able to enjoy it even more. Emily's friend Mercedes Randall recalls fondly Emily's love of their strolls together and Emily's love of the outdoors:

Her love extended to all things living—to birds and plants, to wild flowers, which she could name and knew intimately, to ferns, lichens, insects, and to inanimate objects like pebbles, rocks, and seashells. Never did a nearsighted person see so much in the natural world. A country walk with her was a revelation of the richness of life [Randall, *Improper Bostonian: Emily Greene Balch*, 19].

This loving child faced a tragedy in her life at the age of 17. Her mother, Nelly Balch, died shortly after giving birth to a child who died also. Emily was so affected by these events that her father paid for her to go abroad for a respite. It was on this trip that Emily's true international education began. Not only did she learn of other places and people, but she learned also of war. While she was overseas, England faced an "inevitable" war with Russia. If war had come, Emily would have been unable to return to her country for some time. Perhaps it was this narrow escape from an unwelcome detention that helped her remain calm during many other turbulent times ahead in her life.

Emily wrote home about the miserable beginning of her trip:

To go back to the beginning of the voyage, it was cold at first. Saturday evening we had a snowstorm in fact. I sat up on deck all alone wrapped in my rug and [another] one Mr. Cormack insisted on my taking. I was afraid to go below, however I had to at last. I did not undress but lay outside the bed all night without even having energy to take out my hairpins I believe. The next day I spent on the couch in my room principally ... [Letters to and from Emily Balch, 1885, Swarthmore College Peace Collection].

Emily's March 22, 1885, letter to Alice reflects the gradual return of wit and humor. She wrote about a clock that she saw in the city of Basel. Emily explained to Alice that Basel was built on both sides of the Rhine River. Because the people on the opposite banks disliked each other,

... one side to plague the other, set up on the riverbank a clock with a man's face above it which all the time kept putting out its tongue at the people opposite.... It keeps sticking its tongue out a little way and rolling its eyes (of course by machinery inside) and at the end of every minute [the clock] ran [the tongue] out so far I almost thought it would never stop but keep on till it reached Jamaica Plain [her home in the United States]. It was so absurd we all stood there and laughed and laughed and I think you would have ... [Letters to and from Emily Balch, 1885, Swarthmore College Peace Collection].

Emily was not one to travel and then do nothing further with her life. Upon her return to the United States, she entered Bryn Mawr College and in 1889 graduated with the first graduating class.

The greatest honor that Bryn Mawr awarded was its European Fellowship for a year of study abroad. Bryn Mawr would present this prize to a senior with distinction in academics and in other important areas. Emily received notice that she would receive the fellowship!

The April 12, 1889, "Report to the Trustees" contains the recommendation of the Executive Committee that the Bryn Mawr European Fellowship go to the faculty-recommended student: Emily Greene Balch. This written information accompanying their selection noted that Emily had "entered college three years ago with advanced standing. She is twenty-two years of age, a woman of unusual ability, of extraordinary beauty of moral character, of great discretion and balance of judgment, very unselfish and in every way fit to be a representative of the College and to engage in study in Europe" ("The Report to the Trustees," April 12, 1889).

Humble as always, Emily wrote home that she longed for the award but that another student, Emily James Smith ("Jim"), was more deserving than she. Emily went to President James E. Rhodes and Dean Carey Thomas to tell them that the fellowship should go to another and that she "yielded in favor of Jim Smith."

Emily received the reply that if she would not accept the fellowship, the Board of Trustees would not award the Bryn Mawr European Fellowship for the year. Emily finally did agree to accept the Bryn Mawr European Fellowship, but it was not until after Emily James Smith and she sat down and cried together (Randall, *Improper Bostonian: Emily Greene Balch*, 70).

Elizabeth Balch, Emily's sister, responded to Emily's letter informing the Balch family of the Bryn Mawr European Fellowship and Emily's acceptance of the honor. The joy of Emily's father and her sister Elizabeth is apparent in the letter that Elizabeth sent to Emily. Elizabeth described how, upon returning from the opera the previous evening, she had found an envelope on the gas fixture; the message to her announced that Emily had accepted the award. Elizabeth reported, "I nearly stood on my head but was prevented by

Papa's coming in with a beaming face so we had an empathy meeting instead." Typical of the closeness and caring attitude of the Balch family, Elizabeth also confessed, "Of course I am sorry for Jim Smith but do not let that trouble you for ... they think that you deserve it" (Letters to Emily Balch, 1889, Swarthmore College Peace Collection).

As pleased as Emily now was with her Bryn Mawr European Fellowship, she decided to postpone her study abroad in order to stay at home and spend a year in private work with Professor Franklin Giddings of Bryn Mawr. Emily herself edited—in her own hand-writing—an article by Elizabeth Stix Fainsod and titled "Emily Greene Balch"; the composition made the May 1947 issue of the *Bryn Mawr Alumnae Bulletin*. Emily's additions explained her postponement of the trip abroad and the impact of the trip on her. In regard to her life's work, Emily indicated to her interviewer that she "should have liked to work in the field of literature, but it was a time when there was much exposure of the nursery sweat shops and slums, and I felt that this was a time to try to be useful in the movement for better human relations. All my efforts since that time have been in connection with different phases of that work" ("Corrections on Fainsod article by E.G.B." and "Emily Greene Balch" by Elizabeth Stix Fainsod in *Bryn Mawr Alumnae Bulletin*, May 1947, 1–3, 14, from Emily Balch Papers in the Swarthmore College Peace Collection).

Emily spent 13 months in Paris as a part of her Bryn Mawr European Fellowship. During this time, she wrote the book *Public Assistance of the Poor in France*, published by the American Economic Association in 1893.

Emily's apprenticeship in Paris increased her interest in social work. She wrote, "I thought to myself, 'I know a lot about the Working Man in capital letters, but I don't know a working man by sight.' So I went into the office of the Children's Aid Society as an apprentice under a pioneer in that field of work, Charles W. Birtwell" (Emily Balch to Elizabeth Stix Fainsod, approved by Emily Balch on paper and quoted in "Emily Greene Balch" by Elizabeth Stix Fainsod in *Bryn Mawr Alumnae Bulletin*, May 1947, 1–3, 14, from Emily Balch Papers in the Swarthmore College Peace Collection).

After her apprenticeship, Emily wrote a small text on both institutional methods and the legalities of dealing with delinquent children.

Emily's letters from abroad continued to reflect her fondness for life and her attention to detail. Vivid descriptions and her dainty drawings characterized her communications. Without reading of her love for living things and some of her vivid descriptions, one cannot fully appreciate this Nobel Peace Prize winner. One such letter to Mary Anne contained a vivid portrayal of a scene from nature and also told a humorous story:

> Yesterday I was caught in two hailstorms—one in the morning and one in the afternoon—and today it is raining and blowing so that the poor horse-chestnut trees which line the streets are all torn and drop their blossoms into the sidewalks. But before these last few days we had some piping hot weather and thought summer was here.
>
> One disadvantage was that a family opposite hung a parrot in his cage out of their window and he was terrible. The first day we thought it was a child; he cried and sobbed and caught his breath and then screamed again in the most natural way. The next day he kept calling, "Papa. Papa." Then very gruffly, "What?" Then "Papa" over and over like a child in a tantrum and he kept that up steadily. I told Lena that the child that was the original of the perform-ance ought to have a good whipping and then it occurred to me that the parrot was giving us the whole little drama only backwards. We had heard the outcome of the fit of naughtiness the day before. I should think a parrot like that would cure any child however naughty.
>
> Our little birds are very flourishing, except that they have begun to molt. They hang out of the windows all day and I am sorry to say that we have sometimes forgotten to take them in at night....

We also rejoice in the possession of a charming little ... heather with long pinkish bells. Did you ever see them? I imagine it needs very little water but I like it [Letters to and from Emily Balch, 1890, Swarthmore College Peace Collection].

In 1890 a letter from Emily to her sister Maidie contained both a description of a view from the Eiffel Tower and an occurrence in her quarters; these two passages and her drawing express her wit and her awareness of the world about her.

The shadows of clouds over the city were very pretty and so were the ploughed fields out in the beginning of the country beyond the city and so was the ring of hills that walls in Paris.

Yesterday [my traveling companion] Lina [Fabens] called to me to come into her in the bedroom and I went in and there was a big pigeon sitting on the table. He was very pretty, a sort of pearl gray and very tame. I tried to get him to eat crumbs out of my hand but instead of doing that he pecked my fingers quite hard. Finally as he did not seem to want to go, Marie and the concierge caught him and kept him till the afternoon and then they let him go. The funniest thing was to see him stand by, as solemn as a judge, one foot on the table and one on a book [Letters from Emily Balch to Maidie Balch, 1890, Swarthmore College Peace Collection].

In this same letter, Emily tells of a visit from Mrs. Canfield and her two children; this meeting would prove to be a fortunate encounter. The 12-year-old daughter—Dorothy Canfield (Fisher), who later became a prominent American novelist and children's author—became an important person in Emily's life in the years to come. Emily noted at the time that the child reminded her of "Editha or Little Lord Fauntleroy. She is the same mixture of perfect childlikeness with the considerateness and sense of responsibility..." (Letters from Emily Balch to Maidie Balch, 1890, Swarthmore College Peace Collection).

In December 1892, after her return to the United States, Emily—with the encouragement of Helen Cheever, Helena Dudley, Mary Morton Kehew and others—started Denison House in Boston, Massachusetts. This settlement resembled the Hull House that Jane Addams had helped to found in Chicago in 1889. Jane would be a lifetime friend and co-worker for peace.

In the short, one-paragraph acceptance speech that Emily prepared for reading at the Nobel Peace Prize Award Ceremony, she cited Jane Addams. Emily expressed her grateful appreciation for the great honor of receiving the award, and she acknowledged particularly her pleasure in being associated with that previous Nobel Peace Prize winner—and dear friend (Balch, "Nobel Lecture, April 7, 1946").

Emily later told Mercedes Randall that the first choice for head worker of the Denison Settlement House was Helena Dudley, a Bryn Mawr classmate. When Helena could not accept immediately, Emily assumed the position. Helen Cheever, a schoolmate and friend, became Emily's able co-worker (Randall, *Improper Bostonian: Emily Greene Balch*, 82).

In the beginning, the primary purpose of the Denison House in Boston was to serve those who needed help. For instance, when local people were out of work, Denison House staff members helped them find employment and feed their families. Soon Emily and the others were eagerly trying to improve certain unhealthy social conditions. Even though (or perhaps because) Emily's family had been a part of the "proper" Bostonians, or "the socially and intellectually privileged," Emily made the choice to touch and to serve those in need (G.G., n.p.). Her clients would include prostitutes, paupers, prisoners, labor leaders, strikers, juvenile offenders, battered wives, the homeless, the elderly and pacifists—with whom Emily had empathy. Emily was happy to help with needed reforms, but she especially enjoyed the times when she could bring out her books and materials and teach those at Denison House.

Emily made an important decision; she resolved to give up her full-time work at

Denison House, to continue her studies, and to consider the profession of teaching. Gunnar Jahn noted in the Nobel Peace Prize Presentation for Emily that practical work alone could not exhaust her aspirations; she felt the need to acquire knowledge and to achieve even more through sharing knowledge and her love of learning with others (Jahn, 1).

Emily took course work both at Radcliffe and at the University of Chicago; she even enrolled for two semesters at the University of Berlin. Before returning to the United States, Emily and Mary Kingsbury, a fellow student, decided to visit London. The two were able to observe in July 1896 the International Socialist Workers' and Trade Union Congress; they had obtained press tickets so they could attend the sessions. The two young women saw some of the Socialist leaders, labor leaders, and original Marxists at the last of the International Socialist and Labor Congresses; they observed the emotion and the workings of the sessions, which often had as many as 800 people in attendance. At last Emily boarded the ship home. She fully expected to complete the Ph.D. upon her arrival in the United States and afterwards to enter the teaching profession.

Fate intervened. On the voyage back to America, Emily talked at length with Katharine Coman, a professor from Wellesley College and the one-person economics department there. Katharine told Emily of an opening in social sciences. Emily applied for the teaching position, and Wellesley accepted her application. Her salary at Wellesley for reading papers was $500 for half-time work. Many of her courses in the beginning were merely introductory courses (Randall, *Improper Bostonian: Emily Greene Balch*, 107), but Emily was realizing her dreams of teaching. Jahn noted that Emily began work at Wellesley "first as a lecturer and then as professor of social economics. Teaching was her principal occupation up to the First World War. But her teaching went hand in hand with practical social work in the field, membership on official commissions, and authorship of publications" (Jahn, 1).

Emily's classes were unusual for the era. First of all, most college students had never had the opportunity to be taught by a woman professor of economics. Second, she included information not usually found in the traditional economics courses. How to work with the poor, the prisoners, and the ill were practical suggestions that Emily integrated into the curriculum of her classes. This information was part of the "new" areas of sociology and of the immigrant in America. Third, in her course on the history of socialism, Emily required her students to read from Karl Marx. Marx's writings were not a part of most reading lists in America at that time, but Balch considered his works essential to a history of socialism course. Emily's classes were unusual in a fourth way: Emily employed many new teaching methods. She took her classes to prisons, reform schools, and other community sites where many Wellesley students had never before visited.

Emily's courses were popular, but she was not without critics. When H. G. Wells wrote his history of Wellesley, Emily was surprised to find that he criticized her for having the students read Marx. Some did not understand her incorporation of public service and community visits into her classes. Emily, however, lived what she taught. Every day she worked with the laborers and with those who were in need. Many of her students seemed to welcome her challenge of service.

A former student wrote of her experience in volunteering at Denison House as a part of Emily's class:

> Miss Balch and another famous Wellesley professor, Vida D. Scudder, were greatly interested in Denison House, the college settlement in Boston. During my sophomore year a call went out for college girl volunteers to take charge of some of the clubs and help with the cleri-

cal work on the case records—records which were then a comparatively new idea in charitable enterprises. I promptly offered my services. Going to the settlement meant not only giving up an entire afternoon each week but it ended my Saturday afternoon bats to Boston theatres, since I couldn't afford trips "to town" oftener than once a week. I stuck to the volunteer work, fascinated by the little Syrian and Italian girls I taught and by the first-hand contact with problems of child welfare, housing and health ["Coming of Age at Wellesley," 227].

Emily received mixed ratings on her teaching at Wellesley College. She shared her self-evaluation of her teaching at Wellesley in a 1947 article in *Bryn Mawr Alumnae Bulletin*; she was quick to note that "in some ways I was not a good teacher but I was a stimulating teacher alive to new currents" (Fainsod, "Emily Greene Balch," 2).

Emily's students seemed, in some ways, to concur with her self-assessment. One student enthusiastically wrote of her work with Miss Balch and her impressions of this teacher. These comments from a former student who attended her classes give the reader personal insight into the life of Emily Greene Balch:

Miss Balch was an utterly unpretentious woman, spare of figure, unmindful of clothes and fripperies. Besides her learning, which was broad and deep, she had a very wide personal acquaintance with civic and humanitarian leaders in Europe as well as America....
With a multiplicity of duties in various civic causes as well as in her college courses, Professor Balch would frequently overlook some of the mechanical details of teaching—roll-call, class assignments, periodic reviews. How well one remembers her dashing into the classroom at the last minute loaded down with all sorts of papers, pamphlets, reports, even heavy reference books. Often she would forget to return our examination papers, and the required reading in the reference books would also slip her mind. Sometimes she might seem to forget her class altogether; we would sit patiently the required five minutes after the last bell, and then learn somehow that our teacher was delivering a lecture in Boston or New York or attending a conference of civic leaders in Chicago ... [but] her teaching was all the better for her excursions into the buzzing centers beyond the placid college walls ["Coming of Age at Wellesley," 226–27].

Emily had a particular interest in immigration, labor problems, economic history and theory, and consumerism. With her interest in Slavic immigration, she traveled widely from 1905 through 1907 to Europe and throughout the United States. Her research resulted in the 536-page volume *Our Slavic Fellow Citizens* in 1910.

Jahn noted in the 1946 Nobel Peace Prize Presentation Speech for Emily Greene Balch that she was the first professor in America to give students lectures on immigration problems. Jahn also assessed the volume *Our Slavic Fellow Citizens* as "a landmark in the scientific analysis of immigration problems." The work seemed to illustrate, according to Jahn, Balch's methodology: visiting most of the Slav centers in United States, doing research for a year, seeing things for herself, meeting the people, and studying first-hand their conditions (Jahn, 1). To prevent students' having a one-sided view of the community, Emily also started a course to study "normal" societal conditions.

In 1910 Emily's career seemed to be advancing, but sorrow was a part of her life and figured into her advances at Wellesley. Katharine Coman, her co-worker, friend, and the head of the Wellesley Economics Department, died. The administration asked Emily to complete the balance of Katharine's term. By 1913 Emily had received the appointment of Chair of Political Economy and Political and Social Science at Wellesley and the rank of Full Professor. This rank was an achievement for anyone, but it was particularly noteworthy for a woman—especially a woman at that time.

Jahn noted in the Presentation Speech for Emily Greene Balch in 1946 that the year 1914 was "more than 1939, the great turning point of our era. It marked the end of an epoch..." (Jahn, 1).

War and the threat of the involvement of the United States in the conflict changed the pattern of Emily's life. Just as the discovery of social conditions that needed improvement brought her to the work at Denison House and to the field of economics and just as her love of learning brought her to teaching, now the eruption of World War I lured her into new fields: international relations, pacifism, and woman suffrage. In his Nobel Peace Prize Presentation Speech (1946), Jahn observed that the war "brought [Emily] a fresh challenge, giving her life a new goal. Like so many others she saw the war as a futile interruption to the construction of a better world" (Jahn, 2). Emily herself stated that "this was a tragic break in the work which to me appeared to be the real task of our time: to construct a more satisfying economic order" (Jahn, 2).

Jahn concluded that "she devoted all her strength to the work for peace" (Jahn, 2). Vladimir G. Simkhovitch, Professor of Economic History at Columbia, described her work in this way: "I have never met anyone who has, as she has done, for decade after decade given every minute of her life to the work for peace between nations" (Jahn, 2).

For Emily the year 1915 was monumental. In January she helped to form the Women's Peace Party in Washington, D.C.; this new organization, the result of a meeting of 3,000 women in the Grand Ball Room of the New Willard Hotel, elected Jane Addams as National Chairman. Interestingly, five of the six New York newspapers gave no coverage to the event. *The Independent Magazine* (January 25, 1915) reported that the group "issued a manifesto, unsurpassed ... in power and moral fervor by anything that has been issued here or abroad since the Great War began." The group established a platform that Holt described as radical, sound, and constructive (Holt).

The International Woman Suffrage Association, led by Carrie Chapman Catt, was to have met in Berlin in June 1915. Because of World War I, however, the women felt it necessary to cancel the meeting. Dr. Aletta Jacobs, President of the Dutch National Society for Woman Suffrage, believed it necessary during such a stressful time for women to meet together to show their solidarity and their mutual friendship. Scottish attorney Chrystal Macmillan and a group of women from Great Britain, Germany, Belgium, and Holland concurred in the necessity of such a meeting. This committee issued an invitation to women of various nations to attend a meeting at The Hague (a neutral location in the Netherlands). Jane Addams accepted their invitation to preside over the event.

As a representative of both the Wellesley Woman's Peace Party and the Women's Trade Union League of Boston, Emily received a leave of absence from Wellesley from President Ellen F. Pendleton.

The Wellesley College News reported on April 8, 1915:

> Miss Emily Green [sic.] Balch, head of the Economics Department of the College, has been appointed a delegate to the Women's International Peace Conference to be held at The Hague, April 28, 29, 30. Miss Balch is one of fifteen delegates appointed by the Executive Committee of the American Branch of the Women's Peace Party to attend the Peace Congress, which is convening for the purpose of asking the belligerent nations on what terms they would be willing to make peace, and to try to organize the influence of the women of the world to attempt to secure permanent peace. Miss Jane Addams is to be president of the conference. Among the delegates are Miss Sophinisba Breckinridge and Miss Rose Abbott, both of whom are graduates of Wellesley, and who are now associated with Miss Addams at Hull House.
>
> During the absence of Miss Balch, her classes will be taken by Miss Jane Isabel Newell, who has been temporarily released from her work as Field Agent of the Children's Bureau at Washington. Miss Newell is a graduate of Wellesley and has almost completed her work for a doctor's degree at the University of Wisconsin ["Miss Balch Delegate to Peace Conference," *The Wellesley College News.* n. p.].

The *Chicago Record-Herald* on April 13, 1915, recorded Jane Addams' serene remarks on the eve of her departure:

> We do not think we can settle the war. We do not think that by raising our hands we can make the armies cease slaughter. We do think it is valuable to state a new point of view. We do think it is fitting that women should meet and take counsel to see what may be done [Addams, *Chicago Record-Herald*, April 13, 1915].

On April 14, 1915, Emily, Jane Addams, and 40 other American women began their revolutionary, controversial, dangerous voyage to attend the First Congress of Women at The Hague. Their route would take them across underwater mine fields and through war zones on the Holland-American steamship *Noordam.*

At one point on the voyage, an English boat approached the *Noordam* and trained a machine gun on it. English sailors came aboard, searched the liner, and removed two German stowaways. Other vessels approached the *Noordam*; five of them, in fact, lined up at its side at one time.

When the *Noordam* at last was able to move forward, the women thought the worst was over. The next morning, however, near the cliffs of Dover, an English cutter stopped and detained them for four days. The women were finally able to send censored telegrams to those people who, they hoped, could help their situation; it was to no avail. The torpedo boats, dispatch boats, and destroyers surrounding them included vessels from the United States, Norway, Greece, and Spain. Vessels from the Coast Guard, cutters, and even privately owned ships helped to supply the stalled voyagers with newspapers and supplies. A prevalent rumor suggested that the detainment of the women was to prevent their meeting at The Hague. The apprehended women, however, considered this delay an overassessment of their proposed conference. People everywhere questioned how pacifists en route to a neutral country could receive such a reception; some women even sent telegrams to Great Britain to ask for assistance. The British ambassadors claimed, however, that they had no power to help (Fisher, 3).

News of the women and the *Noordam* seemed to increase the verbal attacks on the delegates—not on those who delayed their passage. The press hurled names like "Pro-Hun Peacettes." People criticized them for working for peace at a time when many countries and men were at war. Dorothy Canfield (Fisher), whom Emily had met abroad in 1890 and about whom Emily had written to her sister Maidie, presented her own views about why there was so much opposition to the work of her friend Emily Balch.

> Take it from me, the social atmosphere of the late nineteenth century [and early twentieth century] did its best to prevent women from sharing in the efforts of the human group they belonged to. They were not veiled, no, but older men said (I've heard them say it many's the time) that "I never like to see a woman outside her home—unless she's on her way to a church service. The street's no place for a woman. Her place is her home, and that's where she should stay." Any form of courage in girls or women was frowned on and called "boldness." This word was a synonym for social indecorum. Any form of intelligence in a woman was disapproved of as "mannishness." ... Without knowing about it, they can have no appreciation of what Emily Balch's example has meant, has accomplished [Fisher, 3].

On Monday the *Noordam* finally was at last able to continue its voyage. The American delegates arrived in time to attend the first session at The Hague. They were appalled, however, when they discovered that the 180 English, female delegates had not even received permits to travel to The Hague and to attend the conference. The American women smiled wryly to think that some in their midst had sent telegrams appealing to British ambassadors for help during the detainment of the *Noordam*. Nevertheless, more than a thousand women of all nationalities had managed to gather at The Hague.

At the Congress, the delegates developed a series of proposals to bring about peace, a major outcome. One of these proposals was a conference of neutral powers to offer mediation in time of war. Second, the Congress sent delegations to 14 European governments; their representatives talked with the Pope, a king, two presidents, and 21 premiers and ministers. Emily went with a delegation to the Scandinavian countries, to Russia, to London, and—eventually—to President Woodrow Wilson. President Wilson later conceded that the propositions "of this far-seeing group" inspired his Fourteen Points Plan (Women's International League for Peace and Freedom, "Emily Greene Balch").

Emily wrote in 1943 about this event:

> For one brief, accidental moment in my life ... I consorted with men in the seats of power. We talked with Prime Ministers and Foreign Ministers in St. Petersburg and Copenhagen and Christiania and Stockholm and The Hague and London, and King Haakon chatted with us familiarly. In England George Bernard Shaw and his wife invited us to tea and Lowes Dickinson dripped rain from his drenched coat and depression from his burdened spirit, standing on the hearth-rug. In Washington I had an interview with Woodrow Wilson, whom I had just missed the privilege of having as a teacher at Bryn Mawr ... ["Information Release for Emily Greene Balch," 1].

A third outcome of the Congress at The Hague was a plan for a future meeting. The women decided to gather again at a peace conference as soon as the war ended. A fourth outcome of the International Congress of Women at The Hague was an important volume; Jane Addams, Emily Balch, and Alice Hamilton wrote *Women at The Hague* (1915). A fifth outcome, according to Jahn in his Nobel Peace Prize Presentation Speech to Emily, was the founding at The Hague of the Women's International League for Peace and Freedom in 1915—even while war was raging. The W.I.L.P.F. would provide a meeting place for women (those from neutral countries, those from Allied nations, those from the Central powers); such a meeting seemed possible at this time when war had not reached its height. Jahn observed that the remarkable thing about this organization was that it was the "only group of any importance within the belligerent countries to meet and reach agreement on a just and practical program for peace" (Jahn, 2).

In August 1915 Henry Ford had turned his attention to war in Europe and had pledged his entire fortune to the pursuit of peace. Rosika Schwimmer, a dynamic Hungarian suffragist and journalist living in America, had proposed mediation to end the war. She had created a document titled *The Neutral Conference for Continuous Mediation*. When Schwimmer heard about Ford's pledge, she secured a meeting with him and obtained his support of her work.

A few days after Schwimmer's visit with Henry Ford, Louis P. Lochner suggested another idea: a peace ship. Ford immediately secured the *Oscar II*, and Schwimmer and he sent invitations to prominent citizens to be a part of the voyage and of its peace negotiations. Most turned him down. Ford, 60 peace ambassadors, 37 journalists, and Ford's personal staff of 20 individuals set sail. When the ship docked at Oslo, however, there was no welcoming committee. Norway did not believe that the plan would work. Copenhagen citizens had decided to ban any meetings with the group from America. Ford abandoned the group because of "illness" and returned to the United States. Although the Peace Ship Experiment had been a total failure and most Americans ridiculed the project, Emily was willing to participate in later peace attempts organized by Henry Ford in Stockholm.

In 1915–16 Emily accepted the role as an active leader in the Women's International Committee for Permanent Peace. In 1916 she received a leave of absence from Wellesley to join the International Committee on Mediation that Henry Ford arranged in Stockholm; this International Committee on Mediation followed Ford's highly criticized Peace Ship venture (Balch, "Miss Balch on the Ford Peace Conference," 444).

During the Stockholm Conference Emily developed and wrote up a plan for paying reparations from a pool obtained from belligerents. She also devised a proposal that was similar to the mandate system later adopted by the League of Nations; her plan appeared to be a forerunner of the trusteeship system used by the United Nations (Fainsod, 2). Emily's publication *International Colonial Administration* (1916) described a proposal similar to the mandate scheme adopted at Versailles. Her *Rehabilitation Fund Contributed by Neutral Countries as a Substitute for War Indemnities* (1916) also was characteristic of her work: practical and concrete (Randall, *Emily Greene Balch of New England, Citizen of the World*, 5).

During her 1916–17 sabbatical Emily enrolled in classes at Columbia University, but she spent most of her time working for peace. She was outspoken in her opposition to America's entry into the war. She served on the Council of the Fellowship of Reconciliation, participated in some of the activities of the Collegiate Anti-Militarism League, and issued *Approaches to the Great Settlement* (1918), a book that examined various proposed peace terms. Feelings were high; some people ridiculed peace proposals, and others advocated them. Her *Approaches to the Great Settlement* stirred further controversy. "Unwilling to embarrass her patriotic college after American entry into the war, Emily Balch took another year's leave of absence without pay, 1917–18" (John Randall, *Emily Greene Balch of New England, Citizen of the World*, 5).

Mercedes Randall recalls making her first acquaintance with Emily about this time:

> I vividly remember the first time I ever saw Emily Greene Balch.... Some forty college students and recent graduates, members of the Collegiate Anti-Militarism League ... were meeting for dinner.... Talk naturally turned to the Russian Revolution.... The air was tense. From a far corner of the long table, Emily Balch arose to speak. Most of us knew her as a distinguished sociologist, Professor of Economics at Wellesley, and warm supporter of the pacifist efforts of young people. We could not guess that her academic career was soon to come to a dramatic close, and that her larger, more enduring work for world peace was about to begin. To my youthful eyes, she looked then exactly as she does today [1947], a slight New England woman, unassuming in manner, with ... an exquisite courtesy and graciousness in her bearing.... On all her hearers, Emily Balch had made an indelible impression. For one listener, certainly, this revelation of a quality of mind and a still rarer quality of spirit had set a standard of inspiration that was to last throughout the years [Mercedes Randall, "Emily Greene Balch: As a Student Saw Her in 1918," 1].

When the time came for the Wellesley Trustees to re-consider the renewal of Emily Balch's contract, however, they did not reappoint her. Emily was in Switzerland on May 8, 1919, when she received the cable with the news of the termination of her teaching appointment to Wellesley.

Emily's reaction to this cable was just what one would expect from her: She refused to contest the decision. As far as Emily was concerned, the episode was over, and she never voluntarily brought up the subject again. If someone pointedly asked Emily about her dismissal from Wellesley, she would promptly note that she was not "fired" but that Wellesley had, in her words, simply "failed to renew her contract." Her forgiving spirit was evident in any of her responses about leaving Wellesley. The 52-year-old woman never complained about the loss of income or prestige that the action had cost her.

Fainsod quoted Emily Balch's exact, humble, kind-as-always words on the subject:

...It is not true ... that I was dismissed. My reappointment was advocated by the President and the Alumnae Trustees but was opposed by other members of the Board of Trustees. Although certain outside professors ... urged me to make this a test case for academic freedom, I did not regard it as such and preferred to accept the Trustees' decision without remonstrance. But ... it was bitter to me that it should have been I who finally over-strained the large and generous tolerance of Wellesley College [Fainsod, 3].

John Randall summarized Emily's loss of her professorial position:

At its conclusion, the trustees of Wellesley College, because of her activities for peace and her outspoken pacifist position—all the more unpalatable in the light of her progressive economic views—refused, after her twenty-two years [*Wellesley Alumnae Quarerly*, 307-08, says twenty-one years] of devoted teaching, to renew her appointment. In characteristic generous understatement, she wrote in 1933, "At the end of this year my existing appointment expired, and much as I grieved that the well-known liberality of Wellesley College should have been overstrained by me, I could not be surprised when, after much discussion and much friendly advocacy of my reappointment, the trustees decided against it." The decision was carried by a majority of only two, the President and all the alumnae supporting her retention....

Emily Balch's professional life as a teacher was thus cut short, at 52; in the America of 1918 there was no opportunity of resuming it elsewhere. But this formal ending of her academic career merely freed her to devote all her time to her larger and more enduring educational work. In the meanwhile, through the generosity of Oswald Garrison Villard she was given a position on the staff of the New York *Nation*, then [1917–18] at the height of its vigorous crusade for a just and lasting peace [John Randall, *Emily Greene Balch of New England, Citizen of the World*, 5].

Charlotte H. Conant, '84, wrote about the March meeting to consider Emily's reappointment in the June 1919 issue of "The Report of Alumnae Trustees":

The appointment of Miss Emily Greene Balch as Professor of Political Economy and Political Science had expired in 1918, and consideration of her appointment had, by a vote of the Trustees, been postponed.
At the meeting March 1919 (this year), after some discussion, it was voted to take up this question of Miss Balch's reappointment. A special meeting for that purpose was held April 21. Notice was given in advance that this was the subject to be brought up, and almost all the members of the Board were present. The fullest opportunity for discussion was given. In the end, by a small majority, the motion to reappoint was lost [Conant, n. p.].

In May 1919 the International Congress of Women met in Zurich. They titled their group the Women's International League for Peace and Freedom (W.I.L.P.F.), adopted a constitution, and set up National Sections. Jane Addams served as president. When the members of W.I.L.P.F., also called the "Women's League," learned that the Trustees of Wellesley had not renewed Emily's contract, they extended an invitation to her to serve as secretary. Emily accepted and fulfilled the position until 1922, when she began to suffer health problems. She had exchanged her careers of social worker and teacher for a third career: a worker for world peace. Her work included traveling to other countries to study the conditions there, taking courses to increase her knowledge, offering courses to others, attending congresses, corresponding, publishing, speaking, and writing.

The Wellesley Alumnae Quarterly noted in July 1919:

The term of service in Wellesley College of Emily Greene Balch has ended, after twenty-one years, as Instructor and Professor of Economics.
Those of her colleagues whose names are given below, of various opinions and habits of mind, take this occasion to express their esteem for Miss Balch as economist, teacher and woman.

During these years through her published work she has achieved an international reputation for careful, exact and original scholarship.

Many students have gone out trained by her in honest, critical methods, inspired by her to continue their studies in the field of economics, and effectively prepared to take a sane and wholesome part in the guidance of public opinion.

Even when differing from her in opinions or action we have respected her essential fair-mindedness, her courageous and conscientious regard for truth. We feel we have had in our midst a person of rare distinction and nobility.

We desire, therefore, to express our belief that Wellesley College has incurred a grave loss. [Fourteen names followed.]

Miss Balch who has been the American representative on the Executive Committee is now to be the permanent secretary of the organization called "The International Committee of Women for Peace and Freedom," with headquarters in Geneva [*The Wellesley Alumnae Quarterly*, 307–08].

Although Emily and her Bostonian family had been most closely associated with the Unitarian Church, Emily joined the Society of Friends in 1920. She had found a way to integrate her religion with her public activism. Emily wrote to Jane Addams, also a member of the Society of Friends, of her new religious commitment:

[W]hat is central to the Friends is central to me—the wish to listen as it were, to understand and receive as much as we can and to try to live out, as far as we can, all that one has of enlightenment ... ["Emily Greene Balch," *The Bulletin of the Atomic Scientists*, April 1979, 9].

Changes came also in other aspects of the personal life of Emily Balch. She had to help to decide the fate of the house in which she had lived since 1879. Her Aunt Catherine died in 1924, and the roomy old house did not seem adequate for a single occupant. Her brother Francis, his wife, and their three children decided to make the house their home. Marion (Maidie) would move in with her brother and his family, but where Emily would live was not certain.

Agnes Perkins of the Wellesley English Department, Agnes's friend Etta Herr, and (later) another friend decided to build a home in Wellesley, Massachusetts; they offered Emily a wing with its own private entrance, four rooms, and two stories. Emily moved into that house in 1925 and resided there until her move to Vernon Nursing Home in Cambridge, Massachusetts, about two decades later. Mercedes described Emily's Wellesley home:

Emily set up her household goods, lit her hearthfires, and welcomed her friends. She arranged her poetry books in an old family secretary, her share of the family silver and Annie's beautiful old green and white tea set in another, hung her father's large Blake scroll to cover the wall beside the eastern windows next to the antique walnut couch.... [S]he lived and worked, departed and returned, in sickness and in health, in war and peace, tending her tulips and valley lilies beside the little doorway, whacking the bushes in the "Thicket" ... [Mercedes Randall, *Improper Bostonian: Emily Greene Balch*, 302].

Emily remained active in both national and international organizations working to bring about world peace. She led a mission of investigation to Haiti at the request of the International Committee of the W.I.L.P.F. (Hull, 4). In the Nobel Peace Prize Presentation Speech, Jahn noted her contributions to investigating the troop occupation of Haiti:

She never embarked on a campaign until she was sure of her facts. She first traveled to Haiti with a delegation whose report, the greater part of which she herself wrote, gives conclusive proof of her ability to get to the root of the problem and of her consummate skill of devising a practical and democratic solution that would greatly benefit the people. These are aptitudes which must surely be the envy of many a politician. Then came the struggle to get the solution accepted [Jahn, 3].

In his Nobel Peace Prize Presentation Speech, Jahn described Emily's efforts to investigate 11 years of troop occupation in Haiti and, later, to work for their withdrawal. Although he conceded that much of the encouragement for the project had come from the W.I.L.P.F., Jahn emphasized that it was Balch who "provided the driving force behind everything that was achieved" (Jahn, 3).

Together with Paul Douglas of Chicago, Emily edited *Occupied Haiti* (1927). It contained recommendations "which President Hoover largely paralleled in his plan for final evaluation of U.S. Troops from that country" (Hull, 4). The final result, Jahn stressed, was that "the American government carried out practically all the delegation's recommendations and withdrew its troops" (Jahn, 3).

Jahn noted that it would be a grave error to think that Emily achieved her victories merely by exerting pressure on those in power or by working only through leagues, congresses, or committees. She herself worked hard to achieve those things. She also tried to educate others who were making an impact on the world. She initiated and taught in the international summer schools that the W.I.L.P.F. ran during the years between World War I and World War II. To increase her knowledge of world affairs, she traveled extensively to gain first-hand information on the conditions of life wherever she was—and to stress understanding of others. She made it a point to contact women in some of the countries, to meet with the leaders of the countries when possible, and to make presentations—both abroad and at home—on the merits of the League of Nations, internationalism, and peace (Jahn, 3–4).

For the peace advocate Emily Balch, there were many frustrations in the years to come. When in 1931 the Japanese occupied Manchuria, Emily foresaw another world war. Her adamant opposition to both isolationism and American neutrality placed her in opposition to the American sector of the Women's League. Emily was not a pacifist in the face of evil; she believed that everyone had an obligation to try to stop wickedness (Jahn, 4).

A 1935 event brought deep satisfaction to Emily. Wellesley invited Emily to deliver the formal Armistice Day Address. The college—"whose large and generous tolerance" Emily had "overstrained" and the very institution that had "failed to renew her contract" (Fainsod, 3)—had now extended its arms to Emily, and she gladly returned its embrace.

Mercedes Randall found in the materials that Emily gave her a sentence written in the third person; the passage was quite typical of Emily's usual way of understating her pleasure: "After her return to America, Wellesley College invited her [Emily] to give the formal Armistice Day Address, which pleased her [Emily]" (Mercedes Randall, *Improper Bostonian: Emily Greene Balch*, 325).

In 1936 Emily succeeded Jane Addams as Honorary International President of the Women's International League for Peace and Freedom. Her slight figure was a familiar sight anywhere that women were at work designing peace strategies. Although meetings, publishing, corresponding, public speaking, and many receptions filled Emily's life, she still found the time to keep her diary, talk with her friends, and enjoy nature.

Emily reacted intensely to the atrocities of the 1930s and the 1940s. She began to work enthusiastically for those—especially the Jews—who fled to the United States. She anticipated the many problems that she knew would arise and began to seek solutions to them even before they emerged.

Would she continue to choose international unity at all costs and advocate pacifism to others? As a leader in the W.I.L.P.F., Emily received scrutiny by people everywhere. The "Emily watch" intensified after the Japanese bombed Pearl Harbor on December 7, 1941.

Women especially wondered if she would continue to advocate peace. Emily's consistent answer was that unless one battles evil, there is no hope for the survival of ideals. She stated:

> International unity is not in itself a solution. Unless this international unity has a moral quality, accepts the discipline of moral standards, and possesses the quality of humanity, it will not be the unity we are interested in [Norwegian Group of the W.I.L.P.F., "Emily Greene Balch," 5].

John Herman Randall, Jr., quoted Emily in his 12-page biography *Emily Greene Balch of New England, Citizen of the World*:

> When the war broke in its full fury in 1939, and especially after the disaster at Pearl Harbor, the U.S.A. became a belligerent, I [Emily] went through a long and painful mental struggle, and never felt that I had reached a clear and consistent conclusion. "How can you reach inner unity," I said, "when in your own mind an irresistible force has collided with an immovable obstacle?" It appeared to me that after the Japanese attack any government would have found it impossible to refuse to fight—impossible, that is, given the existing degree of development of mankind, and its failure to have any effective and generally understood technique for constructive non-violent *action*, such as Gandhi had aimed at. On the one hand, I refused to buy war bonds. On the other, I contributed, however modestly, to so-called community war funds, a large part of which were devoted to wholly peaceful social aid—which typifies my mixed reaction. I thus lost the respect of my many "absolutist" pacifist friends. That of the military-minded I neither had nor desired [John Herman Randall, *Emily Greene Balch of New England, Citizen of the World*, 9].

The public recognized Emily's labors through the years. A clipping by the unknown author C. E. M. commented on her notable work as International Secretary of the W.I.L.P.F.:

> This [job] has at times involved taking on somewhat thankless tasks, and wearing herself out in work for which she felt herself not best fitted. To the onlooker it was grievous to see her using up her strength and health in the routine of office work when her political wisdom, her knowledge of economics, her gift of literary expression could have found scope in so many other ways in the service of peace. Yet on the other hand, to our scattered members all over the world the personal contact E.G.B. maintained, as International Secretary, with each one of them and their work (often by long letters written by hand in the evening after an exhausting day's work) made the W.I.L.P.F. the inspiration it could not have been to them in any other way. [C.E.M. Untitled clipping with unknown source of publication in the papers of the Swarthmore College Peace Collection. Possibly the work of Chrystal Macmillan, an attorney from Scotland].

Emily's interest was, then, an active one; she did not know how to respond passively to any situation. She began to draft proposals for peace; her writings reflected not only on the surrender that would have to come but also on the inevitable rebuilding that would follow to bring about the international settlement.

Jahn observed in describing Emily that she valued ethics. He also recalled that she had definite feelings about the United Nations Organization and had said some things publicly about it:

> [T]he future shape of the new organization will not depend upon what the documents appear to state, but on what the members make of it. Practice in cooperation is what will give the United Nations its character. Plans have not been set up for a utopia but for Europe, Russia, America, and all the other countries with their conflicting interests and ideas. And it is precisely because the proposals we have before us are fairly modest that they may perhaps be realized [Jahn, 4].

More work lay ahead for Emily. Jahn said that her hard work should be an inspiration to us all. He reminded us all that we should "pay her homage and express our gratitude for her lifelong, indefatigable work for the cause of peace. She has taught us that the reality we seek must be earned by hard and unrelenting toil in the world in which we live, but she has taught us more: that exhaustion is unknown and defeat only gives fresh courage to the man whose soul is fired by the sacred flame" (Jahn, 5).

Emily somehow found time for the small things in life. She never seemed to despair when situations appeared at their worst. In fact, according to those who knew her best, she maintained her sense of humor and her love of fun. An incomplete clipping dated 1936, maintained in the papers of the Swarthmore Peace Collection, and written by "C.E.M." (possibly Chrystal Macmillan) describes Emily when she was happy:

> No one really knows E.G.B. who has not been with her in holiday mood, when her sense of fun has free rein and she reveals herself as the most delightful of playmates [C.E.M., Untitled clipping with unknown source of publication. Swarthmore Peace Collection. Dated December 17, 1936].

Hannah Hull remembered:

> In all the serious work on which she has been engaged, she has maintained a saving sense of humor such as few possess. Tense moments in Board meetings and Conferences are frequently eliminated by her kindly witticisms. When an impasse seems inevitable, she looks up from her sketching of curious little flowers and original designing in which she has seemed chiefly absorbed, and proposes a "third way" which is without compromise and is satisfactorily adopted by the whole group. Her approach to problems is practical and free from sentimentality, making her one of W.I.L.P.F.'s ablest as well as best beloved leaders [Hull, 5].

Jahn made a comparison between Emily and Cordell Hull in the Nobel Peace Prize Presentation Speech:

> What was said of Cordell Hull last year is, I think, also true of her: she cares little whether the credit goes to her or to someone else, as long as the object in view has been attained [Jahn, 5].

In addition, an article in *The Bulletin of the Atomic Scientists* noted that Emily tried to remain positive and quoted the advice she had received in a letter; she wrote: "One must not multiply pain by being too good a *conductor* of it" ("Emily Greene Balch," *The Bulletin of the Atomic Scientists*, 10).

Hull, and others, noted, "There is nothing too small or too great for her to undertake." Hannah Hull went on in her unpublished paper to describe Emily's "greatness and simplicity":

> It was not so long ago, even after responsibilities and honors had been thrust upon her, that one bitterly cold day on one of the thoroughfares of Boston, having stamped out of a drugstore refreshed and warmed by a cup of hot chocolate, she encountered a shivering Salvation Army lass who was extending to passers-by a papier-mâché turkey for pennies, to feed the hungry on Thanksgiving Day. Many on such occasions have felt keen sympathy; but few would have taken the time to stop as she did and insist that the girl herself should accept the hospitality of a cup of hot chocolate inside. Moreover, when told that the kind offer would be gratefully accepted upon the condition that she meanwhile would hold out the turkey for the pennies, who of us would have accepted the challenge? Who, but Emily Balch, with her combination of greatness and simplicity? A far cry this, from being envoy to kings and potentates, to begging pennies on a city's street [Hull, 6].

Recognition came to Emily! The W.I.L.P.F. honored her at public luncheons on both her seventieth (1937) and her seventy-fifth (1942) birthdays—long before she received the

Nobel Peace Prize. Emily, however, did not rest on her laurels; she continued her work, to teach, to speak.

At an international congress of women in Luxembourg in 1946, she made a profound analogy between the Alps and human nature. Kettelle, in her article describing the event, quoted Emily and noted that those who listened "found new evidence of her understanding":

> Human nature seems to me like the Alps. The depths are profound, black as night and terrifying, but the heights are equally real, uplifted in sunshine. It is not realistic to concentrate on the recent revelations of the depths of evil to which human beings can descend. To do so leads to stumbling feet, weakness and discouragement.
>
> The recent years have also brought us amazing revelations of the good and great possibilities of human nature. The instances of pure physical courage have been innumerable.... More significant are the revelations we have seen of moral courage, self-forgetfulness, of victorious human love and sheer goodness ... [Kettelle, 15].

While Emily traveled and spoke, others were making some important decisions that would impact her life and the world. Mercedes Randall describes some of the incidents that led to the announcement of the Nobel Peace Prize winner of 1947.

> At the national Board meeting in Richmond, Indiana, in October, 1945, it was suggested that as the W.I.L.P.F. had once captured the honor of the Nobel Peace Prize through Jane Addams, it might do so again through its honorary International President, Emily Balch, of equal Nobel Peace Prize caliber. M. M. Randall was asked to be chairman of the campaign to place [Emily's] name before the Nobel Committee of the Norwegian Parliament. Never was a task undertaken with such implicit faith in its worthiness.
>
> On the last day of November, the chairman was electrified to find out that the deadline for proposing candidates for the 1947 Peace Prize was January 31, 1946. This meant a lightning campaign of six weeks (allowing two weeks more for documents to reach Oslo by air mail) with the Christmas holidays intervening, in which to devise procedures, get a sponsoring committee, secure funds, prepare documentary materials in cooperation with Miss Balch, print letterheads, engage typists, notify and give European branches directions for acting, and secure nominations from duly qualified persons.
>
> In spite of almost a solid week spent at the telephone lining up national organizations to act as a sponsoring committee, I succeeded in getting only four organizations (besides the W.I.L.P.F. International) willing to risk their names in vain: The National Federation of Settlements, the National Council of Women of U.S., the Women's Trade Union League of America, and the National Association for the Advancement of the Colored People. This was the only discouraging and disillusioning part of the task.
>
> I arranged to spend the first week-end in December with Miss Balch, to assemble biographical materials, compile a complete list of all her published books, articles and pamphlets, and get the names of qualified sponsors [The Nobel Committee of the Norwegian Parliament has stringent requirements for the sponsors.] who were familiar with her career ... [Mercedes Randall, "Report to the National Board, February 15, 1947," 1, in the papers of the Swarthmore College Peace Collection].

Mercedes wrote of going to visit Emily "in the teeth" of a New England storm that had begun after Mercedes had left her home. She wrote of the submission of the letters of request for support to John Dewey so that he could personally sign them; not all those invited to respond, however, elected to do so. She also told of more than 100 letters that she sent to other organizations and individuals to ask for their written support—even though they were not technically eligible. Among the 24 individuals who submitted letters was Dr. Alice Hamilton (the first woman professor at Harvard Medical School) and John Dewey, world-renowned educator. By January 8, Mercedes had mailed to Oslo a thick packet of materials including the 12-page biography authored by John Herman Randall, Jr., Mercedes' husband [Mercedes Randall, "Report to the National Board, February 15, 1947," 2, in the papers of the Swarthmore College Peace Collection].

In 1946 Emily read the biography that John Herman Randall, Jr., had prepared. Emily's reaction to her own biography was, "You have made a beautiful thing out of very brittle material.... I had no idea I had ever said so many sensible things" (Mercedes Randall, *Improper Bostonian: Emily Greene Balch*, 405).

Mercedes submitted other materials on January 12. She noted that Emily had "[d]evoted selfless labors over a period of years and voluminous correspondence to work for refugees, especially to Jewish rescue, both as an immediate crisis and as a long-range Problem...." She acknowledged:

> There are unique grounds for considering Emily Greene Balch, a pre-eminent candidate for the Nobel Peace Prize. It would be hard to find another American, man or woman, who has worked so continuously, so realistically, so devotedly, day in and day out, for a period of thirty years (1915–1945) towards the goal of international co-operation and peace. She has applied to that task the powers of a mind well- balanced, scholarly, imaginatively creative, with the world-embracing sympathies.
>
> Miss Balch's special gift consists in formulating new approaches to political and economic problems of international importance. She has the ability to see all facets of a politically intricate question and then work out a unifying formula. This judicial ability to see both sides of a question is coupled with a statesmanship that can propose solutions satisfactory to contending viewpoints [Mercedes Randall, "Emily Greene Balch (1867– [1961]): Brief Sketch of Her Activities and Writings," 2, in the papers of the Swarthmore College Peace Collection].

On November 14, 1946, Emily was a patient with a bronchial infection in the Wellesley-Newton Hospital. From her hospital bed, she heard the news that she would be a co-recipient (with John R. Mott) of the 1947 Nobel Peace Prize (Mercedes Randall, "Report to the National Board, February 15, 1947," 2, in the papers of the Swarthmore College Peace Collection).

Emily believed that most people did not even know her; she saw herself only as a plain, private citizen who had merely tried to show others that anyone can contribute to peace. It was perhaps most ironic—and gratifying—to Emily that Mildred McAfee Horton, President of Wellesley and Commander of W.A.V.E.S., had sponsored her for the award. It had, after all, been Wellesley College that had failed to renew her appointment because of her peace activities; now the very same college had recommended her for the 1947 Nobel Peace Prize because of her activities for world peace.

At 7:00 P.M. on December 10, 1946, the American Nobel Anniversary Dinner began in the Grand Ballroom of New York's Hotel Astor. The theme of the program was "Progress for Peace." Among the 15 speakers were Hal B. Wallis (producer of the film *The Story of Louis Pasteur*), Pearl S. Buck, and Edward R. Murrow. The menu for the $8.50 meal was Coupe of Fruit California, giblet soup, celery, Filet of Sole Bonne Femme, Mushrooms Poullette, Roast Turkey Americaine, dressing, cranberry sauce, candied yams, new peas, Bombe Patriot, Petit Fours, and Demi Tasse. The occasion was the commemoration of the fiftieth anniversary of the death of Alfred Bernhard Nobel. An important speaker was Norwegian Ambassador His Excellency Wilhelm Morgenstierne, who reminded the attendees of the purpose and the past winners of the Nobel Peace Prize; he now celebrated the new recipients.

On December 13, the Norwegian Group of the W.I.L.P.F. issued an unrestricted six-page enclosure to Dispatch Number 407. The enclosure, titled "Emily Greene Balch," paid tribute to its namesake:

She has shown us that the ideals we try to reach must be attained through strenuous work within the world as it is. But she has given us more: She has shown us that you never give up, that defeat is inspired to further efforts if a sacred flame is burning in your heart [Norwegian Group of the W.I.L.P.F., "Emily Greene Balch," 6].

In 1946 Irwin Abrams submitted "A Note on E.G.B." This paper (a typewritten draft) noted how Emily's friend "Mercedes Randall ... had organized the whirlwind campaign that won [Emily Balch] the [Nobel Peace Prize] and Randall's husband, Professor John H. Randall of Columbia ... had contributed an eloquent biographical account for the Nobel Committee" (Irwin Abrams "A Note on E.G.B.," 1946 draft in the papers of the Swarthmore College Peace Collection).

In the spring of 1947, 80-year-old Emily traveled to Norway to deliver the customary address. King Haakon received her and recalled their meeting some 31 years before when she served as W.I.L.P.F. ambassador to Norway (Johnson, 25).

On April 7, Emily delivered her Nobel Address, "Toward Human Unity or Beyond Nationalism." Everyone listened eagerly as she spoke about peace, war, and fear. She said that fear alone was not a legitimate reason for peace and encouraged a resolution banning the use of the nuclear weapons and the draft.

> I have spoken against fear as a basis for peace. What we ought to fear, especially we Americans, is not that someone may drop atomic bombs on us but that we may allow a world situation to develop in which ordinarily reasonable and humane men, acting as our representatives, may use such weapons in our name. We ought to be resolved beforehand that no provocation, no temptation shall induce us to resort to the last dreadful alternative of war.
>
> May no young man ever again be faced with the choice between violating his conscience by cooperating in competitive mass slaughter or separating himself from those who, endeavoring to serve liberty, democracy, humanity, can find no better way than to conscript young men to kill [Balch, "Nobel Lecture," 12].

Emily begged for patience as the world pursued peace, developed generous ideals, and designed a sphere that

> ... will open up great untapped reservoirs in human nature. Like a spring released from pressure would be the response of a generation of young men and women growing up in an atmosphere of friendliness and security, in a world demanding their service, offering them comradeship, calling to all adventurous and forward reaching natures.
>
> We are not asked to subscribe to any utopia or to believe in a perfect world just around the corner. We are asked to be patient with necessarily slow and groping advance on the road forward, and to be ready for each step ahead as it becomes practicable. We are asked to equip ourselves with courage, hope, readiness for hard work, and to cherish large and generous ideals [Balch, "Nobel Lecture," 12].

This 80-year-old Nobel Peace Prize winner urged her audience to be flexible and adventurous—traits often attributed only to a younger generation—in this time of change. She cautioned against rigidity and discouraged enforced peace. She discouraged endeavors to prevent the spread of ideas and experiences; she used the words "iron curtains" to describe the closing off of knowledge (Balch, Nobel Lecture, 6). She begged for a duplication of the refusal of violence like that of "the great-souled Indian Gandhi. He gave his life trying to find ways to oppose domination and coercion without resort to hate or violence" (Balch, "Nobel Lecture," 4). She asked for "a tolerance which (while it is not mere apathy and indifference) means unwillingness to force one's belief, however, precious it seems to oneself, on others" (Balch, "Nobel Lecture," 5).

In her lecture, Emily memorably compared the differences in society to threads. She reminded her audience that one cannot weave if all the threads run in the same direction. Different threads crossing in different directions, however, can result in different patterns and a woven cloth. Emily noted that "differences as well as likenesses are inevitable, essential, and desirable." The problems, she noted, came when the clashes take the form of war (Balch, "Nobel Lecture," 6).

> Indeed in the light of all that mankind has achieved and desired it seems almost incomprehensible that it is today so largely occupied in preparing for war in more hideous forms than ever before. Huge sums of money and treasures of human cleverness and industry are invested in inventing new and more ghastly poisons, methods of disseminating diseases and perfecting instruments of destruction instantaneous and almost unlimited.
>
> The attempt to put an end to war is a special and urgent task which we must solve and solve soon [Balch, "Nobel Lecture," 6].

She concluded her remarks with optimism and her dreams for a "brightening" future (Balch, "Nobel Lecture," 12).

Before her return to the United States, Emily spoke several times: in Oslo, Stockholm, Helsinki, Copenhagen, Odense, Hamburg, Bremen, Hanover, Stuttgart, Frankfurt, and Heidelberg. She readily acknowledged that she considered the Prize an incentive for further achievement, work, and planning—not an end in itself.

Emily's share of the Nobel Peace Prize money was $16,851.49. She told Fainsod that she had given $10,000 to the W.I.L.P.F.; the rest of the money she earmarked in a variety of ways for peace (Fainsod, 3).

Emily spoke at a Philadelphia luncheon of the Women's International League for Peace and Freedom on April 26, shortly after her return to the United States. She received the title "Citizen of the World" on the printed luncheon program (News release, 1).

Emily's work continued even into her late eighties. The world remembered her services. In 1952 the W.I.L.P.F. sent messages to Emily to commemorate her eighty-fifth birthday. One of the messages was from Dorothy Canfield (Fisher), the young child whom Emily had written home about on her trip abroad in 1890.

> Of all the world-gatherings which tonight salute dear, much-loved Emily Balch, none has a more tenderly affectionate message for her than I, nor from so very long ago. Did anyone else in this gathering, more than sixty years ago, realize that she was of a spiritual eminence and distinction so rare that her very presence with us, as part of human life, is reassuring, is comforting, is strengthening.
>
> I think I can probably claim the first place, chronologically, in the great company of her admirers, of those who have counted on her integrity, intelligence, vision, and courage as a vital part of the bulwarks we are all trying to build up against the evil, violence, fraud and stupidity of our sad human world.
>
> She has cast a steadfast ray of brightness over its dark mistakes and its anxiety for a miraculously long term of years. I love her. I am thankful to have this opportunity to send her my affection and trust which began when I was eleven years old [Fisher, "Message to Emily Greene Balch," 1].

Emily always wanted to be fair and just; she always wanted to be open to new ideas. To Pearl Buck, Margaret Clapp quoted 87-year-old Emily as saying: "When I grow old, I hope I shall not become rigid in my thinking." ("Emily Greene Balch" as quoted by Margaret Clapp to Pearl Buck, December 11, 1956).

On May 24, 1955, the American Unitarian Association presented its Seventh Annual Unitarian Award to recognize distinguished service to the cause of Liberal Religion. The award went to Emily. The presentation read:

Economist, sociologist, poet, teacher and humanitarian, she has devoted a lifetime to crusading for civil liberties, interracial brotherhood, social and civic righteousness, and world peace.

During her years as Professor of Economics and Political and Social Science at Wellesley College, she began her efforts in behalf of world peace, and in 1915, with Miss Jane Addams, founded the Women's International League of Peace and Freedom, of which she is presently Honorary International President.

Her constructive statesmanship, her intellectual leadership, her work for the League of Nations, and the United Nations Organizations have spanned the continents of the world and in 1946 she was co-recipient with John R. Mott of the Nobel Peace Prize in recognition of her "contribution to the benefit of mankind."

Miss Balch's Unitarian background, her present Quaker and Unitarian affiliations, her religious insights and her contagious faith that men of good-will can fashion peace, make it especially appropriate that she be honored by the Association at this particular time....

Those about her, from her, shall read the perfect ways of honour ["Emily Greene Balch," *The Christian Register*, 20].

In her acceptance speech, 88-year-old Emily looked forward—not backward. Her speech, titled "Vision of a Vast Brightening Field," indicated that she still had work to do:

We are told that the young men see visions, but visions come also to the old.

I see a vision of a vast brightening field ready for the harvest. I believe we are at the opening of a wonderful amazing era for the growth of all that Unitarianism stands for, of nobler and deeper thinking and of spiritual growth.... In our hands lies a kind of prosperity we have little dreamed of.... The time has come to break down the dikes and let the healing waters flow over us. I see in us, young and old, the seed of the world that is to be [Balch, "Vision of a Vast Brightening Field," 20].

In October 1955 the W.I.L.P.F. set up a fund to commemorate the fortieth anniversary of its founding. They named the fund "The Emily Greene Balch Fund."

In 1956 the W.I.L.P.F. began making plans to celebrate in 1957 the ninetieth birthday of its Honorary International President and co-founder Emily Balch. A red and gold album held the many birthday greetings to Emily. The greetings came from around the world and from such individuals as Albert Schweitzer and Eleanor Roosevelt (Barshak, n. p.).

Hannah Clothier Hull and Katharine Arnett, Quaker Pacifists and W.I.L.P.F. members, took the *Senator* from Philadelphia to Boston at 2:00 P.M. on January 7, 1957, so that they could present the collection to Emily on her birthday. Her family had reserved the morning hours of her birthday for their celebration with Emily. Emily had set 2:00 P.M. on January 8 for the visit of Hannah, Kitty, and Florence Sellect, the President of the Cambridge Branch of the W.I.L.P.F. Hannah described how Emily, who was expecting them, rose, flung open her arms to them, and received them with joy (Hull, "Our Visit to Emily Greene Balch").

In a room already full of flowers, telegrams, and letters, the visitors received frequent interruptions by the delivery of more expressions of good wishes. Emily examined the book with the letters and especially seemed to like the first page, which was labeled, "Emily Greene Balch, Practical Idealist, January Eighth, 1957." The honored visitors rejoiced in her delight in seeing and reading the letters and in reminiscing lovingly about elder stateswomen and "old times." The visit lasted about an hour and a half; every once in a while, Hannah wrote, Emily "would stop ... to stroke the book and remark again on the frontispiece or some special things which certain individuals we would name had done ... she would turn to one of us and say, 'Oh, please express my special appreciation to her, for I am afraid I can not write separately to each one.'" (Hull, "Our Visit to Emily Greene Balch").

Mercedes Randall reported that while Emily was in Vernon Nursing Home in Cambridge, Massachusetts, she had written on a scrap of paper, "Never lonely, never unoccupied, never bored"; she wrote to Mildred Olmsted, however, that life in a nursing home was sometimes "duller than ditch-water." Mercedes also reported that Emily had once remarked unexpectedly to a visitor at Vernon Nursing Home that her life had been "considerably enriched by dreams, my own and those of other people" (Mercedes Randall, *Improper Bostonian*, 442–43).

Balch wrote shortly before her death that she was living her last days "in a world still hag-ridden by the thought of war, and it is not given to us in this atomic world to know how things will turn out. But when I reflect on the enormous changes that I have seen myself and the amazing resiliency and resourcefulness of mankind, how can I fail to be of good courage?" ("Emily Greene Balch," *The Bulletin of the Atomic Scientists*, 11).

Katharine Balch Shurcliff, Emily's niece, visited her in Cambridge early in January 1961. She described her aunt as "peaceful, serene ... and ready to gently go" (Mercedes Randall, *Improper Bostonian: Emily Greene Balch*, 445).

On January 9, 1961, the day after Emily's ninety-fourth birthday, Mercedes received a telegram dated 6:30 P.M., January 9, 1961, from Marion Balch informing her that "Emily died peacefully at 5:15 P.M. Monday night." Emily Greene Balch had died as she had lived: peacefully.

Bibliography

Addams, Jane, Emily Greene Balch, and Alice Hamilton. *Women at The Hague: The International Congress of Women and Its Results, by Three Delegates to the Congress from the United States.* New York: Macmillan, 1915.

Balch, Emily Greene. "Corrections by E.G.B. to Fainsod article." Emily Balch Papers (1947) in the Swarthmore College Peace Collection.

_____. Letter to Maidie. Letters to and from Emily Balch, 1890, Swarthmore College Peace Collection.

_____. Letter to Mary Anne. Letters to and from Emily Balch, 1890, Swarthmore College Peace Collection.

_____. "Miss Balch on the Ford Peace Conference." *The Survey*, July 19, 1916, 444. In the papers of the Swarthmore College Peace Collection.

_____. "Nobel Lecture, April 7, 1948." Available online at http://nobelprize.org/peace/laureates/1946/balch=acceptance.html.

_____. "Towards a Planetary Civilization." *Four Lights*, Vol. 2, No. 2, June 1942. In the papers of the Swarthmore College Peace Collection.

_____. "Vision of a Vast Brightening Field." *The Christian Register*, July 1955, 20. In the papers of the Swarthmore College Peace Collection.

Balch, Marion C. Telegram to Mrs. John H. Randall. January 9, 1961, 6:33 P.M. In the papers of the Swarthmore College Peace Collection.

Barshak, Hanna G. "Messages Pour in for Emily Balch Birthday." No date, no source for this published article. In the papers of the Swarthmore Peace Collection.

C.E.M. Untitled clipping with unknown source of publication, dated December 17, 1936. In the papers of the Swarthmore Peace Collection.

"Coming of Age at Wellesley," p. 227. In the papers of the Swarthmore College Peace Collection.

Conant, Charlotte H. "Report of Alumnae Trustees." *Wellesley Affairs*, June 1919, no page. In the papers of the Swarthmore College Peace Collection.

"Emily Greene Balch." *The Bulletin of the Atomic Scientists.* April 1979, 9. In the papers of Swarthmore College Peace Collection.

_____. *The Christian Register*, July 1955. In the papers of the Swarthmore College Peace Collection.

_____. *Intelligencer*, Volume 103, Number 51, no pagination. In the papers of the Swarthmore College Peace Collection.

_____. As quoted by Margaret Clapp to Pearl Buck, December 11, 1956. In the papers of the Swarthmore College Peace Collection.

Fainsod, Elizabeth Stix. "Emily Greene Balch." *Bryn Mawr Alumnae Bulletin*, May 1947, 1–3, 14. Swarthmore College Peace Collection.

Fisher, Dorothy Canfield. "Emily Greene Balch." *Bryn Mawr Alumnae Bulletin*, Winter 1956, 3. In the papers of the Swarthmore College Peace Collection.

_____. "Message to Emily Greene Balch, Nobel Peace Prize Winner: For the Celebration of her 85th Birthday by the Women's International League for Peace and Freedom of Massachusetts 1952)." In the papers of the Swarthmore College Peace Collection.

G. G. "Review of *Improper Bostonian: Emily Greene Balch.*" *Wellesley College Alumnae Magazine*, May 1965, no page. In the papers of the Swarthmore College Peace Collection.

Heaths, Edith de G. Letter to Emily Balch, n.d. In the letters of the Swarthmore College Peace Collection.

Holt, Hamilton. *The Independent Magazine*, January 25, 1915, boxed notice. In the papers of Swarthmore College Peace Collection.

Hull, Hannah. "Emily Greene Balch." Unpublished, date given as "1940?" In the papers of Swarthmore College Peace Collection.

_____. "Our Visit to Emily Greene Balch." A three-page, unpublished, typewritten paper. In the papers of the Swarthmore College Peace Collection.

"Information Release for Emily Greene Balch." (Unpublished, no date.) Swarthmore College Peace Collection.

Jahn, Gunnar. "The Nobel Peace Prize 1946 Presentation Speech." Available online at http://www.nobel.se/peace/laureates/1946/press.html.

Johnson, Emily Cooper. "Review of *Improper Bostonian: Emily Greene Balch.*" *Bryn Mawr Alumnae Bulletin*, Spring 1965, 25.

Kettelle, Martha. "Emily Balch: World Christian Citizen." *Advance*, June 1947, 15. In the papers of the Swarthmore College Peace Collection.

Letters to and from Emily Balch, 1890, Swarthmore College Peace Collection.

Minutes of the Bryn Mawr Faculty Meeting, Spring 1889. In the papers of the Swarthmore College Peace Collection.

"Miss Balch Delegate to Peace Conference." *The Wellesley College News*, Vol. 23, No. 24, April 8, 1915. In the papers of the Swarthmore College Peace Collection.

News release for Saturday Afternoon and Sunday Papers. Philadelphia, April 26, 1947 (?). In the papers of the Swarthmore College Peace Collection.

Norwegian Group of the W.I.L.P.F. "Emily Greene Balch," p. 5. In the papers of the Swarthmore College Peace Collection.

Press Release: Emily Greene Balch, Women's International League for Peace and Freedom, August 3, 1937. In the papers of the Swarthmore College Peace Collection.

Randall, John Herman, Jr. *Emily Greene Balch of New England, Citizen of the World*, 1946, 12. Twelve-page booklet in the papers of the Swarthmore College Peace Collection.

Randall, Mercedes M. "Emily Greene Balch," p. 2. Paper dated 1969 and found in the Swarthmore College Peace Collection.

_____. "Emily Greene Balch (1867–[1961]): Brief Sketch of Her Activities and Writings." Paper dated 1945 in the papers of the Swarthmore College Peace Collection.

_____. "Emily Greene Balch: As a Student Saw Her in 1918," A Piece for 1947 "Fire Lights," p. 1. In the papers of the Swarthmore College Peace Collection.

_____. *Improper Bostonian: Emily Greene Balch*. New York: Twayne, 1964.

_____. "Report to the National Board, February 15, 1947," pp. 1–2. In the papers of the Swarthmore College Peace Collection.

"Report to the [Bryn Mawr] Trustees," April 12, 1889. In the papers of the Swarthmore College Peace Collection.

The Wellesley Alumnae Quarterly, July 1919, 307–08. In the papers of the Swarthmore College Peace Collection.

Women's International League for Peace and Freedom. "Biography of Emily Greene Balch." (Unpublished one-page paper.) The papers of the Swarthmore College Peace Collection.

Mairead Corrigan Maguire *and* Elizabeth (Betty) Williams (1976)

Unlikely Peacemakers in Ireland

"One cannot drop a bomb on an ethnic conflict.
The weapons we have developed,
as a means of solving our problems,
are no longer of any use to us."
[Maguire, *The Tanner Lectures*, 254]

 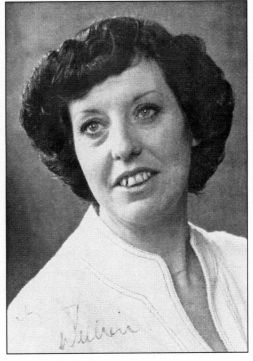

Left: Mairead Corrigan, Nobel Peace Laureate 1976. *Right:* Betty Williams, Nobel Peace Laureate 1976.

After decades of terrorism and armed conflict, it is almost impossible to understand the reasons for the persistent hostilities that have plagued Ireland for the past 600 years. Some place the blame for the historic situation on the United Kingdom. For centuries the British gobbled up lands and people in its thirst for growth, economic resources and world power. When it conquered Ireland in the fifteenth century, it forced a new language, a new religion and a new political organization-government on its people. The conquered peoples embraced the new Roman Catholic tradition, so much so that when Henry the VIII in 1534 declared Anglicanism or Protestantism as the new religion in England, most refused to convert. This religio-political divide may have sown the seeds for the later violent eruptions among the peoples of Ireland (Buscher, 18–19).

While the peoples of Ireland matured as a nation, the strength of the United Kingdom began to decline. Most Irish thought that they should be in control of their own laws and destiny. They were ready to abandon a "parent" government. This hope for political and economic freedom came to the British as a request for "Home Rule."

The English Parliament considered legislation that would have given Ireland "Home Rule" between 1912 and 1914. Not everyone wanted autonomy. Groups in Ireland who were financially and politically tied to the United Kingdom opposed the legislation. Many feared the loss of their business contracts and political power, especially in Northern Ireland. The Orange Order, primarily Protestants, began protesting independence of any kind.

Tensions mounted, and 1916 saw the start of a full-scale civil war, termed "The Easter Rising in Dublin." The United Kingdom quickly retaliated against the seekers of independence and executed most of its leaders. Popular reaction to the executions served to unite Southern Ireland against the British. By 1918, the majority of the Irish demanded total independence. Freedom came in 1921 to Southern Ireland, after a bitter war. Twenty-six counties became known as the Irish Free State and later the Republic of Ireland. Dublin would become the capital in 1948. Six counties in the north resisted and accepted "Home Rule" rather than total independence. This new country is now known as Northern Ireland or Ulster (McKittrick, 3–5).

With such a history of violence, there was hope that the new political structures would work for the peoples of the two Irelands. Unfortunately, hope did not prevail. Many people, both from the north and the south, did not like the concept of a divided Ireland. Groups advocating the reunion of the countries began to form. In the south, there were the Republicans and also the Nationals, originating within the Roman Catholic traditions. The Irish Republican Army (IRA), a paramilitary group advocating violence as a solution, emerged from the Republicans.

To the north, other organizations wanted to reunite Ireland also. They called themselves the Unionists. Most of these groups grew out of a Protestant tradition. The Loyalists supported violence. And out of this group came the Ulster Paramilitary Force (UVF), the Ulster Defense Association (UDA), and the Ulster Freedom Fighters (UFF) (Buscher, 15). Groups aligned with Protestants dominated the Parliament of Northern Ireland. Their methods and politics resulted in discrimination of all types against the Catholics in education, housing, and employment.

Land ownership determined representation in the Parliament of Northern Ireland, and Protestants owned most of the land. Roman Catholics had no official political power. Consequently, many Roman Catholics had poor living conditions, little money, and a pauper's existence, while their Protestant bosses owned cars and lavish homes.

Threats, beatings, firebombs, abductions, assassinations, and terrorist activities, ripped Ireland for more than 40 years, killing almost 4,000 people, the majority Irish (McKittrick, 329). The IRA believed that these were "just" acts of war against "British Imperialism."

The Civil Rights Movement in the United States inspired the Roman Catholics in the north to further action. Dissatisfied Catholics in Ulster began demanding equal housing, equal pay, equal education, and equal representation in Ulster's Protestant controlled Parliament.

The IRA, headquartered in southern Ireland, began to recruit more and more people who saw liberation and freedom from Protestant domination as the 'just' cause. Murder, destruction of property, and death threats were the tools of their trade. Northern Ireland disintegrated under the masterful hands of the IRA terrorists and the brutal British patrols.

Great Britain attempted to stop the violence. In 1971, the United Kingdom instituted "administrative internment." This law gave British troops in Ulster the right to arrest and imprison anyone who looked suspicious. In a matter of hours, average citizens lost their basic freedoms. They could be jailed without a charge or a trial. Britain took these strong measures to bring order to the war that held the streets and the lives of the Irish hostage. In response, the entire parliament of Ulster resigned. Britain wasted no time. It took full control of Ulster and sent 270 people to occupy and run the government in Northern Ireland.

Living in Ulster was frightening. Daily shoot-outs between British troops and the IRA drove many people away from Ireland. Thousands migrated to New Zealand, Australia, and Canada to find peace. Those who remained were often called "xenophobes" because they feared their neighbors and the outside world. The war had created a prison of hostility.

At the height of this nightmare, Mairead Corrigan, Betty Williams, and newspaper reporter Ciaran McKeown found each other. Drawn together by disaster, they began talking about peace—peace through peaceful means. Ciaran McKeown wrote, "We have to do things that people don't expect us to do. We have to be stronger and braver than anyone else" (Deutsch, 43).

Mairead Corrigan Maguire
Voice of Peace to the World
January 27, 1944–

"We are, in fact, absolutely capable of killing each other."
[Maguire, *The Tanner Lectures*, 259]

A pointless violent tragedy propelled Mairead Corrigan and Betty Williams, everyday working women, onto the world's stage. How could they have prepared for the clamoring of the press, the stresses of instant change, and the status of "international celebrity" that came rushing into their lives? Moments such as these can destroy a person. Corrigan and Williams chose not to remain passive at a time when the lives of children were sacrificed for what they believed was a meaningless fight. They chose the path of greatness.

It takes only a few seconds to change a life forever. Ann Maguire's life would never be the same after that fateful afternoon when she bundled up her three children for a walk around the block. While Joanna (age eight), Andrew (age six), and John (age two) walked and played, an out-of-control vehicle plunged over the curb, pinning them to a fence. Danny Lenno, an I.R.A. recruit, had just been shot by a British patrol. He slumped over the wheel of the car as it smashed into Ann and her family. Ann was severely injured and hospitalized for several weeks with internal injuries and broken bones. She survived, but her children did not. They were buried while she remained in the hospital, struggling for her own life.

The swirling moments of the Maguire tragedy also changed Mairead Corrigan's life. While traveling back to her home in Northern Ireland, the news about the deaths of the little children blasted from her car radio. She learned later that the story was about her own sister Ann's children. Ann's husband Jackie Maguire, in shock at the death of his children, and at the possibility of losing his spouse, found it difficult to respond to the press. Mairead became the spokesperson for the family. Within hours of the accident, every news station in Ireland was broadcasting her face to the world. She was so overcome with grief that she had little to say. Through her tears she called for the violence to stop. "It's not violence that people want, only one percent of the people of this province want this slaughter" (Deutsch, 4). She would later visit the mother of Danny Lennon, the young man who died at the wheel of the car that killed her niece and nephew. She also had lost her child.

The death of helpless children dug deep into the consciences of the Irish people. Betty Williams witnessed the tragic accident and was so enraged that she began collecting signatures from women calling for peace. Mairead saw Betty being interviewed on television and invited her to the funeral of the children. A friendship was born.

Ciaran McKeown did not receive the Nobel Prize but he was a vital player in all of the peace efforts that followed the death of the children. A reporter with the Irish Press, Ciaran had studied the peace philosophies of Gandhi and Martin Luther King, Jr. With a college degree and experience in politics, he was the person who had organizational and writing skills.

Ciaran was hopeful that Mairead and Betty would want to begin some type of peace movement. As soon as he met Betty, he knew that she was strong enough to lead peace efforts in Northern Ireland. After talking with Mairead and Betty again at the funeral, he offered to work with them. Following the first big march (over 1,000 women and men) on Finaghy Road on August 14, 1976, they phoned him. Soon the concept of "Peace People" was born, although the press preferred to label the movement "Women for Peace" (Deutsch, 70–80).

Ciaran helped plan many peace marches through December. He created, wrote, and edited the "Peace by Peace" magazine that sometimes contained biting articles attacking both politicians and religious officials.

Mairead had always advocated bringing peace to Ireland by loving one's neighbor. This philosophy was challenged to the extreme when her brother was arrested by the British and ended up missing. She admits that there were times that she wanted to strike back, to join the IRA.

Busy in her career as a secretary, she spent much of her free time in volunteer efforts for the Legion of Mary, a Roman Catholic Social Advocate group. Even before the accident, she took words of love and peace to prisoners in the Long Kesh internment camp near Belfast (Deutsch, 32) and spent many nights with people in the ghetto. As a young woman, she was privileged to travel to the 1972 World Council of Churches in Thailand where she spent three weeks. In 1973 she went to Russia for the Legion of Mary and made a film about Catholics. Later, she traveled to churches and spoke to groups about her discoveries in Russia. These experiences certainly helped to prepare her for the role that was thrust upon her.

The Legion of Mary, a missionary organization in Dublin, was founded in 1921. In a section of its handbook, The Legion, in military terms, describes part of its mission:

The Legion aims to bring Mary to the world as the infallible means of winning the world to Jesus. Manifestly, the legionary without Mary in his heart can play no part in this. He is divorced from the legionary purpose. He is an unarmed soldier, a broken link, or rather as a paralyzed arm—attached to the body, it is true—but of what use for work!

The study of every army (and no less that of the Legion) must be to bind the individual soldier to the leader, so that the latter's plan passes smoothly into concerted action. The army acts as one. To this end is all the elaborate machinery of drill and discipline directed. In addition, there is found in the soldiers of all the great armies of history a devotion of a passionate sort for their leader, intensifying their union with him, and rendering easy the sacrifices which the execution of his plan called for. Of this leader it could be said that he was the inspiration and soul of his soldiers, in their hearts, one with them, and so forth. These phrases describe the operation of his influence and in a measure express a truth.

But at best such unity is only an emotional or mechanical one. Not so the relation between the Christian soul and Mary its Mother. To say that Mary is in the soul of the faithful legionary would be to picture a union infinitely less effective than that which actually exists, the nature of which is summed up by the Church in such titles of Our Lady as: "Mother of Divine Grace," "Mediatrix of all Graces." In these titles is expressed a sway of Mary over the life of the soul, so complete that even the closest of earthly unions—the mother and the babe unborn—is inadequate to describe its intimacy [www.legion-of-mary.ie].

It appears that the Legion was a grass roots organization that provided social services to Catholic parishes. Posted on their "Local Event Guide" are prayer group meetings, rosaries, and events that publicly advocate peace. A long essay describing how to become a saint explains, "In the heart of every right-thinking Catholic, God has implanted the desire to become a Saint." (Duff, "Can We Be Saints?"). Many females within Roman Catholicism, rather than becoming a sister or nun, take informal vows to serve the church in a variety of ways. Perhaps Mairead, early in her life, was one of these people who dedicated herself to the church and this lay organization?

Prior to the death of her niece and nephews, Mairead regularly witnessed absurd and inhumane practices by the government. Great Britain ignored the needs of the common people in Northern Ireland. For example, the politicians decided to build a highway through a suburb of Belfast. Bulldozers made their way right down the middle of a neighborhood. The new road divided the neighborhood into two sides with no crosswalks for the people. Many children subsequently died or suffered injury while attempting to cross the street.

Mairead understood the reasons as to why many Catholics rebelled against the strong hand of the British. Killing your neighbors was not the solution. There had to be a better way. The United Kingdom, after thousands of complaints, attempted to demonstrate its interest in the plight of Catholics by building high-rise apartments. The purpose of the apartments was to house people who currently lived in less than human living conditions or were uprooted because of bombings in the city. While Catholics liked having a roof over their heads, they did not appreciate the location of the buildings. The housing was built far away from stores, cinemas, and playgrounds. Most of the people who lived in the buildings did not own an automobile, neither did they have the money for transportation. The new apartment buildings were soon in disrepair. The sparkling new concrete structures quickly became crumbling tombs that segregated their residents from the rest of the world.

Mairead worked long hours to bring recreational areas, meeting halls, and shops to areas desolated by fire, bombings, or poverty. She even took children to the beaches. This does not seem to be very important, but it is life-changing to a child who lives on an island and has never seen the sea. She considered her work with children, the Legion of Mary, an extension of her Christian faith.

At 33, Mairead was still living with her parents in the Catholic ghetto in Belfast. She did not have high academic aspirations when she was young, having dropped out of school at the age of 14. She studied business for one year and, later in life, received certification in Ecumenical Studies from the Irish school of Ecumenics. She also became affiliated with the Methodist Theological Education and the Northern Ireland Council for Integrated Education. While some Roman Catholics had experienced discrimination and prejudice because of their faith, Mairead claims that she did not, because she always had good paying positions and had personally never experienced violence.

Mairead did experience the brutalities of the never-ending war between Britain and the IRA. During a funeral, she witnessed British soldiers throwing tear gas on the altar of the church. She also saw soldiers beating and molesting women as they searched them. The British also pushed the parents of her friends down a flight of stairs. Then she witnessed the death of her best friend.

The IRA continually retaliated against the brutality of the British army with its own violent actions. It bombed key political places and killed politicians. No one was safe. In a moment, violence could erupt in anyone's front yard.

After the death of the Maguire children in 1976, Mairead left her job to become a full-time worker for peace. She and Betty Williams—with the advice of news reporter Ciaran McKeown—planned marches, rallies, talks, television appearances, and literature with the sole purpose of stopping the war. By the end of March of 1977, the Peace People had gathered more than 300,000 signatures on their Declaration of Peace (Aaseng, 59) and at least 8,000 people volunteered to create peace cells all over Ireland. "Throughout the troubles, we have heard the voices of women calling for compassion instead of conflict, for collaboration instead of coercion, for cooperation instead of competition," said Mairead (Vildulich, 2). Authored by Ciaran, the "Declaration of the Peace People" embodied their hopes and beliefs. It is still the banner of the Peace People website.

> We live a simple message to the world from this movement for Peace.
> We want to live and love and build a just and peaceful society.
> We want for our children, as we want for ourselves, our lives at home, at work, and at play to be lives of joy and Peace.
> We recognize that to build such a society demands dedication, hard work, and courage.
> We recognize that there are many problems in our society which are a source of conflict and violence.
> We recognize that every bullet fired and every exploding bomb make that work more difficult.

We reject the use of the bomb and the bullet and all the techniques of violence.
We dedicate ourselves to working with our neighbors, near and far, day in and day out, to build that peaceful society in which the tragedies we have known are a bad memory and a continuing warning ["Peace People Declaration"].

Collaboration was a strategy advocated by Ciaran. Lasting peace would only come when everyone in Northern Ireland was involved. All over Ireland, small neighborhood cells were formed with the purpose of creating peace. While many of these did serve to bring people together, they often lost their direction and wanted more guidance from the central organization. Eventually, over the years, they disintegrated.

Slowly, discrimination in housing for the Roman Catholics was reduced. The election procedures changed. Newly established offices handled complaints of harassment or discrimination. Mairead and Betty began to see progress as they worked tirelessly together. Within 15 months of the beginning of their campaign against war, violent incidents and deaths were cut in half. The two women were making inroads into conquering hate.

The months of feverish work took its toll on Mairead. She found herself beaten, the object of vicious criticism, and accosted by people who called her a traitor. After every meeting, she felt drained and empty. She was giving much to her country, but her country had little to give back to her. Although Mairead felt lonely, the rest of the world was beginning to take notice of her relentless energy. In late 1976, an alliance of newspapers and civic groups from all over the world collected over $300,000, the Norwegian People Peace Prize, to give to Mairead and the Peace People in Ireland. She had become an example of world peace.

Jealousy and dissension grew among the volunteers of the Peace People. Mairead and Betty were accused of wearing better clothing and leaving behind the needs of Ireland when they flew around the world. Only a few months after they received the donation, the Nobel Peace Price Committee named Mairead Corrigan and Betty Williams recipients of the 1976 Nobel Peace Prize. Egil Aarvik, Vice Chairman of the Norwegian Nobel Committee, presented the prize to the women with these words:

Love of one's neighbour is one of the foundation stones of the humanism on which our western civilization is built. But it is vital that we should have the courage to sustain this love of neighbour when the pressure to abandon it is at its greatest... Betty Williams and Mairead Corrigan Maguire are still attempting to show what ordinary people can do to promote the cause of peace [http://nobelprize.org/peace/laureates/1976/press.html].

When outsiders asked about the meaning of this prize for the women, Mairead said that it was a way to change the world through non-violence.

The organization of Peace People needed the money, but Betty and Mairead differed on what to do with it. Eventually, some of the money bought a house for the offices of Peace People. Both Mairead and Betty had been unemployed for some time; Betty had actually gone in debt to support her lectures and travels, so she also needed the money. Without consulting Betty, Mairead told the world that the money would be donated to Peace People. This announcement was the beginning of the end of their association.

Months after the Nobel Prize was collected, charges of financial mismanagement were leveled against the women. Powerful organizers resigned when they were not able to control the destiny of Peace People. No one could have prepared them for the beatings and harassment they faced from both sides in the war. For one brief moment, the light of faith in their God, in neighbor, and in country twinkled. But it soon faded.

Mairead and Betty were idealists and had created no real workable plan to bring

peace to Ireland. They thought that the marches, the cells, and their guest speaking engage-
ments would quickly turn the tide. Opposition forces claimed that they wanted "Peace at
any price!" and dogged their progress. They accused the women of selling out Ireland and
the Catholics.

Father John Dear writes about how Betty and Mairead were received in the north:

> In Belfast, where Catholics and Protestants still walk on opposite sides of the streets, where
> the long memory of past bloodshed keeps the demonic spirit of vengeance alive, where retalia-
> tion is too often the principal topic of conversation over a pint of Guinness at the corner pub,
> Mairead's vision of non-violence was not well-received, particularly in the 1980s and early
> 1990s. She was dismissed, ridiculed, and ignored, while those who called for vengeance and
> violence found an audience. But Mairead has remained faithful. She continues in her quiet,
> gentle way to announce a vision of peace, even in the face of violence, resentment, and rage
> [Dear, "Mairead Corrigan Maguire"].

Having never run a big volunteer organization, the founders of Peace People were
often late to their appointments. Reporters would fly halfway across the world to do an
interview with Mairead and Betty, but then the women would only give them a few minutes of their time, if any. The organization had practical problems with phones and the
day-to-day workings of the office, which was staffed by volunteers. The headquarters of
Peace People was a great gathering place. People felt comfortable in the house. Consequently, many tasks were left undone because people wanted to talk.

By 1978, Betty and Mairead resigned as leaders. Full-time staffers were appointed to
run the organization with the stipulation that Mairead and Betty would respond to requests
for assistance. Yet their assault on war brought continued violence into their own lives.

Her sister Ann, who had survived the accident that killed her children, went on to
have two more children. But the psychological pain of losing her children, of never seeing them buried, haunted her. Mairead wrote about the demise of her sister:

> On January 21, 1980, at around 3:00 P.M., Ann took her own life, and her spirit found peace
> at last. Her husband Jackie, a motor mechanic in a local firm, was at work. One of her daugh-
> ters, Joanne (two and a half), was at nursery school, and baby Marie-Louise (nine months old)
> lay upstairs in her cot. Her ten-year-old son, Mark, returned from school to find his mother
> sitting in a chair, dying or dead from her wounds. Ann had taken an electric knife and cut her
> wrists. We were told it would have taken about thirty minutes for Ann to "bleed to death."
> Before dying, she took the kitchen mop and tried to clean up her blood from the floor. An
> unfinished note to her family lay beside her. It read, "Forgive me. I love you" [Maguire, *The
> Vision of Peace*, 22].

In 1981, Mairead married Ann's husband, Jackie Maguire, and soon became mother
to two children, Francis (b. 1982) and Luke (b. 1984).

Today Mairead is still involved with peace efforts in her country, but the notoriety
brought to her because of the Nobel Peace Prize changed the direction of her life. She has
become a world spokesperson for peace while coming to understand the uncontrollable sys-
temic problems caused by governments and big business. Her lectures have been collected
and published in several volumes. Having traveled to more than 25 countries and met people such as John Paul II, Jimmy Carter, and Queen Elizabeth II, she is regularly invited
to academic institutions to receive honorary doctorates and to lecture around the world.

The themes of her lectures have changed dramatically. "We lost many members
because many people would prefer to pray to God and hope the problems go away. They
do not see the genuine, structural inhumanities present in our society. Perhaps this is
where Christianity has failed most" (Maguire, *Vision for Peace*, 13).

She has gone on to criticize the wealthier nations for arming the "third world" (Maguire, *The Tanner Lectures*, 256). In 1995 she visited Burundi, Africa, a country racked by civil war, and asked the people what they needed. They said, "Don't send us any guns. Don't send us any military forces" (Maguire, *The Vision for Peace*, 50). Mairead began to realize that all of the peoples of the world are interconnected in some way. In her essay on "Grassroots Peacemaking in a World of Ethnic Conflict," she writes,

> Eighty-five percent of these weapons in the Third World come from the wealthy "First World" nations. We must delude ourselves no longer. We are arming the Third World. In return, a high percentage of their budgets and international aid are coming back to the West. While some of these countries cannot feed their people, they can and do buy our guns and send money back to us. This is so unjust. It causes so much suffering. The world's people need to unite their voice to stop the genocide of the poor [Maguire, *Vision for Peace*, 50].

In an address remembering the fiftieth anniversary of Gandhi's assassination, Mairead hoped for a new idealism regarding peace efforts. Yet, she concluded that we "live in an insane world" (Maguire, "Gandhi and the Ancient Wisdom," 160). She asks penetrating questions such as,

> Is it not insanity to go on producing nuclear and conventional weapons that if used can destroy millions of people, if not the whole planet? ... while millions of children die of disease and starvation each year? Is it not insanity that developed countries—including Britain, currently the third largest exporter of arms of the world—sell huge amounts of armaments to poor and developing countries, which in turn use much of the money allocated to them for aid to pay for these arms? [Maguire, "Gandhi and the Ancient Wisdom," 160].

Mairead calls for the univocal disarming of the nations of the earth! She thinks that the world, including her own country, has been fooled into thinking that the "Just War Theory" is valid.

> What is needed in Ireland—and the Christian world—is for all church leaders and Christians to renounce the lie of the just war theory. Fr. John McKenzie describes the just war theory as "a phony piece of morality." And that is why we need a new theology of non-violence and peace [McGuire, *Vision for Peace*, 29].

She argues that perhaps the church has done violence in the name of God, but Jesus was non-violent and Christians should follow his example and refuse to kill. There needs to be a conversion among the peoples of the earth to a non-violent way of thinking (Maguire, "Gandhi and the Ancient Wisdom," 162).

Mairead believes that love can transform a person, a people, or a nation. Misguided government polices in Iraq caused the suffering that took place during and after the first Persian Gulf War. In 2001 she wrote a letter to Umm Reyda in Iraq after having visited a shelter in Baghdad. This is an excerpt:

> When we met, you were living in a little portacabin on the site and acting as a guide for visitors to the shelter. You told us that one night during the Gulf War many hundreds of people had gathered in the shelter to celebrate the end of Ramadan. That night the shelter was struck by two American bombs. Of the hundreds present, only 14 people survived the inferno. Your son, your daughter Reyda, and thirteen of your relatives were among the dead. We were moved to tears when we saw the photographs of the victims, most of whom were women and children. You told us that you had worked since that day to keep the truth alive—for them and the world. I remember so well your passionate plea for the story to be told about what happened and your call for "no more wars." How much we need to hear your voice in our world today. Since then, I am haunted by the memory of the burnt imprints of bodies, fused into the concrete walls [Maguire, "Letter to an Iraqi Woman," 337].

Mairead also worries about the economic power of big business and links the current dictatorship in Burma/Myanmar to the investment in this country by the big oil-producing companies. The violent regime of Myanmar that has killed and raped Karen women and tortured its inhabitants is now financed by oil. Mairead visited a refugee camp on the border and found 5,000 refugees who had fled for their lives with 60 percent of them being orphaned children under 12 years old (Schoeder, 2). "We are fast moving into a world where big businesses control national and international economies. They quickly become more politically powerful than national and international governments and political institutions and find themselves at the service of brutal military forces" (Maguire, *The Tanner Lectures*, 257).

The conflict in Ireland is between Christians—Catholics and Protestants. Mairead has come to believe that people should be taught about the faiths of other peoples. She relies on her own spiritual path for understanding. She has reached the conclusion that reconciliation and forgiveness are supreme values. The rigidity of beliefs must give way to tolerance. "As [the young people] move away from traditional religions, we realize that there are many paths to God" (Maguire, *The Tanner Lectures*, 264).

How do we solve our problems without killing each other? At home in Northern Ireland we try to accomplish this through teaching non-violence at every level of our society—courses on conflict resolution, prejudice reduction, human rights. This is a new direction for us. In teaching respect for life and respect for diversity we will create a tolerant and more compassionate world [Maguire, *The Tanner Lectures*, 260].

E-mail Mairead at Info@peacepeople.com.

Elizabeth (Betty) Williams

Protector of the Children of the World

May 22, 1943–

"I've never known people who hate as much as we do."
[Deutsch, 58]

"Shoot Betty"
(a slogan painted on walls in Belfast in 1977)
[Ashby, 282]

Betty Williams had a happy life with Ralph Williams, a sailor. Ralph appreciated her independent and spunky spirit. Eleven months out of the year, her Protestant husband was off sailing around the world. Because his salary was good for Northern Ireland, Betty decided to focus most of her time on raising their two children. She often took part-time jobs to bring in a little extra cash. While she had no problem *finding* a job, she did have trouble *keeping* a job. People said that she was "head strong" or "insubordinate."

At age 15, Betty's mother died, leaving the responsibility of her sister Margaret and the home to her. She learned how to share her gentle side with others whom she loved, but she could also be tough. Betty had to develop strengths in order to manage work and home. "I don't believe that women should cut themselves off from the world when they become wives and mothers. They should keep their minds open and learn new things" (Deutsch, 51).

Betty was no stranger to violence. It had touched her personally in many indescribable ways. Violence had killed two of her cousins. Protestants shot one of her family members. A car bomb set by the IRA took the life of the others. A crowd burned down the new home of her sister! She was livid after the fire, and admits that she smuggled members of the movement to the South. In a moment of anger, she could give as much as she had gotten from another.

> If there's one person in the movement who is not a true and complete pacifist, I'm that person.... My reaction, when I'm attacked, is to give as good as I get.... I still have to struggle for self-control [Deutsch, 56].

Yet violence touched the lives of the opposition too and Betty came to realize that every life is important and should be protected. One day when the fighting was especially heavy, Betty watched the British police shovel the remains of young men into plastic bags. "For the first time I realized the British are human beings too" (Deutsch, 53–54). She says she will always be haunted by that day.

Betty longed to get involved. When the Reverend Joseph Parker led a personal crusade against violence, she supported him. She listened to his sermons and walked with him as he protested violence. She believed in his messages, but her belief did not thrust her into action. Rejected and apparently a failure in his peace efforts, Reverend Parker left the country. Betty commented,

> I sometimes reflect on how the English must hate themselves for having sent colonists here seven hundred years ago. Since then, they've had nothing by trouble. And they don't understand why. The English live in the future, while we live in the past. Every two or three hours, we resurrect the past, dust it off, and throw it in someone's face [Deutsch, 59].

One day while Betty was out walking with her own children, she saw the British patrol chasing a runaway truck. The patrol had shot the driver. Slumped over the wheel, the man was no longer in control of the vehicle. Seconds later a woman and her three children lay pinned between the truck and an iron fence. Only the mother, Ann Maguire, survived.

The death of the Maguire children triggered something inside Betty. She had had enough! She was going to do something to stop the insanity! With pen in hand, she searched the streets of Belfast for people who cared about Ireland. By the next morning she had gathered thousands of signatures (some say 10,000!) of women who were determined to bring peace to Ireland.

That same evening, on national television, Mairead Corrigan was interviewed about her sister, Ann Maguire. She pleaded with the people of Ireland to stop the war. Mairead heard of Betty's personal response to the death of the children and invited her to sit with her at the Maguire funeral. From that day on, Mairead and Betty became friends in search of peace. Together they began to plan peace efforts in Ireland.

Betty and Mairead's work began with signatures, but it soon blossomed into a full-scale assault on war. The women planned a protest march with the sole purpose of drawing attention to the possibility of peace. Betty knew that everything they were doing was dangerous. She feared that at any moment, either side could decide to eliminate her. She received death threats on the phone and day after day watched people plaster "Shoot Betty" on city walls. At first she shrugged them off, but she soon realized that her life was on the line. The danger, however, did not stop her. She organized a march in downtown Belfast along Finaghy Road. Thousands of women, including some clergy, joined her. It was a victorious day.

The glory soon faded as crowd of onlookers began to abuse Betty and the rest of the courageous women. They spit on them, pulled their hair, and shouted obscenities. Some of the marchers were dragged into alleys and beaten. The march did not stop. While most of the women were a little dirty and roughed up by the end of the day, no one had been killed. Miraculously, these determined people had brought violence to a halt—if only for a brief hour or two.

Betty spent days and nights organizing talks and marches, writing letters, and reaching out to both the Protestants and Catholics. Newspaper reporter Ciaran McKeown became her staunchest supporter. Together these three people forced the inhabitants of Ireland to think about peace.

In less than two years, fighting in the streets began to slow down. According to the Peace People website, "Within the first six months there was a 70 percent drop in the rate of violence" ("Peace People History"). People again walked alone in the middle of the day. For her very successful efforts, Betty received the Nobel Peace Prize. Words from her acceptance speech surely haunted the peoples of Ireland:

> Mairead Corrigan and I may take some satisfaction with us all the days of our lives that we did make that initial call, a call which unlocked the massive desire for peace within the hearts of Northern Irish people, and as we soon discovered, in the hearts of people around the world ... not least in Norway....
>
> As far as we are concerned, every single death in the last eight years, and every death in every war that was fought represents life needlessly wasted, a mother's labor spurned.... We are for life and creation, and we are against war and destruction, and in our rage in that terrible week, we screamed that the violence had to stop ["Betty Williams–Nobel Lecture"].

The Peace People confronted and overcame many problems. The most challenging were not financial or organizational but involved personal relationships. Sometimes people do cruel things in order to make a point. Once, in a gesture of peace, Betty invited a few women from both sides of the war to come to her home to talk. A few hours later, she was left badly bruised, beaten, and lying on the floor alone in her house. The price of peace can be too high for many, but Betty decided to take the risks. She still believes that people must trust one another. She still believes in the force of love.

Betty said that she would never forget her roots. She was born in the ghetto, and the ghetto is where she did most of her work. But her personal life changed in 1982 when she and her husband Ralph divorced. Subsequently, she married James T. Perkins. Betty chose not to stay in the midst of the battle. After years of violence and death threats, she left her country for a new life with her children and husband in Florida.

Currently residing in Huntsville, Texas, she directs the World Centers of Compassion for Children International. Her current podium consists of diatribes against child soldiering, seeking to educate and to protect the rights of children. She is targeting laws and setting up neutral children's zones where war will not affect them. Her passion for peace and human rights continues. Because of her dedication, Betty has traveled all over the world, "a guerrilla for peace."

Peace People, at its peak, boasted 10,000 members. They smuggled people out of the country who were on death lists. They set up social agencies. They were determined to erase violence wherever it occurred—from the family living room to the halls of parliament.

Total peace still eludes the people of Ireland, but if you look hard, you can see it on the horizon. Even after Mairead and Betty received the Nobel Peace Prize, hundreds of people continued to be killed in their neighborhoods. The IRA attacked the residence of the Prime Minister at 10 Downing Street and bombed a train station in Great Britain. But today Northern Ireland has again begun to thrive economically. People are finding jobs and businesses are starting to invest capital.

Talks began in 1993 between the National Social Democratic Party and members of what had been the Provisional IRA. These negotiations resulted in the 1993 Joint Declaration of Peace. By 1994, the IRA announced that it would bring a halt to all military operations. A New Framework for Peace Agreement was hammered out during the early months of 1995. And by 1996 all parties were calling for a complete ceasefire. A Northern Ireland Assembly was established in 1998 under the Good Friday Agreement. Elections have now been held in Northern Ireland with equal representations from both Protestants and Catholics. In 2004 there were only two deaths related to the historic conflict ("The Troubles"; "Northern Ireland Peace Process"; "Good Friday Agreement").

Perhaps the Peace People have won!

E-mail Betty at: bwccc@eircom.net

Bibliography

Aaseng, Nathan. *The Peace Seekers*. Minneapolis: Lerner Publications, 1987.

Ashby, Ruth, and Deborah Gore Ohrn, ed. *Herstory: Women Who Changed the World*. New York: Viking, 1995.

"Betty Williams Presentation for Plowshares." Available online at http://www.plowsharesproject.org/php/BettyPresentation.php.

Buscher, Sarah, and Bettina Ling. *Mairead Corrigan and Betty Williams: Making Peace in Northern Ireland*. New York: The Feminist, 1999.

Dear, S.J., John. "Mairead Corrigan Maguire." Available online at http://www.peacepeople.com/Mairead.ByJohnDear.html.

Dekar, Paul. "Mairead Corrigan Maguire and the Northern Irish Peace People." *Peace Magazine* (July–August 1992): 7–8.

Deutsch, Richard. Trans. Jack Bernard. *Mairead Corrigan and Betty Williams*. New York: Barron's, 1977.

Duff, Frank. "Can We Be Saints?" Available online at www.legion-of-mary.ie/Publications/CWB Saints/FDSaints.html.

Hill, George. *An Historical Account of the Plantation in Ulster at the Commencement of the Seventeenth Century*. Shannon: Irish University Press, 1970.

http:—
"Betty Williams–Curriculum Vitae." http://www.nobelprize.org/peace/laureates/1976/Williams-cv.html

"Betty Williams–Nobel Lecture." http://www.nobelprize.org/peace/laureates/1976/Williams-lecture.html.

Engle, Dawn, and Ivan Suvanjieff. "An Interview with Betty Williams." Conducted July 4, 1995. Available online at http://www.peacejam.org/pages/laureates_betty/laureates_betty_interview.htm.

"Good Friday Agreement." http://www.en.wikipedia.org/wiki/Good_Friday_Agreement.

http://www.legion-of-mary.com.

"Mairead Corrigan–Curriculum Vitae." http://www.nobelprize.org/peace/laureates/1976/Corrigan-cv.html.

"Northern Ireland Peace Process." http://www.en.wikipedia.org/wiki/Northern_Ireland_peace_process.

"The Troubles." http://www.en.wikipedia.org/wiki/The_Troubles.

World Centers of Compassion for Children Website. http://www.centersofcompassion.org/.

Kennedy, R. Scott, and Peter Klontz-Chamberlain. "Northern Ireland's Guerrillas of Peace." *Christian Century*, August 31–September 7, 1977: 746–51.

Maguire, Mairead Corrigan. "Gandhi and the Ancient Wisdom of Nonviolence." *In Peace Is the Way: Writings on Nonviolence from the Fellowship of Reconciliation*. Edited by Walter Wink. New York: Orbis Books, 2000: 159–62

_____. "Iraq After First (1991) Gulf War." In *The Iraq War and Its Consequences. Thoughts of Nobel Peace Laureates and Eminent Scholars*. Edited by Irwin Abrams and Wang Gungwu. London: World Scientific, 2003.

_____. "Letter to an Iraqi Woman." In *Women on War: An International Anthology of Women's Writings from Antiquity to the Present*. Edited by Daniela Gioseffi. New York: The Feminist Press, 2003: 337–40.

_____. "A Non-Violent Political Agenda for a More Humane World." In *Waging Peace II: Vision and Hope for the 21st Century*. Edited by David Krieger and Frank K. Kelly. Chicago: The Nobel Press, 1992: 47–57.

_____. "Peacemaking from the Grassroots in a World of Ethnic Conflict." In *The Tanner Lectures on Human Values*. Edited by Grethe B. Peterson. Salt Lake City: University of Utah Press, 1997: 253–66.

_____. "Politics with Principles." In *World Without Violence: Can Gandhi's Vision Become Reality?* Edited by Arun Gandha. New Delhi: Wiley Eastern Limited, 1994: 47–54.

_____. *The Vision of Peace: Faith and Hope in Northern Ireland*. Edited by John Dear. New York: Orbis Books, 1999.

McDade, Jim. "Lives Dedicated to Peace," *Newsweek*, vol. 132, issue 20 (November 16, 1998): 20.

McKittrick, David. *Making Sense of the Troubles: The Story of the Conflict in Northern Ireland*. Chicago: New Amsterdam Books, 2002.

Opfell, Olga S. *The Lady Laureates. Women Who Have Won the Nobel Prize*. Metuchen, New Jersey: Scarecrow, 1978.

"Peace People Declaration." Available online at www.peacepeople.com/PPDeclaration.htm.

"Peace People History." Available online at www.peacepeople.com/PPHistory.htm.

Schroeder, Steven. "Toward a Higher Identity: An Interview with Mairead Corrigan Maguire." *Christian Century* (April 1994): 414–17.

Vidulich, Dorothy. "Though Nobel went to men, Women helped bring peace." *National Catholic ReporterI*, vol. 35, issue 4 (November 13, 1998): 16–20.

Mother Teresa
(Agnes G. Bohjaxhiu)
(1979)

Icon of the Oppressed

August 26, 1910–September 5, 1997

Mother Teresa (Agnes G. Bohjaxhiu), Nobel Peace Laureate 1979.

The Castaways of War

When hostile neighborhoods erupt into lethal violence, when super-powers invade nations, when big business and governments create dynasties that suck the wealth out of a country, a tragic consequence is the creation of uncounted castaways. Most bureaucracies attempt to ignore the suffering that their policies, laws, and procedures produce. This practice of "ignoring" can place an entire nation at risk for disease, civil war, and violent crime. Such disregard occurred in India.

Harmless but desperate people fill the streets of all the major cities in India. Many have no recorded birth and do not know their families. They have migrated to India seeking a better life only to win a spot on the ground out of the cold wind. They beg. They search for anything of value for themselves and their babies. There are no adequate words to describe the suffering of these people who share their space with the refuse of water buffalo, abandoned cows, goats, pigs, and dogs.

India has had more than its share of greedy and bloodthirsty rulers. Historically, the Moguls and Maharajas, in the Middle Ages, enslaved the local people to feed and entertain them and to build their monuments, fortresses, and palaces. Sultan Qutbuddin Aibak, a Muslim conqueror in 1209, built the Qutab Minar in Delhi, the tallest tower in India. It stands almost 238 feet high and is a symbol of ferocious Muslim power. The surrounding mosque is built from the remains of Hindu temples that the invaders had destroyed. Humanyun's Mausoleum, the Taj Mahal, and even Red Fort in Jaipur astound the traveler. According to historians, it took 20 years and 20,000 people to build the Taj Mahal, a mortuary for the wife of Shah Jahan in Agra.

According to most archaeologists, the Aryans, who migrated from the north into the Indian subcontinent over four millennia ago, dominated and subjugated the peoples. The British Empire, from the nineteenth century onward, attempted to bring order to a very diverse and multi-religious landscape in India. But in the end, the subjugated peoples wanted self-rule.

The Victims of War

Agnes G. Bohjaxhiu (Mother Teresa) experienced this political struggle for independence first-hand in 1943. In Calcutta, a local fight between Muslims and Hindus led to the massacre of over 5,000 people and the injury of 15,000 more. While the war raged outside Agnes' windows, she attempted to protect 300 starving students. Finally she mustered enough courage to go outside her compound to find food. It was a day that she would never forget. "Then I saw the bodies on the streets, stabbed, beaten, lying there in strange positions in their dried blood. We had been behind safe walls..." (Egan, 24–25).

> Accounts of those apocalyptic days describe how violence shook the city to its foundations. Shops were set afire with kerosene bombs while the owners were inside. Sewers were flooded with the crush of bodies tossed into them. In the open streets men and women, pierced with metal-tipped lathis, or with any variety of lethal blade, were left to bleed to death. Entrails spilled onto the sidewalks and half-dismembered bodies sprawled across gutters [Egan, 25].

Blood stained the walls and streets wherever she walked. Fortunately, Agnes ran into a few soldiers who agreed to bring rice to her students.

Refugees poured into India after it declared its independence from Great Britain in

1947. This new freedom had brought chaos to everyone. About 8,000,000 people fled to India from Pakistan and West Bengal because of the riots and religious persecution. The neat and trim streets of British Calcutta became homes for people in search of a new life. More than 400,000 people out of 9,000,000 lived on the Calcutta streets. A few years after this episode, Agnes would leave her teaching position and begin a new career as founder of the Missionaries of Charity and servant of homeless, starving, diseased, and dying people.

The Early Years

Agnes Gonxha Bohjaxhiu was born on August 26 (baptized on August 27), 1910, in Skopje, Albania, which is now the capital of Macedonia. Long before her journey to the streets and alleys of Calcutta, Agnes had learned generosity and self-sacrifice from her widowed mother.

Agnes was born into a comfortable family with a father who provided well for his family. According to her brother, Lazar, their family owned two adjoining houses. Her father, Nikola, spoke five languages, which facilitated his success as a building contractor and importer of food. He was also engaged in a movement to restore identity and power to the Albanians. Returning from a trip to Belgrade, Nikola began hemorrhaging profusely. No one could save him. Many suspected that his political enemies had poisoned him (Egan, 7–9).

Drana, Agnes' mother, was devastated for almost a year. Her husband's partner assumed full ownership of the businesses and left her without income. Drana eventually turned to embroidery and sold her cloth and carpets to support her family. Her life became wholly intertwined with the local Catholic Church that the Jesuit priests staffed. Drana and Agnes made yearly pilgrimages to the shrine at Our Lady of Cernagore. Both participated in the social and fund-raising aspects of their parish. They were always careful to set aside food or money for those less fortunate.

During this time, Agnes began hearing stories about Jesuit Missionaries in India. A movement termed "Sodality" romanticized the efforts by Jesuits and others to liberate suffering people in faraway places. This type of life excited the mind and heart of Agnes as it had done to so many young men who became Jesuit missionaries. Agnes, however, could not be a part of the Jesuit order because it was a male-only community. Some sources suggest that there were very few sisters in her area, and Agnes knew very little about the demands and constraints of becoming a nun. After some research, she discovered the ministry of the Sisters of Loreto in India, and applied to enter their training program. After her acceptance into the Sisters of Loreto, 18-year-old Agnes traveled to Ireland to begin her language study. Those studies lasted only six weeks, and then she was off to Calcutta.

The route by ship to India was very long. Agnes was making a decision that would take her away from her home and family for the rest of her life. In those days, sisters were "cloistered," meaning that they stayed within the confines of the convent and did not receive furloughs. In a way, her old life was dying as she stepped forward to find a new life in an unknown country.

To symbolize this death of the old life, most sisters take a new name when entering a religious community within Roman Catholicism. In 1931, Agnes took the name of Teresa of Lisieux, the name of a young Carmelite sister who had died at the age of 24 while serving the people of Hanoi.

A Career in Teaching

The Loreto nuns were proud of their female graduates. When India finally became a free state in 1947, several of the Loreto graduates were made judges in the High Courts of Delhi and Calcutta. Others were elected to Parliament. Teresa was one of those responsible for the foundation of excellence in Calcutta.

While the Loreto Sisters, according to their mission, developed a school system to educate wealthier clients, they took very little of the money for themselves. Their ultimate goals included the education of as many females as possible, not just those who could pay their tuition. The Sisters charged the wealthy and used the rest of the money to fund education for women who could not pay.

Teresa's first assignments were at Loreto Entally and St. Mary's High School, where she taught geography, history, and catechism. Her training came from the sisters and Jesuits at their college in Darjeeling. She took her final vows in 1937. Teaching gave way to the responsible position of principal, but Teresa found herself, after 20 years, still yearning to work with the unfortunate people living next to the walls of her school. Many sources suggest that Teresa always wanted to be a missionary to the poor, but she did not know how to do it.

The Train to Darjeeling

In 1946, on a day now celebrated as "Inspiration Day," Teresa was riding on a train bound for Darjeeling, a hill station in the Himalayas. Teresa claims that on that train ride she began to understand that she had to leave the life of the convent. There was something more waiting for her. Teresa came to the decision to quit her job and leave the community of the Sisters of Loreto. The decision was both happy and heartbreaking. She had spent so many years pouring her life into the schools that it seemed like a death to her. She mourned the loss of her friends and students. With permission from the Bishop of Calcutta, Teresa received permission to live outside the convent for one year. She retired her nun's habit and would never wear it again.

Her education had not prepared her for working among the uneducated, starving, and often diseased people who lived in cardboard boxes, lean-tos, and abandoned buildings. How and where can one begin to teach, to heal, to help people who cannot help themselves?

As a symbol of solidarity with the "outcasts" of India, Teresa chose a simple white sari with blue trim as her new symbol of dedication and vocation. If she were going to work among the castaways, she thought that she must look like them. Preparation for this seemingly impossible task included studying elementary nursing with the Medical Missionary Sisters, but she must also have learned from the Sisters of the Poor, with whom she lived for a year or so. The Sisters of the Poor worked among the abandoned elderly.

The congregation is included in the class of hospitallers. Its constitutions are based on the Rule of St. Augustine, and the sisters take simple and perpetual vows of poverty, chastity, and obedience, to which they add a fourth, hospitality. They receive into their houses aged men and women who have no other shelter. Sixty is the youngest age at which they are admitted, after which they are members of what is known as the "Little Family," the superior being called by all the "Good Mother." To the best of their ability they assist the sisters in the work of the home. For the support of their foundation the sisters are dependent absolutely on charity, having no fixed income or endowments, and most of what they receive they procure by begging. The constitution was definitively approved by *Pius X*, 7 May 1907 [*Catholic Encyclopedia*].

In many Indian families, there is a common practice of turning over the house and business to younger family members once a person reaches a certain age. This last stage of life can be compared to a "sannyasin," who leaves his home, goes naked, begs, and begins a search to find "oneness" with his Deity. Many older people in India leave their homes voluntarily so that they will not be a financial burden on their children. Varanasi, formerly Banares, is a city where millions of people migrate to die. (It has been compared to the holy city of Makkah in Saudi Arabia.) They believe if they can touch the water of the Ganges, they will have a better rebirth. Families often cannot support the elderly and force them to leave. Many missionaries report that they find the dying elderly in garbage cans or thrown along the side of the road. In Varanasi, you can see thousands of people wrapped in threadbare blankets waiting for death. While there are a few government-supported homes for the elderly, they are very small compared to the numbers who come to die. Teresa certainly learned from their work because her mission centered on the elderly and expanded to include all peoples.

Many of Teresa's students grieved over the loss of their beloved teacher. One by one, ten female students, many who had not finished their studies, came to work with her. After finally severing ties with the convent, in 1950 she created a new order: the "Missionaries of Charity."

Missionaries of Charity

The organization of the Missionaries of Charity today includes thousands of lay workers in over 100 countries. Nearly 1800 sisters and 250 brothers took vows to help the needy in those early years. Teresa and her dedicated associates created schools, homes for children, and clean and healthy places for the sick and dying—especially those who had leprosy or AIDS. Teresa thought that people should keep busy so she taught them to make craft items in their homes. Currently, businesses and the government in India heavily support these cottage industries. According to *Nationmaster Encyclopedia*, Missionaries of Charity currently number 4500 nuns, an undetermined number of brothers, in 133 countries ("Encyclopedia: Missionaries of Charity").

The people of Calcutta began to call Agnes "Mother Teresa." The name of "Mother" has many meanings in the Indian culture. Like a loving, normal mother, Teresa gave her life to the poor, her children. Her neverending love lasted for over 25 years.

In the name of love she washed the infected and diseased bodies of children, of parents, of the old and the young. It became a sacrament for her. She equated touching the unfortunate with touching God. It was a Divine moment for her.

Her emphasis on monetary sacrifice and self-sacrifice catapulted Mother into the lights of world cameras. She was sincere, passionate and simplistic in her approach to problem-solving. It seemed as if she believed that holding the hand of a dying person was the key to curing poverty, alienation, lack of education, discrimination, unemployment, under-employment, child marriage, sati, and the abuse of the elderly.

In Asia, the appellation of "Mother" has always contained a hint of the divine within it. To be a "Mother" was to be an important person in the community but it was more.

The person with this title may have come to be seen as the incarnation or the embodiment of the Divine. In Hindu mythology, the Gods could become incarnated into everyday people or even animals. This is certainly true of many Buddhist sects where a human being becomes a bodhisattva, a Buddha in the making, who helps others reach the state of bliss or nirvana. Many swamis (holy men and women) are viewed as the embodiment of the Divine. In many ways Mother Teresa embodied the holiness of a Roman Catholic saint, a Hindu sannyasin, and a bodhisattva. Her journey to find the Divine was found each day in the faces of those who had been victimized by society. That encounter created a saint.

The Missionaries of Charity and Teresa

The year 1950 marked the birth of the order of the Missionaries of Charity. Father Celeste Van Exem read the decree marking its formation.

To fulfill our mission of compassion and love to the poorest of the poor we go:

- seeking out in towns and villages all over the world even amid squalid surroundings the poorest, the abandoned, the sick, the infirm, the leprosy patients, the dying, the desperate, the lost, the outcasts;
- taking care of them,
- rendering help to them,
- visiting them assiduously,
- living Christ's love for them, and
- awakening their response to His great love [Egan, 42].

It is no coincidence that Mother Teresa secured an old religious temple dedicated to the worship of the goddess Kali to begin her work. There she began her ministry to the dying by offering them a clean bed and the touch of a caring human being. She began this loving empire with only five dollars in her pocket.

The numbers of dying and needy people were overwhelming. The missionaries desperately needed headquarters and a place to live. With the help of Albert D' Souza, the Archbishop of Calcutta, she acquired for a very small sum of money a huge compound from a Muslim fleeing Calcutta. Some suggest that the amount Teresa paid for the house, courtyards, and outer buildings would have covered only the land upon which the structures were built.

Mother Teresa loved the poor, any kind of poor. She understood that there was also a poverty of the spirit or soul. Her houses helped those who were handicapped—either physically or emotionally. She encouraged others not to forget those who were hungry for bread or love. With a wistful eye, she told the world that she would "never forget." Above every crucifix in every Missionaries of Charity House all over the world, she placed these words, "I Thirst."

Mother Teresa refused to take any money for herself. Like the sisters who worked with her, she owned only three changes of clothing: one for working, one for mending, and one for washing. Donations from around the world financed her projects. She refused to accept money in the form of grants or annuities that would require record-keeping. Pope Paul VI gave her a white Lincoln limousine, a donation he had received. She promptly raffled it off and gave the proceeds to her organization.

She was very successful in attracting large donors, volunteers, brothers, and sisters. One of the reasons for her success was her generally apolitical and ecumenical approach to her mission and the people whom she served. People were able to focus upon her simplicity, her honesty, and her obvious care for unlucky people.

Mother Teresa broke the barriers of the caste system within the Indian-Hindu socioreligious system. Hindu social structure is cataloged in the Law Code of Manu. The Code of Manu did not create the social structure, but it did help to perpetuate its mythology. While outlawed in 1950, the caste system still functions as the glue that keeps Hindu society together. Not only do Hindus know their caste, but also their rank among the hundreds of sub-castes or jatis that number 3,000.

Brahmins, the highest caste, were historically the wealthy landowners, the educated, the teachers, and, most of all, the priests who led others in Vedic rituals. Even today, if a Brahmin woman marries someone from a lower caste, her friends and neighbors would argue that she had compromised her lineage and history. When she changed her name to her husband's, she was no longer a Brahmin.

On the lowest rung of the caste system are the Sudras, who usually occupy positions of service or work in the fields as peasants. Outside this ancient system are the "untouchables." These are the people who do all of the tasks that most Hindus will not do. They butcher meat, bury the dead, clean nuclear power plants, and assist terminally ill patients, such as those with AIDS. On this lowest rung also is anyone who is not born in India. The people in India never fully integrate those who move to India into the society of India. These forgotten people become the "untouchables" because they do not cleanse themselves in the proper Hindu way; neither do they worship one of the 330 million gods and goddesses of India.

While there are social service agencies in India, these establishments are not a priority for many of the people. The Hindus believe in "samsara," the cycle of birth and death which indirectly militates against helping someone in trouble. That person could have been reborn into this life as an "untouchable" because his prior life was so bad. The Hindus believe that such a reborn person needs to have a chance to live this life, in whatever condition it is, and then hope for a better birth in the next life. Perhaps the individual may even come back as a Brahmin!

The Hindus believe that their intervention into the person's journey in life may actually hurt someone who is "paying for" his deeds in the past. Suffering becomes a positive experience in this person's struggle for a better birth, a better life.

When Mother Teresa began to hold out her hand to the "untouchables," she bridged a gap. Hindus might term Mother Teresa herself as an "outcaste" because she was not born in India. (Later in life, Mother Teresa herself felt that it was necessary to become a citizen of India.) By choosing to minister to the most undesirable people in India, she could have been severing the line to the wealthy. In fact, it did not work that way in her career. The more she focused media reports on the plight and anguish of the "untouchables," the more money came her way. The world began to call at her door. During the fighting between Israel and Lebanon in 1982, she stunned a global audience by rescuing 37 special-needs children hospitalized in Beirut.

For her work, Mother Teresa received many prizes, recognitions, and honors, among them the Padmashri (Lord of the Lotus) Award for distinguished service in 1962; the Pope John XXIII Peace Prize in 1971; the Kennedy International Award in 1971; the Jawaharlal Nehru Award for International Understanding in 1972; the Order of St. Francis of Assisi in 1974; the Medal of Freedom from the United States in 1985; honorary U.S. citizenship in 1996; and of course, in 1978, the Nobel Peace Prize.

The Nobel Peace Prize

In 1979, the Nobel Peace Prize Committee awarded the prize to Mother Teresa. John Sanness, Chair of the Norwegian Nobel Committee, described Teresa as a person who recognized the value of each individual. At her hands, he said, some of the most miserable persons in the world received compassion. In defending their decision to give Mother Teresa the Nobel Peace Prize, the committee members focused upon what they termed "the spirit" of Mother Teresa that respected the "poorest of the poor." Her life helped the world to focus upon the "human dignity" that it should afford to everyone. This respect for life promotes peace on the most basic level we can understand (Nobel Prize website).

Graciously, Mother Teresa accepted the prize with these words:

Though I'm personally unworthy, I'm grateful and I'm happy to receive it (for the world's poor). Our poor people are great people, a very lovable people. They don't need our pity or our sympathy. They need our understanding love and they need our respect. We need to demonstrate to the poor, that they are somebody to us, that they too have been created with the same loving hand of God, to love and be loved ["Mother Teresa–Nobel Lecture"].

Rather than holding the traditional banquet to honor the Peace Prize winner, the Nobel Committee abandoned the event at Mother Teresa's request. She used the money instead to feed Christmas dinner to the hungry.

A Saint in the Making

Sometimes the mind is stronger than the body. Mother Teresa would not listen to her body, and in 1983 her health began to fail. She suffered a heart attack while she was in Rome for a visit with Pope John Paul II. Another heart attack in 1989 was almost fatal and resulted in the implantation of a pacemaker in her chest. Realizing that her body needed rest, Mother Teresa decided to resign, but her sisters would not allow it.

In 1991, while she was in Tijuana, Mexico, she developed pneumonia and congestive heart failure. Hospitalization in La Jolla, California, followed. After recovering, she fell in Rome in May 1993 and broke three ribs. One month later she contracted malaria. In September she underwent surgery in Calcutta to clear a blocked blood vessel.

In 1996, a broken collarbone, another bout with malaria, heart failure, and continued breathing problems brought about her permanent retirement. On March 13, 1997, she stepped down as head of the order Mission of Charity.

Sister Nirmala succeeded Mother Teresa as head of the Mission, which had 500 clinics, orphanages, homes. and centers in 100 countries of the world. The Mission in 1997 included 4,500 nuns and 500 brothers.

At the age of 87, the best-loved woman of the century died on September 5, 1997, of cardiac arrest. Her funeral was on September 13, 1997, the fifty-first anniversary of her train ride to Darjeeling. Her work, however, did not die. At the turn of the century (2001), the Missionaries of Charity were feeding 500,000 families, treating 90,000 leprosy patients, and educating 2,000 children each year in Calcutta alone.

Immediately after the death of Agnes Bohjaxhiu (Mother Teresa), many Catholic voices around the world began to clamor for her recognition as a saint. The Pope, the supreme authority of the Catholic Church, is the person who must declare that the individual lived in fidelity to God's grace, exercised heroic virtue, is with God in heaven, and should receive veneration throughout the whole Church. The Pope enrolls the person on the canon, or list, of Saints. In the Church's liturgical celebrations, the person receives a feast day at the time of beatification—one step toward canonization, or receiving sainthood. The normal rules require five years to pass after a person's death before an investigation can even begin.

On the first anniversary of her death, the Vatican announced a tribute to Mother Teresa. A memorial Mass in St. Peter's Basilica, a celebration from St. Peter's Square, and homage from Pope John Paul II marked the event. In 1999, Father Miguel Garrito launched the idea of a new holiday: "Brother's Day." This day—in honor of Mother Teresa—would occur on September 5 each year. Observers would mark the day with acts of mercy.

The clamoring for recognizing the sainthood of Mother Teresa increased. In March 1999, Pope John Paul II waived the five-year rule. The first phase (Diocesan Phase) included the gathering of information, interviewing of witnesses, and obtaining of documents by the local church. The second stage (the Roman Phase) required the transferring of the information from the local church to the Congregation for the Causes of Saints for findings after a study of the information. The Vatican must consider the findings of the Congregation for the Causes of Saints. This Congregation for the Causes of Saints necessarily considers the evidence and information before developing a position paper to give (or to deny) permission to begin the beatification process. This group agreed in July 1999—barely a year and a half after her death—that it was appropriate for the canonization process to begin.

The next step is the bestowing of the title of beatified (blessed) on the individual. This title requires a proven miracle coming as a result of someone praying to the deceased for help and occurring after the death of the candidate. The miracle of healing that the Holy Father recognized occurred on the first anniversary of Mother Teresa's death. A woman in India woke to find a huge abdominal tumor gone after members of the Missionaries of Charity prayed for the intervention of Mother Teresa to help the sick woman.

On October 19, 2003, only six years after her death and only three days after Pope John Paul II celebrated the twenty-fifth anniversary of his papacy, Mother Teresa received beatification in Rome. Mother had become an icon on the world stage. She received canonization as a "saint" by the Roman Catholic Church before a crowd of 300,000 devotees in St. Peter's Square in 2003. Pope John Paul's declaration resulted in the shortest beatification process in the history of the Catholic Church. Officially Mother Teresa became "Blessed Teresa of Calcutta" after the Beatification Ceremony.

The final step in becoming a saint is after the occurrence of a second miracle and after the Pope at last confirms the acceptance. After this last step, Agnes G. Bohjaxhiu would lose her title of "Blessed Teresa of Calcutta" and would become "Saint Teresa of Calcutta."

The Other Mother Teresa

The Roman Catholic Church declared Mother to be a saint-in-the-making, but in reality she had become an icon for the rest of the world. Rarely did anyone question Mother

Teresa's strategies, beliefs, or organizations when she was alive. Even if criticisms had sur-faced, the general public would have disregarded the negative comments.

Yet, after her death, stories have surfaced about her "seeming" brutality to her own sisters. In various places, she forced sisters to give away furniture and beds. This meant that, even in missions in Western countries, both the needy and the sisters had to sleep and sit on the floor at all times. One of the sisters, Susan Shields, who managed dona-tions for almost ten years, charges that Mother did not use the money that was donated to the Missionaries of Charity, "Most of the money sat in our bank accounts" (Shields, *Free Inquiry*). Many suggest that Mother Teresa did not use the money that she collected for the Missionaries for Charity; instead, she gave much of it to the Vatican. Sisters tell stories about how Mother Teresa knew there were funds to buy food or equipment but that Mother would force the sisters to go to local merchants to continue begging for help.

Mother was a missionary to the needy and spokesperson for her faith, but she some-times neglected the cries of other sisters for equality. While many sisters in the world were arguing with the Vatican about ordination and the inclusion of women in the all-male hierarchy of the church, Mother argued both implicitly and explicitly for submission. She loved the traditions of the Catholic Church and became the anti-model for feminism. She never challenged the belief that women should sacrifice themselves for their family. After all, she believed that she had sacrificed herself for the "little poor," the children of the world. Conformity—not change—was central to her message.

Years ago, Barbara Harrison had the courage to highlight problems within Mother Teresa's ministry:

> Mother Teresa's allegiances are deeply traditional. She has angered feminist nuns by exhort-ing them to demonstrate more complete obedience to their bishops; she does not appear to comprehend the women who wish to be ordained as priests; she has consistently urged Indian women to be homemakers and to leave to men "what they do best." All of this, on her part, may be a failure of the imagination [Harrison, 11].

It may also be a failure of experience and education. While Mother did have training in history and geography, she was not a theologian, politician, social worker, psychologist, or academician. Even her attempt to interpret Biblical references reflects no historic foun-dation in any type of interpretative methodology.

Clearly Mother accepted the age-old Christian belief that females are the source of evil. Most medieval scholars blamed "Eve" for giving the "apple" to Adam as the founda-tion for "evil." Mother put her own twist on this interpretation. During her acceptance speech of the Nobel Peace Prize, Mother placed the blame for the lack of peace upon "females":

> We are talking of peace. These are things that break peace, but I feel the greatest destroyer of peace today is abortion, because it is a direct war, a direct killing—direct murder by the mother herself. And we read in the Scripture, for God says very clearly! Even if a mother could forget her child—I will not forget you—I have carved you in the palm of my hand. We are carved in the palm of His hand, so close to Him that an unborn child has been carved in the hand of God. And that is what strikes me most, the beginning of that sentence, that even if a mother could forget something impossible—but even if she could forget—I will not forget you. And today the greatest means—the greatest destroyer of peace is abortion. And we who are standing here—our parents wanted us. We would not be here if our parents would do that to us. Our children, we want them, we love them, but what of the millions.... And this is what is the greatest destroyer of peace today. Because if a mother can kill her own child—what is left for me to kill you and you kill me—there is nothing between ["Mother Teresa—Nobel Lecture"].

Mother used her speech to highlight beliefs central to her faith. There appears to be no understanding of the "awful" circumstances that push women towards abortion. Neither does she recognize the possibility of rape, incest, mutation, the threat to the mother's life, etc. For most people who had leprosy in India, their children would be born deformed or with the disease. It appears that she had little understanding of the grief, personal, and economic stress that bearing a deformed child would have for a family.

Charges have also arisen that the houses that the Missionaries of Charity staffed were unsanitary. The goal of the mission was to alleviate the suffering of those who were dying, but what would the mission do with those who were very ill and needed hospitalization? Both the dying and the sick lived together in situations that were less than sanitary ("Encyclopedia: Mother Teresa"). Baptizing the dying was a common practice.

> Although the Missionaries of Charity assist persons of any faith, they have baptized 40,000 inmates in homes for the dying.... According to a former Missionary of Charity, at the home for the dying, "Sisters were to ask each person in danger of death if he wanted a 'ticket to heaven.' An affirmative reply was to mean consent to baptism which happened on the spot" [Kwilecki, *Journal for the Scientific Study of Religion*, 11].

Sisters also complained that the Missionaries of Charity considered the prayers and rituals to be more important than the individual. If the bell rang for prayers and a sister did not immediately come to chapel, she was punished for disobeying. Sisters explained that many times they would be feeding a baby or helping some other needy person, and they would have to stop immediately their work to leave and attend prayers.

Others have criticized Teresa because she seemed to be unaware of the larger socioeconomic picture. She often remarked that she admired the suffering of the poor. The fact that she chose to work with the poor on an individual basis indicated that she sometimes neglected the larger picture. She could have used her influence in the government to change the political system or to change the economic system that kept the poor on the streets, but she did not.

Many people remarked that Mother Teresa was a deeply traditional Roman Catholic who would not question her church or her country. Her critics asked why did she not seek the source of the poverty instead of focusing on individuals. Many of her critics suggest that the number of people that the organization claims to have helped are inaccurate—even exaggerated.

Mother Teresa, according to an analysis by Susan Kwilecki, was a "calculating, profit-seeking religious entrepreneur" (p. 17). She based Mother Teresa's success on the belief by many that she was a conduit to God.

> Mother Teresa did not correct popular perception of her spiritual giftedness; indeed, sometimes she encouraged it, for example, by making known her presumptuous prayer that God release a soul from purgatory each time she allowed herself to be photographed [Kwilecki, 18].

Most of the books that have been written about Mother are in a tone that would place them in the category of "hagiography." In spite of all of her faults and the criticisms leveled against her, the masses still worship her. Now, as a saint-in-the-making, she is intervening to the Divine on behalf of those Roman Catholics who pray to her.

Bibliography

Desmond, Edward D. "A Pencil in the Hand of God." A *Time* Interview with Mother Teresa. Available online at http://www.time.com/time/reports/motherteresa/t891204.html.

Egan, Eileen. *Such a Vision of the Street: Mother Teresa—The Spirit and the Work.* New York: Doubleday, 1985.

Fleming, James. "Blessed Is She Among Women: Peace Prize for Mother Teresa." *Macleans* 92 (October 29, 1979): 31.

Harrison, B. G. "The Stubborn Courage of Mother Teresa." *McCalls* (August 1985): 8–11.

http:—

"The Art of Loving." *Sojourner's* Magazine, November–December 1997. Available online at http://www.sojo.net/index.cfm?action=magazine.article&issue=soj9711&article=971141b.

"Encyclopedia: Missionaries of Charity." Available online at http://www.nationmaster.com/encyclopedia/Missionaries-of-Charity.

"Encyclopedia: Mother Teresa." Available online at http://www.nationmaster.com/encyclopedia-/Mother-Teresa.

"Flash: Mother Teresa Was Human." Available online at http://www.christianitytoday.com/ct/2003/002/32.18.html.

"History of India. A Chronological Outline." Available online at http://www.askasia.org/image/maps/timeind.htm.

http://www.sfyam.org/currentevents/detail.as?id=37

"Mother Teresa: Angel of Mercy. Highlights of Mother Teresa's Life." Available online at http://www.cnn.com/WORLD/9709/mother.teresa/chronology/index.html.

"Mother Teresa: Angel of Mercy. Mother Teresa: a profile." Available online at http://www.cnn.com/WORLD/9709/mother.teresa/profile/index/html.

"Mother Teresa: Angel of Mercy. Mother Teresa in her own words." Available online at http://www.cnn.com/WORLD/9709/mother.teresa/quotes/index.html.

"Mother Teresa: Angel of Mercy. Saint of the gutters: Legacy extends beyond India to the World." Available online at http://www.cnn.com/WORLD/9709/mother.teresa/impact/index.html.

"Mother Teresa: Angel of Mercy. A special voice for the poor." Available online at http://www.cnn.com/WORLD/9709/mother/teresa/perspective/index.html.

"Mother Teresa Biography." Available online at http://www.nobel.se/peace/laureates/1979/teresa-bio.html.

"Mother Teresa Biography." Available online at http://www.galegroup.com/free_resources/whm/bio/motherteresa.html.

"Mother Teresa, a citizen of Skopje." Available online at http://www.mymacedonia.net/links/tereza.html.

"Mother Teresa–Nobel Lecture." Available online at http://nobelprize.org/peace/laureates/1979-/teresa-lecture.html.

"Mother Teresa–Quotes on Abortion." Available online at http://www.gargaro.com/mother_teresa/quotes.html.

"Path to Peace Foundation." Available online at http://www.thepathtopeacefoundation.org/about.html.

"Teresa of the Slums: A Saintly Nun Embraces the Poor." A Classic *Life* Photo Essay. Available online at http://www.life.com/Life/classic/motherteresa/index.html.

"What's Mother Teresa Got to Do with It?" Available online at http://www.time.com/time/archive/preview/0,10987,364389,00.html.

Jennings, Jack A. "A Reluctant Demurrer on Mother Teresa." *Christian Century* (March 1981): 258–60.

Kwilecki, Susan, and Loretta S. Wilson. "Was Mother Teresa Maximizing Her Utility? An Idiographic Application of Rational Choice Theory." *Journal for the Scientific Study of Religion* 37 (1998): 205–22.

Le Joly, Edward. *Mother Teresa: A Woman in Love.* Notre Dame, Indiana: Ave Marie Press, 1993.

_____. *Servant of Love: Mother Teresa and Her Missionaries of Charity.* New York: Harper and Row, 1977.

Loesch, Robert K. "Seven Nobel Women." *Christian Century* (November 17, 1982): 1158–59.

Maalouf, Jean. *Mother Teresa: Essential Writings.* New York: Orbis Books, 2001.

McCarthy, Abigail. "Neither Paul nor Cephas: Division over Mother Teresa." *Commonweal* (September 25, 1981): 520–21.

McCreary, Alf. "Mother Teresa Invited to Address Ulster Protestants?" *Christianity Today* (August 7, 1981): 38.

Shields, Susan. "Mother Teresa's House of Illusions: How She Harmed Her Helpers As Well as Those They 'Helped.'" *Free Inquiry Magazine*, 18 (1998): 1–4.

Spink, Kathryn. "A Christmas Message from Other Teresa of Calcutta." *Good Housekeeping* (December 1983): 144–45.

_____. *The Miracle of Love*. California: Harper and Row, 1981.

_____. *The Wisdom of Mother Teresa*. Louisville, Kentucky: Westminster Press, 1998.

Srububasa, Murthy B. *Mother Teresa and India*. Long Beach, California: Long Beach, 1983.

Vardey, Lucinda. *Mother Teresa: A Simple Path*. New York: Ballantine Books, 1995.

Alva Reimer Myrdal
(1982)

Diplomat, Teacher, Writer, Pioneer Feminist,
Peace Advocate, Wife, Mother

(January 31, 1902–February 1, 1986)

Alva Reimer Myrdal, Nobel Peace Laureate 1982.

Very few human beings could rival Alva Myrdal's enthusiastic contributions both to the social welfare of Sweden and to world peace. She treated life with a precious reverence. John Kenneth Galbraith was quick to note how Alva Myrdal's own life fuses

> ... three of the truly remarkable people of our time—Alva Myrdal, urgent in the pursuit of women's rights and peace, ambassador, Swedish cabinet minister and Nobel Peace Prize winner; Gunnar Myrdal, her husband, the most innovative and diversely concerned economist of his generation, also a Swedish minister and also a Nobel Prize winner; and Sissela, their daughter, distinguished for her books on sociology and philosophy and as a teacher at Brandeis University and Harvard [Galbraith, Bok, back cover].

Alva Myrdal received the Nobel Peace Prize in 1982 when she was 80. The award came jointly to Alva and the Mexican diplomat Alfonso Garcia Robles (Parry, 487; Aarvik, 1). Her work in the United Nations, her success as an ambassador, her contributions made when she served as the world's only Minister for Disarmament, her peace advocacy, and her writings, particularly *The Game of Disarmament* (1976) and *War, Weapons and Everyday Violence* (1977), were chief reasons for her nomination. Her contributions included becoming chair of Sweden's Peace Forum Movement in 1981 (Bok, 317, 340) and founding the Stockholm International Peace Research Institute in 1964 (Bok, 294–95, 317).

Alva had been born to Lowa Jansson (1877–1943) and Albert Jansson (1876–1943). The family later changed its name to Reimer. Alva noted that her parents had different political beliefs and even subscribed to two different newspapers because of their diverse opinions. It was unusual that Lowa, a woman, was able to express herself well at a time when most females were more reticent.

Lowa, tried the new fads in child-rearing on her firstborn: Alva, who was born on January 31, 1902. Alva received a cold rubdown each morning, cod liver oil, and oatmeal porridge. Lowa picked up Alva only at regular intervals for fear of spoiling the child. When a doctor diagnosed six-month-old Alva with malnutrition and stomach cramps, he ordered additional food in her diet. Lowa had lost both a brother and a sister to tuberculosis; to protect her daughter, she avoided caresses and kisses (Bok, 15–22).

Alva's beloved sister Rut was born two years later. Another child—this time a boy named Folke—came two years after Rut. Alva and Rut noted the preferential treatment their parents and society at large gave to a boy. She never "had an open, confident relationship with the family" (Bok, 23). Two other children—daughter Maj (1909) and son Stig (1912)—were born after Folke.

Her father bought and managed a cooperative store, and the board members met in the Reimer dining room; Alva hid under the table and listened to the discussions. She claimed that it was under this table that she began to take politics and the rules of order seriously and learned that contributions of both men and women were necessary for world order (Bok, 26).

The family, however, would soon move elsewhere. In fact, during her first 12 years of life, Alva moved at least once—and sometimes twice—a year. One of the most traumatic moves was from the city to the country to help Lowa's father after the death of his second wife. Alva, Folke, Rut, and Lowa disliked their new surroundings; at one point Alva and Folke disliked their new home so much that they ran away (Bok, 26–29).

Alva loved reading and earned good grades. Her mother, however, discouraged Alva's reading. Lowa believed that excessive reading harmed the eyes; she also feared that library books might carry germs and that the volumes in their own locked bookshelves might not be appropriate for a child. These prohibitions on reading seemed to encourage, not discourage Alva. She did much of her reading in secret and was sometimes able to "borrow" and return books from the cabinet without being caught. There was little hope of Alva continuing her education after elementary school. Lowa thought seven years of education was enough for her daughter. Alva's father hoped that all his children would go into farming. Because the high schools served primarily the upper middle class and the upper class students, he considered the environment in schools to be hostile to his intent for his offspring (Bok, 29, 35–37).

Alva felt alone in her desire to pursue an education. Fortunately, she found encouragement in a former teacher, Per Sundberg. He had encouraged Alva to correspond with him after her move from the area. For three years she wrote of her interests in education, literature, religion, and other things. He told her to pursue education that she did not find at home. Determined to go farther with her education, Alva embroidered and sewed for pocket money; she used some of her income to pay for a correspondence course in astronomy. She paid for a commercial program at the town's institute and secured some financial help from her family in the form of a loan (Bok, 36–37, 47).

Alva found employment in the local tax office of Eskilstuna after the completion of her courses in bookkeeping, shorthand, and typing. She also took some literature and language courses. With her income, she was able to give some back to her family, put some aside, and buy some books of her own. She once said of this incessant love of books that she could hardly "keep from reading." Lowa had always forbidden her children from using library books because of the danger of germs, and Alva still lived at home. Alva found, however, that she could hide the banned books in the folds of her clothing and smuggle them into the attic until she was ready to read (Bok, 36–38).

About this time, Alva formed a close friendship with Märta Fredriksson. This young woman loved books and learning as Alva did, and their camaraderie lasted a lifetime. Märta encouraged Alva in her plans to further her education. Although Alva had Märta's support, she did not have the backing of her parents; they wanted her to take the courses needed for teacher certification but to remain at home. Alva did not want to teach; she was resolute, however, about furthering her education and began to write away for information and to explore boarding schools that offered courses other than teacher education and commercial courses. She even found a family friend who agreed to lend her the money to continue her education. When she approached her parents with a completed application that lacked only their signatures, the melodramatic scene that followed was engraved in Alva's memory forever. Her mother tore the application in half and told her she would never sign. Furthermore, she told Alva that she must not go to any school away from their home. Alva's father remained neutral in the controversy (Bok, 38–46).

Later, however, Alva's father realized that Alva was set in her determination to continue to study and learn. He worked out a strategy to please everyone. With some other parents who were interested in an education for their daughters, he approached the town school board and successfully encouraged the establishment of a "private gymnasium" for the young women in Eskilstuna. Alva's mother was pleased because Alva would remain at home. Alva was pleased because she could further her education.

Each student's first writing assignment was on a topic of choice. Alva elected to write on the League of Nations and to focus on peace prospects through designs, coalitions, and confederations—not through violence and fear (Bok, 44–47).

Alva constantly worried about money. Her father required his children to repay the money that they "owed" him. She worked in the summer to help reimburse him for her education, but this caused her to get behind on her reading. She had no money during the regular year for any expense that was not an absolute necessity.

This concern with money would remain with Alva all her life. Alva later insisted that her own children reimburse her just as she had reimbursed her father. Alva kept small ledgers with every expense—large and small—entered within; her daughter Sissela found all the small black notebooks that Alva never threw away. When the amounts owed seemed to be more than the children could return, Alva informed them that she would deduct the sum from their inheritance (Bok, 46–47).

Alva and her younger sister Rut began writing two young Norwegian men as a youth organization activity; Alva wrote to a man named Andreas Arnesen. In her biography of her mother, Sissela stated emphatically that except for her father, her teacher Per Sundberg, and, later, her husband, "no one had greater influence over Alva than Andreas." Their letters continued until Alva met Gunnar and ceased the correspondence in the summer of 1919 (Bok, 48–49).

Rut and Alva were sleeping late on a summer morning when their father banged at the door and asked them to get up and make coffee for three beggars who had slept in the loft of their barn. The girls turned over and went back to sleep. In a few minutes, their grandfather called out that three university students had slept in their barn and that they needed a breakfast tray. The girls leaped from their bed, dressed quickly, and prepared coffee and rolls. One of the three was Gunnar Myrdal. Alva and Gunnar were taken with each other—for life. He invited Alva to come with them on their bicycle tour, and this young woman—who had never even kissed a boy—agreed to go! The two-week tour lasted longer than planned; Alva and Gunnar even spent some time with his parents, Sofie and Carl Adolf Pettersson (Bok, 50–59). Gunnar had changed the name *Pettersson* to *Myrdahl* and later to *Myrdal* when he started college (Jan Myrdal, *Childhood*, 89).

Gunnar was the firstborn of four children and the family favorite. Alva found him remarkable. Their daughter Sissela wrote that he felt *himself* to be remarkable. A friend of Gunnar's commented that he made a person feel "as if one had been invited to a feast of imagination, intellect, and playfulness" (Bok, 59).

Alva looked forward to completing her education so that she could begin a new period of her life with Gunnar, whom she liked immensely. Because Gunnar admired that which was scientific and rational, she decided to put an end to that which implied emotion in her own life. As a start, Alva decided that she must destroy all of the poems, stories, and novels that she had written; she even burned her diaries.

From the time that Alva first met Gunnar, she tried to be a companion to him, but, at the same time, she tried to be an "active seeker in the world." Fulfilling both roles was a demanding task—as any working wife knows. Alva's life would be even more difficult in the days to come (Bok, 61–62).

Alva was an able scholar. She quickly realized that she had already mastered the content of most of the courses. She found that she could speed up the process of her education and save her parents some money by compressing two years' work into one. After completing her official oral examinations that she could not take in Eskilstuna, Alva received with highest honors her degree in Stockholm. At 14 she had thought such an achievement would never be possible for her; now at 20 she had achieved an important goal in her life (Bok, 48).

Gunnar and Alva planned to marry in 1923 when Gunnar earned his law degree and could support himself, but Gunnar's father convinced them that Alva should complete her degree—the "Filosofie Kandidate" (a rough equivalent of the B.A.)—before they married. The couple finally wed on October 8, 1924. They invited only two guests to the ceremony. Alva invited Märta Fredriksson, and Gunnar invited his friend Alf Johansson. Sissela took this exclusion of her grandparents to indicate that her parents' ties to them were only of the nature of responsibilities (Bok, 61–63).

Gunnar was not elated with his law degree. In fact, Sissela noted that her father later stated that he was "'intellectually crushed and deeply depressed'" at this time in his life (Bok, 75). The young couple talked, explored Gunnar's genealogy, and traveled to England. Alva noted they had to bond together in the foreign country. She would always remember the trip as her first experience with racial discrimination, a topic that Gunnar and she would later explore in depth in their research and writing (Bok, 68).

Sissela realized that throughout her parents' relationship and marriage her mother had subjugated her own needs to Gunnar's whims and desires. Gunnar expected her to do all the housework, to help him in his profession—virtually to take second place in their marriage and to make him the center of attention. It was much later before she asked the rhetorical question of why she gave up so much. Gunnar seemed to take for granted Alva's subservience (Bok, 72–75).

Alva continued to subjugate her work and desire to her husband's; her silence concerning her own needs continued. She later asked a rhetorical question: "Why did it seem natural ... to give up so much...?" (Bok, 72–74). Sissela noted that her father in later years seemed to continue to take for granted Alva's subservience and "that Alva should continue to help him after their marriage and do all the housework seemed to him only natural" (Bok, 72). Sissela indicated that "Alva even nourished his urge—increasingly insatiable with the passage of time—to be the center of attention ... she took second place within the marriage" (Bok, 74).

It was, in fact, Alva's concern for the social conditions of the time that provided Gunnar the issues for his research. Alva—despite her housework and her own responsibilities—assisted with the library work, the languages, the sorting of materials, the typing, and the editing of Gunnar's text. Gunnar was thoroughly absorbed with his work; it was only through her participation in his work that Alva could share his life with him (Bok, 75).

Alva and Gunnar's first years together were not idyllic materially. Gunnar was studying for an advanced degree at the University of Stockholm. The little ledgers that Alva kept through the years listed loans, expenses, and pawn tickets for that period of their life. In 1926, Alva suffered a miscarriage (Bok, 76–77).

Success followed this tragedy in their life. Jan Myrdal, their son, writes of the achievement in his autobiography, *Childhood*.

The entire family rejoiced in Gunnar Myrdal's completion of his doctorate. Jan presents his father's defense of his dissertation as a significant event; this event was three months before Jan's birth. Jan notes that his father was his professor's favorite and that his dissertation was important. He goes on to explain that Gunnar had the highest possible mark and that he became a lecturer at Stockholm University. Jan remarked that Gunnar's international reputation was growing and that on April 11, 1927, he was well on his way to having one of the most significant scientific professions of his generation (Jan Myrdal, *Childhood*, 93).

When at last Alva was able to bear the living son they called Jan in July 1927, her diary reflected her happiness:

Darling Jan, beloved child, you wonderful little life, Gunnar's and mine, sacredly in common and yet a little self of your own, drawing your own dear, dear breaths—thank Goodness for you! [Bok, 77].

In the fall after the birth of Jan, Gunnar secured a teaching position at the University of Stockholm. He had earned the highest academic honors in the spring with his dissertation on price formation theory, and the university was eager to have him employed there (Bok, 78).

Sissela indicated that Gunnar wanted to be at the center of Alva's world. He resented any demands on her time or interests that were not his own. With no help at home, a child who slept very little, physical recovery from the birth, and many responsibilities, Alva was exhausted most of the time. Gunnar responded to his wife's situation with irritation and even jealousy (Bok, 79).

Great honors came to them in 1929–30. Alva received a Rockefeller Fellowship to focus on social psychology methodology in the United States. Gunnar, too, received a Rockefeller; he would pursue economics and social science methodology, also in the United States. The chance and prestige of even one half of a couple receiving such an award was uncommon; for a husband and wife both to receive a Rockefeller Fellowship was extremely rare (Bok, 80).

Alva and Gunnar made a decision that Alva would regret the rest of her life. She decided to leave her two-year-old child with her in-laws for a year while she and Gunnar went to America for their study and writing (Bok, 81)

Sissela attributed her mother's absence from Jan's life for a year to the fact that she did not understand the importance of the parent-child bond. Even the family pediatrician advised that Alva go with Gunnar. Jan's doctor said that leaving Jan with Gunnar's parents on Gesta farm for a year would benefit Jan, and he reminded Alva that the trip would be the opportunity of a lifetime. Alva longed to pursue her studies, and with Gunnar pressing her to go with him, she made her decision (Bok, 81).

The year was a hard one for Jan. He described being left as being "lent out." His grandfather died, and his grandmother sold the farm. Next, Sissela—whom Jan referred to as "their own child"—was born (Jan Myrdal, *Childhood*, 58–59, 116).

The couple went first to London for three months to write and prepare for the American trip. Gunnar turned his lectures into a book that became a classic: 1930's *The Political Element in the Development of Economic Theory* (Bok, 82–84).

Alva Reimer Myrdal's prophetic voice began not with a concern for world peace but with a cry for the children of her own country, Sweden. Alva wrote an article titled "Emotional Factors in Education" and began a revision of Freud's *Interpretation of Dreams*; she planned to submit the study of Freud as a dissertation topic (Bok, 82–84).

Alva and Gunnar's arrival in New York was just days before the stock market crash of 1929. Their host was the sociologist Robert Lynd, the author of *Middletown*, the celebrated study of a community in the Midwest. With all the research on child development and on social work on children, Alva focused her work on both topics. She was appalled at the poverty she encountered in America and at the racial and the religious discrimination she saw. This information would affect her work—and Gunnar's—in the days to come (Bok, 85–89).

Gunnar spent his days finishing *Political Element in the Development of Economic Theory*. While he was in America, he was trying to discover and understand as much as possible about economics—particularly its theory—and related research (Bok, 89).

Alva was meeting and working with some of *the* names in child development and social theory: Alfred Adler, Charlotte Bühler, Dorothy Thomas, W. I. Thomas, and others. She began thinking about doing a study of her own town in Sweden as Lynd had done in *Middletown*. Sissela found a list of 14 research tasks that Alva had listed for future work. Alva reveled in her studies and the joy she found in her work. She indicated jokingly to others, however, that she was finding more problems than solutions to problems (Bok 89–93).

As the return time came near, Alva began to focus on the difficulties that they might encounter with restoring their relationship with Jan. She worried about their reunion and wrote in her diary of her concerns about her son having "two mothers." She hoped, however, that her study of child psychology might help prevent some mistakes. She also planned to publicize in her country of Sweden the information she had found on the dangers of denying tenderness to children and of trying to structure rigorously their young lives (Bok, 94–95).

Alva found out that Bert Hammer, the professor who had encouraged her dissertation, *Sketch of a Critique of Freud's Dream Theory*, had died suddenly. The professor who had taken Hammer's place rejected Alva's proposal. Her next approach was a study based on Florence Goodenough's tests; her committee denied this topic also.

When Gunnar received an invitation from the Institute for International Studies of the University of Geneva, they were both delighted. This meant that Alva could study with Jean Piaget, the greatly admired child development psychologist (Bok, 96–98).

The next years would not be idyllic, however. Alva suffered another miscarriage, and her physicians found she had a large tumor. She also had an infection and a fever. Gunnar was distraught. One of Gunnar's colleagues wrote that Gunnar was so distressed over the possibility of losing Alva that he brought his gloom to work with him. The co-worker noted that Gunnar was able to create around him a feeling of dread *or* happiness because of his strong personality and his intense feelings. His love for Alva was evident to all in the workplace (Bok, 100).

Alva refused surgery for the tumor for fear that she would not be able to bear children. With no penicillin or modern antibiotics, treating infections was not easy in the 1930s. Her condition persisted.

There were, however, periods when she was able to walk with Gunnar and to consider conditions about her. She called herself a Social Democrat because she was opposed to certain groups having special privileges and other groups not having these opportunities. Alva considered her union with Gunnar a good one. She told a friend that when the social psychologist (Alva) and the economist (Gunnar) joined together, they created a sociologist (Bok, 102).

Alva began to study the population decline that concerned Europeans between the two wars. She called this decline "a birth strike." To remedy the situation, she set up a course of study to train parents; her program in the fall of 1931 was "what I think was the first course of that kind that existed [in Sweden]" (Bok, 103).

Alva enjoyed speaking in public and advocated not only day care for children (so that their parents could pursue their work) but also proper training of personnel (so that parents could know their children were receiving proper care). Both Gunnar and Alva advocated this national socio-economic program for children regardless of the parents' economic means (Moritz, 639–40). When periodicals turned down the Myrdals' articles on the population crises and child care because they were too lengthy, they decided to combine the works into a book. They finished the volume in the summer of 1934 as they walked, vacationed, and worked in the Norwegian Alps. The book *Crisis in the Population Question* appeared in late 1934—just before the birth of Sissela in December of the same year (Bok, 104–15).

Crisis in the Population Question received critical acclaim. It was indeed shocking to some to find a woman's name on a book that she had written with her husband; usually the husband would simply acknowledge her in the preface. Alva's name actually appeared with Gunnar's (Bok, 104–15).

The shock continued when the public read the information inside the book. The authors suggested that toys were essential to the development of children and were not a luxury. They advocated nurseries to care for the children while the parents worked and suggested that training was necessary for the child care workers. The book, bearing a woman's name, had a focus on the birthrate. In 1933 Sweden, the rate was 13.6 per 1,000; during the previous century it had been 30 per 1,000. Many people were horrified that a woman would mention birth control or advocate bearing children. To suggest such "radical" actions as free school lunches, sex education in the schools, free health care, and a law prohibiting the firing of a pregnant woman was outrageous to a large segment of the population. As Alva traveled about lecturing on the book, someone was sure to ask her why she was not home with her newborn daughter Sissela and her son Jan (Bok, 115–26).

Jan wrote his views of his parents and his sister Sissela in his autobiography. His impressions are not favorable. He noted that Gunnar called Sissela "Little Hypocrite" because she—like her mother Alva—was able to charm those she met. He claims that she lacked her own style and that she is in every respect her parents' child: as phony as a "three-Crown coin" (Jan Myrdal, *Childhood*, 115–16).

The Myrdals built "the most radical family house" of the 1930s. It was their home from 1937 until about 1947. The home had several levels with the parents' room on the top floor; off the master bedroom was a terrace with a ship's rail. There was a movable wall in the bedroom for privacy if either partner needed it. The opinion of those who saw the home, however, was that the Myrdals were too inaccessible to their children and too unconventional in the way they arranged their home. Their top floor also included a workroom and archives with shelves lining the walls (Bok, 124–126).

The ground floor had a nursery and an enormous drawing board on the wall. There were bedrooms for Jan, the maid, and the housekeeper; a wading pool; a yard for ball games; white linoleum stairs (down which the children could ride mattresses); and a play school (Bok, 121–23). Everything was not happy within the house, however. The old arguments between Gunnar and Jan escalated (Bok, 124–26).

Alva noted that it was Gunnar and not she who was asked to chair the Housing Committee formed in 1935; her call was to serve only as a consultant. Alva took her consulting role as being a way to secure both of their services for the price of one (Bok, 124–26).

In 1936 Alva helped to establish the Social Pedagogical Institute in Stockholm to train preschool teachers. She indicated that men as well as women might take the courses. She advocated a life outside of the school for teachers and dared to suggest that young women and men might work with the children. When others criticized her work, she merely encouraged them to make the program better. Alva directed the school from 1936 until 1948 and continued to promote progressive educational theories and reforms in child care (Raven, 81; Uglow, 395; Bok, 126–30).

Alva allowed little Kaj, who was younger than Sissela, to be one of the children whom Frances Ilg studied. Ilg published her findings along with Arnold Gesell. People across the country began to read child studies by Ilg, Gesell, Piaget, Margaret Mead, and Dr. Benjamin Spock. Although Alva included child development information in her Seminar for Social Pedagogy, she also included information about society in the curriculum (Bok, 130–32).

Alva set about to assist women. She helped to organize the International Federation of Business and Professional Women and even chaired the organization. Through this group, the Swedish Civil Service helped bring about an important change: A new law made it illegal to dismiss women because of pregnancy, marriage, or childbirth. Alva chaired the group (Uglow, 395) in 1937; in 1938 she served as the vice-president (Bok, 140–41).

Meanwhile, however, Gunnar was becoming more and more discontented. He wanted to accept the invitation of Fredrick Keppel, the President of Carnegie Corporation, to begin a long-range study: "The American Negro Problem." Gunnar emphasized, "The Negro problem is this: From the point of view of the American creed the status accorded the Negro in America represents nothing more and nothing less than a century-long lag of public morals" (Gunnar Myrdal, *An American Dilemma*, 24).

Gunnar began to realize what a tremendous task lay before him with the research and writing. He expressed his horror at discovering the depths of the problems and evils that he saw in America. Gunnar admitted that he was "shocked and scared to the bones by all the evils I saw" (Bok, 134). He believed it was necessary to travel "through most of the Southern states." They talked with "a great number of white and Negro leaders in various activities; visited universities, colleges, schools, churches, and various state and community agencies as well as factories and plantations." The group talked with "police officers, teachers, preachers, politicians, journalists, agriculturists, workers, sharecroppers, and, in fact, all sorts of people, colored and white..." (Gunnar Myrdal in a memo to Keppel, August 12, 1937, *An American Dilemma*, ix). This time while Gunnar did his research, however, he had his family with him in the United States.

While in America, Gunnar made friends with Ralph Bunche, a brilliant, radical professor of political science at Howard University. With Bunche and others, Myrdal began to map the ambiguities, the inconsistencies, and the paradoxes he found in what he called the "Negro problem in America" (Bok, 136–7). Gunnar emphasized that the Negro *problem* in America means "that the Americans are worried about it." The problem "is on their minds and on their consciences" (Gunnar Myrdal, *An American Dilemma*, 26). Gunnar's project and the resulting book *An American Dilemma* would become, according to his daughter, his life's finest achievement. This period was the most stimulating in Gunnar Myrdal's life (Bok, 132–33).

Gunnar emphasized in the Introduction to *An American Dilemma*, "The Negro problem is an integral part of, or a special phase of, the whole complex of problems in the larger civilization. It cannot be treated in isolation" (Gunnar Myrdal, *An American Dilemma*, xlix). He also used this same method in *Asian Drama*. He emphasized one must approach all subjects—including politics, history, health, education and social stratification—in mutual relationships and not in isolation (Bok, 136–37).

Alva used the same approach that Gunnar was using in her work on her new book. Her volume would have the title *Nation and Family: The Swedish Experiment in Democratic Family and Population Policy* (Alva Myrdal, *Nation and Family*, 1941). The problem that Alva addressed was not the Negro problem but instead was the female problem. Alva stated that women not only experience problems but also *are* the social problem. Sissela speculated that Alva's words in this volume seem to reflect the difficulty that her mother had with combining a career, love, and parenting* (Bok, 139–40).

With the war, the family returned to Sweden in 1940. Jan, who was about 12 at the time, did not want to leave the United States; Jan insisted that he had his naturalization papers and demanded that he be allowed to remain in the United States (Jan Myrdal, *12 Going on 13*, 33).

Before using some corporal punishment, Gunnar told his son:

> Of course it would be possible to arrange for you to stay and we could probably afford it, but that's not the issue.... It's a moral question. We come from peasant stock, we don't flee the country in times of danger. It would look bad if we left you here in America in wartime. It would be immoral for us to leave you here. It would imply that we were seeking privileges for ourselves [Jan Myrdal, *12 Going on 13*, 33].

Alva told the reporters that millions of other Swedish children (and even European children) were exposed to danger that their children could face also. (Jan Myrdal, *12 Going on 13*, 65).

The family returned to Sweden in May 1940. Jan wrote of his journey on board the MS *Mathilda Thordén* (Jan Myrdal, *12 Going on 13*, 7). After the Myrdals' return to Sweden, Sissela remembered seeing her mother writing at her large wooden desk, made of birch and placed just across from Gunnar's desk. The couple often worked together, especially during the winter of 1940–41 (Bok, 153).

Gunnar, increasingly dissatisfied with life in Sweden, decided to return to America. When he arrived in the U.S. in February of 1941, he immediately began to urge Alva to join him. He told her it was too dangerous for the children to travel at this time. He insisted that she accompany him, though, voiced his need of her, and said that without her, he could not write or even think (Bok, 153).

At first Alva postponed joining Gunnar and told him she had her work with the Siminar and her writing. She had family problems: Her sister Maj was very ill (and died during this time). She reminded Gunnar that Jan was 13 and, as a teenager, he needed her. Sissela was six, and Kaj was only four. Sofie was in her sixties. Gunnar, however, viewed "as a betrayal" the fact that she was remaining in Sweden with the children and with her work instead of coming to him (Bok, 153–57).

Gunnar may have given her an ultimatum: Come to America with him or face divorce. She was not ready to consider an end to their marriage. She therefore left their children with Sofie (Bok, 155–56) and suspended her work that had been a success. Through her planning and suggestions, over 400 trained fellows went to help underdeveloped countries (Selvidge). She began the difficult journey to America. Alva always referred to this trip as her second biggest mistake; leaving Jan for a year when he was only two was the first (Bok, 155–56).

When Alva was 81, she wrote to her daughters about the moves she made without the children. She noted that she did not want to go with Gunnar in 1941, but he did everything in his power to make her do so. Alva admitted that her obedience was—as always—unquestioned (Bok, 356).

---

*Alva's book Nation and Family: The Swedish Experiment in Democratic Family and Population Policy *would not appear until shortly after Pearl Harbor in 1941. With all the unrest in the world, the press gave very little attention to her book (Bok, 153).*

At the time, Alva saw supporting her husband as her main task. She wanted to make his load lighter and to help him in his varied, multi-dimensional efforts that he could not complete without her. In an April 1983 letter to her daughters, she reflected on the costs of her life to her family. She noted that they had had to pay a price but said that her son Jan was her "almost constantly bleeding cross" (Bok, 357).

Jan had resented being left behind while his parents returned to the U.S. His book *12 Going on 13* is the third book in a series of three; Jan insists that the books are not strictly autobiographical but merely books about childhood. He does express his contempt at being left in "Hitler Sweden" while his parents traveled to New York—home (Jan Myrdal, *12 Going on 13*, 167).

The journey for Alva was hazardous. The June 1941 day before she was to depart Germany entered Soviet territory; she had to postpone leaving. She had many delays and detours on her trip. She wrote of her journey and sent the articles to newspapers. These essays would later appear in her book *Samples from Great Britain* (Bok, 156–58).

She also began writing *Women and Wars* while she was in England. This book, never finished, explored her observations of the roles of women in wartime. She noted that although women were not entrusted with major roles in peacetime, they made major contributions during war (Bok, 158–59). More than 30 years later, she would explore the dangers of the weapons of war in *The Game of Disarmament* (1976).

It was mid–October of 1941 before Alva at last joined Gunnar. Her children missed her terribly. Sissela told about her fears of being captured during the war and of losing her family to the world struggle. Alva expressed this loneliness through poetry (Bok, 156–59, 161).

In 1941 Gunnar and Alva published together their second book: *Contact with America*. When they worked on the volume in the U.S., they did not know whether their country of Sweden would enter the conflicts in Europe (Bok, 140–48). Their book encouraged optimism. According to Sissela, the Myrdals regarded the book as a hasty contribution to an emergency situation (Bok, 148).

In October 1942—almost a year exactly after her departure from Sweden—Alva at last returned with her husband. This period of attempting to restore the family ties was particularly painful for Jan and Gunnar. Alva tried to mediate, but there seemed no way to defuse the situation. She attempted to set aside the problems at home in order to write and teach. Jan at last left home and dropped out of school when he was 16 (Bok, 161–66, 174).

In 1943 Gunnar traveled again to the United States. This time his objective was to study post-war planning because the victory of the Allies seemed inevitable. Because he would be gone for only a few months, he did not insist that Alva accompany him. Her letters to Gunnar express her loneliness and her desire to re-create the intimacy of their early years together (Bok, 165). Gunnar, however, threatened "to seek refuge from family life"; still he continued to resent "not having Alva all to himself." Alva felt that she still had to be very careful when dealing with Gunnar (Bok, 166).

Alva continued her work to help others. She assisted Count Folke Bernadotte in planning trips to Germany in white Red Cross buses to bring concentration camp inmates to Scandinavian countries. She started a newsletter titled *Via Suecia*. Printed in four languages, this forum for refugees included lists of missing persons, addresses for those in Scandinavia, memoirs, news, and poetry (Bok, 166–70, 175).

Writing articles for parents, she emphasized supplying children with warmth and joy.

She indicated also—as she had as early as 1933—that to protect a democracy against demands for submission, the new generation must receive training in how to think critically, how to act independently, and how to cope with criticism and opposition (Bok, 175–76).

Sissela had definite views about her parents. In Sissela's opinion, Alva had not assumed the educational role that she advocated that other parents assumed; Alva had not focused on reshaping her two girls but allowed them to drift. Sissela saw her mother as "captivating but not ideal, in spite of all her knowledge about children and their development." Alva seemed to know that she was not a gifted parent. When Alva was home and took time for her family, the girls found her "a joy to be with." Alva, however, hired Karin Anger, a caregiver-housekeeper, to take charge of the girls (Bok, 178–83).

Sissela was aware that Gunnar always wanted his own work and well-being to come first—even before his wife's work or his family's needs. In fact, Sissela was aware that her father was turning away from his family and more toward his work. This was the beginning of a pattern that would persist throughout his life. She described her father as "egocentric" and insecure (Bok, 183–89).

In 1946 Alva learned that she was a possible choice for Sweden's minister of education. She withdrew her name, however, because Gunnar might become the minister of commerce and both could not serve at the same time.

Gunnar did not become minister of commerce after all. He had often irritated those about him by saying anything that popped into his head. The most powerful newspaper in Sweden criticized Gunnar. It indicated that his decisions were unreliable.

Alva also faced the criticism of others. With the reintroduction of rationing in March 1947, many of the newspapers accused Alva of relying on advance information and stocking up on supplies. Harassment included the home delivery of stinking meat in greasy packages that the police had to open, angry letters, and frequent newspaper articles about them. Sissela said that the family saw "our name clearly singled out, denounced, and in turn defended. We heard accusations we knew were groundless and others we were not sure we understood" (Bok, 190–92).

Gunnar finally received an offer to serve as the director of social affairs in the secretariat of Trygve Lie, the newly appointed secretary-general of the UN. He turned it down, however, explaining that his expertise was in international economics and not social affairs. Alva received the offer also, and she too declined; in her case she did not want to separate herself from her family again. She next received the offer of another position: assistant director of UNESCO in Paris. She would have loved this position, but she again declined because of her family. Gunnar asked her to tell them that he was interested in directing the U.N. Economic Commission for Europe (ECE) in Geneva. The offer came, Gunnar accepted, and the family moved to Geneva. Their new home, which offered a view of Lake Geneva and Mount Blanc, had large rooms for the children on the third floor (Bok, 193–194).

Alva had given much—her work with the Seminar and all the effort expended in moving her family and all its possessions to Geneva—in order to accompany Gunnar, but he seemed to have eliminated Alva and his family from all parts of his life. He included only things relating to the ECE. His secretary Anika de la Grandville seemed to provide much of the help that Gunnar required (Bok, 195–200). Alva told Sissela that she had not asked Gunnar about Anika. In the forty years that followed, Gunnar never offered any explanation, and Alva never inquired (Bok, 200).

Sissela later realized that the children were not aware of their mother's suffering. Alva had not demanded attention for herself. She had endured her grief silently, without any expressions of answer or sorrow (Bok, 201).

Sissela had her own concerns—school, foreign languages, and new teachers. Later, looking back on this time, she understood that the light in their family was growing dim; Alva was subdued, Gunnar was absent, and even Karin the housekeeper was anxious and without her usual joy. Gunnar forgot birthdays, and his official obligations determined the social life of the entire family (Bok, 201–03).

It finally became evident that Gunnar and Alva would live separately for longer than they had planned; they decided to break up their Geneva home. Alva and Gunnar seemed not to notice the loss that Sissela felt (Bok, 217).

Opportunities for work continued to arise for Alva. She wrote articles, worked to advance the prestige of the new international organization (Organisation Mondiale de l'Education Primaire, or OMEP) on early childhood education research and reforms that she had helped to start, gave lectures, and began to explore with sociologist Viola Klein the possibility of a book on the roles of women in society (Bok, 204–06, 225). Jan saved a clipping from the May 29, 1940, issue of *Dagens Nyheter*. The article quoted Alva: "'Now I will send the children to the country and finish writing a book on women's work during wartime,' says Mrs. Myrdal, who has stepped off the train after her long and secret trip across the Atlantic, looking just as fresh as if she had only come from Götenborg" (Jan Myrdal, *12 Going on 13*, 87).

When Kaj was 13 and Sissela 15, Alva realized that her relationship with Gunnar had changed. Gunnar had never respected her obligations or her work, and now he seemed to have put her aside. She believed that now—at the age of 47—she could begin a career of her own. She left for New York on February 1, 1949, the day after her birthday, to assume a position of exceptional responsibility. She would be heading the Department of Social Affairs for the U.N. (Raven, 81).

Alva wrote to her daughters in April 1983—even after the brain tumor had made it extremely difficult for her to write—about accepting the position:

> One thing has to be drummed into my children: mine was not a "career." My life has, rather, been filled with *campaigns*, both before and after the time of my professional work—that first began when I was exactly 47 years and one day old. That this offer came (after I had declined two others, one position as significant as that of vice director for UNESCO, out of considera- tion for the family—that is so long as the positions would have required that I be the one caus- ing the family to move) was something of such dreamlike satisfaction that I could not resist it. But by then Gunnar had already relocated the family— a departure that tore away the ground for all my meaningful work. Would there remain only hostessing duties? For no job was fore- seen [Bok, 336].

Alva was eager to begin and wrote later "that I first became a free person in 1949. And so *happy*, in New York, in Paris, in New Delhi" (Bok, 206–07). Kaj and Sissela real- ized, however, how torn their mother was between her family and her life work (Bok, 214).

In her lectures Alva stressed that half of the world goes to bed hungry, half are illit- erate, and 200 million are homeless. Now she hoped that she was in a position to help them personally. She intended to use her positions to help others (Bok, 207–09).

In the summer of 1950, Alva moved to Paris. Her role there was Head of the Division of Social Sciences of the United Nations Educational, Scientific, and Cultural Organization (UNESCO). Sissela, who remained behind, viewed her mother's leaving as abandonment and felt that she and her siblings were too young to be left alone (Bok, 214).

After Alva departed for Paris, Gunnar "turned increasingly to his secretary, Anika de la Grandville, to make all the necessary arrangements and to serve at his side as a hostess. We [the children] grew used to seeing her arrive for Sunday luncheons and other gatherings, always elegantly attired and ready to welcome the guests" (Bok, 210–11). Sissela reflected that her parents didn't live under the same roof but visited each other as if nothing has changed. She remembered their assuring each other that they were only an overnight train trip apart (Bok, 211–12).

Disaster struck. In November 1952, Gunnar was a passenger in a vehicle driven by Ingvar Svennilsson, an economist. The pair was on their way to Sweden when they wrecked. Gunnar suffered a severe hip injury; a university hospital in Lund was treating him. Alva heard the news in Paris and hurried to his hospital room in Sweden. The next month she traveled to India for UNESCO, but her departure came only after Gunnar was well enough to return to Geneva (Bok, 218).

On March 18, 1953, Sissela at last arrived in Paris to spend time with her mother— and she found Alva leaving for a two-month trip around the world on behalf of UNESCO. Sissela indicated in her diary that she was very sad at being left alone so soon after her arrival (Bok, 222–23).

Alva found when she reached New York that she could not enter the country. She had an appointment to speak to the U.N. Commission on "The Status of Women," but those in charge of allowing her to pass would not yield. Alva could not understand why the immigration officials denied her entry. Finally, in order to pass, she had to sign an agreement that gave her a "temporary release on parole" (Bok, 223).

When Gunnar heard of the incident, he was furious. He asserted that Alva was an international civil servant and her legal rights were in violation. Gunnar immediately appealed to Dag Hammarskjöld, Secretary-General of the United Nations, and asked him to take the necessary steps. Hammarskjöld issued a statement noting that the agreement between the U.N. and the United States had the specification that there should be no impediments in the way of officials going to the headquarters of the U.N. (Bok, 223–24).

Speculation as to why Alva found herself halted resulted in two theories. Perhaps the interference with Alva's progress was because 26-year-old Jan had political leanings toward the Communist Party. Another possibility was that misinformed agents believed that her support of the Swedish Social Democratic Party implied membership in the Communist Party. As soon as Alva reached Paris, she issued a statement insisting that she did not belong to the Communist Party; she indicated that denying a mother her rights unless she rejects her child was an unacceptable policy. On July 29, a statement from the deputy representative of the United States at the U.N. proclaimed that Alva Myrdal is "persona grata to the United States authorities" (Bok, 224).

Although Alva was enjoying her work, Gunnar was depressed. He began to realize that he had aged since his injury. Now his health was poor, and Alva was no longer with him. Gunnar interpreted her absence as a rejection of him. As his self-confidence diminished, his boastfulness and verbal attacks on others increased. He was unable to do research and often quoted his own works as references. He tried to diet strictly and to give up smoking. He worried about financial support for his work. His depression increased (Bok, 218–22, 237).

In May 1954, Sissela met Derek Bok, a B. A. from Stanford in 1951 and LL.B. from

Harvard in 1954; professor of law at Harvard from 1958; Dean of the Harvard Law School from 1968–71; President of Harvard, 1971–91; namesake for the Derek Bok Center for Teaching and Learning ("Bok, Derek Curtis," *Columbia Encyclopedia*, 2000-2004). They planned a 1955 Paris wedding with both sets of parents present. The next year, Alva had another cause for celebration: the publication of *Women's Two Roles: Home and Work*, the book that she and Viola Klein had been planning and writing for some time (Bok, 224–25).

The women had originally suggested *Women's Two Lives* as the book title. Their publisher, however, thought their title might suggest a double life and chose instead *Women's Two Roles: Home and Work* (Bok, 225). The two authors stressed in the volume the importance of "Children first" in all discussions of the employment of women (Alva Myrdal and Viola Klein, *Women's Two Roles: Home and Work*, 116). Myrdal and her co-writer also outlined some ways to use women workers, especially during wartime and when the women wish both to fulfill a lifelong dream of achievement and to rear a family.

To rear a family and to achieve career success, the two authors suggested an innovative plan: to start afresh at 40—after rearing their children. They note that the increased life expectancy would make this possible and desirable; this was an option women had not had in past decades. "Education, family, and work can be blended to a harmonious whole in one lifetime if each is given its own place in a chronological sequence. In practice, this precept is nowadays very often acted upon" (Alva Myrdal and Viola Klein, *Women's Two Roles: Home and Work*, 13, 39). Some retraining and additional education may be a necessity for women who have been out of the job market for a while and were now seeking to return to work (Alva Myrdal and Viola Klein, *Women's Two Roles: Home and Work*, 13, 39, 165).

Myrdal and Klein found in 1940–50 that many women in their forties already returned from necessity to the work world. The two authors quoted labor statistics showing that the percentage of working widows and divorced women was more than twice that of working married women (Alva Myrdal and Klein, *Women's Two Roles: Home and Work*, 13, 39). Sissela Bok observed that her mother did not apply these guides to her own life because she "would not have wanted to postpone work outside the home in the manner that this book sets forth." Nevertheless, after several decades, the book may still be of use—and may even have new relevance (Bok, 228–30).

In 1955 Gunnar was planning a volume on underdeveloped countries. He had visited India in the past and was planning that as his next study. He encouraged Alva to apply for positions in that country so that they would not have to endure a lengthy separation. In the summer of 1955, Alva accepted an invitation to serve as an ambassador; she would be the first woman to serve as an ambassador for Sweden. With an embassy located in New Delhi, the position would fit perfectly with Gunnar's work also. Gunnar, meanwhile, continued to experience health problems and bouts of depression; he had to remain behind until he could tie up loose ends. Alva eagerly prepared for her new position even though she had some concerns about resuming her marriage to Gunnar (Bok, 230–37). She would serve as Swedish ambassador to India from 1955 until 1961 (Raven, 81; Moritz, 640).

On November 30, 1955, Alva wrote to Gunnar from the plane as she flew to New Delhi. Her enthusiasm and eagerness to begin a new phase of her life was evident, but her desire to relieve his anxiety was evident also. She reminded him that they had found each other on a fence and that they had also found that which they wanted to achieve. She assured him that they could now meet in a house that had been readied for them, and that they could shut out the world on "this continent of wonders" (Bok, 239).

Alva's reception in New Delhi was a complete surprise. Arriving at the Delhi airport at midnight, she expected to find only a couple of sleepy attendants and perhaps a representative to help her find her quarters. Tired and sluggish after hours of travel, she discovered that friends from the women's movement were there to shower her with support, affection, and congratulations. She described the welcome as an "ovation-like whirl of women, garlands, and press photographers" (Bok, 240).

The next day when she arrived at the embassy, her reception was different: lukewarm. The secretary who had filled in for her until her arrival conveyed to her that he found her inexperienced. The complexities of the world at the embassy were unfamiliar to her. The fact that she was a woman did not make her work easier. In the beginning she felt "marginalized" (Bok, 240–41), but as she served the countries of Ceylon (Sri Lanka), Burma (now called Myanmar), and India (Bok, 240–41), she became "a spectacular success" (Bok, 248). Alva came in contact with many world leaders during her years in diplomatic service, but Jawaharlal Nehru was the one who impressed her above all others (Bok, 250). She remained in the position from 1955 until 1961 (Moritz, 640).

Gunnar was to close up the apartment and follow her to Delhi for a visit in January; it would be October 1957 before he could actually move to Delhi to be with her. Instead of merely packing up the letters, Alva's diaries, account books, and clippings, however, Gunnar began to read them. He despaired that he had squandered the love that she had offered him and professed in the diaries and letters. He realized the pain that his unfaithfulness and inattention had caused. It was he who had thrown away their life together and made her begin a life on her own. He feared death, and he felt alone and insecure. He readily admitted his errors and his feelings in his letters to her; he stressed that he was still functioning well on the job, that he could run the ECE, give lectures and write, but he was sad within (Bok, 246). Alva wrote and encouraged him. "Darling, you will get your confidence back. And your beloved you have. There is *much* left Gunnar" (Bok, 244–45).

When Gunnar arrived in Delhi in October 1957, he had already done some background work for his study *Asian Drama: An Inquiry into the Poverty of Nations* (Bok, 260). When the book finally appeared in 1968, Gunnar had spent 15 years on it. He had not only noted problems in the country but also had tried to suggest ways to resolve them (Bok, 260–61). The two problems that he saw as important were (1) how to increase efficiency of labor and (2) how to bring about full employment. Necessary to the solution of the problems were three things: advancing the low status of women; tackling the issues of health, nourishment, social inequalities, illiteracy, and family planning; and eliminating the scorn of the people for manual labor (Bok, 267).

Things seemed better for the Myrdal family. Alva and Sissela were writing back and forth, their letters reflecting their love for each other. The two were open and frank about their feelings and their life. Kaj's husband-to-be came to India to work on his doctoral dissertation on the red laterite soils; Kaj moved to India to be near her family and her future husband. Jan began to write for publication; Alva wrote Sissela: "Write he really can"* (Bok, 246–47, 263).

Alva became very sick. She had high fever, a swelling in her throat, difficulty swallowing, and weakness. She did not want to indicate a lack of confidence in the doctors in India, but she grew steadily worse. At last she went to Sweden for medical care. It took

---

*Jan Myrdal was a prolific writer. He had 14 books in English, five novels in Swedish, 35 nonfiction works in Swedish, and three plays in Swedish as of May 21, 2003. "Jan Myrdal," Contemporary Authors Online, 3–6.

weeks of misery before the medical staff could offer its diagnosis and she could complete her treatment. The diagnosis was that what had begun as diphtheria had spread to her whole nervous system. What followed were weeks of tube feeding, a near-coma state at times, and many tests. It was a year before Alva regained complete feeling in her feet and hands (Bok, 269).

In 1961, Alva and Gunnar returned to Sweden. She realized the dehumanization that could result from the obsession with a project, but she also knew that for her it would be a risk to have no project at all. She took two lectures she had prepared and had them published (August 1961) in a short book, *Our Responsibility for the Poor People: A Social Close-up of Development Problems* (Bok, 277).

In May 1961, Östen Undén, the foreign minister, asked Alva to prepare a report on disarmament proposals that he might present for Sweden in his farewell speech to the U.N. General Assembly (Alva Myrdal, *The Game of Disarmament*, xxiii; Bok, 278). She was 59 and "had no idea that she was about to begin more than two decades of the most absorbing and difficult struggle of her life, centering on disarmament" (Bok, 275). In *The Game of Disarmament*, the book that followed the long years of her "crucial personal involvement," she noted that she had not begun her work with "a critical attitude or a missionary zeal, but with a rationalistic bent, hoping that by using diplomatic professionalism and advice from experts in many fields it would be possible to advance the progress of disarmament" (Alva Myrdal, *The Game of Disarmament*, xi).

Later, she was able to tell Sissela in a letter that she had finished work for Undén was completed. She had "delivered the ammunition" for the Undén Plan; this proposal for a "non-atom club" stressed the role of non-nuclear nations in the disarmament debate. Undén hoped that nations free of nuclear weapons might serve as role models for other nations, might agree not to make or harbor nuclear weapons, and might urge others to halt the nuclear testing—both atmospheric and underground (Bok, 283).

In November 1961, Alva won the election for a seat in the Swedish Parliament (Bok, 283), By March 1962, she was eager to join in the deliberations of the Eighteen-Nation Disarmament Committee (established in 1961). Eight non-aligned nations—Sweden, Brazil, Burma, Egypt, Ethiopia, India, Mexico, and Nigeria—would join the Ten-Nation Committee on Disarmament. The Ten-Nation Committee included the Foreign Ministers of France, the Soviet Union, Britain, the United States, Bulgaria, Czechoslovakia, Poland, Rumania, Canada, and Italy (Alva Myrdal, *The Game of Disarmament*, 344; Bok, 290–91).

Alva found that the general public did not have access to the various viewpoints. The media did not provide the varying opinions because the two major powers—the United States and the USSR—dominated the discussion. The reasoning of the world, therefore, was "encapsulated in a bipolar model.... On the one side there is the United States; on the other side the Union of Soviet Socialist Republics. These two countries are truly in a category by themselves as superpowers; they alone have the might to annihilate each other and all other countries" (Alva Myrdal, *The Game of Disarmament*, xii).

A prevailing bipolar model was evident "by such phrases as 'the other side,' 'the adversary position,' if not 'the enemy.' In this model, the recent détente has not meant any change, although it has led to a more polite use of language, which by itself is all to the good" (Alva Myrdal, *The Game of Disarmament*, xii). She noted that attempts to make suggestions were often "thwarted because of the resistance of the two superpowers ... they struggle against each other, they are in a kind of conspiracy, dividing between them the responsibility for saying nyet and no. They apparently want to continue the arms race, to make mutual concessions, minor as they are, within bilateral negotiations, undisturbed by the majority of nations" (Alva Myrdal, *The Game of Disarmament*, xiii). Alva said she "felt there were better futures to choose than the ones of a Russian-led world revolution or an American-led stride forward to a century of unrestrained capitalism" (Alva Myrdal, *The Game of Disarmament*, xxii). She hoped through *The Game of Disarmament* to acquaint independent experts and citizens across the world with various views from many groups not previously publicized (Alva Myrdal, *The Game of Disarmament*, xviii).

In her opinion, change was not readily apparent. "The horizon has darkened further. There has been no attempt on the part of the superpowers to fulfill their promises of negotiating seriously to reverse the nuclear arms race.... I feel that we cannot give up" (Alva Myrdal, *The Game of Disarmament*, xviii).

Alva criticized the Soviet Union, the United States, and Germany for making the world a "plaything." She called their talks "therapy" and insisted that they had made no real changes. She believed that both the USSR and the USA wanted to be the most important power in the world. They enjoyed competition. She called their game "shared insanity" because their irresponsibility could destroy the entire world (Selvidge).

Alva said that the world spent too much of its resources in making weapons of war. She tried to demonstrate that the results of spending more and more money on arms would harm everyone. The amount of money that both the USA and the USSR spent on arms each year was greater than the amount they spent on education or health and 15 times larger than all of the aid they give to underdeveloped countries. The arms race reduced the standard of living. Not only did the race affect a country's economic standards, she argued, but it also depleted a country's natural resources (Selvidge).

Another disadvantage she noted was that developers of weapons were depleting the world's resources of bauxite, copper, iron and manganese. In their quest for a more potent and lethal weapon, these developers hired the best people in science to solve their problems. They were using up the best minds in the world. Myrdal believed governments were misdirecting science and technology (Selvidge).

Although the costs of war were enormous, preparing for a war had its positive economic effects upon some countries. People made money producing and selling arms. To stop the production would almost assuredly mean a period of unemployment and rising costs for a country. Huge corporations made fortunes as they encouraged political leaders to build new weapons. Taking lives for profit did not seem ethical or moral to Alva; she was appalled (Selvidge).

In their quest to gain power, both the USSR and the USA placed nuclear weapons in other countries. Many of these nuclear devices were sitting in countries that did not have nuclear technology. Myrdal and others proposed a "Nuclear Freeze Zone" where some countries would be free from nuclear weapons. The only region of the world where there were no arms at that time was Antarctica—a region with no governments, no countries, and no people. As it stood, the superpowers could launch a limited nuclear attack (not a full-scale attack) at each other, and Europe would be the most likely battlefield. Both powers placed over 10,000 atomic weapons in European countries. Their actions placed people everywhere at risk (Selvidge).

In addition to working toward making Europe free from nuclear weapons, Myrdal spoke out against inhumane warfare. She reminded others that International Law outlawed cluster bombs, dumdum bullets (high speed bullets which blast a large hole in human beings), and terrorist bombings. She called for an elimination of all biological and chemical weapons (Selvidge).

Alva later wrote to Sissela that during the 12 years that she worked with disarmament, "she had never felt so uplifted by any task" (Bok, 291) and wrote to Gunnar that she found her work "absorbing" (Bok, 293).

In December 1964, she became head of a group that would later become the Stockholm International Peace Research Institute (SIPRI). In 1967 when she joined the Swedish cabinet and could no longer serve, Gunnar (who had almost completed *Asian Drama: An Inquiry into the Poverty of Nation*) took over as chair. The two main concerns of the group at that time were disarmament and international development (Bok, 294).

In 1966, Alva received the appointment to Minister for Disarmament—the first and only such position in the world. By the time she took office in January 1967, she was almost 65; she held this position until 1973. A year later her work included a new role: minister of church affairs; she held this job from 1969 to 1973 (Uglow, 395). This job made sense to Balch because churches were involved in disarmament (Bok, 295–96). She looked forward to exploring the theme of equality "between faiths, between believers and nonbelievers, and—still fiercely contested by a minority within the church—between men and women priests..." (Bok, 297).

Out of this work came the report *Towards Equality*. The report cited the need for nine years of compulsory education for all children in Sweden; because most adults only had the compulsory six years of education, the report advocated adult education. *Towards Equality* called for higher family allowances, parental leave with pay after the birth of a child, higher salaries, tax reforms, and other advances. When the cabinet suggested revisions, she called the rewritten version "pure aspirin"; she declared emphatically that she would resign rather than support a watered-down version (Bok, 299).

Another thing that may have resulted from this appointment was the final separation between Jan and his family. Alva believed that the breach occurred when Gunnar and she returned from America. Upon their arrival at the Arlanda airport near Stockholm, Gunnar called his son and suggested getting together. What the parents did not know was that Jan had been arrested because of his participation in an anti–Vietnam protest and the resulting scuffle with police.

Jan saw the matter-of-fact call as belittlement and rejection. Alva wrote that had they known of Jan's trouble, they would have taken his side. She had not taken any part in the decision of police action (Bok, 333–34).

Jan's version of the incident was totally different; he described it in detail in *Childhood*. He recounted that Alva had invited Gun (his wife) and him to dinner at the Aurora restaurant in August or September 1968. At that time Alva was the Minister of Disarmament.

Jan recalls that his mother was never a stingy person when she invited someone out. Shopping with her was always pleasant, and her company was enjoyable. Jan, however, noted that his mother seemed to want something. They ate, chatted, and shared a good bottle of wine.

At last, Alva remarked that Prime Minister Tage Erlander had been concerned about Alva seeing Jan. Erlander suggested it might be good if Alva did not see Jan for a while.

Jan was a controversial figure at that time. He had just returned from Cambodia and was active in a movement for solidarity with the Vietnamese. He had also spoken forthrightly after the Six Day War about the rights of Palestinians and publicly opposed in the press the foreign policy of the Swedish government.

Jan's response was that it was probably best that they never see each other again (Jan Myrdal, *Childhood*, 158–60).

Somewhere about this time, Alva and Gunnar began preparing a will that disinherited the children. The signed will carried the date September 15, 1966. They had financed the education of their children and had provided other support to them when it was necessary. Now they wanted to help those who had a greater need. They would give away considerable amounts of their income to needy groups, to scholarly institutions, to writers and artists, and to research on peace (Bok, 332–33).

The family knew that Alva was opposed to inherited wealth. She considered this income as an undesirable privilege; her work with the Swedish Equality Report reinforced that opinion. Nevertheless, after the death of Alva in 1986 and Gunnar in 1987, the family found it "dismaying" to have to ask the representatives of the estate for permission to remove some personal articles from the belongings (Bok, 332–33).

In 1968, Gunnar's *Asian Drama: An Inquiry into the Poverty of Nations* (2,284 pages and 16 appendices) at last appeared in print. Alva had helped him with the sections on education. Gunnar apologized for the length of the study but added that it had become "to me personally a destiny, the course of which I had not foreseen or planned at the beginning" (Bok, 276). Sissela wrote that *Asian Drama*, like *An American Dilemma*, would become a classic. She admits, however, that the book met a chilly reception because it criticized some of the failed reforms and passed judgment on the ruling leaders (Bok, 289).

Gunnar and Alva together won the German Peace Prize in 1970 (Uglow, 395; Bok, 338). Another honor was forthcoming.

In the fall of 1974, while Gunnar and Alva were in New York, Gunnar received the news that he and the arch-conservative Austrian economist Friedrich von Hayek would share the Nobel Prize in economics. Although special mention was made of Gunnar's books *The Political Element in the Development of Economic Theory* (1930), *An American Dilemma: The Negro Problem and Modern Democracy* (1944), and *Asian Drama: An Inquiry into the Poverty of Nations* (1968), 76-year-old Gunnar claimed that receiving the award with Hayek was not adequate recognition for his work; he urged his family not to attend the ceremonies. He even advocated abolishing awards in which politics played a role—as he believed had been true in this case (Bok, 306).

Alva, too, had received many awards. In 1975 the Ralph Bunche Institute at the City University of New York honored the couple. In 1977 they accepted a joint professorship at the Lyndon B. Johnson School of Public Affairs at the University of Texas, Austin (Bok, 338).

She had received the D.H.L. from Columbia University in 1965 and from Temple University in 1968. She had accepted another degree from Gustavus Adophus University in 1971 and from Brandeis University and the University of Gothenburg in 1975; she would receive still another honorary degree from the University of East Anglia in 1976. Some of the awards and awards still to come included the West German Peace Prize in 1970, the Wateler Prize from Hague Academy of International Peace in 1973, the prize from the Royal Swedish Institute of Technology in 1975, and the Monismanien Prize for the protection of civil liberties in 1976 ("Alva Myrdal," *Contemporary Authors*).

During 1975, Alva's work on *The Game of Disarmament* received top priority in the lives of both Alva *and* Gunnar; he read Alva's work as carefully as he would have read his own—even though his many suggestions and changes increased her work. Alva wrote that she had learned to sit at her desk for long hours and had excluded food preparation, sun bathing, and other activities from her schedule. She vowed never to write a thick book again (Bok, 308).

In *The Game of Disarmament*, Myrdal expressed her concerns about nuclear warfare, war, bipolar positions, nuclear testing, the costs for weapon development to people and society, her distaste of making profits from taking the lives of people, the loss of scientific minds to weapon development, inhumane weapons, and other types of warfare, particularly biological and chemical. Solving these additional problems requires "initiatives by governments ... but behind governments stand groups of concerned citizens, in particular, scientists..." (Alva Myrdal, *The Game of Disarmament*, 292). She cautioned that all of us "must watch for any [threats] ... to overtake what is the common, long-range ideal of building for peace and protecting human beings" (Alva Myrdal, *The Game of Disarmament*, 292).

Alva noted that the third act of the play *The Game of Disarmament* was not a completed one. In fact, she believed, it had not begun. "I would still hope [the actors] ... would win victory over the arms race, so senseless and cruel, and to bar a complete militarization of the whole world" (Alva Myrdal, *The Game of Disarmament*, xxvi). She reminded the reader that this intellectual and moral dilemma is the major one of our time; because "it has been created solely by mankind, it lies within our power to solve it" (Alva Myrdal, *The Game of Disarmament*, 334).

The book received critical acclaim. Schurmann in *The New York Times Book Review* called it "an eloquent plea for disarmament." He also observed that the author

> ... argues on rational grounds, sketches out feasible scenarios for scaling down the arms race and, in particular, urges that every effort be made to banish "cruel weapons" from warfare. There is more to the book than arguments for disarmament. Myrdal sees much of the arms race as collusion between the two superpowers, the United States and the U.S.S.R., to serve their own concerns and interests [Schurmann, 5].

Gibson in *The Library Journal* also gave it a positive review:

> This important book is based on the author's participation in multilateral disarmament negotiations for more than 12 years as a Swedish representative.... Her basic position is one of pessimism, but she gives good and cogent reasons for continuing disarmament efforts. The writings is authoritative, the documentation is extensive, the lengthy quotations permit many of the people involved to speak for themselves, and the entire book conveys a sense of urgency. It is unfortunate that the United States appears to be the chief villain, but on balance, this book is the best one available on the needs and problems of disarmament.... [A]ll libraries should have a copy available [Gibson, 2468].

The *Economist* presents a less favorable review:

> The reasons why nations spend so much on arms are, in fact, more complex than Mrs. Myrdal will admit; and so is the problem of how to get them to stop.... She [has a] blithe way of ignoring things that don't fit [*Economist*, 95].

Alva was still concerned about the split in her family. She wrote to Jan in 1977 and urged him to resume at least minimal relations with his parents. Jan did reply to the letter; he was not inclined to meet with them again. Sissela reported that Jan never felt sure of Gunnar and Alva. If Jan met with them, Gunnar might begin his cruel teasing or even go into a fit of rage. Alva decided it was inappropriate to appear in public with Jan, and he became less disposed to meet with them (Bok, 334–35).

Gunnar and Alva formed and endowed the Myrdal Foundation in 1978. The purpose of this organization was to provide support to citizens' groups and to disseminate information on disarmament and international security.

In the spring of 1980, Alva learned that she would be the first Albert Einstein Peace Prize winner. The prize would honor the individual "who has contributed most significantly to the prevention of nuclear war and to the strengthening of international peace" (Bok, 315). Even though Alva was about to undergo a hip operation after an accident that resulted in a broken bone, she planned to travel to New York for the May ceremony. Many friends and family members accompanied her (Bok, 315–16).

In 1981 Alva became chair of a Peace Forum she formed with the help of the Swedish labor movement. She also helped establish Women for Peace. This popular movement stretched throughout European communities.

When Alva did not receive the Nobel Peace Prize after nominations several years in a row, the public developed its own prize and a financial award of $60,000 for Alva Myrdal. She received the prize—the Norwegian People's Peace Prize—in Oslo in February 1982 and immediately donated the money to the Peace Forum.

In 1982, a reissue of *The Game of Disarmament* appeared. In the new preface, there was a message of hope:

> The ruin of the planet is there for all to contemplate. But so, too, is its potential richness if we learn to cooperate. We still have a choice. But we must act now as never before [Preface, *The Game of Disarmament*, 1981].

That summer brought, along with the accolades for her winning the prize, a devastating blow to the Myrdal family. Jan's book *Childhood* presented the Myrdals in a different, intensely personal way. Although Jan says the book is more fictional than autobiographical, he used Alva and Gunnar Myrdal as characters; the publisher of *Childhood* notes on the end page that Jan

> ... insists that this book is "a story about childhood, not an autobiography...." It is also part of the background of this book that it was a major Scandal.... Myrdal had to fight to get *Childhood* published, and it was almost marginalized in a small, limited edition. But he circumvented attempts to suppress the book by reading it on the radio and serializing it in a major daily, forcing the controversy into the open. *Childhood* soon became a best-seller and finally was accepted as a classic.
>
> The second book in Myrdal's childhood series, *Another World*, won the Literature Foundation's Great Prize for the Novel. The third, *12 Going on 13*, won the Esselte Prize for Literature and was distributed free to 100,000 of Sweden's middle school children—a strange fate for Sweden's most outspoken oppositional figure [*Childhood*, endpage].

Alva was in poor health when the furor surrounding Jan's book hit the press. She had fallen and was suffering from a concussion; the fall could have been a result of the medicine she was taking to relieve her high blood pressure. She was deeply saddened by the book's contents. *Childhood* brought letters of criticism to Alva and her family, but they also received notes of condolence and compassion from strangers and friends [Bok, 342–43].

In October 1982, Alva received a call announcing that she and her U.N. colleague Alfonso García Robles would receive the Nobel Peace Prize. This made Gunnar and Alva the only husband-and-wife recipients of Nobel Prizes in entirely different fields. It helped salve some open wounds (Bok, 342).

In Egil Aarvik's presentation speech in Oslo (December 10, 1982), Aarvik, Chair of the Norwegian Nobel Committee, announced that Myrdal and Robles were receiving the award not only because of "their magnificent work in the disarmament negotiations of the United Nations, where they have both played crucial roles and won international recognition," but also because of their contributions of "informing world opinion on the problems of armaments and of arousing the acceptance by the general public of their joint responsibility for the train of events" (Aarvik, 1).

Aarvik noted the span of time and service over which Alva had worked. He recognized that after working on behalf of Norway during World War II, she received a well-deserved honor: His Majesty King Haakon VII's Freedom Cross. He called her "a staunch spokesman of peace and disarmament," "a researcher and disarmament expert," "a staunch champion of women's liberation and equal rights," "a brilliant diplomat," and "the first woman to be appointed head of a department in the United Nations" (Aarvik, 2).

Aarvik acknowledged that it was "typical of great personalities that it is easy both to agree and disagree with them." He stated firmly, however, that everyone would agree on one point: "[H]er name has become a rallying point for men and women who still cling to the belief that in the last resort, mind is bound to triumph over matter." He continued, "Today in her eighty-first year, she can look back on a life which must of necessity have been not only rich but also dramatic. It must have alternated between hope and disappointment, and almost certainly, too, between encouragement and discouragement" (Aarvik, 2–3).

Alva continued to have angina pains, spells of dizziness, heart arrhythmia, and a brain tumor. Not in the best of health, from the Oslo podium she said first that her Acceptance Speech would be brief. She explained, however, that "the brevity of my speech is in no way a measure of the depth of my gratitude." She expressed thanks to the Chairman of the Nobel Committee for his "bold acknowledgment of the principles which must support all efforts to attain peace and disarmament," to "the Norwegian Nobel Committee for granting me this year's Nobel Prize for the cause of peace," to the "large groups of people who have ... brought forth a strong popular movement for peace," and to "those great numbers of experts and authors in many countries who have destroyed false misconceptions and provided us with powerful arguments for a cessation of this competition in over armament" (Alva Myrdal, "Acceptance Speech," 1). Interestingly, Alva called on the words of the first woman Nobel Peace Prize winner, Bertha von Suttner. Alva said, "Now sounds the cry 'Down with nuclear weapons!'" (Alva Myrdal, "Acceptance Speech," 1).

At the time of the award, Gunnar was suffering from Parkinson's disease, yet he used the occasion of Alva's award to speak publicly with the press about Jan's writings. During this time of celebration, he again brought the focus of the media and the public on the "dirty laundry" (Bok, 347–49).

The amount of the Nobel Peace Prize was about $78,000. Gunnar wanted Alva to deposit the sum in their joint account. She disagreed. After setting aside a small amount for secretarial help, Alva designated half for a study on the deployment of nuclear weapons at sea and the remainder for studying the "culture of violence." As always, Alva's focus was anti-violence (Bok, 351–52).

Early in 1984, Alva suffered a stroke that forced her to retire from public life. Her brain tumor and her heart problems added to her incapacitation. Her condition worsened, and she slipped into a state of unconsciousness; she never awoke. The day after her eighty-fourth birthday—and 45 years to the day after she began her career in 1949—Alva died (Bok, 360).

The bishop of Stockholm Krister Stendahl conducted the service. A part of his tribute read:

Alva Myrdal had very clear eyes. They reflected the clarity of her thinking, the orderly and methodical way she handled every project, the happy faith in reason that carried her through life.

In her eyes, you also encountered warmth, thoughtfulness, her ability to understand the situation of others. You felt encompassed not only by her thoughts but also by her heart.

... When you talk about Alva Myrdal, people become inspired. To them, she signifies happiness about life's potential, a bright faith in the future. A person can hardly hope for a better monument [Strendhal, as quoted in Bok, 361].

Gunnar's last months were peaceful but achingly alone. His memory was weak, and he could not remember family and friends who visited. He died on May 17, 1987, when he was 89 (Bok, 361).

In her Foreword to *The Changing Roles of Men and Women*, Alva Myrdal issued a challenge that is, as yet, unmet; her call is still important to the world today. It is one we should heed.

Let people ... be prompted to pierce the veil with which conventions and traditions and comfortable conformism conceal our visions of the future, a future which could be more reasonable and profitable for society and more creative and rewarding for the men and women who inhabit it [Alva Myrdal, "Foreword," *The Changing Roles of Men and Women*, 15].

Bibliography

Aarvik, Egil. "Nobel Peace Prize Presentation Speech." December 10, 1982. Available online at http://nobelprize.org/peace/laureates/1982/press.html.

"Alva Reimer Myrdal." *Contemporary Authors Online.* Reproduced in *Biography Resource Center.* Farmington Hills, Michigan: Thomson Gale, 2005.

"Bok, Derek Curtis." *The Columbia Encyclopedia.* 6th Edition. New York: Columbia University Press, 2001–04.

Bok, Sissela. *Alva Myrdal: A Daughter's Memoir.* A Merloyd Lawrence Book. Reading, Massachusetts: Addison-Wesley Publishing Company, 1991.

Dahlström, Edmund, ed. *The Changing Roles of Men and Women.* Boston: Beacon Press, 1962.

Gibson, Edward. "Review of Alva Myrdal's *The Game of Disarmament.*" *Library Journal*, December 1, 1976, 101: 2468.

"Jan Myrdal." *Contemporary Authors Online.* Reproduced in *Biography Resource Center.* Farmington Hills, Michigan: Thomson Gale, 2005.

Moritz, Charles, ed. *Current Biography Yearbook: 1986.* 47th annual cumulation. New York: H. W. Wilson, 1986.

Myrdal, Alva. "Acceptance Speech." December 10, 1982. Available online at http://nobelprize. org/peace/laureates/1982/press.html.

_____. *The Game of Disarmament: How the United States and Russia Run the Arms Race.* New York: Pantheon, 1976. Revised and enlarged edition, 1981.

_____. *Nation and Family: The Swedish Experiment in Democratic Family and Population Policy.* New York: Harper and Brothers, 1941.

_____, and Viola Klein. *Women's Two Roles: Home and Work.* London: Routledge and Kegan Paul, 1956.

Myrdal, Gunnar, with the assistance of Richard Sterner and Arnold Rose. *An American Dilemma: The Negro Problem and Modern Democracy.* New York: Harper and Brothers, 1944.

_____. *Asian Drama: An Inquiry into the Poverty of Nations.* New York: Pantheon, 1968.

Myrdal, Jan. *Childhood.* Chicago: Lake View, 1991.

_____. *12 Going on 13.* Chicago: Ravenswood Nooks, 1989. English translation copyright 1995.

Parry, Melanie, ed. *Larousse Dictionary of Women.* New York: Larousse Kingfisher Chambers, 1996.

Raven, Susan, and Alison Weir. *Women of Achievement: Thirty-five Centuries of History.* New York: Harmony Books, 1981.

"Review of Alva Myrdal's *The Game of Disarmament.*" No author. *Economist,* August 13, 1977, 264, 95.

Schurmann, Franz. "Review of Alva Myrdal's *The Game of Disarmament.*" *New York Times Book Review,* March 6, 1977, 5.

Selvidge, Marla. "Unpublished paper on Alva Myrdal." Warrensburg: Central Missouri State University, 1999.

Uglow, Jennifer S. *The Northeastern Dictionary of Women's Biography.* Third edition. Boston: Northeastern University Press, 1999.

Aung San Suu Kyi (1991):

Political Leader, Prisoner, Pacifist

(June 19, 1945–)

Aung San Suu Kyi, Nobel Peace Laureate 1991.

The doors to the conference room burst open, and men carrying rifles rushed into the meeting. Bullets sprayed the people and the walls. Bleeding, General Aung San—the young father of three children and the leader of the Anti-Fascist People's Freedom League (AFPFL)—collapsed to the floor and gasped his last breaths. U Aung San had given his life trying to help his country, his people, and his family to attain freedom from the military rule in Burma. Now he and six other leaders of the AFPFL could no longer help their country in its quest for freedom (Ling, 26).

General Aung San (February 13, 1915–July 19, 1947) had been a leader in Burma's struggle against the government that had illegally seized power. His personal search for peace and democracy had ended. His life was over without even a final goodbye to his wife and children. His influence, however, would continue in the days to come (Parenteau, 56–57).

General Aung San's daughter—named Aung San (for her father) Suu (for Tuesday, the day of the week on which she was born and for her grandmother) Kyi (for her mother)— was an innocent victim of the 1947 assassination of her father. Although Suu (June 19, 1945–) was only two at the time of her father's death, she soon realized the results of violence in the world. Her young, widowed mother—Daw Khin Kyi—kept the memory of her husband alive in her home and in Burma. To ensure that young Suu and her family remembered that U Aung San had given his life for others, she held a memorial for him each month; Buddhist monks helped with the monthly memorial services. Daw Khin Kyi did not want anyone to forget that her husband had been a victim of violence and a martyr for freedom for the people of Burma. Khin Kyi even served the people of Burma by assuming her late husband's seat in parliament for a time; later she went on to a career of service to others by pursuing the nursing profession (Parenteau, 59).

From an early age, Suu's family encouraged the young girl always to communicate with others. Reminders of the violent death of her father and the model of her widowed mother rearing three children without a spouse caused Suu to detest violence and to try to get along with others—and there were many people in their household with whom to practice these skills. Aunts and uncles helped run their home; they came and went regularly. As a nurse, Khin Kyi opened their home to nursing students of all nationalities. Suu had the opportunity to associate with people of various religious beliefs. Suu herself was Buddhist, but her grandfather was Christian; Suu often read his Bible aloud to him (Parenteau, 57–63).

The joy of associating with others coupled with her personal experience with those who killed rather than talked must have encouraged Suu's desire to communicate with others and to find harmony. She especially believed in talking with those with whom she had the greatest disagreements. Aung San Suu Kyi saw early in her life the rewards of respecting others and promoting understanding. She read her father's words and learned from others about his leadership style: humility and "profound simplicity." She vowed to serve others humbly and, when needed to do so, to lead wisely.

Besides her father, Suu had another model of dedication to duty and country; this other great teacher was her mother. Tragedy struck Suu's family again in 1953 when Suu's nine-year-old brother Aung San Lin drowned in a local pond. Suu was devastated; Aung San Lin was next to his sister Suu in age and had been very close to her. Though grief-stricken at the loss of her son, Daw Khin Kyi felt such devotion to her country and to her duty that she finished the workday before returning home to view her son's body and to be with her family. Suu always remembered those traits of her mother (Parenteau, 58, 137).

In 1960, Khin Kyi received an appointment as ambassador to India. Fifteen-year-old Aung San Suu Kyi accompanied her to New Delhi. Suu attended high school there at the Convent of Jesus and Mary. After graduation, she enrolled in New Delhi's Lady Shri Ram College (Parenteau, 63) or Delhi University (Ling, 34).

One of the people she studied there would influence her life and actions for years to come. This model was Mohandas K. ("Mahatma," which means "Great Soul") Gandhi, a martyr for peace and understanding. When the people of India tired of British rule of their country, Gandhi led the masses on their journey toward freedom. Mahatma Gandhi was not an emperor, a president, a prime minister, or an emperor. He was merely a man who loved India and its people and wanted freedom and respect for them. Suu read about his peaceful means of accomplishing his goals (Parenteau, 64).

When Great Britain sought to enforce its rule in India by shooting the unarmed masses who protested the presence of British troops, Gandhi began to talk and to try to help. He practiced peaceful resistance to brutality and hate; he encouraged others not to take up arms of war. Rather than using violence to try to achieve changes in government and to bring consideration for his people, Gandhi resorted to voluntary starvation. His peaceful practices hurt only himself, but they showed his determination to earn the proper respect for the people of India. Gandhi went days at a time without food to show his concern for his land and the people. Though nominated for the Nobel Peace Prize five times, Gandhi never received it (Parenteau, 63–65).

After Gandhi's last nomination for the Nobel Peace Prize, his life—like the life of U Aung San—ended with his assassination. The Nobel Peace Prize Committee had never presented an award posthumously—and Gandhi did not receive the prize after his death either. In deference to Gandhi, however, the Nobel Peace Prize Committee made no award in 1948; the committee members "respectfully left open" the place that would probably have been his.

On March 2, 1962, the military overthrew Burma's elected government and seized power. Suu feared for her people in Burma (Parenteau, 65– 76).

Suu continued her pursuit of a broad education, learned of life in other countries, and began to consider how she could serve others. She attended St. Hugh's College in Oxford from 1964–67; St. Hugh's was one of five single-sex colleges at Oxford University in England. Ann Pasternak Slater, a classmate at St. Hugh's and a friend of Suu's through the years, described her during her college years as "genuinely innocent" and "laughably naive" ("Suu Burmese," Slater, *Freedom from Fear*, 293). Slater wrote also that Suu was "kind by conviction as well as by nature" and possessed "pertinacity" ("Suu Burmese," Slater, *Freedom from Fear*, 297).

While Suu was in Oxford, her friends Sir Paul Gore-Booth and his wife Patricia welcomed her to their home. Sir Paul had been ambassador to Burma and had a high commissioner in New Delhi, India; Suu had met him when he held those positions. At their home she met Michael Aris, a young British student who was majoring in Tibetan studies (Ling, 40). Michael became her friend and, some five years later, her husband (Stewart, 45). During the summers when she was not in school, Suu traveled to Africa and Spain. While she was in Algiers, Suu's kindness evidenced itself to many: She helped build homes for the widows of Algerian soldiers.

Suu earned the B.A. in Philosophy, Politics, and Economics from Oxford. After graduation, she spent 1969–71 working as Assistant Secretariat to the Advisory Committee on Administration and Budgetary Questions at the United Nations in New York. She also found time to volunteer her services at Bellevue Hospital in New York, where she befriended and helped the mentally ill hospitalized there (Parenteau, 65–76; Stewart, 48).

While Suu worked in New York, she corresponded with Michael Aris, who was residing in Bhutan. Michael saved the 187 letters he received from Suu in the eight months while she was in New York and he was in Bhutan in the Himalayan Mountains. In her letters, Suu wrote often of her felt obligations to the Burmese people (*Freedom from Fear and Other Writings*, xviii–xix). Michael described "inevitability" in her role as peace icon to her people; Suu seemed to sense her role-to-be even during their courtship. Michael quoted from Suu's letters in his Introduction to her *Freedom from Fear and Other Writings*:

> I only ask one thing, that should my people need me, you would help me to do my duty by them.
> Would you mind very much should a situation ever arise? How probable it is I do not know, but the possibility is there.
> Sometimes I am beset by fears that circumstances and national considerations might tear us apart just when we are so happy in each other that separation would be a torment ... [*Freedom from Fear*, Aung San Suu Kyi, xix].

In 1971, Suu made a trip to Burma; she visited with Michael in Bhutan on her way back to New York. She accepted Michael's proposal of marriage before she returned to the United States (Stewart, 55). They married in London on January 1, 1972 (*Freedom from Fear*, xix).

After their marriage, Suu traveled with her husband, now a British Tibetan scholar, to Japan and to India. The couple then moved to Bhutan and enjoyed their time there. By foot, Jeep, or donkey they traveled with their Himalayan terrier, Puppy, into the mountains. Michael tutored the royal family there and headed the Translation Department. Suu became the Research Officer on United Nations Affairs for the Bhutan Foreign Ministry (Ling, 44).

Despite living elsewhere, Suu still felt an obligation to Rangoon and to her country of Burma. Michael understood his wife's commitment and sense of duty to Burma. He accepted the fact that she might someday have to go back to her homeland to lead and to serve her people.

The couple returned to London in 1973 for the birth of Alexander, their first son. In 1974 Michael accepted a position in Tibetan and Himalayan Studies at Oxford University. Three years later, Suu gave birth to Kim, their second son, in Oxford.

When Oxford turned down Suu's application to pursue graduate work, she decided to do some research and writing (Parenteau, 76). She worked to catalogue the Burmese books in the Bodleian Library at Oxford University from 1975 until 1977 (Stewart, 58).

Suu wanted to learn more about her father, who had given his life for others. In 1984, after much study and research, she was able to publish her first book, *Aung San* (Parenteau, 76).

Suu is the first to admit that "[w]riting about a person to whom one is closely related is a difficult task, and the author is open to possible accusations of insufficient objectivity.... For myself, I can only say that I have tried to give an honest picture of my father as I see him" [*Freedom from Fear*, 3].

Determined to know more about her father, the martyr Aung San, Suu decided to interview those in Japan who had known him. In 1985, after teaching herself to speak

Japanese, Suu and their son Kim—then about eight years old—traveled to Japan to gather information on her father's (Kim's grandfather's) trips there in 1941–42 (Parenteau, 72). In 1991 she was able to publish her second edition of *Aung San of Burma: A Biographical Portrait by His Daughter.*

While the younger son traveled with his mother, Michael and 12-year-old Alex remained in India. Michael had a fellowship at the Indian Institute of Advanced Studies in Simla. Kim and Suu joined Michael and Alex in India as soon as their work in Japan was complete.

Michael, Suu, and their two sons moved to England where Michael, an Oxford scholar, continued his writings on the Himalayas and Tibet. Suu continued to study and read. She wrote *Let's Visit Burma* (1985), *Let's Visit Nepal* (1985), *Let's Visit Bhutan* (1986), and several scholarly papers during this time (Parenteau, 77). Burma was receiving publicity; on December 11, 1987, the country received the questionable recognition from the United Nations of becoming the Least Developed Country (Stewart, 67). The once "Golden Land" had become a land in agony (Schraff, 90).

Suu entered the graduate program at London University's School of Oriental and Asian Studies. She was eager to pursue graduate work and planned to prepare her doctoral dissertation on Burmese literature (Parenteau, 77). The young couple might have continued their life in the world of academics but for two events.

On March 12, 1988, a petty fight at a teahouse near the Rangoon Institute of Technology changed the course of Suu's life. A few days later (March 31) Daw Khin Kyi suffered a severe stroke. After receiving the phone call about the life-threatening illness of Khin Kyi, Suu left immediately to nurse her gravely-ill mother in Rangoon (Parenteau, 78–84).

During the trivial argument on March 12, the son of the teahouse owner had stabbed college student Win Myint. The next morning, the college students found that the person who had wielded the knife was free. They feared that the teahouse owner's son would not receive punishment because his father was a member of the People's Council and belonged to the Burma Socialist Program Party (Myanma Sosialit Lanzin Pati)—the party in power. The students gathered before the People's Council and demanded compensation and apologies. The employees called the police; when the riot officers arrived, the angry students began to throw bottles. Gunshots rang out, and a student (*Maung* Phone Maw) died from the gunfire (Parenteau, 84–85). At least two other wounded students later died in the hospital from loss of blood and infection; chained to their beds, they could not seek help (Stewart, 70).

The death of their comrades seemed the breaking point. College students and college graduates in Burma had been growing increasingly disgruntled. They had had little opportunity to use their skills in the country with the new government. This dissatisfaction was coupled with the reduced value of the currency and the use of military power to enforce the government. The fight in a teahouse turned into a protest against the government.

Police brutality mounted. This violence should not have surprised the students. In an earlier incident, the military had killed a thousand students who protested the rise of the new government and demanded the proper burial in 1974 of U Thant, the Burma-born third secretary-general of the United Nations (Parenteau, 84–85).

Despite the military threat to the well-being of protestors, the assembled students from the Rangoon Institute of Technology and Rangoon University began a march from

Rangoon University to the Institute of Technology (Stewart, 71). They used the bloody shirt of the slain student as a banner (Parenteau, 84–85).

The police surprised the protestors as they marched from Rangoon University, up Prome Road, and by Inya Lake. The military officers trapped the students, fired shots, beat the girls and the boys, and drove some protestors from the White Bridge over Inya Lake. A hundred students died from beatings and from drowning; witnesses said some of the soldiers held the students under the water until they died (Stewart, 71). The government, however, did not admit either to the number of lost lives or to the claims of violence that the students leveled against them.

On March 17, the students assembled for the funeral of *Maung* Phone Maw only to learn that the body had been cremated. The students demanded compensation for the boy's family, a funeral, economic reform, and democracy. The police broke up the assembly, sent a thousand students to jail, closed the universities, and called in the army. Hundreds of protestors suffered wounds; many would later die from these injuries. The students called the day "Bloody Friday" and gave Sein Lwin, the police chief, the nickname "The Butcher of Burma."

By the time that Suu arrived on March 31 to tend her ailing mother, peace seemed to have returned to Burma. Suu did not feel peaceful, however. She found that her mother was very ill and required constant care. Moreover, Suu saw the unrest begin to mount again. The hospital where her mother stayed was the site of many demonstrations. The government at last reopened the universities on May 30 (Parenteau, 84–85).

Released students began to tell and write of their mistreatment. The government, however, would admit only to three deaths and 400 arrests. The students demanded that the government submit an honest report by June 17. On that day the government again closed the universities; the government officials would not change their earlier statements.

Meanwhile, the arrested students continued their claims that the police had treated them inhumanely; they reported that 42 students had suffocated in a crowded van and that mutilations and torture were common among those imprisoned (Parenteau, 85).

On June 17 the government ordered the universities again to close. The student demonstrations, however, did not cease. This time workers, citizens, and even Buddhist monks joined in the protests. Suu realized that the demonstrators were about to turn violent, but she remained at her mother's side and watched the unorganized people try to advance their cause. Her top priority was the care of her mother; the time was not right for her efforts for her country to begin (Parenteau, 86).

On June 20 the police (Lon Htein) sealed off the university. The protestors—armed with slingshots and sharpened bicycle spokes for use as projectiles—continued their demonstrations. It seemed the protestors had won and Ne Win resigned (Parenteau, 87).

General Ne Win appointed police chief Sein Lwin the "Butcher of Burma," as the new chair of the Special Congress (Stewart, 74). Sein Lwin was probably the only person in the land more despised by the masses than Ne Win, who had been in power since 1962 (Parenteau, 88).

Thousands of college students—supported by high school students, Buddhist monks, and workers—assembled in a show of protest. The protests continued over the next month, but still Suu remained involved with the care of her mother.

It became apparent that Khin Kyi was not going to recover. The two left the hospital and went to the family home on University Avenue in Rangoon. Suu believed that her mother would be more comfortable spending her last days in familiar surroundings. Once established in her mother's house, Suu became more involved in the political situation; her first priority, however, remained the care of her mother.

On the eighth day of the eighth month of the year 1988, at 8 minutes past 8:00 A.M., 100,000 peaceful protestors of the military government of Burma assembled on the streets of Rangoon. Similar assemblies occurred across the country. Although Suu was not present at any of the demonstrations, her message of non-violence was present in the actions of the participants.

The government demanded that the people leave. Many believe that if the officers had not done that, the assembly would have adjourned as it had begun: peacefully. Instead of dispersing, however, the crowds now seemed to increase. The army began to fire haphazardly into the crowds. An estimated 3,000 unarmed citizens died under the bullets of the soldiers over the next four days; the people called this tragic series of events the "Four Eights" strike (Parenteau, 92–93).

Afterwards, the army indiscriminately dumped bodies—both wounded and dead—outside the Rangoon General Hospital. Observers noted that when nurses came out to claim the patients and beg for a halt to the violence, the armed soldiers would turn the fire on the unarmed health care workers (Parenteau, 96).

Suu sent an open letter to the Burma Socialist Program Party (BSPP) on August 15. She urged non-violence from the demonstrators and the military and asked for the release of the political prisoners (Ling, 53).

Sein Lwin, the head of the government of Burma, finally resigned. Many saw the resignation of the "Butcher of Burma" as the only alternative to civil war in the country. Maung Maung, who was an attorney, newspaper publisher, and historian, replaced him in September 1988 (Parenteau, 96–97).

Suu issued a very modest statement to the government. Her letter quoted Ne Win, a former leader of Burma and a friend of Maung Maung, the current ruler of Burma: "If we should have to choose between the good of the party and the good of the nation, we should choose the good of the nation." The government ignored her pleas for peace and prisoner release (Parenteau, 98–99).

Suu appeared briefly at Rangoon General Hospital on August 24, 1988. She told the people of her intention to speak again on August 26; this next speech would be at the Schwedagon Pagoda. Some followers immediately went to the pagoda to camp out and wait for the event (Parenteau, 101).

Between 500,000 and one million people gathered on August 26 to listen to Suu's first political speech. Among those present were Michael and their two sons; they had come to support her (Parenteau, 102–03). Suu began her speech with a greeting to the "Reverend monks and people" and immediately gave the purpose of the assembly: "to show that the entire people entertain the keenest desire for a multi-party democratic system of government" ("Speech to a Mass Rally at the Schwedagon Pagoda," page 192 in *Freedom from Fear and Other Writings* by Aung San Suu Kyi, London: Penguin Books, 1995). Next Suu openly professed her love for Burma and reminded the audience of the place that her family had occupied through the years. Several times during her speech she called for the Burmese people to "always be united and disciplined" and quoted her father:

> We must make democracy the popular creed. We must try to build up a free Burma in accordance with such a creed. If we should fail to do this, our people are bound to suffer.... Democracy is the only ideology that is consistent with freedom. It is also an ideology that promotes and strengthens peace. It is therefore the only ideology we should aim for [Aung San

Suu Kyi, "Speech to a Mass Rally at the Schwedagon Pagoda," page 194 in Aung San Suu Kyi's *Freedom from Fear and Other Writings*].

Suu begged for

... no splits and struggles between the army, which my father built up, and the people who love my father so much. May I also from this platform ask the personnel of the armed forces to reciprocate this kind of understanding and sympathy? [Aung San Suu Kyi, "Speech to a Mass Rally at the Schwedagon Pagoda," page 194 in Aung San Suu Kyi's *Freedom from Fear and Other Writings*].

Her first appeals—for democracy and peace—remained her constant pleas to the army, the people, and the leaders. She asked the masses to forgive the army for the deaths and encouraged the government to give the people reason to trust again. She denounced the violence that the protestors, the armies, and the police displayed. Her words stopped some of the people from fighting against the soldiers in the streets.

Suu called herself "my father's daughter" and viewed her work as a continuation of the work that her father had begun. She reiterated her aims of achieving democracy for the country without further violence or deaths (Parenteau, 102–03).

Kreager had definite views on Suu's position in Burma. He called her a "clear leader, advocating non-violent methods." He saw her as one who commanded "widespread admiration and support." Kreager, however, described her position as "at once formidable and extremely vulnerable." He noted that she was—and continues to be—"at the mercy of a military regime which retains power by the use of force" (Kreager, "Aung San Suu Kyi and the Peaceful Struggle for Human Rights in Burma," 318–10).

After her mass appeal, the government began to free prisoners, but it released criminals as well as protestors. Crime in the country mounted. Perhaps the government hoped that Suu would receive the blame for the problems that resulted.

General Saw Maung had served under Ne Win; now head of the army, General Saw Maung ousted Maung Maung's government and ended the Burmese Socialist Program Party, the *Ma Sa La* (Parenteau, 108–09).

General Saw Maung called his new government the State Law and Order Restoration Council (SLORC). He promised a referendum on democracy, as had his friend, dictator Ne Win (Stewart, 84). The people, however, were dubious about General Saw Maung's actually giving them the referendum and about the leadership. They wanted democracy immediately, and they wanted to elect their own leader (Parenteau, 96–97). The State Law and Order Restoration Council (SLORC) and its army now ruled. The violence in the streets continued. Some placed the dead at 10,000. Many protestors began fleeing to Thailand (Parenteau, 108–09).

On September 24, Suu became secretary of the newly-formed National League for Democracy (NLD). She worked from her mother's home to help the NLD, the political party that called for an end to violence and the restoration of law and order. The NLD was a legal organization, but the military government sometimes called for the arrest of NLD leaders. Nevertheless, Suu counseled, advised, and urged non-violence among NLD members. She tried to spread the word throughout the world that Burma's people were suffering abuse (Parenteau, 111).

Lintner described Suu as "the only one who could unify all segments of Burmese society: the urban as well as the rural population, the young student radicals and the older, much more moderate pro-democracy advocates" (Lintner, *Burma in Revolt*, 277 as cited in Stewart, 87).

From September until December, confusion ruled. The government and the military were particularly brutal to college students who opposed their control and who demanded a voice in the government. The government placed thousands of these students in prisons; the military corralled the naked youth like cattle and shipped them to the front lines for a war begun 40 years before their "draft."

Suu's mother's health continued to fail. Even after her valiant struggle for life and even with the tender care of her daughter Suu, 75-year-old Daw Khin Kyi died on December 27, 1988.

About 100,000 people lined Rangoon's streets on January 2, 1989, for the funeral. Suu asked the crowd to be calm and disciplined. She reminded them that they were "sending my mother on her last journey" (Parenteau, 112–13).

After the funeral, Suu began to work for democracy with all her strength. The house on University Avenue became a center for political activity. Suu traveled from village to village to speak with the people each day. She continued to advocate unity and discipline, but her message always included non-violence (Parenteau, 89–90).

The State Law and Order Restoration Council (SLORC) worked against Suu in every way possible. The military played loud music to drown out her words when she tried to speak. They arrested her. They put up barbed wire fences to keep her out of the towns and the villages. The SLORC threatened to harm anyone who came to her speeches. They made good on their promises and imprisoned many of the people who gathered to listen.

The SLORC began to work against Suu and the NLD with words. They said that Suu was not a patriot of Burma because she had married a foreigner and had lived outside the country. They printed many of their lies where the people would be sure to read them. The members of SLORC declared that the NLD was a group of Communists. They blamed Suu and NLD for all the problems in Burma (Parenteau, 117).

During 1989, a year of upheaval, the SLORC even changed the name of the country: Burma became Myanmar. The explanation was that many cultural groups besides the Burmese lived within its borders (Parenteau, 117). The SLORC declared that English-speaking people should use Myanmar instead of Burma when referring to the country. The Burmese people were furious about a name change in which they had no voice (Stewart, 87).

At last, the SLORC agreed to an election in the spring of 1990, a year away. The Council did not, however, announce an exact date. The Council recognized the NLD as a legal party, but the SLORC refused to allow the NLD to campaign for the election.

Suu tried to organize the masses through secret videotapes and through broadcasts on short wave radio bands; she even dared to name Ne Win as the person to blame for their woes. Suu's jacket and hat became a fashion statement and a symbol of the NLD Party (Parenteau, 117).

Suu conclusively proved her determination and fearlessness on April 5, 1989 (Parenteau, 117). When an assembled group of the NLD began walking down the street, six armed soldiers knelt and aimed their rifles directly at her. She did not hesitate. She continued walking calmly in the direction that she was going. An army major countermanded the order and the soldiers lowered their rifles without firing (Silverstein, *Freedom from Fear*, 309). Myint Oo, a captain in the SLORC, received a promotion for his planned attack on Suu (Stewart, 88).

The story of Suu's bravery in the face of danger spread far and wide. The event brought even more supporters for the NLD. The soldier who did not fire received a demotion.

The government declared that the National Union Party was the only political party that could meet and publish papers. The members published rumors about Suu and printed papers with obscene drawings of her (Parenteau, 117).

Still, the NLD won most of the seats in the election in May 1989. The military government remained in power and refused to allow the NLD to assume its elected positions. The SLORC would not concede the election and punished the NLD members (Parenteau, 14–15).

On Martyr's Day in July 1989, Suu planned to speak at the grave of her father. The SLORC feared what might happen when she spoke. They decreed that no assembly on Martyr's Day was legal. Those who assembled might face death, life in prison, or three years at hard labor. Two days before the scheduled speech, mass arrests began. The police cut phone lines to many homes and businesses. The army invaded the villages and towns (Parenteau, 119–20).

On June 20, 1989, the SLORC made a new ruling. The organization decreed that the government could detain anyone for up to three years without a trial or without charges. The SLORC immediately placed Suu under arrest (Ling, 65). (Schraff on page 86 mistakenly gives the date as July 20, 1988.) Suu received punishment without a charge or a trial. Suu could not leave her home; her family could be her only visitors. Her sons Kim and Alexander remained with her (Parenteau, 120–21).

Suu was not surprised by her arrest. She asked to enter the prison with the NLD members who were there; she believed her presence might help them to receive better treatment. She worried about her sons; before her captors cut her phone line, she let her relatives know about her detainment and asked that they contact Michael for her. She asked that they secure the boys if something happened to her. Her calmness reassured her boys; they remained peaceful also (Ling, 66–67).

Michael rushed to her side. He had flown to Scotland for the funeral of his father, but he returned immediately when he learned what had happened. He found his wife confined to their home and in the third day of a hunger strike (Parenteau, 120–21). He saw her engagement in the struggle in Burma as "unavoidable"; her inevitable participation caused her "to draw on ... her very finely cultivated sense of commitment and her powers of reason." He saw her as being both "blessed and burdened with her unique status as the daughter of the national hero" (Aris, "Introduction," Aung San Suu Kyi's *Freedom from Fear*, p. xx).

Michael wrote in the Introduction to Suu's *Freedom from Fear*:

[I]t came as no surprise when Suu told me she was resolved to enter the struggle. The promise to support her decision which I had given in advance so many years ago now had to be fulfilled. Like Suu perhaps, I had imagined if a day of reckoning were to come, it would happen later in life when our children were grown up. But fate and history never seem to work in orderly ways ... factors conspired with the sad circumstances of her mother's final illness to make her engagement unavoidable [Aris, "Introduction," Aung San Suu Kyi's *Freedom from Fear*, p. xx].

Like Mahatma Gandhi before her, Suu was using passive starvation to demand humane treatment of NLD members. Her peaceful means to bring about change became world news. When *Time* publicized her arrest, the SLORC began to be more lenient. Finally, the Council assured her that NLD members would receive fair treatment. She stopped her fasting after losing 12 pounds in 12 days when she learned of their promise to give more consideration to the NLD members. Michael wrote:

The days I spent alone with her that last time, completely isolated from the world, are among my happiest memories of our many years of marriage. It was wonderfully peaceful.... We had all the time in the world to talk about many things. I did not suspect that this [time between July 20 and September 2, 1989] would be the last time we would be together for the foreseeable future [Aris, "Introduction," Aung San Suu Kyi's *Freedom from Fear*, p. xxv].

Kim and Alexander needed to return to school, and Michael needed to return to work. The three left Suu, who was still under house arrest, on September 2, 1989; the SLORC agreed to allow Suu to receive and send letters to her family (Parenteau, 121).

Suu was eager for her boys to return to England and safety. The three left Suu with hopes of a reunion at Christmas, but it was not to be. The government canceled both Kim's and Alexander's visas. Only Michael was able to return that year (Ling, 69).

Burma began to plan its first "true" election since 1960. "Laws," however, prevented the campaigning of certain candidates. Voters at the polls found that many names on the ballot, like Suu's, did not appear. In the election on May 27, 1990, the NLD won large victories. The NLD had won more than two-thirds of the popular vote and more than 80 percent of the seats in the legislature (Parenteau, 122).

The SLORC, however, did not accept its defeat. The Council declared that the election was to choose those who would form a committee to write a new constitution. It would not, however, allow the committee to meet. The human rights group Asia Watch noted that throughout Burma, arrests, torture, beatings, and sleep deprivation continued as punishments for those who opposed the government; the party in power had issued more than 100 death sentences for protestors. In July, Suu found that her house arrest would continue for another year (Parenteau, 123). The SLORC hoped that separating Suu from her husband and children, placing barbed wire about the house, cutting the phone lines, and preventing visitors would cause her to leave Myanmar (Burma). Suu remained determined, however. She had seen the examples of her parents before her (Stewart, 91).

Life under house arrest was difficult for Suu. Neighbors reported that until 1991 she played the piano daily, but her music suddenly ceased. Michael found on his later visit the reason for the quiet: The strings and keys of her piano had broken and worn out from constant use (Parenteau, 127).

Suu tried to maintain her dignity. She refused to accept any food or financial aid from her captors and paid for everything she used. When Michael finally received permission to visit, he filled his luggage with food for his wife. When he left, he took with him the writings that Suu had produced in her long hours alone.

To maintain her health, Suu exercised vigorously each day, read, and studied the literature she loved. She wrote to encourage others and to advance peace (Parenteau, 126). She refused favors from her captors (Ling, 75). Her weight of 106 pounds sometimes dropped below 100; her hair fell out from malnutrition (Stewart, 96). Her vision became poor, and she developed degeneration of the spinal column (spondylosis) because of an improper diet. Finally she developed heart problems that led to breathing difficulties. Still she refused to accept money from her captors (Ling, 76).

Her maid Maria made arrangements to sell Suu's furniture, her bathtubs, and her air conditioner (Ling, 76); the SLORC gave Suu the money for the items. However, the SLORC did not sell the possessions but stored them instead. Suu refused to accept the furniture back; she insisted she would buy it back when she had the money (Stewart, 96).

The world began to recognize the sacrifices Suu was making for her people. On October 12, 1990, the Rafto Human Rights Prize went to Suu. On July 10 the European Parliament granted her the Sakharov Human Rights Prize. On October 14, 1991, the Norwegian Nobel Peace Prize Committee announced Aung San Suu Kyi as the newest Nobel Peace Prize winner (Parenteau, 125). Michael Aris held a news conference at Harvard University in Cambridge, Massachusetts, where he was a visiting professor. He admitted that he was deeply concerned about his wife whom he had not seen or heard from in almost two years; he said he was not sure if she was alive and had no idea if she knew about the honor (Ling, 78). Suu did know about the award; she had heard the announcement via her short-wave radio (Ling, 79).

The world eagerly awaited the Nobel Prize ceremonies on December 10, 1991, but fear and anxiety marked the event. More than 1500 dignitaries assembled in City Hall in Oslo, Norway. These guests from across the world wanted to witness the presentation (Parenteau, 11).

The winner—Daw (Mrs.) Aung San Suu Kyi—was not in attendance. The military in Burma (Myanmar) had held her under house arrest since July 1989. Her picture, her husband, and her two sons (Kim, then 12, and Alexander, then 16) represented Suu to the audience. Her two sons accepted the prize on her behalf. Francis Sejersted, chair of the Nobel Peace Prize Committee, presented the gold medal to Alexander and the honorary diploma to Kim. The response of the audience of 1500 was a standing ovation (Ling, 80). Alexander stated that the dedication and sacrifices of his mother had made her a worthy symbol to the Burmese people (Parenteau, 11–12).

The same night as the Oslo celebration, the Prime Minister of Oslo, Gro Harlem Boundtland, led hundreds of Burmese supporters of Aung San Suu Kyi and of the National League for Democracy (NLD) in a march. Law enforcement officials arrested about 900 marchers; two students died in the demonstrations (Parenteau, 12–13).

Michael had assembled some of Suu's writings in a collection called *Freedom from Fear* (1991; reprinted in 1995 with the addition of several articles that others wrote about Suu). Alexander read to the gathered audience some of her words from the book. An important message was that fear—not power—corrupts a person or nation. Her words urged fearlessness; the Nobel Peace Prize Committee acknowledged Suu as a model of determination and bravery in her pursuit of peace.

Suu used none of the Nobel Prize money for herself. With the more than $1 million, she established the Burma Trust for Education (Ling, 97). Suu had received more than 20 humanitarian awards by 1991. As with the Nobel Peace Prize honorarium, however, she refused to accept any of the money for herself. She declared that the money should improve the health and education of the people of her country (Stewart, 102). The only income she had for food and necessities was the royalties from the book *Freedom from Fear* that Michael had edited; the royalty checks went into her bank account in Rangoon so that the maid could make withdrawals from this account for Suu's needs (Stewart, 100).

The SLORC publicly insisted that Suu could have attended the presentation ceremonies. What the government did not admit, however, was that it might not have permitted Suu to re-enter the country. Suu elected to remain in Myanmar, confined to her home, so that she could be close to her people (Parenteau, 129).

A group of Nobel Peace Laureates tried to visit Suu in December 1992. The group included Betty Williams and Mairead Corrigan, the 1976 Nobel winners; the Dalai Lama (the 1989 Nobel Peace Prize winner), Oscar Arias Sanchez (the 1987 Nobel Peace Prize winner), and Bishop Desmond Tutu (the 1984 Nobel Peace Prize winner). The government rejected their visa applications. The group visited Burmese refugees in Thailand and called publicly for Suu's release (Stewart, 107; Ling 84). They repeated their appeals at the UN Commission for Human Rights in Geneva, Switzerland (Parenteau, 129).

On Valentine's Day of 1994, the government allowed Bill Richardson, a member of the United States Congress, to visit Suu. This was the first contact Suu had had with a non–family member, besides the maid, since 1989 (Parenteau, 129).

Through the mediation of a Buddhist monk, Suu, and others, the SLORC released Suu on July 10, 1995, and she was able to conference with her captors (Stewart, 111). Archbishop Desmond Tutu wrote about her release and the conference:

Aung San Suu Kyi is free. How wonderful—quite unbelievable.

It is so very like when Nelson Mandela walked out of prison on that February day in 1990, and strode with so much dignity into freedom. And the world thrilled at the sight.

The world is exultant, too, at the news of Suu Kyi's release from the six years of house arrest which prevented her from becoming the leader of her beloved country after her National League for Democracy [392 of 485 seats, Stewart, 98] a landslide victory in the 1990 elections....

How wonderful that Aung San Suu Kyi's first public utterance after her release should be a clarion call to all the major role-players for dialogue and reconciliation! ["Foreword to the Second Edition," Tutu, p. xv, from Aung San Suu Kyi's *Freedom from Fear*].

The world hoped for her immediate release, but it was not to be. Further tragedy struck Suu's family. Michael developed prostate cancer. In very ill health, he asked to enter Burma and to visit his wife one last time. Michael had not seen his wife since 1995; his allotted time was very limited because the cancer was severe. The governmental authorities continued to deny his request to visit his spouse, but they told Suu that she might leave the country to visit Michael. Suu sadly decided to remain inside the boundaries of her country. She knew the authorities would never allow her to recross its borders and return to Myanmar (Burma). She—like her mother before her—chose not to neglect her country and her duty.

Her followers have often feared for her life. With her phone lines severed and her visitors restricted, oral communication with others has not always been possible. Her writing has helped console her, encourage others, and inform the public as to what was happening. Another book *Letters from Burma* (1998) is evidence of her work and words.

Suu's life of confinement has not been easy. Michael died on March 27, 1999, in London. Like his father-in-law Aung San before him, Michael was not able to say goodbye to his wife. Suu was not present to bid him goodbye personally and to tell him again of her love.

From September 2000 until May 2002, while the NLD was meeting secretly to break the political deadlock, Suu found herself again under house arrest. European officials arrived in Myanmar on March 13 to try to encourage democratic reforms, to work to end the nation's isolation, and to help with what Suu had tried to accomplish for years.

In the first years of the twenty-first century, then, there was still no peace in Myanmar. On March 10, 2002, Myanmar authorities arrested U Ne Win and his family. The man who ruled for 26 years until his 1988 retirement found his home sealed. The government stated that the family (the son-in-law and his sons) and some of the leaders of the current government were plotting to seize control of the government. Even U Ne Win's wife and daughter discovered that the government had restricted them to their home; they could not have visitors and could not use their phone. The government described its actions as a way to protect the people.

In 2002, Myanmar still remained under the tight military reign of the State Peace and Development Council (SPDC), a political group that was formerly the SLORC. Suu continued her efforts to communicate with the government on behalf of the people.

Suu was not free. The government of Myanmar continued to place restrictions on her. She did not believe—even in the new century—that she would ever be able to return to her country if she should leave. Myanmar did not have the liberty to elect its own government. The people could not elect the government and the officials they wanted. Suu began to appeal to the outside world for sanctions to bring pressure on the SLORC. Suu discouraged travelers from visiting Myanmar for vacations and as tourists. She hoped this would be a sign of non-support for the military government and would limit the government financially (Ling, 92).

In May 2003 she again found herself in "protective custody" as confrontations between the military government and the NLD increased (http://www.who2.com/aungsansuukyi.html).

To show their support, the singers Eric Clapton and Paul McCartney and the popular bands U2, Indigo Girls, R.E.M., and Pearl Jam launched an album on October 25, 2004. The album symbolizes the freedom that the musicians endorse for Burma. They titled it "For the Lady: Dedicated to Freeing Aung San Suu Kyi and the Courageous People of Burma." These artists specified that profits from the sales of the album would benefit the non-profit group the United States Coalition for Burma (USCB), which seeks an end to the military rule of the deprived people of Myanmar ("On Two"). Among the 27 tracks on the Rhino Records CD is a song titled "Walk On"; the band U2 dedicated the song, which the military regime of Myanmar (Burma) banned, to Suu. Even singing this song (or *any* song about the quest for freedom) can bring a minimum jail term of seven years in Myanmar.

Jeremy Woodrum, the founder of the USCB, commented from his Washington office about the banning of the album and the songs about freedom. He said, "The fact that the country's dictators are threatened by songs from Paul McCartney, Eric Clapton, Sting and others shows how weak they truly are" (Kammerer).

At the time of the release of the album, Suu had spent most of the past 14 years under house arrest ("Album to Benefit Burmese Activist"). Though her house arrest had been hard on Suu, she believed that she has had a full life. She had lived with courage and had tried to teach this fearlessness to her own sons (Spera, 25).

Peace seems hard to find in Burma, but Suu has not given up hope. She remains committed to freedom for all people (http://www.dassk.org/contents.php?id+870).

She encourages peace and freedom in her country and for the world. She has allowed PeaceJam, an international education organization that works to address the problems that teenagers face, to use her name. She likes the fact that the organization helps to bring peace, meaning, and integrity into their lives. She hopes that the group will inspire a new generation of peacemakers and that they will transform their communities, their countries, and the world. Some other female Nobel Peace Prize winners (Mairead Corrigan, Betty Williams, Rigoberta Menchu, and Jody Williams, for instance) have also endorsed the work of PeaceJam (Ling, 99; www.peacejam.org).

Many people have attempted to write biographies of Aung San Suu Kyi. Suu herself, however, does not plan to write of her life until she knows "the final outcome."

Bibliography

"Album to Benefit Burmese Activist." *The Ottawa Citizen*, September 24, 2004, page D4.

"Aung San Suu Kyi: A Who2 Profile." Available online at http://www.who2.com/aungsansuukyi.html.

Aung San Suu Kyi. Web site http://www.dassk.org.

Kammerer, Peter. "Rock Stars' Album for Suu Kyi Banned." *South China Morning Post*, October 21, 2004, 10.

Kreager, Philip. "Aung San Suu Kyi and the Peaceful Struggle for Human Rights in Burma." In *Freedom from Fear and Other Writings* by Aung San Suu Kyi. London: Penguin Books, 1995, 318–59.

Kyi, Aung San Suu. *Freedom from Fear and Other Writings*. London: Penguin Books, 1995.

Ling, Bettina. *Aung San Suu Kyi: Standing Up for Democracy in Burma*. New York: The Feminist Press at the City University of New York, 1999.

Lintner, Bertil. *Burma in Revolt: Opium and Insurgency Since 1948*. Boulder, Colorado: Westview Press, 1994.

"On Two." *Houston Chronicle*, September 24, 2004, Section A, 2.

Parenteau, John. *Prisoner for Peace: Aung San Suu Kyi and Burma's Struggle for Democracy*. Greensboro, North Carolina: Morgan Reynolds, 1994.

"Peace Jam–One Person Really Can Make a Difference." Web site www.peacejam.org

Schraff, Anne. *Women of Peace: Nobel Peace Prize Winners*. Hillside, New Jersey: Enslow, 1994.

Silverstein, Josef. "Aung San Suu Kyi: Is She Burma's Woman of Destiny?" In *Freedom from Fear and Other Writings* by Aung San Suu Kyi. London: Penguin Books, 1995, 310–17.

Slater, Ann Pasternak. "Suu Burmese." In *Freedom from Fear and Other Writings* by Aung San Suu Kyi. London: Penguin Books, 1995, 292–300.

Spera, Keith. "Spare Notes." *Times-Pacayune* (New Orleans). October 29, 2004, page 25.

Stewart, Whitney. *Aung San Suu Kyi: Fearless Voice of Burma*. Minneapolis: Lerner, 1997.

Tutu, Archbishop Desmond. "Foreword to the Second Edition." In *Freedom from Fear and Other Writings* by Aung San Suu Kyi. London: Penguin Books, 1995, xv–xvi.

Rigoberta Menchú Tum
(1992)
Human Rights Activist for Indigenous People
(January 9, 1959–)

Rigoberta Menchú Tum, Nobel Peace Laureate 1992.

The eight-year-old girl looked up at the hot sun overhead and wiped her damp face with the back of her hand. Her head hurt. Bending down for long hours to find the coffee beans that had fallen to the ground made her feel dizzy and sick to her stomach. Beside her in the coffee fields were adults and children bending over and picking beans from the bushes. Like Rigoberta, they were trying to earn enough money to feed themselves and their families (Schraff, 93).

Picking 35 pounds of coffee beans per day was difficult for even a teenager. Retrieving 35 pounds of beans from the ground was almost impossible for any eight-year-old. Yet young Rigoberta Menchú Tum was determined to earn the 20 centavos that the owner of the *finca* (plantation) paid for 35 pounds of coffee beans (Brill, 18). Rigoberta set for herself the goal of gathering 35 pounds of coffee beans; often she would not go to the shelter that housed the workers until she had reached her goal. By the time she was 12, Rigoberta could pick 70 pounds of coffee in a day and earn 35 centavos.

The roof of the *galera* (shelter), that housed the workers was made of banana leaves. There were no side walls. Three to four hundred men, women, and children slept in the shed at night. Even when no one was talking or whispering during the night, there was still noise from the breathing, snoring, coughing, and turning of exhausted workers. Tired, unwashed people who craved sleep at the end of 15-hour workdays in the blazing sun soon fell asleep in the hut. There were no days of rest. The laborers worked every day for a month before the lorry would take them back to their villages.

Outsiders viewing the sleeping quarters might never have realized that they were in the largest and richest country in Central America. The gap between the wealthy and the poor there remained great. Half of its 11 million people were Maya and lived in the Sierra Madre, the central and western highlands of the country.

Sometimes as she worked, Rigoberta thought about the ride that had brought her mother (Juana Tum Cotojá), her brother, and her to this place. Each family carried its own clothing, cooking utensils, and water jugs with them. There had been no stopping on the trip—unless the driver himself wanted to stop. Even then, he usually would not allow anyone to get out of the lorry.

The workers were unaccustomed to riding. On the bumpy, unpaved roads winding around the countryside, many became ill. The driver would refuse to stop, and they had to sit in their own vomit for the rest of the trip. Sometimes the trip would last for more than a day and night. Most of the passengers soiled themselves before it was over. Still they had to remain in the lorry. The heat and the odor were overwhelming. Most families carried their animals—usually dogs, cats, pigs, and chickens—with them because no one was left at home to care for the stock. Their noise and odor made things worse.

The field workers found no good way to wash when they arrived at the camp. There was no running water; bathing or washing clothes was almost impossible. The workers had to sleep in the same filthy clothes that they worked in each day. The smell of unwashed human bodies huddled together was almost unbearable even in the open shed. One night Rigoberta lit a candle and saw that the faces of the sleeping workers around her were black with mosquitoes.

Any sickness in the group spread rapidly. Babies died, and mothers lost their jobs for leaving the fields long enough to bury them. Young children cried in pain, but no one answered their wails. There was no other way of life (Menchú, *I, Rigoberta Menchú*, 34–49).

Before Rigoberta could remember, a brother of hers had died in the fields. A crop-dusting plane had flown over and sprayed the fields where he and others were working.

The young boy choked to death on the clouds of chemicals. The employers and overseers did not care how many workers died. The work went on, and the plane continued to dust the crops whenever the owner of the fields thought it necessary.

Rigoberta's mother—Juana Tum Cotojá—told how, when her child died, the overseer charged her for medicine even though they had not received any. The "boss" fired Juana and charged her for placing her child's body in the ground. Juana had to walk home—a trip that had been two days by lorry (Schraff, 93–94).

Even as an adult, Rigoberta remembered her two-year-old brother, with his stomach distended from malnutrition. Juana Tum Cotojá knew that her son was dying, but she could not remain with him even in his last moments. If Juana had stayed with him, she would have lost her job. She knew he would die on the long trip home if they tried to walk—and she had no idea how to get home again. Under no circumstance would the "boss" furnish transportation for those who had lost their jobs (Menchú, *I, Rigoberta Menchú*, 38).

Once when Rigoberta was seven, a brother and a sister were too sick to go with their parents to the plantations to work. The parents had to have some money; the only thing to do was for the other children to accompany their father to the mountains to gather wood. They would tie the sticks together and drag the bundle back to the market to sell. It was always a long, dangerous trip. They could hear wild animals howling around them. Once Rigoberta was separated from her father and her other brothers and sisters. Her loving father hunted for her until they were all together again. Rigoberta always remembered how frightened she had been (Brill, 8–9).

When Rigoberta was only 12, she took a job in the capital city as a servant. The family that employed her refused to pay her for the first two months because they said she was "training." She barely had enough to eat; they fed her only hard tortillas and a few beans. She noticed that the family dog ate better than she; it had rice and meat. The family never gave her a kind word, and she had to sleep on a bare mattress in the room where the family kept its garbage. Rigoberta was very homesick and cried often as she lay on her hard mattress (Brill, 20–21). Rigoberta later said matter-of-factly that she never had a childhood.

Rigoberta's job was particularly difficult because she did not speak their language, Spanish. Her job was to do all the cleaning, but she could not always understand the orders. When at last she seemed to perform satisfactorily, the woman in the family gave her two months' pay; she then took it back and bought clothes for Rigoberta. Her employer told her never to wear her traditional Guatemalan dress in the house again (Brill 20).

When Rigoberta finally received her pay after eight months, she promptly returned home (Brill, 22). She found even worse conditions than when she left. Government officials were coming to the peasants and demanding that they "sell" their land for a mere pittance. If the Indians refused, the soldiers attacked them, destroyed their homes, and killed all their animals. Often they even destroyed their dishes and cooking utensils. The Indians began to band together in large numbers to resist the attacks. Rigoberta's father, Vicente Menchú, was a trusted leader of the tribes.

The group continued the peaceful tradition of the Quiché Indians, who had always been peaceful—as had most of the neighboring tribes. The Quiché did not own guns or weapons. They loved their land and respected the plants and animals living there. The lack of violence in the Indian community extended to all people and all life; the Quiché did not even cut flowers growing in the area except on special occasions. It had been easy, therefore, for the Spanish to conquer them in 1523 and to force them into slavery.

Vicente tried to remind his people of the pride they should feel. He reminded them that tourists to the area saw examples of astronomy and architecture that were the most advanced in the ancient world. Particularly appealing to outsiders, he reminded them, were their ancient forms of writing, their calendar, their use of zero in their numeration system, the examples of soil conservation, and the pyramids still in existence. Most visitors left with souvenirs of their fabric and clothing. Their pride and love of the Indian culture was important to the Mayas.

Officials, however, did not like Vicente encouraging peasant resistance to government "purchase" of the land. The soldiers imprisoned him and tortured him almost to the point of death. When they at last released him, Vicente did not give up his mission. He worked in secret under cover of night. One night soldiers spotted him and tortured him; he was unable to walk because of his many broken bones. His suffering endeared him even more to the peasants; they talked the priests into taking him to a hospital. When he was at last well enough to come home, he received another threat: If his work continued, he could expect death for himself or for his children. Yet Vicente and his children continued to help others (Menchú, *I, Rigoberta Menchú*, 110, 111).

Vicente helped organize the CUC (Committee for Peasant Unity), an organization that would emphasize non-violence and used undercover operations. Vicente no longer lived at home; he did not want his presence to endanger his family.

Rigoberta's brother Patrocinio, who was working to unite the Indian workers in the country, was a target for the government. In 1979, soldiers captured Patrocinio and tortured him day and night for 16 days. The soldiers called everyone to see all his wounds; the boy was out of his mind with pain and probably did not recognize his own family. Then the soldiers poured gasoline on him and burned him to death in front of Rigoberta, her family, and the community (Menchú, *I, Rigoberta Menchú*, 170–82).

Rigoberta continued to follow the example set by her father. She tried to lead her people to live in harmony with those about them. She joined a clandestine group. She tried to help others to read the Bible, create weapons for self-defense, and use the Bible as a guide. She recalls how her village captured a soldier who came to harm them. She remembers also the slaughter of a young village woman by the soldiers when she would not become the mistress of a soldier (Menchú, *I, Rigoberta Menchú*, 152).

By 1978, the Menchú family no longer lived together. Vicente and Rigoberta had gone into hiding. About this time, Rigoberta recalls, she began to learn Spanish and to help organize her people and the CUC, founded in 1979. This was the year, she explains, that Lucas Garcia came to power. Rape, murders, military bases, tortures, massacres, and kidnappings increased.

Vicente continued to try to encourage peaceful means despite the slaughter of his son Patrocinio. He went to the Spanish Embassy on January 31, 1980, in a peaceful protest. The soldiers threw grenades into the building, and he was burned alive inside (Erlandson, 4).

Rigoberta's mother turned to violence. In April 1980, soldiers kidnapped Juana Tum Cotojá, tortured her, cut off her ears, and left her in the woods for insects and animals to finish what they had begun. She was dead when her friends and family found her. She was 43 years old (Menchú, *I, Rigoberta Menchú*, 196–99; Schraff, 93–111).

At last the women workers became more powerful in their peaceful resistance to the atrocities and hardships that the government and the businesses had doled out to them. They decided to strike for a minimum wage increase of five quetzals. The strike of 80,000 workers brought production to a halt for 15 days. Landowners began to realize that they could not function without their workers. The workers tried to barricade the mountain roads to prevent the soldiers from reaching them.

Many of the people had to go in hiding; the troops looked especially hard for Rigoberta. They looked in the homes of the nuns. One of these homes housed Rigoberta. When the troops searched the buildings, Rigoberta let her waist-length hair down and knelt in prayer in the church with two other companions. The soldiers did not recognize her. She was able to escape in 1981 to Mexico, but she knew her work was still in Guatemala (Schraff, 93–111).

Rigoberta traveled across Europe and the United States with other Guatemalans to talk about the problems in their country. While Rigoberta was on her first European tour in 1982, she shared the first part of her life story with Elisabeth Burgos (later Burgos-Debray) in Paris. Arturo Taracena, a Guatemalan who lived in France, had arranged for her to talk with Burgos (Brill, 37–39). Most of those who bought Rigoberta's book were foreigners. The book was not popular in her own country.

Menchú was 23 years old when she shared her story with others in the Spanish language. She began the book by stating boldly in the first pages, "My name is Rigoberta Menchú. I am twenty three years old. This is my testimony. I didn't learn it from a book and I didn't learn it alone. I'd like to stress that it's not only *my* life, it's also the testimony of my people...." Menchú also stated she had never been to school and had been speaking Spanish only three years (Menchú, *I, Rigoberta Menchú*, 3).

Rigoberta tried to make sure that others knew that she was speaking for both her people and herself in a language that the world could understand—the language of her oppressors. Because most outsiders did not understand the language of the Mayas, she had to use the Spanish language to ensure distribution for her story. Rigoberta tried to use her words as weapons to reveal what she had witnessed; the oppression, the torture, the murders, and the discrimination were still problems in Guatemala in 1982 (Wright, viii).

Rigoberta Menchú was important to the Mayas. She "gradually became a symbol of all those who had lost everything except their dignity and their will to continue the struggle against the military. For progressive Ladinos she was a symbol of democracy and freedom of expression. By 1990 many of them were finally buying and reading *I, Rigoberta Menchú*, though the text never became a best-seller outside the university campuses" (Arias, "Roberta Menchú's History within the Guatemalan Context," 13).

During the second week of October 1991, Rigoberta attended the Second Continental Meeting in Guatemala. The conference launched her candidacy for the Nobel Peace Prize. At the Guatemalan meeting, "indigenous women" even brought children to Rigoberta to bless. "[T]hat gesture ... signified the degree of recognition that she had finally achieved among her own people..." (Arias, "Roberta Menchú's History Within the Guatemalan Context," 15).

Rigoberta received a nomination for the Nobel Peace Prize in 1991. Her nomination came from Adolfo Perez Esquivel, who had won the Nobel Peace Prize in 1980 for his work to advance human rights, particularly in Argentina (Schulze, 78). Another Nobel Peace Prize laureate (1984), Bishop Desmond Tutu, suggested her also (Brill, 41).

In her second biography, *Crossing Borders*, Menchú told how seven journalist friends went with her to the diocese headquarters of the Catholic Church in San Marcos on the day before the scheduled announcement of the 1992 Nobel Peace Prize winner. Rigoberta had had to change her lodging place the day before because of threats on the boarding house where they were staying. She told of going to bed and being awakened by a phone call from the Norwegian ambassador in Mexico. "'In nine minutes ... it will be announced that you won the Nobel Peace Prize. Let me be the first to congratulate you. You have nine minutes to prepare yourself, after that the news will be out.'" When she hung up the phone, all her friends rushed in to hear what had happened. "Well! We've got the Nobel Prize," she reported (Menchú, *Crossing Borders*, 17).

Rigoberta, in a borrowed *huipil* (a blouse with a low neck and short sleeves that indigenous women often wear) and a *corte* (a full-length skirt) flew in a rented helicopter to Guatemala City where she would meet the press. Thousands of people were waiting for her to arrive. When she got into a bulletproof car to greet the crowds, the people almost lifted the vehicle off the ground in their eagerness to congratulate her and to be near her. Rigoberta had to get out and greet them personally (Menchú, *Crossing Borders*, 17).

Unfortunately, not everyone rejoiced with Rigoberta. Anonymous enemies tried to defame her; they even sent her bouquets of the traditional Guatemalan funeral flowers, baby's breath and marigolds. Some declared she was a terrorist (Schulze, 78). Death threats against her were numerous, particularly in Guatemala and Mexico City where she lived. Bodyguards were necessary (Brill, 40).

Conservative critics opposed her receiving the Nobel Peace Prize. They said that she had participated in the violence inflicted by guerrillas in Guatemala (Abrams, 1). The Norwegian Nobel Committee believed otherwise, however. In his presentation speech, Francis Sejersted, chair of the Norwegian Nobel Committee, stated that Rigoberta Menchú Tum had managed to maintain a "disarming humanity" in a brutal world. The committee recognized the fact that Menchú had not turned to violence when faced with violence; instead, she had worked to help her people through her political and social work. The Norwegian Nobel Committee presented her with the Nobel Peace Prize on December 10, 1992—the 500th anniversary of the European colonization of the Americas (Sejersted, 1).

In the exquisite Oslo Town Hall, Rigoberta received the Nobel Peace Prize from Francis Sejersted, the chair of the Norwegian Nobel Committee. While the king of Norway, several hundred guests, and the Norwegian Parliament (Storting) looked on, Rigoberta stood proudly barefoot and dressed in a multi-colored huipil and ankle-length *corte* (skirt). She listened carefully to the words meant for her: "[I]n recognition of ... work for social justice and ethno-cultural reconciliation based on respect for indigenous peoples" (Schulze, 78–79).

Rigoberta may have been among the first to acknowledge why she had won the prize. She recognized that it had come "not as a reward for me personally, but rather as one of the greatest conquests in the struggle for peace, for Human Rights, and for the rights of indigenous people, who, for 500 years, have been split, fragmented, as well as the victims of genocides, repression, and discrimination." She saw the Nobel Peace Prize as a way to continue the struggle toward the achievement of peace (Menchú, "Acceptance and Nobel Lecture").

By receiving the Nobel Peace Prize, Rigoberta—known for her work in promoting (1) the rights of indigenous persons, (2) peace, and (3) respect for all people—became both the youngest person ever to receive this distinction and the first indigenous woman or man to earn the award. As an adult, Rigoberta claimed that the cause she worked for was one born out of wretchedness and bitterness. The malnutrition, discrimination, deaths, and poverty she said she had experienced throughout her life as an Indian in Guatemala served to intensify her efforts. She noted that her work was to ease the apprehensions of her family and other peasants—particularly those of the 22 ethnic groups in the country (Stoll, *Rigoberta Menchú and the Story of the Poor Guatemalans*, viii).

Rigoberta decided ahead of time that if she won the Nobel Peace Prize, she would set up an independent foundation with the $1.2 million that accompanied her gold medal (Brill, 41). Others who had won the Nobel Peace Prize before her had established strong institutions to back them so that they could conduct their peace campaigns. Rigoberta founded the Vicente Menchú Foundation (named for her father). The main purposes of the institution are to encourage Indians in Guatemala to participate in the political process by registering and voting and to set up educational programs for children—especially refugee children. Rigoberta decided to rename the Vicente Menchú Foundation the Rigoberta Menchú Foundation; her reasoning was that outside of Guatemala her name was better known than the name of her father (Schulze, 80). After the Nobel Peace Prize presentation, the government agreed to give land to Guatemalans who wanted to return. Rigoberta led about 2400 indigenous people into Guatemala in January of 1993. She was pleased with the recognition of her people (Brill, 43–44). To serve her people better, she moved to Guatemala in 1994 despite the risk to her safety.

Many consider Rigoberta an unlikely peace laureate. Neither Rigoberta—nor anyone else—had been able to end the Guatemalan civil war that had raged for decades. She had been active in a public career for only ten years and was only 23 when she told her story. Rigoberta's profile was not that of the usual individual recognized internationally for achievements. The stories she told were of death, rape, torture, and fire—unpleasant topics at best.

Some continue to bring up the question of whether Rigoberta was actually an advocate of peace. "[H]er 1982 testament clearly advocates violence. Invoking the Bible for precedents, Rigoberta makes Molotov cocktails, endorses bomb threats as a tactic, and debates whether to execute an old woman suspected of being an informer. (Fortunately for the future peace laureate, the suspect is judged innocent)" (Stoll, *Rigoberta Menchú and the Story of the Poor Guatemalans*, viii, 213).

The question of whether the story is true is an awkward one—especially for those who think the Nobel Peace Prize for Rigoberta was a good idea. David Horowitz (author and commentator on Fox News, C-Span and "Nightline") wrote for FrontPageMagazine .com an article (January 12, 1999) titled "I, Rigoberta Menchú, Liar." He begins the article by calling Rigoberta Menchú Tum's story "a fabrication" and "one of the greatest hoaxes of the Twentieth Century." What he finds so extraordinary is that

> ... the revelation of Rigoberta's mendacity has changed nothing. The Nobel committee has already refused to take back her prize; the thousands of college courses that make her book a required text for American college students will continue to do so; and the editorial writers of the major press institutions have already defended her falsehoods ... [Horowitz, 1].

He noted that Elisabeth Burgos-Debray, who helped Rigoberta ready her story for the book *I, Rigoberta Menchú*, was a French leftist and the story itself is a "Marxist myth."

> Unfortunately for this political fantasy, virtually everything that Rigoberta has written is a lie. Her lies, moreover, are neither incidental nor accidental. They are lies about the central events and facts of her story, and they have been concocted to shape its political content, to create a specific political myth. This begins on the first page of her text [Horowitz, 2].

Stoll asks rhetorically, even if the "laureate's famous story is not true, does it matter? Perhaps not." He felt compelled, however, to indicate some of the problems he found in *I, Rigoberta Menchú*. He does not call Rigoberta a prevaricator but asks if the falsehoods might be the fault of the editor or the translator. Stoll suggests the possibility that the Mayan oral tradition is not grounded in the same definition of fact as some other cultures;

he wonders if Menchú might have been tired, might have been selective in what she reported, or might have experienced communication problems. He also suggests that trauma might have caused the mistakes in information or that she was trying to protect the Catholic Church by omitting her education by the nuns (Stoll, *Rigoberta Menchú and the Story of the Poor Guatemalans*, viii, 190, 191).

Some people, however, were particularly opposed to Stoll's critique of Rigoberta's story.

> What Stoll undertook to do, and what many cannot forgive him for, was to intervene in Rigoberta's story ... he did not set out to destroy her. But scholarly rigor made it impossible for him to avoid asking basic questions once he became aware of the many discrepancies in her story [Patai, 274].

There are other controversies over Menchú's book *I, Rigoberta Menchú*. *New York Times* reporter Larry Rohter, after much research and a study of Stoll's report, observes that Rigoberta "received the equivalent of a middle-school education as a scholarship student at two prestigious private boarding schools operated by Roman Catholic nuns" (Rohter, 59). He concludes that Menchú's claim on the first page of her first book that she "never went to school" and that she "could not speak Spanish or read or write until shortly before she dictated the text of *I, Rigoberta Menchú*" are untrue because she did have some education. Furthermore, Rohter acknowledges that "it is extremely unlikely that she could have worked as underground political organizer and spent up to eight months a year laboring on coffee and cotton plantations, as she describes in great detail in her book" (Rohter, 59).

Many attribute the furor over Menchú's book to Rohter and his front-page *New York Times* story "Tarnished Laureate: Nobel Winner Finds Her Story Challenged," published on December 15, 1998. This story served, in their opinion, as the catalyst for the rash of appearances on radio news shows or articles in magazines and newspapers. "Larry Rohter's article on the *New York Times*'s front page put the controversy in motion.... Stoll's investigation of Rigoberta ... had already circulated through various channels ... and it had already received several rebuttals. Without Rohter's article, Stoll's book ... would have achieved only a very limited notoriety" (Ferman, 158–59).

Further factual questions with *I, Rigoberta Menchu* arise. Vicente, Rigoberta's father stopped working on plantations long before she was born in 1959 (Stoll, *Rigoberta Menchú and the Story of the Poor Guatemalans*, 25). Vicente could not have accompanied Rigoberta on some of the trips to the plantations—if she herself actually went on the trips (Rohter, 62). There are also problems with the story of Rigoberta's younger brother Nicolás dying from malnutrition (Danilo Rodríguez, "About Rigoberta's Lies," 70). Rigoberta's younger brother—whom Menchú says she saw die of starvation—"turns out [according to some researchers] to be alive and well, the owner of a well-kept homestead here" (Rohter, 62).

Menchú responds to questions about her brother's fate by saying, "I have a brother, Nicolás I, the one who died, and another, Nicolás II, who is still alive. That is very normal in Guatemala, that names are repeated in families" (Aznárez, 112).

There appear also to be problems with Rigoberta's story of her brother Patrocinio being burned to death in front of the community and the family (Danilo Rodríguez, "About Rigoberta's Lies," 70) Rigoberta had devoted a whole chapter in *I, Rigoberta Menchu*, to the death of her brother. She titled the chapter "The Torture and Death of Her Little Brother, Burnt Alive in Front of Members of Their Families and the Community." A researcher reported "being surprised when a routine atrocity check ... failed to corrobo-rate the immolation" of Patrocinio. Although the researcher was able to find that the death occurred, he was not able to corroborate the method of the execution (Stoll, *Rigoberta Menchú and the Story of the Poor Guatemalans*, 8). In fact, more than one researcher found that "a second [brother], whose suffering she says she and her parents were forced to watch as he was being burned alive by army troops, was killed in entirely different circumstances when the family was not present" (Rohter, 59). Rodríguez, too, notes that the immolation of Patrocinio and "many episodes in the book are pure invention" (Danilo Rodríguez, "About Rigoberta's Lies," 70).

Menchú finally admitted that she had not seen the immolation. She asserts, how-ever, "My mother saw it. And she can no longer speak about it.... That was one truth, my mother's truth. And if you ask me if I believe Stoll or my mother, it is obvious that I believe my mother" (Aznárez, "Rigoberta Menchú: 'Those Who Attack Me Humiliate the Vic-tims,'" 110, 111).

Rigoberta insists that she has a right to her own story and to tell the story in light of what she lived, of what she has heard, and of her own interpretations. She insists, "'*I, Rigoberta Menchú* is a testimonial, not an autobiography. I have my truth of what I lived for twenty years. The history of the community is my own history.'" Later in the inter-view, Menchú asserts, "'Everything for me that was the story of my community is also my own story.'" She continued, however, to downplay her education (Aznárez, "Rigoberta Menchú: 'Those Who Attack Me Humiliate the Victims,'" 110, 111, 113).

Even the editor notes errors. Burgos said that she had begun to receive information by the end of the 1980s that did not corroborate the information in *I, Rigoberta Menchú*. Burgos cites Stoll's well-documented book; he "proves that it isn't true that Rigoberta never went to school, that it isn't true that her brother Nicolas died of hunger—in fact he is still alive—that it is even less exact that Rigoberta worked as a maid in the capital ... that she did not witness the murder of her other brother ... and that her idealized image of her father is not true either" (Martí, "The Pitiful Lies of Rigoberta Menchú," 79).

In her first autobiography-testimony, Menchú told of another brother dying in the field from spray from the air. Another reader-researcher realized that Rigoberta "forgot or ignored the small detail that in Guatemala coffee trees are not sprayed from the air. And that is not the only falsehood..." (Palmieri, "Lies by the Nobel Prize Win-ner," 74).

Stoll suggests that the contrasts between the accounts of others and the contents of Rigoberta's testimony might simply reflect the time that she spoke. He noted these incon-sistencies when he was only a graduate student and says that he did what any "sensible graduate student" would have done: drop it (Stoll, *Rigoberta Menchú and the Story of the Poor Guatemalans*, 182–83). The main problems that Stoll noted were:

(1) Rigoberta describes in detail the death of her mother and the disposal of her mother's body in *I, Rigoberta Menchú*. Stoll does not question the death of Juana or that there were witnesses to her death. He wonders, however, if all these details would be avail-able for the death of a kidnap victim. He suggests that all the gruesome elements might have been a way for Rigoberta to have a degree of closure; he also likens these horrible details to those she gave about the death of her brother Patrocinio.

(2) Rigoberta waffles on her father's connection with the CUC. Although she at times described her father as a founding member of the CUC, in 1992 she conceded that he

never was that, just "a very active member." Stoll concludes, however, that Vicente's rank in the CUC was not really important.

(3) Rigoberta maintains that the land controversies were with the plantation owners and government. Stoll found, however, that some of the court records indicate that the conflicts were actually between Vicente and his in-laws.

(4) Rigoberta states that Burgos had also included the life stories and testimonies of other people in the book; this multiple-narrator hypothesis could explain the discrepancies (Stoll, *Rigoberta Menchú and the Story of the Poor Guatemalans*, 88, 94–95, 127, 182–183).

(5) Menchú tells of her father going peacefully to the embassy and dying there; others tell a different story. "[H]er father and those in his company ... arrived at the diplomatic installations of the Spanish embassy armed with machetes and Molotov cocktails ... and died in the terrible tragedy when one of the [Molotov cocktails] fell on a plastic rug ... which started the fatal fire" (Palmieri, "Lies by the Nobel Prize Winner," 74).

To research the cause of the fire, Stoll showed two arson investigators in California some photos of the event, talked with observers, and examined newspaper stories. He concluded that Vicente and his comrades did carry weapons with them and did not enter the embassy peaceably as Rigoberta maintained. Stoll indicates that there is another terrible possibility: "a revolutionary suicide" and the murder of other protestors and hostages (Stoll, *Rigoberta Menchú and the Story of the Poor Guatemalans*, 88).

The cause of the fire is, of course, still under debate. On December 13, 2004, however, the Associated Press Worldstream reported that a Mexican judge had issued an arrest warrant for Donaldo Alvarez Ruiz, the former Guatemalan Interior Minister. Ruiz had served General Romeo Lucas García from 1978 to 1982. Spain had issued the warrant for Ruiz for his alleged role in the siege on the Spanish Embassy in Guatemala. This police raid in 1980 killed 37 people, including Vicente Menchú. The international news from AP Worldstream indicated that Vicente was at the Spanish Embassy with a group of Guatemalan Indians who were "asking the diplomatic mission to help stop attacks against the Indians accused of being Marxist guerrillas. Instead, police staged an operation to retake the embassy, during which the protestors were killed" (Associated Press Worldstream, December 13, 2004).

Not everyone condemns Rigoberta or denies her claims. Montero defends her by writing, "To say that Rigoberta lies seems to me a much bigger lie than the imprecisions in her autobiography" (Montero, "Her," 76–7). Montero also suggests that perhaps some problems might have come from the fact that "Rigoberta is nothing but a poor Indian woman in her forties with braids" (Montero, "Her," 77). Ferman, on the other hand, insists that Stoll's book *Rigoberta Menchú and the Story of the Poor Guatemalans* "exhibits methodological problems" and is "inconclusive in most of its inquiries—it presents tentative theses that sometimes cancel each other, uses vaguely defined or completely undefined sources, and it is extremely clear and direct in terms of its political agenda" (Ferman, 158).

In defense of Rigoberta, Galeano writes: "Those who stone Rigoberta ignore what they are praising. After all, as the old proverb says, it is the tree that gives fruit that receives all the stones" (Galeano, 102). Others see the work to verify Rigoberta's story as an international campaign against her. Dante Liano remarks, tongue-in-cheek, "Obviously, we shall always need an American anthropologist to explain what our lives are really about.... We in Guatemala always had someone who came to study us like insects.... Then the *New York Times* ... and other American and European newspapers ... simply spread the word around the globe" (Liano, 122). Liano comments also on Rohter and his writings in the *Times*: "The strategy is simple: humiliate the witness, make him stammer, cast the shadow of doubt on his testimony, so shame itself can be questioned" (Liano, 123).

Another writer notes: "A gringo, suspiciously claiming to be an academic, writes a dissertation with the only goal of discrediting our Nobel prize winner. Even if he claims he does not mean to destroy Menchú, his effort to evidence details where he claims she altered the truth is highly suspicious, as is his claim that he is not racist" (Carrera, 108).

Lovell and Lutz conclude, "What is the point of it all? Does not Stoll, in effect, exhibit exactly the same selectivity in constructing his text as Menchú does in constructing hers? As best we can discern, Stoll could easily have arranged his findings to support what Menchú has to say as much as criticize her for how she goes about saying it" (Lovell and Lutz, 195). They indicate that "Menchú's account is many things, but above all else it is an act of political protest aimed at capturing the attention of an international audience that she believes, rightly or wrong, can ameliorate the dire situation of her people" (Lovell and Lutz, 186).

Warren, too, criticized Stoll—not Rigoberta Menchú. He notes that Stoll "refuses to read Menchú's autobiography as an instance of testimonial literature in which, by design, there is room for maneuver between collective and individual veracities" (Warren, 204). He warns the reader: "Stoll's dominant focus is on *the facts* so as to question the veracity of the testimonial account" (Warren, 208). Warren calls Stoll "a rigorous investigator" and warns that "Stoll envisions himself as the truth teller ... who decides when 'problems in [Menchú's] account should be brought to wider attention'" (Warren, 207–08).

Beverley and others have sought to interpret Stoll's work. Beverley writes: "What seems to bother Stoll above all is that Menchú has an agenda. He wants her to be a 'native informant,' who will lend herself to *his* purposes (of information gathering and evaluation); but she is ... concerned with producing a text of 'local history'" (Beverley, 221–22). He cautions: "Although Stoll talks a lot about 'facts' and 'verification,' it turns out that he also has an ideological agenda. He believes that the attempt of the left to wage an armed struggle against the military dictatorship in Guatemala put the majority of the highland Indian population 'between two fires,' driven to support the guerrillas mainly by the ferocity of the [army]" (Beverley, 223).

Ann Wright, Rigoberta's translator, remarks "Sometimes ... the wealth of memories and associations which come tumbling out in this spontaneous narrative leave the reader a little confused as to chronology and details of events" (Wright, viii). Wright readily admits that at times she had to change and reorder portions of the work to make sure that the meaning could be readily understood. She closes her "Translator's Note" with: "Rigoberta has a mission. Her words want us to understand and react. I only hope that I have been able to do justice to the power of their message. I will have done that if I can convey the impact they had on me when first I read them" (Wright, viii–ix).

The stories that young Rigoberta told to the world were full of the violence and the hatred that Rigoberta professed that the landowners in Guatemala had showed to the peasants. She tried to reveal the stories of the sufferings of her people to all those who would listen. Rigoberta suggested, "Any problems with the text ... are the responsibility of Elisabeth Burgos, the Venezuelan anthropologist who interviewed ... transcribed and edited the resulting twenty-six hours of tapes [Ferman says 24 hours, page 166], and secured a publishing contract" (Rohter, 61). Burgos, on the other hand, indicates that "she [Burgos] still has the original recordings ... and is willing to make them available to a university so that other researchers can have access to them" (Rohter, 61). Burgos describes in detail to Stoll how she turned the tapes into a book and how the manuscript went to Arturo Taracena to send to Menchú's organization for a security check. Burgos stated that it was Rigoberta who brought the corrected manuscript and some letters from Mexico directly to Burgos. After this last visit, however, Rigoberta became cool and distant. Rigoberta's vita reflects that she was the winner of the Casa de las Américas Award, when the award actually went to *Burgos*, as editor (Stoll, *Rigoberta Menchú and the Story of the Poor Guatemalans*, 185–88).

Rigoberta complained that Burgos had stopped sending royalties. Burgos, however, stated that she had always sent full royalties through "an arrangement with Danielle Mitterand and the Mitterand Foundation. Incensed by Rigoberta's accusations, she now stopped the remittances." Rigoberta requested that Burgos sign the rights to *I, Rigoberta Menchu* back to her. Burgos, however, could not sign the rights over because of the numerous book contracts throughout the world. Stoll suggests multiple narrators may have contributed to the errors (Stoll, *Rigoberta Menchú and the Story of the Poor Guatemalans*, 182–88).

In her 1998 book *Crossing Borders*, Rigoberta describes how she spent about two months trying to read and understand the manuscript of *I, Rigoberta Menchú* after Burgos had finished it. Rigoberta describes how she "took out bits that referred to my village, details about my brothers and sisters, and names of people. That is why the book lacks a more specific identity and I feel it will be my duty to provide this before I die.... Giving their names away in a book could have had them killed" (Menchú, *Crossing Borders*, 114).

Some of the questionable information does not offend either Burgos or Stoll. Burgos notes that Rigoberta "belongs to a different cultural tradition, pre-literary tradition, an oral tradition, in which history has a collective nature, facts are stored in a common memory and belong to the entire community. Everything she told has happened, even if it did not happen to her personally" (Martí, "The Pitiful Lies of Rigoberta Menchú," 80). Others defend the style of storytelling that Menchú uses; for instance, Skinner-Kleé calls this phenomenon a "communal memory" (Skinner-Kleé, "About David Stoll's Book *Rigoberta Menchú and the Story of the Poor Guatemalans*," 97).

Another writer defends Rigoberta by saying: "David Stoll is probably right about some objections he raises to Rigoberta Menchú's 1983 *testimonio*.... And sympathetic readers may feel justifiably disappointed, even offended, if, in fact, they have been somewhat deceived. This is hardly reason to dismiss Rigoberta..." (Sommer, 237). Some readers contend that "a measure of creative writing and reading is ... unobjectionable in most first-person narratives..." (Sommer, 238). Sommer goes on to say: "Stoll is probably right to quibble over Rigoberta's facts, given the tension between her particular political agendas and her universal, almost saintly, Nobel laureate stature, and given also the nature of his own work as fact-finder and analyst" (Sommer, 240). She does not dispute Stoll's information about Vicente Menchú's battles with in-laws over land. "To his credit, Stoll's game acknowledges that judgments should derive from a historical record that can and should be as complete as possible, even when completion includes countervailing narratives" (Sommer, 239, 241). She warns, however, "Stoll's ideally disinterested, almost innocent, game of fact-finding gets mired in the tangled terrain of persistent social and cultural difference.... Information gathering, in Stoll's hands ... comes very close to policy recommendations" (Sommer, 242).

Carol A. Smith has used Menchú's book in her classes for many years. She is aware of the controversy; she explains, however, that she always emphasizes that Rigoberta says that the story is that of her people (Menchú, *I, Rigoberta Menchú*, 3). Smith tells her "students to read the book as if it is a general rather than particular depiction of life in Guate-mala, noting that in *testimonios* it is typical for a person to present the experience of a whole people as if it happened to a single individual." Smith does not "teach ... a literal-ist reading that Stoll feels compelled to refute" (Smith, 152).

In 1996, Allen Carey-Webb and Stephen Benz edited a 392-page volume on teach-ing *I, Rigoberta Menchú* in the classroom. They comment, "More than two decades after a twenty-three-year-old Rigoberta Menchú told her story, despite challenges, attacks, and negative publicity, her testimonial remains an excellent, provocative, and most credible classroom resource" (Carey-Webb, 328) They also note: "[I]t would certainly be wise for teachers to at least read Stoll's book" but that teachers should not "feel obligated to include Stoll's research or the publicity it has generated in their classrooms." They remark that Stoll has "created a climate in which teaching Menchú's testimony has become a suspect activity" (Carey-Webb, 327).

Stoll himself comments, "If anything, the controversy has made [*I, Rigoberta Menchú*] a better assignment for teaching constructed history, that is, how a memoir can be both partial and true. A few students may ask, Why are you assigning us a hoax? Should you still be wondering how to explain why *I, Rigoberta Menchú* is not a hoax, read my book" (Stoll, 2001, 400).

Burgos observes that *I, Rigoberta Menchú* "has been useful so that people could know what was happening in Guatemala. Until that time, there was only curiosity in Europe about Argentina and Chile..." (Martí, 80). Many recognize that Menchú and Burgos were "able to accomplish a huge feat by making the book" (Earle, 305).

Some caution, however, that the inaccuracies in *I, Rigoberta Menchú* might have neg-ative consequences. "The bad thing is that today, those mistakes, half-truths, or full lies uttered by Rigoberta Menchú can discredit not only her own person but an entire move-ment, or color all the information that addresses the suffering of Central America's Indi-ans" (Martí, "The Pitiful Lies of Rigoberta Menchú," 81).

Some say the reasons for the misunderstandings in *I, Rigoberta Menchú* are mixed. One reason might have been: "She wanted to promote her cause *and* she wanted to proj-ect a certain image of herself. Both objectives were served, in her view, by distorting her life story, and even lying about it when that seemed expedient" (Patai, 284). There were results: "[T]he main damage done by Rigoberta's misrepresentations is to the cause of human rights" (Patai, 279).

Whatever the reasons for the discrepancies, the "errors" in *I, Rigoberta Menchú* find repetition in the literature about her. The biographies by Julie Schulze, Marlene Targ Brill, and Michael Silverstone, for example, repeat the stories of Patrocinio's being burned in front of Rigoberta, her parents, and the community. They also include the graphic details of Juana's death.

Some people go so far as to suggest that because it is a lie that Rigoberta never went to school and because it is a lie that her brother was burned to death in front of her, many other events in the book are "pure invention." These critics state that she should admit these "falsehoods" publicly (Rodriguez, "About Rigoberta's Lies," 70, 72).

Rigoberta, however, affirms, "Not even Mr. Stoll's book says I am a liar...." Later in the same interview, she says that Stoll implies that "all of us victims lie. He has already reached a conclusion ahead of time, and he adorns everything to reach that particular con-clusion. And the most aberrant of all is that not only are we all ignorant, as Mr. Stoll says.... [H]e is also saying we are liars, not just ignorant and savage..." (Aznárez, 114).

Menchú admits that the scandal has hurt her. She asserts that Stoll's book "humiliates the victims. It wasn't enough to kill them, to leave them dead. It wasn't enough that my mother was killed, my father, my brothers, but they even want to build a polemic around the dead" (Aznárez, 115). She believes that someone is trying to hurt her. "I hate to speculate unless I have evidence. We are not going to say it was the CIA, but we cannot believe that someone wasn't behind this, either" (Aznárez, 115).

The Nobel Peace Prize Committee commented on the controversy. "The campaign against Rigoberta even reached Oslo. There are those who demand that she return the Nobel Prize or that it be taken away from her. The prize has already been given, and properly given, ratified the Norwegian Committee: '[T]he details invoked are not essential,' said their spokesperson" (Galeano, "Let's Shoot Rigoberta," 101).

When Stoll published his findings, "editorialists in Latin America and Spain attacked him as an agent of the CIA and the Guatemalan army" (Morales, 351). Earle had warned Stoll ahead of time that exposing Rigoberta's contradictions might abet the perpetrators. He also cautioned Stoll about "the heaps of derision he [Stoll] would receive for doing it.... [Verifications of] the personal biographical facts were far more trouble than they were worth..." (Earle, 289). Earle knew first-hand the ire that confrontations could cause; when he mentioned at a meeting some inaccuracies in the traditional beliefs that Rigoberta describes in *I, Rigoberta Menchú,* "The vehemence of the response from the man who organized my talk took me aback. In front of the whole group he insisted that the book was 'authentic' down to the last jot and I must have gotten it wrong, since I was the white foreigner. She was the Maya, she was the authority" (Earle, 291). Earle suggests that perhaps Rigoberta was "misrepresenting these cultural practices intentionally, a form of disguise, her 'secrets'" (Earle, 296).

Rigoberta's recognition and work did not end with the Nobel Peace Prize. She has since received several honorary doctorates. She has participated regularly in PeaceJam, an international education program built around Nobel Peace Laureates; these Nobel Prize winners work personally with youth to educate, to inspire a new generation of peacemakers, and to transform themselves, their communities, and their world. Over 100,000 youth have participated in the programs. On July 23, 2004, Menchú participated in the Peace-Jam in downtown Guatemala City. The three-day meeting welcomed 150 young people from eight countries. Betty Williams, a former Nobel Peace Prize winner, joined Rigoberta for that conference ("Two Nobel Peace Laureates Meet Activists in Guatemala," Agence France Presse, July 24, 2004).

Rigoberta's recent personal life has been rewarding for her. Upon the death of her parents, Rigoberta had decided never to marry or rear a child. Three years after receiving the Nobel Peace Prize, however, she began to appear in public with an adopted infant, Mash Nawaljá (Tomás Water Spirit).

Soon after the adoption, she married Angel Francisco Canil Grave. Angel was a fellow refugee from Guatemala who had sought safety in Mexico.

Menchú's recent life has not been without problems. She still receives death threats. A nephew was kidnapped in Guatemala City where Rigoberta had gone to a family wedding. The family was able to recover the child, but the incident caused concern for Rigoberta; she could now visualize someone kidnapping her own child (Stoll, *Rigoberta Menchú and the Story of the Poor Guatemalans,* 265).

Even during brutal situations in her life, Rigoberta tried to preserve her own humanity. She constantly remembers her past, but she continues each day to achieve her life goals and remains "a vivid symbol of peace and reconciliation across ethnic, cultural and social dividing lines" (Sejersted, Presentation Speech for Roberta Menchú).

Rigoberta Menchú reflected and considered solutions following the events of September 11, 2001. She made a public statement:

> I firmly condemn the horrible terrorist attacks that have taken thousands of innocent civilian lives and have provoked an unpredictable spiral of violent consequences.... I express my profound condolences and solidarity with their victims, their families and the American people. I call upon serenity and wise judgment to avoid a rushed and insensate response.... I call upon the use of all available resources leading to a dialogue.... I call upon the media to avoid alarmist sensationalism ... I call upon the world's civil society, Nobel Prize Laureates, and all world leaders, not to rush to conclusions on today's events conforming instead a wide FRONT FOR WISE JUDGMENT in order to stop the cowardly use of violence and avoid further suffering to humanity [Menchú Tum, "A Call for Wise Judgment," 1].

In a recent interview, Rigoberta gave these comments in response to the question of what would be her "message to humankind." She reminded us, "We are living in a troubled world, in a time of great uncertainty. It's ... time to reflect.... Solutions will come [only] when the world becomes educated about global values, the common values of its inhabitants and communities.... We have to focus on solutions in this time of great challenges. If we just wait around, the problems will overwhelm us" (O'Callaghan, 1).

Bibliography

Abrams, Irwin. "Rigoberta Menchú Tum." A paper presented for the conference "Peace and War Issues: Gender, Race, and Ethnicity in Historical Perspective" held at Rutgers University, November 11–12, 1994.

Agence France Presse. "Two Nobel Peace Laureates Meet Activists in Guatemala," July 24, 2004.

Arias, Arturo, ed. *The Rigoberta Menchú Controversy*. Minneapolis: University of Minnesota Press, 2001.

_____. "Rigoberta Menchú's History Within the Guatemala in Context." In *The Rigoberta Menchú Controversy*, Arturo Arias, ed. Minneapolis: University of Minnesota Press, 2001, 219–36.

Associated Press Worldstream. "Mexican Judge Issues Arrest Warrant for Former Guatemalan Interior Minister," December 13, 2004.

Aznárez, Juan Jesús. "Rigoberta Menchú: Those Who Attack Me Humiliate the Victims." In *The Rigoberta Menchú Controversy*, Arturo Arias, ed. Minneapolis: University of Minnesota Press, 2001, 109–117.

Beverley, John. "What Happens When the Subaltern Speaks: Rigoberta Menchú, Multiculturalism, and the Presumption of Equal Worth." In *The Rigoberta Menchú Controversy*, Arturo Arias, ed. Minneapolis: University of Minnesota Press, 2001, 219–36.

Brill, Marlene Targ. *Journey for Peace: The Story of Rigoberta Menchú*. New York: Lodestar Books, 1996.

Carey-Webb, Allen, and Stephen Benz, ed. *Teaching and Testimony: Rigoberta Menchú and the North American Classroom*. Albany: State University of New York Press, 1996.

Carrera, Margarita. "Against Gerardi and Against Rigoberta, Attacks are Continually Made to Make Them Lose Some of Their Luster." In *The Rigoberta Menchú Controversy*, Arturo Arias, ed. Minneapolis: University of Minnesota Press, 2001, 107–08.

Earle, Duncan. "Menchú Tales and Maya Social Landscapes." In *The Rigoberta Menchú Controversy*, Arturo Arias, ed. Minneapolis: University of Minnesota Press, 2001.

Erlandson, Greg, ed. "Catholic Rights Activist Wins Nobel Prize." Our Sunday Visitor, October 25, 1992, 4. As cited by Anne Schraff in *Women of Peace*.

Ferman, Claudia. "Textual Truth, Historical Truth, and Media Truth: Everybody Speaks About the Menchús," 156–70, in *The Rigoberta Menchú Controversy*, Arturo Arias, ed. Minneapolis: University of Minnesota Press, 2001, 156–70.

Galeano, Eduardo. "Let's Shoot Rigoberta." In *The Rigoberta Menchú Controversy*, Arturo Arias, ed. Minneapolis: University of Minnesota Press, 2001, 99–102.

Horowitz, David. "I, Rigoberta Menchú, Liar." Front Page Magazine.com, January 12, 1999. Available online at http://www.frontpagemag.com/Articles/ReadArticle.asp?10=1186.

Liano, Dante. "The Anthropologist with the Old Hat." In *The Rigoberta Menchú Controversy*, Arturo Arias, ed. Minneapolis: University of Minnesota Press, 2001, 121–26.

Lovell, W. George, and Christopher H. Lutz. "The Primacy of Larger Truths." In *The Rigoberta Menchú Controversy*, Arturo Arias, ed. Minneapolis: University of Minnesota Press, 2001, 171–97.

Martí, Octavio. "The Pitiful Lies of Rigoberta Menchú." In *The Rigoberta Menchú Controversy*, Arturo Arias, ed. Minneapolis: University of Minnesota Press, 2001, 78–81.

Menchú Tum, Rigoberta. "Acceptance and Nobel Lecture." Available online at http://nobelprize.org/peace/laureates/1992/tum:lecture.html.

_____. "A Call for Wise Judgment." In *The Peacemakers Speak*. Available online at http://www.thecommunity.com/crisis/rigoberta.html.

_____. *Crossing Borders*. Translated and edited by Ann Wright. New York: Verson, 1998.

_____. *I, Rigoberta Menchú: An Indian Woman in Guatemala*. Edited and introduced by Elisabeth Burgos-Debray. New York: Verso, 1984; 12th impression, 1992.

_____. "Rigoberta Menchú Tum—Nobel Lecture." December 10, 1992. Available online at http://www.nobelprize.org/peace/laureates/1992/tum=lecture.html.

Montero, Rosa. "Her." In *The Rigoberta Menchú Controversy*, Arturo Arias, ed. Minneapolis: University of Minnesota Press, 2001, 76–77.

O'Callaghan, Michael. "Interview with Rigoberta Menchú—Extracts from the Transcript of a Global Vision Video Interview" (1993). Available online at www.global-vision.org/interview/menchu.html.

Palmieri, Jorg. "Lies by the Nobel Prize Winner." In *The Rigoberta Menchú Controversy*, Arturo Arias, ed. Minneapolis: University of Minnesota Press, 2001, 73–75.

Patai, Daphne. "Whose Truth?" In *The Rigoberta Menchú Controversy*, Arturo Arias, ed. Minneapolis: University of Minnesota Press, 2001, 270–87.

Rodríguez, Danilo. "About Rigoberta's Lies." In *The Rigoberta Menchú Controversy*, Arturo Arias, ed. Minneapolis: University of Minnesota Press, 2001, 70–72.

Rohter, Larry. "Tarnished Laureate." In *The Rigoberta Menchú Controversy*, Arturo Arias, ed. Minneapolis: University of Minnesota Press, 2001, 58–65.

Schraff, Anne. *Women of Peace*. Hillside, New Jersey: Enslow, 1994.

Schulze, Julie. *Rigoberta Menchú Tum: Champion of Human Rights*. Evanston, Illinois: J.G. Burke, 1997.

Sejersted, Francis (Chairman of the Norwegian Nobel Committee). Presentation speech for Rigoberta Menchú. http://nobelprize.org/peace/laureates/1992/presentation-speech.html

Silverstone, Michael. *Rigoberta Menchú: Defending Human Rights in Guatemala*. New York: Feminist Press of the University of New York, 1999.

Skinner-Kleé, Jorge. "About David Stoll's Book *Rigoberta Menchú and the Story of the Poor Guatemalans*." In *The Rigoberta Menchú Controversy*, Arturo Arias, ed. Minneapolis: University of Minnesota Press, 2001, 97–98.

Smith, Carol A. "Why Write an Exposé of Rigoberta Menchú?" In *The Rigoberta Menchú Controversy*, Arturo Arias, ed. Minneapolis: University of Minnesota Press, 2001, 141–55.

Sommer, Doris. "Las Casas's Lies and Other Language Games." In *The Rigoberta Menchú Controversy*, Arturo Arias, ed. Minneapolis: University of Minnesota Press, 2001, 237–50.

Stoll, David. "The Battle of Rigoberta." In *The Rigoberta Menchú Controversy*, Arturo Arias, ed. Minneapolis: University of Minnesota Press, 2001, 392–401.

_____. *Rigoberta Menchú and the Story of All Poor Guatemalans*. Boulder, Colorado: Westview Press, 1999.

Wright, Ann, trans. "Translator's Note." In Rigoberta Menchú, *I, Rigoberta Menchú: An Indian Woman in Guatemala*. New York: Verso, 1984; 12th impression, 1992, viii–ix.

Jody Williams
(1997)

Advocate for the Banning and
Clearing of Anti-Personnel Mines
(October 9, 1950–)

Jody Williams, Nobel Peace Laureate 1997.

It was 1981. A 31-year old woman hurried through the subway tunnel with the other Washington, D.C., workers. As usual, there were people giving out fliers for causes, holding posters to announce opinions and events, and reaching out hands for a few coins from those who would give. Absent-mindedly, Jody Williams took a flier and went about her business (Williams, 12). When she later took the time to look at it, she found she had been invited to hear a presentation on Central America and American foreign policy (Fleischman, 49–57). Little did she know that day that this flier would change her life and the lives of people across the world.

As a result of studying the brochure, Jody decided to begin doing what she could to improve the rights of people—especially in Central America—and to help modify the policies of the United States in the region. Jody left her work with a temporary employment agency and began a career in global activism. With a Master's Degree in International Relations from the Johns Hopkins School of Advanced International Studies (Washington, D.C., 1984), a Master of Arts in Teaching from the School for International Training (Brattleboro, Vermont, 1976), and a Bachelor's Degree (in French and Spanish, according to Fleischman) from the University of Vermont (Burlington, Vermont, 1972), Jody seemed right for the job of building public awareness about human rights in Central America (Keene, 171–72).

Protecting others and defending their rights were things that Jody had long been accustomed to doing. Jody had grown up in a small town in rural Vermont and had learned how to care for her older brother (Fleischman, 49–50), whom Jody described as "deaf schizophrenic." (CNN, 3) She worked hard to protect him from the misunderstandings and taunts of others (Keene, 1–2). "I couldn't understand why people would be mean to him because he was deaf. That translated into wanting to stop bullies being mean to ... people, just because they are weak" (CNN, 3). Jody recalls standing up for her older brother Stephen as "her earliest political experience" (Fleischman, 49–50). She said to herself, "Anybody who didn't know how to speak for themselves, I thought, 'I know how. I'll speak for you'" ("Combat Ready," 9).

Jody spent some time in the United Kingdom, Mexico, and Washington, D.C. Her experience in teaching English as a Secondary Language had convinced her not to choose this as her life profession. She also knew upon her graduation in 1984 that work in a large governmental organization was not "her cup of tea" (Keene, 1–2).

From 1984 to 1986 she was one of the coordinators of the Nicaragua-Honduras Education Project and often headed fact-finding delegations. From 1986 until 1992 she served as the deputy director of Medical Aid for El Salvador. Ed Asner had founded this Los Angeles–based group; its job was to help victims of the civil war in El Salvador (Keene, 171–72).

One of Jody's main responsibilities was to help obtain artificial limbs for child victims of exploding landmines. The sight of such maimed young bodies disturbed her deeply. Even more children had not survived the explosions. The setting of landmines in El Salvador and elsewhere continued; the destruction, maiming, and death seemed without end. The International Red Cross had determined (1) that armies had sown more than 100 million landmines in 69 countries (including Central America, Asia, Africa, and the Middle East) and (2) that each year 26,000 people (mainly civilians) fell victim to them. The only way to end the suffering and death would be to cease using the devices and destroy the 100 million–plus mines waiting to explode and claim other victims (Keene, 171–72). Regrettably, the 100 million civilians killed or maimed from 1975 to 1997 cannot be reversed (De Mont, 29).

In Central America and elsewhere, Jody met those who were helping to fit victims of landmines with prostheses. She found that many people were actively soliciting the removal of hidden landmines before more innocent children and adults fell victim.

To Jody, the need was clear. Just because a war was over, she argued, did not mean that the killing stopped. Every 20 minutes, a landmine somewhere in the world injures a person. Jody understood that one hundred million landmines were still hidden in fields where farmers cultivated the soil and in areas where children played. Jody believed that the time was right to ban the further use of landmines, to help those affected by the devices, and to clear those hidden explosives waiting to maim or kill.

In November 1991, representatives of the Vietnam Veterans of America Foundation (based in Washington, DC) and Medico International (a German humanitarian organization) met with Jody to launch a campaign to ban landmines. Hundreds of organizations were already at work and were pulling together to eliminate landmines, promote human rights, and advocate the development of Third World Countries (Jenish, 32–33).

Robert Muller, head of the Vietnam Veterans of America Foundation, was himself a disabled veteran. Muller and Williams decided that merely helping to supply prostheses to landmine victims was not enough. They agreed that the elimination and banning of all landmines was crucial (Keene, 171–74).

At Muller's instruction, Williams banded humanitarian relief organizations, friends, and other interested organizations together for a new coalition: the International Campaign to Ban Landmines (ICBL). Williams served as ICBL coordinator and urged the creation of even more groups to begin to accomplish two goals: a ban on landmines and the creation of a fund to begin to remove the landmines still buried in the earth (Keene, 171–74). She was particularly disturbed because some of the bright colors of the landmine attracted children. One Khmer Rouge general said, "A landmine is the most excellent of soldiers." The landmine is "ever courageous, never sleeps, never misses" ("Land-Mines: A Deadly Inheritance," *Impact of Armed Conflict on Children*, 1).

The ICBL began with two offices in two countries. In October 1992, Jody organized in New York City the first international conference on landmines and their devastation. Six non-governmental organizations (NGOs) participated. A London conference (May 1993) brought representatives from 50 organizations. By 1995 the European Parliament had passed an important resolution: There would be a ban on landmines in European Union member nations (Jenish, 32–33).

Shawn Roberts and Jody Williams together wrote the book *After the Guns Fall Silent: The Enduring Legacy of Landmines*, published by the Vietnam Veterans of America Foundation in 1995. With the figures given in the book, the reader can generalize what might happen in future wars if the landmine threat persists. The goal was to convince the public that the long-term effects of landmines outweigh any military usefulness (Roberts, i).

The ICBL made more progress. By 1997 more than 100 organizations from 60 countries had banded together (Jenish, 32–33).

When Diana, Princess of Wales, visited Angola with the British Red Cross in January 1997, merely by her travel she brought much attention to the suffering and devastation brought about by landmines. In early June 1997, Princess Diana delivered the keynote address at the conference co-hosted by the Mines Advisory Group and the Land Survivors Network (LSN) at London's Royal Geographical Society. At this conference she shared for the first time her experiences in Angola (www.landminesurvivors.org/inside_chronology.php?year=1997).

A few days later, on June 12, Princess Diana delivered the keynote address at Sweet Brier College and called the landmines "stealthy killers." She described how, long after the wars were over, innocent victims suffered wounds and often death from remaining landmines. In fact, she reported that 800 died each month from the terrible injuries and that another 1200 a month suffered devastating injuries. Landmines had been in use by virtually every fighting nation at war since World War I. Hundreds of millions of the mines were stored around the globe. The weapons claimed thousands of victims every year (Diana, Princess of Wales, 1).

Diana recognized that most people were not aware of the threat of landmines; she admitted that until her Angola trip, she had not been aware of the tragedy associated with them. In Angola, with a population of 10,000,000 people, there were 15,000,000 landmines; one out of every 334 people is an amputee. The manufacturers usually designed the mines to be especially dangerous to the de-miner; this increased the cost of disposal. Diana learned that there were 100,000,000 mines in the world waiting to explode (Diana, Princess of Wales, 1–20).

The Princess was appalled! After seeing first-hand the mangled bodies (some of them children), she marveled that they lived in a country with so few medical resources. The lack of painkillers, medicine, anesthetics, prostheses, and medical personnel indicated the increased suffering of these people in underdeveloped countries (Diana, Princess of Wales, 2).

In August 1997 Diana joined the Landmine Survivors Network (LSN). In August 1997, during the last working week of her life, she met with rehabilitation specialists and even visited the homes of some landmine victims. She wrote to Jerry White of the LSN that these meetings and visits had strengthened her resolve to ensure that victims across the globe received the support and the care that they needed. Diana stressed that her interest was humanitarian—not political (www.landminesurvivors.org/inside_chronology.php?year=1997).

A car accident cut Princess Diana's life short on August 31, 1997. Jody called the accident "a tragic loss." The late princess's outspokenness had helped to draw international attention to the work of Jody Williams and the ICBL (International Campaign to Ban Landmines Web site, "Frequently Asked Questions").

The landmark conference in Oslo in September 1997 drew representatives of more than 100 countries. They spent more than 18 days developing the text for the treaty to outlaw landmines globally (Haydon, "Anti-Landmine Campaigners Win Nobel Peace Prize").

U.S. President Bill Clinton refused to commit the United States to a global treaty after the conference in Oslo. Clinton stated on September 17, 1997, "There is a line that I simply cannot cross, and that line is the safety and security of our men and women in uniform" (Giacomo, "Clinton Still Opposes Anti-Landmines Pact").

Williams accused the President of "abdicating his role as U. S. Commander-in-Chief by allowing the Defense Department to make the decision for him" (Haydon, "Anti-Landmine Activists Win Nobel Peace Prize").

On October 9, 1997, Jody Williams celebrated her 47th birthday. The very next morning, she received a 4:00 A.M. phone call from Oslo to inform her that she and the ICBL were the Nobel Peace Prize winners for 1997. At her home in Putney, Vermont, Jody could not watch the announcement on television because she had no set (Fleischman, 1).

Robert Muller, president of the Vietnam Veterans of America Foundation, issued a October 10, 1997, statement that the foundation was pleased that the ICBL had received the honor and hoped that the award "will lead to a full worldwide ban that will include the United States, which has yet to show support for this effort" ("Ban Landmines Campaign," Vietnam Veterans of America Foundation Press Release, October 10, 1997, 1).

The press did not present Jody as a woman without faults. "Williams is no angel. In interviews, her blunt language often lapses into cursing" (Bauldauf, 1).

In her kitchen, Jody and Stella, her white German shepherd, received photographers and reporters on October 10. By 9:00 A.M., nine satellite-dish trucks had parked in her meadow. Jody was careful to inform the news that she was only the co-winner of the Nobel Peace Prize and that the ICBL would share the prize with her. Within weeks, however, newspaper stories would begin to surface about her co-winners accuse her of "media grandstanding" or "hot-dogging" (Fleischman, 1–2).

"Williams used the occasion not to bask in the glow of having received the world's most coveted prize, but to blast the president of the United States.... 'I think it's tragic that President Clinton does not want to be on the side of humanity,' Williams said of the man she calls a 'weenie' for refusing to endorse the land mine ban...." (CNN, 1; Ballafante, 65).

She went on to say, "I've repeatedly said that Bill Clinton is neither a leader nor a statesman, and I'll say it again...." She called the award "a wake-up call for the United States. I would think that Bill Clinton would find it hard to keep saying he's a leader on this if he doesn't sign the treaty" (Rauber).

CNN reported that Williams commented on the fact that President Clinton had not called to congratulate her. "It's easier to ring the winners of the Super Bowl, because he is going to get a rah-rah testosterone answer.... If he calls me he is going to get something different." President Clinton did send her a letter congratulating her; the letter also stated that he maintained his position "that any land mine treaty must provide some exceptions" (CNN, 2).

Jody made *Glamour*'s list of the Top Ten Women of the Year a few weeks after she heard that she had won the coveted Nobel Peace Prize. Ms. Foundation placed her on its list of Top Role Models for Today's Girls (Fleischman, 1–2). There soon would be much controversy around Jody Williams.

Perhaps the attention that Princess Diana and Jordan's Queen Noor helped to draw to the landmines, the ICBL, and Jody Williams was important in influencing the Nobel Peace Prize Committee. Perhaps, also, the attention that Princess Diana, Jody, the Pope, Queen Noor, Nelson Mandela, and Paul McCartney drew to the tragedy of landmines helped increase the number of signatures on the Ottawa Treaty to Ban Landmines. Jody said that what she found so amazing about their participation was that they took up the issue on their own (International Campaign to Ban Landmines Web site, "Frequently Asked Questions"). On December 3, 1997, leaders from 125 countries—all the nations of the world, save 44—signed the document (Biography Research Center). These are the 44 that did not sign:

Armenia	Estonia	Kazakhstan	Lebanon
Azerbaijan	Finland	Korea, North	Libya
Bahrain	Georgia	Korea, South	Micronesia
Bhutan	India	Kuwait	Mongolia
China	Iran	Kyrgyzstan	Morocco
Cuba	Iraq	Laos	Myanmar (Burma)
Egypt	Israel	Latvia	Nepal

Oman	Russia	Syria	United States
Pakistan	Saudi Arabia	Tonga	of America
Palau	Singapore	Tuvalu	Uzbekistan
Papua New	Somalia	United Arab	Vietnam
Guinea	Sri Lanka	Emirates	

Despite the victory, many believed that for the treaty to have meaning, the United States, China, Russia, South Korea, and Israel must sign (De Mont, 29). In 1997, even with the $500,000,000 available for use and the signing of the landmine treaty, most knowledgeable parties knew that the work was just beginning. Organizations and personalities immediately began to disagree on how to spend the money. Lou Grath, the director of the British-based Mine Advisory Group, stated boldly that improving the lives of those already affected by landmines should be the first priority; he believed one of the first steps was to develop new technology to locate the mines (De Mont, 29). Still, by November 2004, Jody Williams was able to report that 143 nations had endorsed the treaty (Federal News Service, 5).

The fact that the United States had not signed, however, deeply disturbed Williams. Her actions and words caused some contention. President Clinton had refused to sign the treaty because "landmines were still needed to protect U. S. troops in various parts of the world, especially on the border between North and South Korea" (Keene, 171–74).

Jenish, too, noted President Clinton's failure to sign the treaty "under pressure from the Pentagon." Jenish recognized that Clinton's refusal came because (1) "American negotiators failed to win an exemption for South Korea, where 37,000 American troops are stationed" and (2) "Washington also wanted a nine-year implementation period" (Jenish, 32–33).

The Current Biography Yearbook noted that President Clinton's reason for not signing was because he "believes the so-called smart mines, which are designed to self-destruct after a predetermined period of time, pose no threat to civilians after a war is concluded." Another reason was his opposition to including the Korean border area in the banned area ("Williams, Jody," *Current Biography*).

It seemed ironic to the rest of the world that Jody's own country was a holdout in the agreement to ban landmines, but it was miraculous that, in only five years since the launching of the ICBL, most of the nations of the world ratified such a treaty. Jody saw the treaty as an important part of the groundwork for what she wanted to be a new future.

Jody's answer to those who asked why her own country had not signed the treaty was that the United States had explained that it needed the landmines for defense against Korea. Jody herself had noted that her nation seemed to favor a plan to eliminate the landmines over a decade—not immediately. Jody explained many times to interested parties how she saw the reluctance of the United Sates to be a fear that if it gave up the landmines, it might next have to face abandoning other destructive weapons for similar reasons (teacher.scholastic.com, 3).

During the treaty negotiations, the Nongovernmental Organizations were given the right to comment—an unusual occurrence.

• The Pentagon claimed that the landmines saved the lives of American soldiers, but the N.G.O. reported that one-third of the U.S. casualties during the Vietnam War were a result of landmines.

- The Pentagon said the landmines were "submunitions"; the N.G.O. reported that the Pentagon had already used the classification of "anti-personnel mines" for the landmines.
- When President Clinton pledged $80 million to remove mines in place, the N.G.O. reported that the plan was inadequate because each landmine cost only $3, but the cost to remove each could be as high as $1,000 (Roth, 23).

In Oslo on December 10, 1997, in his speech to honor Jody Williams and the ICBL, Francis Sejersted, Chair of the Norwegian Nobel Committee, said that Jody had succeeded in proving that she could change "the impossible to possible" (Sejersted, 1). The Norwegian Nobel Committee awarded the Nobel Peace Prize for 1997 equally to the ICBL and to Jody, the campaign's coordinator. The two would divide the $1,000,000 prize (Rogers, 51).

Jody's appearance and her comments at the ceremony created criticism. "At the Nobel awards presentation ceremony, she reportedly called President Bill Clinton a 'weenie' for refusing to sign the treaty, and was only mildly surprised when he did not call to congratulate her on her win" (*Biography Resource Center Online*, "Jody Williams," 2).

On December 31, 1997, Robert Muller "quietly dropped his support of his old friend ... seven weeks after the Nobel committee honored her and the campaign with joint shares in the $1-million prize" (Clines, A8). Muller went on to say, "It seemed contrary to my recollection" that a single individual was nominated for the Nobel Peace Prize (Clines, A8).

Muller commented on her calling President Clinton a "weenie": "When you're a Nobel laureate, you don't use language like that. Maybe if you're a 1960s activist, fine, but this is 1996" (Redmond, 9).

Jody, on the other hand, reported that the minutes should confirm that there was a joint nomination. "The campaign decided it was better to have a face connected with the nomination and obviously it should be mine" (Clines, A8). Others, however, said that she was only to accept the award, not to have a personal share in the award.*

In 1998, Jody and eight other Nobel Peace Prize winners met at the University of Virginia in Charlottesville, Virginia. Robert Muller and Jody Williams received recognition for their work to develop the treaty to ban landmines. Several of the laureates "expressed their disgust with a weapon that sits silent in the ground for decades, only to explode when a child or a herder steps that way" (Cobban, 11).

During the Virginia meeting, Nobel Peace Prize winner Betty Williams spoke about another type of wound: the resentment and coldness that accompany war survivors for years after the end of the war. She had a special name for this condition: "landmines of the heart." The Dalai Lama summed up the thoughts of the group by noting two necessary types of disarmament: both external and internal disarmament (Cobban, 11).

Jody received honorary doctorates from Franklin Pierce College and Wesleyan University (2003); the Royal Military College of Canada (2002); Regis University (2000); Shenshu University in Japan and Rockhurst University (1990); Williams College (1998); and Briar Cliff College, Marlboro College, and the University of Vermont (1997). In 2003,

*There were 130 nominees for the Nobel Peace Prize of 1997. Democratic Senator Patrick Leahy of Vermont had praised Williams, nominated her for the Nobel Peace Prize, and sung the praises of the ICBL (Giacomo, "Clinton 'Rock Solid' Against Landmines Pact"). Another member of Congress, James McGovern, also nominated Jody.

AARP: The Magazine appointed her to its list of America's most innovative people over 50; the previous year, Jody received the Humanitarian Award presented at the Hollywood Film Festival and the Humanitarian of the Year Award that the UN Association of the United States presented at its "Adopt-a-Minefield" Program. The Oldender Foundation of Washington, D.C., named her the "Peacemaker of 1999." Clark University presented her the Flat Lux Award, which took its name from Lark's motto "Let there be light"; the Flat Lux Award honors individuals who have demonstrated exceptional leadership in increasing the understanding of issues vital in the twenty-first century.

In March 1999, Jody answered some questions posed at an interview for *Newsweek International.* When asked if the numbers of existing mines were inflated, she said that the charge was "pathetically laughable. It would be amusing if they weren't killing people every 20 minutes" ("There's Still Too Many," 29).

At the same interview she responded to the criticism "that ICBL spends money on receptions and press conferences instead of on de-mining and victim assistance." She noted that the ICBL had decided to use the money it raised on political activities, not clearing mines. She said the political activities were necessary to ensure a universal treaty. She also said that from 1992 to 1997, the ICBL had spent $6,000,000 globally—"Politics on a shoe-string" ("There's Still Too Many," 29).

Jody remained in the news. On March 26, 2003, Washington, D.C., police arrested Jody Williams and Mairead Corrigan Maguire, the 1976 Nobel Peace Prize co-winner. The two sat with Catholic and Methodist bishops and with a leading rabbi in a circle in the park near the White House and chanted, "Peace, shalom." They held posters of the civilian casualties of the war and roses. Maguire reported that she had asked President George W. Bush to meet with her and that she would like to resolve problems with dialogue. As Jody had the handcuffs applied and as the police placed her in the van, she shouted, "This is what our democracy looks like" (Pleming, 1–2).

Williams said that it was difficult for Americans to protest the war. She said that Americans as children learn little mythologies that make it difficult to disagree with war. She expresses the opinion that George W. Bush, like his father President George H. W. Bush, is trying to reshape the world after the Cold War and to rebuild the American empire. She does not condone the message that to support the troops means that one must also support the war (Turner, 1–2).

By October 23, 2003, only one NATO nation—the United States—had not signed the treaty. Jody feared the United States might not even consider joining the treaty in 2006, the year it had agreed to reconsider, if its search for other alternatives was successful.

Jody's schedule also includes work with the PeaceJam Foundation. That international organization brings Nobel Peace Laureates to work with youth and to pass on their skills and their wisdom. The goal is to inspire a new generation of peace people. The year-long PeaceJam had worked with over 100,000 teenagers between its inception and November 2004. That November, Jody Williams and Iranian Nobel winner Shirin Ebadi led the 92nd PeaceJam Youth Conference in Kenya (Malcolm, 2).

At the University of Houston, Jody is a Distinguished Visiting Professor of Social Work and Global Justice. Her appointment is to the Graduate School of Social Work for the years 2004–07. She served also in a one-year appointment from 2003–04. (International Campaign to Ban Landmines Web site).

When an interviewer asked who she is and what she plans to do, Jody replied that she is still the one "who didn't go to her own graduation. I'm still Jody Williams, who doesn't know what my next job's going to be.... The only thing I do know is that I still, every single day of my life, get up with joy and excitement and wonder about what I am going to do today that's going to make a difference. Nobody can define what makes a difference for you. You have to figure out what makes a difference for you.... What matters is that it gives you joy" (Williams, *Christian Science Monitor*, 12).

Jody gives the following advice: "Have the courage to try to figure out what brings you joy so you can bring it to everybody else" (Williams, *Christian Science Monitor*, 12).

Bibliography

Baldaug, Scott. "Nobel Laureate's Long Trip from Vermont Farm to Fame." *Christian Science Monitor*, XC, October 14, 1997.

Ballafante, Ginia. "Kudos for a Crusader: Jody Williams Wins the Nobel Peace Prize for Her Campaign to Ban Land Mines Around the World." *Time*, October 20, 1997, 65.

"Ban Landmines Campaign Receives Nobel Peace Prize." Vietnam Veterans of America Foundation Press Release, October 10, 1997, 1)

Beard, Mary. "Down Among the Women (Nobel Laureates)." *Kenyon Review*, XXIII, Spring 2001, 239–48.

Clines, Francis X. "In Fighting Land Mines, Friendship Is Casualty." *New York Times*, February 20, 1998, A8.

CNN. "Jody Williams: The Woman Who Waged War on Land Mines." Available online at www.cnn.com/SPECIALS/1997/nobel.prize/stories/williams.profile.

Cobban, Helena. "Nine Nobelists, One Room." *Christian Science Monitor*, November 12, 1998, 11.

"Combat Ready: New Nobel Laureate Jody Williams Never Shrinks from a Fight," *People Weekly*, October 27, 1997, 9.

De Mont, John. "Axworthy's Grand Moment." *Maclean's*, December 15, 1997, 29.

Diana, Princess of Wales. "Responding to Landmines: A Modern Tragedy and Its Consequences." *Gifts of Speech at Sweet Brier College*, June 12, 1997. Available online at http://gos.sbc.edu/d/diana.html.

Federal News Service. "Press Conference on the Landmine Monitor Report 2004." November 18, 2004. Available online at web.lexis-nexis.com/universe/document?_m=711b813759f66cd3d5c 9b3c2fad5b486& ...

Fleischman, John. "You Can Never Live Down the Nobel Prize." *Yankee*, June 1998, 42–51.

Giacomo, Carol. "Clinton 'Rock Solid' Against Landmines Pact." Washington (Reuters), October 11, 1997.

_____. "Clinton Still Opposes Anti-Landmines Pact." Washington (Reuters), October 10, 1997.

Haydon, Simon. "Anti-Landmine Activists Win Nobel Peace Prize." Washington (Reuter), October 10, 1997.

"International Campaign to Ban Landmines." www.icbl.org/campaign/ambassadors/jody_williams.

"International Campaign to Ban Landmines Frequently Asked Questions." www.icbl.org/cgi-bin/faq/landmines/index.cgi?subject+9996244752.

Jenish, D'Arcy. "Landing the Prize: Peace Activists Share in the 1997 Nobel." *Maclean's*, October 20, 1997, 32–33.

"Jody Williams." *Biography Resource Center Online*. Gale Group, 2001, 1–4.

Keene, Ann T. "Peace Profiles: Jody Williams, Carlos Felipe Ximenes Belo, and Jose Ramos-Horta." *Peace Review*, March 1999, 171–76.

Landmine Survivors Network. Chronology 1997. www.landminesurvivors.org/inside_chronology.php?year=1997.

"Land-Mines: A Deadly Inheritance." *Impact of Armed Conflict on Children*, UNICEF Home Page. Available online at http://www.unicef.org/graca/mines.htm.

Malcolm, Teresa. "Youth Urged to Act for Peace," *National Catholic Reporter*, December 10, 1999. 6–8.

McGovern, James. Letter to Mr. Geir Lundestad on January 13, 1997. Letter available by calling Stephen Goose at (202) 371–6592.

Pleming, Sue. "Nobel Winners Arrested at the White House." Reuters news story, March 26, 2003.

Rauber, Marily. "Nobel Hero Blows Up at U.S. Mines." *New York Post*, October 11, 1997.

Redmond, Tim, and Linda Ehrlich. "Pie 'em All and Let God Sort 'em Out: Presenting Our 14th Annual Off-Guard Awards for the Worst of the Year That Was." *SFBG News*, December 30, 1998. Also available online at www.sfbg.com/News/33/13/Features/offies.html.

Roberts, Shawn, and Jody Williams. *After the Guns Fall Silent: The Enduring Legacy of Landmines.* Washington, D.C.: Vietnam Veterans of America Foundation, 1995.

Rogers, Adam. "Science of War, War of Science." *Newsweek*, October 20, 1997, 51.

Roth, Kenneth. "New Minefields for N.G.O.: After Winning the War on Landmines, These Organizations Started New Campaigns." *Nation*, April 13, 1998, 22–24.

Sejersted, Francis. "Presentation Speech on the Occasion of the Award of the Nobel Peace Prize for 1997." http://www.nobelprize.org/peace/laureates/1997/presentation-speech.html.

"There's Still Too Many." Interview with Ken Shulman *Newsweek International*, March 8, 1999, 29.

Turner, Angela. "Laureate Makes a Case for Peace," *Albuquerque Journal*, April 6, 2003, JOURNAL NORTH SECTION, 1.

Who's Who of American Women: 1999–2000. New Providence, New Jersey: Marquis Who's Who, 1998.

"Williams, Jody." *Current Biography Yearbook: 1998*. Elizabeth A. Schick, Ed. New York: H. W. Wilson, 1997–98.

Williams, Jody. "Nobel Laureate Jody Williams on Joy." *Christian Science Monitor*, June 12, 1998, 12.

_____, Paul Wapner, and Gina Coplon-Newfield. "Sign the Mine Ban Treaty." *Issues in Science and Technology*. Fall 2003, 19–22.

"Women Who Changed History. Jody Williams." Available online at http://teacher.scholastic.com/activities/women/jody_transcript.htm.

Shirin Ebadi
(2003)

A New Prophetic Voice in Iran

(June 21, 1947–)

"Poverty negates human rights."
[Twair, "Shirin Ebadi, Iran's
Nobel Peace Laureate," 31]

"Their religion is an ideological tool of power."
[Ebadi, "Tell Them to Use Their Heads," 72]

"Those who kill in the name of Islam, they violate Islam."
[Danbolt Mjøs, "Nobel Peace Prize
2003 Presentation Speech"]

Shirin Ebadi, Nobel Peace Laureate 2003.

Introduction: Iran and its History of Religio-Political Abuse

It was in the summer of 1982, so long ago that *Ha'Aretz*, an Israeli newspaper, has headlines about the executions of Bah'ai in Iran. The Western powers paid virtually no attention to these executions because they understood very little about the religion and its people. Today, 23 years later, followers of Bah'ai are still being jailed, physically abused, and murdered. Their religion is banned and they are prevented from participating in the government or other social institutions (http://www.endgenocide.org/genocide/bahai.html). This type of brutal totalitarianism has characterized the politics in Iran for decades—some would say hundreds if not thousands—of years.

The history of the country now called Iran is too long to explore in this chapter because it can be traced back almost 6,000 years. Various countries occupied and ruled this part of the world because of its proximity to the Tigris and Euphrates Rivers at the mouth of the Persian Gulf. It had access to fresh and salt waterways in the midst of desert conditions, so invading armies from north, south, east and west fought for control of this route, and ultimately to security and domination of the region.

Around the seventh century c.e., Islamic armies conquered Iran. By the sixteenth century, after occupations by the Turks and Mongols, the Shiite sect of Islam became firmly entrenched in Iran under Shah Ismail. (Sunni is the majority division within Islam, Shia represent approximately ten percent of Muslims in the world.) Oil was discovered in the nineteenth century and with that news, Russia, the United Kingdom, and others attempted to get involved in reigning in the profits. Numerous military occupations and internal conflicts plagued Iran, leaving its people and governments unstable.

Iran was occupied by the United Kingdom during World War I and given independence in a document in 1919, but in reality, the Brits continued to dominate Iran. During WWII, British and American troops controlled Iran. By 1954, several countries were managing the oil facilities in Iran, including the United States. In 1953, supported by the United States, the Shah of Iran, Mohammed Reza Pahlavi, began a program of westernization and modernization in his country. His strategy, like his predecessors, was brutal and totalitarian. Many of the reforms were superficial since they did not arise from the people themselves but were imposed upon them.

And while his feminist reforms did bring change, such as opportunities for equitable education, an openness for both sexes to work in government, and the vote for women, the conservative religious leaders felt left out. They had been brutally repressed by the Shah's secret police.

His reforms also produced class conflict among females. There was an insidious cultural hierarchy brewing among the women in Tehran. Those who worked uptown were considered sophisticated and intelligent because they did not wear the veil. Those of the lower classes or workers in supportive and service positions did not abandon the veil and so were seen as "lower" or "unevolved."

> The enforcement of the dress-code or hijab (modesty) after the revolution was in part an attempt to replace markers of difference by dress, although it was widely propagated as a pre-server of public morality and modesty. During the Shah's era, the chador was a highly conspicuous marker of social distinction along class lines. Those who wore a chador were derided by the "west-intoxicated" (gharb-zada) middle classes as "ummul" (pejoratively "traditional") [Torab, "The Politicization of Women's Religious Circles in Post-Revolutionary Iran," 145].

The Ayatollah Ruhollah Khomeini led a resistance movement against the Shah's regime from exile in France. He hinted that the Twelfth Imam, a messianic figure who was prophesied to usher in a period of peace and prosperity, would come sooner if the Shah was deposed. By 1979 he claimed victory, with the exile of the Shah, and returned to Iran in an emotional blitz.

Riding on the wings of this eschatological ideology, Khomeini began to transform Iran into a theocratic state, into the Islamic Republic of Iran. In an overwhelming referendum, the people of Iran gave Khomeini almost unlimited powers. And with these powers he took control of Iran and created a religious state.

Many followed the lead of the Ayatollah and supported his hard-line and fundamentalist view that Iran should return to historic Shia Islam. They did not like the western-style atmosphere of their country under the Shah that separated religion and government.

> [T]he Islamic revolution, marginalized or eradicated leftists and liberals and instituted a draconian cultural-political system characterized by the rule of a clerical caste, the application of Islamic law to the areas of personal status and crime, and compulsory veiling for women. During the 1980's, leftists—whether of the communist or Muslim variety—were purged from jobs, forced underground, compelled to flee Iran to escape arrest, imprisoned, subjected to torture, executed, and assassinated [Moghadam, "Islamic Feminism and Its Discontents," 1137].
> The new government represented a major shift toward conservatism. It nationalized industries and banks and revived Islamic traditions. Western influence and music were banned. Women were forced to return to traditional veiled dress, and Westernized elites fled the country ["Iran," in *Columbia Encyclopedia*, 2005].

In the name of Allah, he quashed any sign of opposition. Approximately 1600 people had been killed by 1981. Among those unfortunates who were eliminated were people who did not practice his brand of Islam. And the Baha'is were an offshoot of Islam that he would not tolerate. He was convinced that Shia Islam was the answer for everything in the state. Khomeini wrote:

> In the society we propose to establish, the Marxists will be free to express themselves because we are convinced that Islam contains the answer to the people's needs. Our faith is capable of standing up to their ideology [Mohammadi, "Tradition versus Ideology," in *Islam Encountering Globalization*, 207].

Within ten years, in 1989, the position of prime minister was eliminated, giving the president even more powers. To oppose or criticize the government, even if a Shia, could be lethal.

> Therefore, in addition to retreating to patriarchal interpretation, as a result of political necessity rules attacked the roots of independent thinking, causing a retreat of critical thought. The threat of individual violence against Muslim scholars advocating free will in the interpretation of Islam and the imposition of an official dogma effectively limited religious interpretation [Sayeh, "Islam and the Treatment of Women," 5].

The Public Ebadi

It was during this time that Shirin Ebadi was fired from her job because she was a woman. Women could no longer hold important and intellectual positions in Iran. Their minds were considered to be too fragile.

Shirin supported the return of the Ayatollah. She may have originally sided with many women "who considered themselves the heirs of the revolution [and who] collaborated with the Islamist state to oppress secular women" (Kian-Thiebaut,"From Islamization to the Individualization of Women," 129).

She was warned that with his return, she would lose her position in society. She did not believe it until it actually happened to her. As the first woman judge in Iran, Shirin was well-known and had thoughts of running the Ministry of Justice. It never happened. With the return of Khomeini, she was demoted to an administrative-secretarial position. This humiliation was too much for her, so she retired from her government position and went into private practice.

> Although I earned much more money than when I was a judge, I was not satisfied because my new job was not as prestigious as my previous post.... I came to the conclusion that I should do something else to prove my social identity.... As a woman jurist, I have always been sensitive to the issue of gender.... I started to write books and articles ... to show the shortcomings of the legal system [Kian-Thiebaut, "From Islamization to the Individualization of Women," 134].

Females and Iran

Islamic scholars chide the west for denigrating Islam using the issue of the rights of females. The issue of the status of females in Islamic states is very complicated. Many students of the Quran point out that in the past, females had more equity. Islamic writers contend that the Prophet, Muhammad, had wives, among them A'isha, who taught the Quran, a position termed a "jurist," and that he established a standard of equality that was abandoned by later leaders within Islam. They argue that the Quran and Hadith (Deeds and Sayings of Muhammad) have been misinterpreted by the current Mullahs. The sacred scriptures intended to liberate, not subjugate, females (Sayeh, "Islam and the Treatment of Women," 8). Some point to Quran 4:1,

> · O mankind! Reverence Your Guardian-Lord, Who created you from A single Person, Created, out of it, His mate, and from them twain Scattered (like seeds) Countless men and women [An-Nabawiyah, *The Holy Quran*, 205].

They also argue that when Europe was in the "Dark Ages," and women had few or no rights, Islam was protecting women and giving them rights to an inheritance and a career.

> At the time Islam announced that women would have certain rights, including a right to education, a right to a dower, a right to choose whether to marry, and a right to manage their own property, the West was mired in that unenlightened period known as the Dark Ages [Sayeh, "Islam and the Treatment of Women," 13].

The hijab (total body covering) for females is also problematic for the west. It is viewed as a symbol of oppression or submission. To date, France has not rescinded laws prohibiting the wearing of a veil (or hijab) in schools. The French also interpret the veiling as oppressive.

> [T]he dominate image of a "typical" Muslim woman combines powerlessness and passivity on an individual level with what seems like a fierce and active loyalty to her community and its shared values, especially religion and culture [Ansari, *Women, Religion, and Culture in Iran*, 1].

But the total covering does not always symbolize "submission" to males. In Iran, the wearing of the chador-hijab was used as a way of expressing freedom of speech when the Ayatollah returned. Females willingly returned to the dress as a sign of their own freedom from the dictates of the oppressive Shah and the imperialistic west. Most of them never suspected that their own government would soon legislate personal dress for women. Even today in Iran, there are Islamic female preachers-teachers who require their female students to wear the hijab as a sign of resistance; as a way of protecting their identity; as a sign of solidarity.

> In the course of the revolution, various categories of women adopted the Islamic veil for different reasons: while secular women used the veil as a symbol of national unity against the Shah's regime, the traditionalists' thick black chador symbolized their Shi'ite ideology and culture, and their aspirations to an exclusive society ruled by Islamic laws....
> When I was a high school student, I used to wear a small scarf and a short dress over my pants. Then when I started participating in the protest movement, I wore the chador. Yet, by wearing it I did not intend to cover my head or body. Like many other women what I meant to do was to mark my identity. We wore the chador as a symbol of our struggle for a just society [Kian-Thiebaut, "From Islamization to the Individualization of Women," in Ansari, *Women, Religion, and Culture in Iran*, 128].

Human Rights and Ebadi

> "I'm a Muslim, so you can be a Muslim and support democracy."
>   ("Iranian Lawyer," 1)

Shirin Ebadi is proud to be a Muslim. She believes that the Quran teaches equality for all peoples, so she set out on a crusade to reform Iran through its own religio-judicial system. Shirin thinks that the rights of females, children, and others can be protected under the current theocracy in Iran if certain laws are changed or reinterpreted. In a sense, she seeks to protect her country and her religion, while at the same time she works for human rights.

In her book *History and Documentation of Human Rights in Iran*, she discusses the inconsistencies in the law and how it punishes people for killing another human being. The law discriminates against certain peoples in favor of others. A married woman has very few rights.

> Premeditated murder should result in "qisas" punishment, except when (1) the perpetrator is a Muslim and the victim is a kafir (lit. unbeliever) or non–Muslim; (2) a father or paternal grandfather kills his child; (3) a sane person slays an insane one; or (4) a man murders his wife. These exceptions to capital punishment are rooted in the Islamic Republic's understanding of the need for social order and a man's ownership of his offspring and spouse—both of which override the rights of non–Muslims, children, the mentally ill, and married women ... [Vaziri, "Review of History and Documentation of Human Rights in Islam," 754–55].

Basing her interpretation of law in Iran upon international human rights laws, she has taken on legal cases that no one else would touch for fear of losing their lives. This choice resulted in a guilty verdict and sentence against her for "preparing videotape cassettes to reveal the involvement of conservative officials in terrorism" (Vaziri, *Review of History and Documentation of Human Rights in Islam*, 754–55). Ultimately she spent very little time in prison but lost her right to work as an attorney for five years in 2000.

One of her cases included an ex-minister of labor, Darioush Forouher, who was murdered with his wife in their home by the government. She also represented the families of serial killings in the '90s; a Canadian journalist, Zahra Kazemi, who was killed while being held by the courts, and Hashem Aghajari, a professor who was sentenced to death for opposing the government.

The Foundation of Discrimination Against Females in Iran

Ebadi has tackled many of the issues underlying the very low status of women in Iran. For instance, the age of puberty is important for determining responsibility for crimes. Iranian law states that a male reaches puberty at 15 and a female at nine years old. "If a fourteen year old boy commits a crime, he will be exonerated from any criminal responsibility, but if the same crime is committed by a ten-year-old girl, she will be held accountable" (Monshipouri, "The Road to Globalization," 2).

In the past, in Iran, a father could sell his infant daughter into marriage. The daughter was not involved in the decision. Ebadi has worked to raise the age of marriage for both sexes. Now girls must be 13 and boys 18 before they can marry. Shirin points out inconsistencies in the legal system.

> If a man helps a woman have an abortion, which would result in the child's death, he is sentenced to a three-six month imprisonment. If, by contrast, the embryo is not killed and grows to become a fourteen-year-old boy or girl and then the father kills him or her intentionally, the father will receive a less severe punishment [Monshipouri, "The Road to Globalization," 3].

Iranian Family Law places females in double-bind situations. Ebadi seeks equity and justice for both males and females. Tradition allows Muslim males to marry four women. Muslim women may only marry one male. The courts require the testimony of two females to equal that of one man. Women are allowed to obtain a divorce in Iran if her husband physically abuses her. But even if she does obtain a divorce, she may be shunned by her family because they do not have the funds to support her. And many women cannot find work, so someone has to take care of them. At the moment there are few agencies that facilitate the escape from an abusive relationship in Iran.

One of Ebadi's cases exposed the Iranian clerics' rigid and often counterproductive interpretation of the Quran-Iranian Law. A divorced woman wanted to obtain custody of her daughter because the father was abusive. She proved in court that he was an addict and had spent time in prison. The court awarded custody to the father because Shari'a (Islamic law) considers children to be the property of the father. Not long after the court case, the child was beaten to death by the father. Based on this case, Ebadi helped to launch a citizen's movement that forced the clerics to recognize the rights of women and children in these cases. She also obtained a conviction of the father (Ahmad, "Shirin Ebadi: a Muslim Woman Nobel Peace Laureate," 2).

The Award

The Nobel Peace Prize Committee took a progressive and politically charged step forward when they chose to honor Ebadi. They hinted in their speeches that they did not appreciate the rhetoric of denigration used by the West towards Islam. At the same time, they chided the hard-line approach that Iran has taken toward women and children. The prize money will guarantee that Ebadi's legal efforts on behalf of women and children will continue. She may lose her license to practice law but she can continue her work towards alleviating the suffering of so many people who have been jailed or silenced.

Ole Danbolt Mjøs, chairman of the Norwegian Nobel Committee, offered a speech in tribute to Ebadi, the first Muslim woman to win the prize. The following are a few of his thoughtful and pointed words.

> Let us hope that the prize will also inspire changes in your beloved home country, Iran, as well as in many other parts of the world where people need to hear your clear voice. And let me hasten to add—this applies to the western world as well....
>
> All people are entitled to fundamental rights, and at a time when Islam is being demonized in many quarters of the western world, it was the Norwegian Nobel Committee's wish to underline how important and how valuable it is to foster dialogue between peoples and between civilizations ...
>
> She has been very clear in her opposition to patriarchal cultures that deny equal rights to women, who represent half of the population. But mothers must also be aware of their responsibilities. They are the ones who bring up young boys to be men and who raise daughters to become strong women....
>
> As a lawyer, judge, lecturer, author, and activist, her voice has sounded clearly and powerfully in her native country of Iran, and also far beyond its national borders. She has come forward with professional force and unflagging courage, and she has defied any danger to her own safety. She is truly a woman of the people!

Iran and the Nobel Peace Prize

The news of Ebadi's prize received a lukewarm reception in her own country. State-run television and radio stations barely mentioned it. Finally, Abdollah, spokesman for the Iranian government, gave an official reaction to her prize: "In the name of the Islamic Republic of Iran's government I congratulate her" ("Iranian Human Rights," 1). President Mohammad Khatami, unimpressed, indicated that it would have been a greater honor to receive the Nobel Prize in science or literature. "The state-run television did not broadcast her acceptance speech last December, because, by not wearing a headscarf, she was in violation of the official dress code for women" (Pal, "Helen Thomas Interview," 1).

More conservative Shi'as are insulted by her refusal to follow the rules of Hijab when she is traveling. Militant students and traditional females often protest her presence in lecture halls. Supporters have had to surround her while students chanted "Death to Ebadi" and "God is great" at Al-Zahra Women's University in Tehran ("Protesters Prevent Speech," *ISNA Website*, 1).

Her Life

Shirin Ebadi was lucky to be born into a family that was educated and economically secure. Documents reveal very little about her mother. It is to her father that Shirin refers when she speaks about her interest in law. Mohammad Ali Ebadi was a lecturer in Commercial Law and authored several books. He passed away in 1993. Her own academic credentials are impressive.

> I sat the Tehran University entrance exams and gained a place at the Faculty of law in 1965. I received my law degree in three and a half years, and immediately sat the entrance exams for the Department of Justice. After a six-month apprenticeship in adjudication, I began to serve

officially as a judge in March 1969. While serving as a judge, I continued my education and obtained a doctorate with honors in private law from Tehran University in 1971 ["Shirin Ebadi-Biography"].

She served as the first female judge for four years and became president of a city court in Tehran. After her demotion to a clerk, she was denied a license to practice law and says that she was "housebound for many years." By 1992, she had finally obtained a license to practice law and began taking on controversial cases, including child abuse, freedom of speech, and murder by the state. She teaches at the University of Tehran and is married to Javad. And, in addition to her other activities, she is mother to two daughters, Narges and Negar.

In her dedication to the children and women of Iran, she has founded or co-founded organizations including Human Rights Defense Center and the Association for Support of Children's Rights. Her written works include 11 books, some of which have been translated into English, including *The Rights of the Child: A Study in the Legal Aspects of Children's Rights in Iran* (Unicef, 1993). She has also written articles for the *Encyclopedia Iranica*, *Bonyad Iran*, and *Studies in the Social Impacts of Biotechnology* (Ebadi, "Autobiography").

Ebadi and Iran Today

Women are entering the universities in Iran in record numbers and becoming a powerful political force. Around 63 percent of students in universities today are female. Educating women has slowed the tremendous birth rate of Iran that catapulted the state into literacy and population crises under the Khomeini regime. Sending women back home, fired from their careers, resulted in 7.2 children per family. Recently, under the more moderate regimes in Iran, that figure has dropped to 3.2 children per family.

> The rule of political Islam, which has proved incompatible with the realities of modern Iranian society, has led Islamic and secular women to join hands, re-appropriate modernity, and challenge gender inequality [Kian-Thiebaut, "From Islamization to the Individualization of Women," 141].

Today in Iran, women are beginning to challenge laws that have subjugated them. Clerics who claim that their authority comes from Allah and thus, absolute power, are being argued out of their positions by very bright women, including Shirin. The arguments they are using are difficult to refute. For instance, if there is only one interpretation of the Quran, then why do laws created by Muslims differ in Egypt, Morocco, or Pakistan regarding females? Even in Iran, the Mullahs admitted that they made mistakes when they fired the women under Khomeini's rule. Now Iran is once again appointing female judges. Does God's law change or do people interpret the Quran only to bolster their own authority? "We must distinguish between humanity's own mistakes and the religion and cultures to which they belong," says Shirin. (Buczek, "Nobel Laureate Urges More Understanding," 1).

Shirin criticizes the all-male ruling clergy in Iran but she does not stop there. She also argues that females are co-conspirators.

> There is no "true Islam," just different interpretations. Since I brought up patriarchy, let me make one thing clear. I am not singling out men, I am addressing the issue of inequality of genders. A patriarchy does not only not accept the equality of sexes, it also has a hard time understanding the principles of democracy and its essence. Women are the victims of this patriarchal culture, but they are also its carriers. Let us keep in mind that every oppressive man was raised in the confines of his mother's home. This is the culture we need to resist and fight [Pal, "Helen Thomas Interview," 2].

The Fearless Shirin Ebadi

"I try to follow his example, to grit my teeth..., to clench my fist, too, until my fingers are blue. But sometimes I hate myself and discover I am still weak."
(Ebadi, "Tell Them to Use Their Heads," 72)

Shirin appears to be afraid of no one. In the United States, journalists, television personalities, and pop stars have lost their jobs because they have criticized the United States' invasion of Iraq. Now that Ebadi has the world as her stage, she is speaking out against what she views as violations of human rights by the United States in the prisons of Iraq and at Guantanamo Bay in Cuba. She is also challenging Iran to open the doors of the prisons and allow hundreds of political prisoners to go home.

She hints that the United States may be dishonest about its reasons for invading Afghanistan and Iraq. U.S. policymakers demonstrate a misunderstanding of the causes of terrorism and how to control it effectively. By invading Iraq, the United States may have, indeed, created an atmosphere where terrorism will thrive.

Her antidote for terrorism is education and support. People who are abused, who have no food, or hope for the future, will certainly gravitate toward groups who will provide the necessities for them. The more educated people become, the more they are exposed to pluralistic thinking, the less they will be attracted to a terrorist groups that teach that their way is the only true way (Pal, "Helen Thomas Interview," 3).

You cannot export democracy with weapons. You cannot pour human rights on people's heads with cluster bombs. Those countries claiming they are sympathetic to human rights and democracy should work through the United Nations [Twair, "Shirin Ebadi, Iran's Nobel Peace Laureate," 33].

Shirin points to the children who have lost their parents and the great devastation of the political and physical infrastructures of Iraq—and then critically says, "[but] the arms industry seems to flourish." Who benefits from the war in Iraq? For her, it is the imperialistic business interests of the United States who are only interested in oil and keeping their weapons' manufacturing companies operating at top speed (Pal, "Helen Thomas Interview," 4).

While President George W. Bush lauds the new democratic government in Iraq, Ebadi predicts that the Iraqis will oust the U.S. occupation in the future. She thinks that the war has served as a catalyst to unite Muslim countries against the United States. America had a positive image around the world after World War II but it has vanished.

I want to take my American friends back to the end of World War II, when the Universal Declaration of Human Rights was formulated. A group of thinkers met to come up with ways and means to prevent yet another war. Mrs. Eleanor Roosevelt played a crucial role in assembling this group of people. And that is why the name of the United States is synonymous with the cause of human rights around the world. Now what has happened to the glorious American civilization that has brought us to the present phase when we see those despicable pictures of mistreated Iraqi prisoners? What do you think Mrs. Eleanor Roosevelt would have said if she were alive in this day and age? The present Administration should apologize to the spirit of Eleanor Roosevelt for what it has done, for the atrocities committed [Pal, "Helen Thomas Interview," 4].

A new voice is being heard in Iran. Perhaps someday Iran will cherish Shirin Ebadi's well-reasoned, truthful, and daring words. Many Shiites believe that a Madhi (messiah), the Twelfth Imam (leader), will come in the future to usher in a new age of universal peace, prosperity, and equity. Perhaps she has come!

Bibliography

Ahmad, Iftikhar. "Shirin Ebadi: A Muslim Woman Nobel Peace Laureate." *Social Education*, Vol. 68. May–June 2004: 1–6.

An-Nabawiwyah, Mushaf Al-Madinah, trans. *The Holy Quran. English Translation of the Meanings and Commentary*. Al-Madinah Al-Munawwarah, King Fahd Holy Quran Printing Complex.

Ansari, Sarah, and Vanessa Martin. *Women, Religion, and Culture in Iran*. London: Curzon, 2002.

Buczek, Nancy. "Nobel Laureate Urges More Understanding: Former Iranian Judge Stresses Islam Isn't a Religion of Violence." *The Post Standard*, May 11, 2004, 1.

Danbolt Mjøs, Ole. Nobel Peace Prize 2003 Presentation Speech. Available online of www.nobel-prize.org/peace/laureates/2003/presentation-speech.html.

Ebadi, Shrin. "Autobiography." Available online at http://nobelprize.org/peace/laureates/2003/ebadi-bio.html.

_____. *History and Documentation of Human Rights in Iran*. New York: Bibliotheca Persica Press, 2000.

_____. "Nobel Peace Prize 2003 Nobel Lecture." Available online at http://nobelprize.org/peace/laureates/2003/ebadi-lecture.html.

_____. "Shirin Ebadi Autobiography." Available online at http://nobelprize.org/peace/laureates/2003/ebadi-bio.html

_____. "Tell Them to Use Their Heads." *Index on Censorship* 33, No. 4 (2004): Interview by Jenane Kareh Tager.

Haddad, Yvonne Yazbeck. *Islam, Gender, and Social Change*. New York: Oxford University Press, 1998.

"Iranian Human Rights Activist Wins 2003 Nobel Peace Prize: Shirin Ebadi Honoured for Work on Behalf of Women and Children." *CanWest News* Service, October 11, 2003: 1–3.

"Iranian Lawyer, Human Rights Activist Awarded Nobel Peace Prize for 2003." *The Guardian*, October 11, 2003: 1.

Kian-Thiebaut, Azadeh. "From Islamization to the Individualization of Women," in Ansari and Martin, *Women, Religion, and Culture in Iran*, 141.

Kim, Uichol, Henriette Sinding Aasen, and Shirin Ebadi. *Democracy, Human Rights, and Islam in Modern Iran. Psychological, Social, and Cultural Perspectives*. Bergen, Norway, Fagbok for laget, 2003.

Moghadam, Valentine M. "Islamic Feminism and Its Discontents: Toward Resolution of the Debate." *Signs* 27 No. 4 (Summer, 2002): 1135–71.

Mohammadi, Ali, Ed. *Islam Encountering Globalization*. London: RoutledgeCurzon, 2002.

_____. "Tradition versus Ideology," in *Islam Encountering Globalization*. Edited by Ali Mohammadi. London, RoutledgeCurzon, 2002: 207–21.

Monghipouri, Mahmood. "The Road to Globalization Runs Through Women's Struggle. Iran and the Impact of the Nobel Peace Prize." *World Affairs* vol. 167, no. 1, Summer 2004: 1–11.

Pal, Amitabh. "Helen Thomas Interview." *The Progressive Magazine*. September 2004: 1–5.

"Protesters Prevent Speech by Iranian Nobel Laureate Shirin Ebadi." *ISNA Website*, Tehran. Translated from the Persian. December 3, 2003:1.

Sayeh, Leila P., and Adriaen M. Morse. "Islam and the Treatment of Women: An Incomplete Understanding of Gradualism." *Texas International Law Journal* (spring 1995): 1–28.

Thamilaran, V. T. *Human Rights in the Third World Perspective*. New Delhi: Har-Anand, 1992.

Torab, Asam. "The Politicization of Women's Religious Circles in Post-Revolutionary Iran." in Ansari, *Women, Religion, and Culture in Islam*, 139–65.

Twair, Pat McDonnell. "Shirin Ebadi, Iran's Nobel Peace Laureate." *Washington Report on Middle East Affairs*, vol. 23, issue 6, Jul–Aug 2004: 32–34.

Vaziri, Haleh. "Review of History and Documentation of Human Rights in Islam." *International Journal of Middle Eastern Studies* 34 (2002): 764–55.

Wangari Muta Maathai
(2004)

To Plant Is to Empower

(April 1, 1940–)

"The rights of those at the bottom of the pyramid are violated every day by those at the top."

[Maathai, *The Bottom Is Heavy Too*, 13]

"We are still too secure, too greedy, too selfish, too blind."

[Maathai, *The Bottom Is Heavy Too*, 21]

"We have a special responsibility to the ecosystem of this planet. In making sure that other species survive we will be ensuring the survival of our own."

["The Right Livelihood Award"]

Wangari Muta Maathai, Nobel Peace Laureate 2004.

The physical effects of violence are obvious when tanks overrun homes, children lie dead in the streets, and bombs incinerate the infrastructure of towns and cities. At this very moment, people are still protesting the United States invasion of Iraq. But violence has all sorts of insidious incarnations that readily exploit, consume, and imprison people in a hopeless cycle of debilitating illness and poverty. These days it is difficult to find someone who will protest against our government for mismanagement of funds or the destruction of the environment.

Every evening the nightly news program leads off with stories about individual cases of shootings or beatings in my town. They are keen on examining individuals who break employment laws or engage in spurious verbiage with someone on the Internet. No news channel ever addresses the big issues of exploitation, inequity, and abuse that happen every day in government, education, and business. It takes more than a sound bite to report on the structural problems that can slowly destroy certain segments of the human race.

Our new governor, only a few months on the job, has disenfranchised thousands of people who cannot pay for medical treatment or therapy. To re-allocate money into his favorite areas, he is leaving the sick and mentally ill to fend for themselves. Undocumented reports say that there are more than 11 people per bed waiting for a room in a mental facility because he is refusing to fund clinics. Of course, these decisions will not hurt his re-election because the people on the lower rungs of society do not vote. But his decisions will eventually harm all of us when people who are mentally ill and physically deprived do not get treatment. They will be sleeping in our garages and knocking on our doors for food and help.

Unresponsive government abuses people but so do the CEOs of huge corporations. People enjoy discussing how their mutual funds or stocks are rising, but no one talks about the insatiable greed and abnormal quest to acquire power that propels those stocks. Instead, we create folk heroes with stories about how they obtained their wealth, or how they managed to circumvent charges brought against them for illegal practices. Everybody wants to be a Martha Stewart whose company stock rose while she was in prison. Everybody wants to be wealthy—don't they? How can the accumulation of wealth harm others? How can a government that labels itself democratic use and abuse its own citizens for monetary gain?

Kenya, Decimation of Resources and the Imperial Administrators

Wangari Maathai's life has been spent unearthing the human traits of greed and power in Kenya. The foreign domination of Kenya peaked in 1915 when Africans and Asians were excluded from owning property. British colonizers gave up complete control of Kenya in 1963, after 300 years of rule, but not their hold on the land and its resources.

A parliament was formed and in 1979 Daniel arap Moi presided as Kenya's second president. All other political parties were outlawed in 1982. In 1991, the one-party system was repealed. The Kenya African National Union had dominated politics in Kenya for almost half a century. In 2002, a new president was elected from the 15-party union of the National Rainbow Coalition. Mwai Kibaki of the Democratic Party became the third president of Kenya. Since his election, anti-corruption laws have been passed and the World Bank has begun loaning money to aid the poverty in Kenya ("Background Note: Kenya").

Today the majority of the fertile land in Kenya belongs to expatriates but is managed by hired locals. When they left Kenya, they appointed Kenyans to run their farms. This created a mirror aristocracy of the colonizers. The new black aristocracy had a vested interest in keeping the peoples of Kenya in a form of slavery.

> In the process, the African leaders abandoned their people, and in order to maintain their hold on power they did exactly what the colonial system was doing, namely to pit one community against another [Anabarasan, "Wangari Muta Maathai," 50].

Wangari terms these very power-hungry people "imperial administrators" (Anabarasan, "Wangari Muta Maathai," 50).

The aristocracy has done very little to prevent the deforestation of Kenya. When Wangari left for college in 1960, her own hometown Nyeri was self-sustaining. It had spring water and many native trees. She remembers no slums or starving children. When she returned only six years later, all the trees were gone and the spring no longer existed (Breton, *Women Pioneers for the Environment*, 12).

In spite of all of the efforts to save the environment, Kenya is losing its land to the desert. Only two percent of Kenya is forested (Mathaai, The Green Belt Movement, 2). There are more than 31,000,000 people in Kenya with 42 percent under the age of 15. Life expectancy for a female in 2002 was 49 and a male 48. Only three percent of the population is older than 65 (Earthtrends: The Environmental Information Portal). The average person earns only $271 a year and the government does not mandate any type of education for its peoples.

Meet the Woman

Wangari studied biology but it was politics that brought her face to face with her brothers and sisters in Kenya. In 1974, she was on the campaign trail for her husband Mwangi where she heard promises made to supporters regarding employment and adequate living conditions. She says, "Perhaps I was naive, I took the political promises that we made to the voters seriously..." (Maathai, *The Green Belt Movement*, 9).

After a seminar arranged by the Standing Committee on Environment and Habitat, Wangari learned how poor the conditions were in Kenya. They highlighted malnutrition as a problem no matter what the economic level. Farmers chose to grow crops that they could sell to others. Sometimes they did not get paid for their harvest. By choosing to grow crops that were not indigenous to the area, they were not growing food for themselves. This lack of variety and availability of vegetables and fruits resulted in malnutrition in most people. According to Jeremy Seabrook,

> A large proportion of Kenya's foreign exchange goes to pay for the country's energy needs, but not for the energy needs of the poor, who have no alternative bio-energy. With a lack of wood fuel, women must alter the eating habits of their families, using tea, bread, rice, maize meal, which are refined carbohydrates. The disruption of balanced feeding patterns soon leads to malnutrition [Seabrook, *Pioneers of Change*, 50].

Because Kenyans had learned how to eat the food of the western world, they had to compete with the west for this food. It was often too expensive for them to buy. They had abandoned crops and trees such as figs, bananas, papayas, papaws, mangos, nadi flames, acacia, thorn, and cedar (Breton, *Women Pioneers for the Environment*, 13). Most of the food they were growing needed to be cooked but fuels were unavailable or were out of their price range. So they cut down trees in the area in order to sustain themselves. This deforestation led to soil erosion and depletion and broadened the scope of malnutrition and poverty.

Information about the disastrous ecological effects of colonialization was not new. In the early 1920s, a program called "Men of the Trees" had been initiated by Josiah Njonjo and, later, Barb Baker, both environmentalists, but it faltered with the death of its founder. Wangari became acquainted with environmental efforts as part of her job as director of the Nairobi Branch of the Kenya Red Cross. She was invited to join a group called the Environmental Liaison Center (Maathai, *The Green Belt Movement*, 8) and that relationship led Maathai to action. She began to develop a tree-planting plan in her own backyard. Eventually it spread throughout Kenya and to other countries in Africa (Maathai, *The Green Belt Movement*, 12).

Seedlings for the Green Belt Movement were originally donated by the government and later by companies such as Mobil Oil (Maathai, *The Green Belt Movement*, 26). Early on, the government also provided an office that they took away from her when the organization began protesting the practices of President Moi. Small checks from women from around the globe poured into Wangari's organization. Some of the current supporters include organizations from the Netherlands, Finland, Austria, the United Kingdom, and Germany (Maathai, *The Green Belt Movement*, 60). Her original goal was to plant one tree per person in Kenya, 30 million strong, and most people claim that she reached it. She says that as many as 80,000 women were planting trees at any one time. They were obtaining their seedlings from over 3,000 nurseries. They deliberately discouraged the wealthy and popular politicians from participating because they wanted the plantings to stay with the local people.

> Because of the great interest that the community members showed for tree planting, a local tree-planting strategy was developed for public land. This involved the planting of seedlings in rows of at least one thousand so as to form green belts of trees. These "belts" had the advantages of providing shade and windbreaks, facilitating soil conservation, improving the aesthetic beauty of the landscape and providing habitats for birds and small animals [Maathai, *The Green Belt Movement*, 27].

It was out of this massive tree planting effort that the name "The Greenbelt Movement" was born. The movement hoped to replenish the land, but more importantly its goal was to support the lives of human beings.

> If you want to save the environment you should protect the people first because human beings are part of the biological diversity. And if we can't protect our own species, what's the point of protecting tree species? [Anabarasan, "Wangari Muta Maathai," 46)].

Wangari had a talent of joining groups and bringing them together with a common task. By 1999 she said that 6,000 nurseries were functioning throughout Kenya (Maathai, *The Green Belt Movement*, 29). The program focused upon volunteers. Primarily women would come to the nurseries and take seedlings with them. A member of the local nursery would follow up to see that the trees were planted. If they survived three months, they were paid a small sum for each tree.

This plan was immensely successful. Women began to plant all sorts of indigenous trees, including fruit- and nut-bearing trees. As time progressed, they began to replenish the soil and food supplies, and furnish wood for heating and cooking. Not everyone understood how to plant and care for trees, so workshops sprung up throughout Kenya and people became more educated about their environment, themselves, and their government.

> Twenty years down the road, the women have gained many skills and techniques that they continue to share among themselves.... Many women have become foresters without diplomas [Maathai, *The Green Belt Movement*, 27].

A common pledge was made among these newfound foresters every time there was a public tree planting ceremony, often called "harambee" ("Let us pull together!"). The pledge reads as follows:

> Being aware that Kenya is being threatened by the expansion of desert-like conditions; that desertification comes as a result of misuse of the land and by consequent soil erosion by the elements; and that these actions result in drought, malnutrition, famine and death; we resolve to save our land by averting this same desertification through the planting of trees wherever possible. In pronouncing these words, we each make a personal commitment to save our country from actions and elements which would deprive present and future generations from reaping the bounty (of resources) which is the birthright and property of all [Maathai, *The Green Belt Movement*, 20].

Risking Your Life

On the surface, designing a program to help people help themselves to a place of economic independence does not seem to be a political activity. Planting trees and discussing local use of indigenous food or wood seems apolitical. But as Kenyans began to plant trees, a political awareness was born.

> The act of planting trees conveys a simple message. It suggests that at the very least you can plant a tree and improve your habitat. It increases people's awareness that they can take control of their environment, which is the first step toward greater participation in society [Anabarasan, "Wangari Muta Maathai," 46].

Wangari explained her basic goals in an address when she received the Edinburgh Medal for contributions in the field of Science:

> The overall objective of the Movement was to raise awareness of symptoms of environmental degradation and raise the consciousness of people to a level that would move them to participate in the restoration and the healing of the environment [Maathai, *The Bottom Is Heavy Too*, 11].

If you visit the Green Belt website, you find the following vision statement:

> Our vision is to create a society of people who consciously work for continued improvement of their environment, and a greener, cleaner Kenya. Our mission is to mobilize community consciousness for self-determination; equity, improved livelihoods securities and environmental conservation—using tree planting as an entry point. Guided by the values of volunteerism, love for environmental conservation, pro-action for self-betterment, accountability, transparency, and empowerment.

As the program became successful, politicians and local bureaucrats began placing roadblocks in the way of the local tree planters and farmers. Some foresters may have been afraid of losing their jobs. As the people became more educated about how to successfully survive, they began demanding more from their government. They wanted new roads and more trees.

Fances Moore Lappé followed Wangari on one of her visits to villages. She saw first-hand how local lives could be changed. The workshops were more about educating people on how to improve their living conditions than about planting trees. In one story, Wangari uses the example of getting on the wrong bus. If you get on the right bus, you end up in the right destination. If you get on the wrong bus, you will run into all types of problems. She begins the discussion with a question such as, "How do people get on the wrong bus?" That is an easy question to answer, retorted the audience: People cannot read, so they have to ask someone. Many people will give them the wrong answer so they have to keep asking until they know for certain that they are getting on the right bus.

Wangari transforms the conversations about the bus into a discussion about making choices in life. People begin to understand that they have been misled and that they can have control over their lives. They just have to learn how to get on the right bus.

In Kenya, planting trees and protecting trees are not neutral acts. They mean confronting authority. Wangari knows. She herself has been arrested many times for protesting the tearing down of public forests. In her successful fight to save a downtown Nairobi park, she was beaten so badly by government police that she had to be hospitalized (Lappé, *Hope's Edge*, 184).

President Moi labeled Wangari as a "mad woman and a threat to the order and security of the country." Various ministers have referred to her as an ignorant and ill-tempered puppet of foreign masters, an unprecedented monstrosity—and accused her of inciting people to rise against the government of men (Sears, "Wangari Maathai," 57).

Wangari was opposed to taking away the tree-lined green space of Uhuru Park that was situated in the center of Nairobi. It is where "poor" people come to find relief from their overcrowded conditions. In 1989, the government planned to build the highest building in Africa, a sort of ego-enhanced image of the current Moi government. Maathai reasoned that it was a misuse of funds since their country had so many other infrastructure problems such as roads, water, and jobs. "In fact, the estimated construction cost of $197,000,000 would almost double the country's international debt" (Wallace, *Eco-Heroes*, 14).

> Unfortunately, for many world leaders development still means extensive farming of cash crops, expensive hydroelectric dams, hotels, supermarkets, and luxury items, which plunder human and natural resources. This is short-sighted and does not meet people's basic needs— for adequate food, clean water, shelter, local clinics, information and freedom [Anbarasan, "Wangari Muta Maathai," 46].

Maathai and others, staged demonstrations at Uhuru Park by bringing seedlings and standing with mothers who protested the arrest of their relatives. It became known as freedom corner. Moi had disregarded all pleas to stop the development and began clearing part of the land for very expensive housing. Some of the protestors burned bulldozers and other equipment valued at over a million dollars (Mutiso, "Wangari Maathai").

One evening, 200 nicely dressed men, armed with swords, clubs, and whips, attacked the female protestors. Wangari was beaten so badly that she had to be hospitalized. Imanyara, a writer, recalls the incident:

> "It is a measure of the depravity of the regime that the women and their sympathizers were gassed and beaten by the police and the personal presidential paramilitary unit. In the meanwhile, hundreds were trampled or crushed..." [Wallace, *Eco-Heroes*, 18].

Wangari understood that "every time you speak out, you expect you may suffer for what you believe in" (Sears, "Wangari Maathai", 58).

You know, when they attack me, I say this is violence against women. When they threaten
me with female genital mutilation, this is violence against women. When they attack me, I
attack them back. A lot of people say, "They could kill you." And I say, "Yes, they could, but if
you focus on the damage they could do, you cannot function. Don't visualize the danger you
can get in...." At this particular moment, I am only seeing one thing—that I am moving in the
right direction [Cuomo, *Speak Truth to Power*, 43].

When she was able to function again, Wangari began protesting against the park.
"As soon as I recover, I shall return to Karura Forest, even if they bury me there" (Mutiso,
"Wangari Maathai"). Plans for the park eventually failed because foreign investors with-
drew.

Wangari understands that choices in her life have also hurt her economically. In a
Ms. Magazine article she acknowledged that she earned only a tenth of what she could
earn on the international market. "It has been very difficult. I have paid a very heavy price
at the personal level, at the family level, in my pursuit of what I believed in..." (Wallace,
Eco-Heroes, 20).

Wangari openly opposed the Moi government again in 1992 when she learned of a
planned military coup by reigning President and a list of people to be liquidated (Wallace, *Eco-Heroes*, 117). The Forum for the Restoration of Democracy stopped it. Yet she
continued to be harassed. Soon after that event, 150 police officers surrounded her home,
beat down the doors and windows, and grabbed Wangari. She spent time in a prison but
was later released to a hospital in 1992 (Wallace, *Eco-Heroes*, 117).

Frances Lappé tells a story about meeting Reverend Timothy Njoya during the terrible days of Daniel Moi. People were afraid to be associated with the Green Belt Movement and so would send a message secretly that they were supporting Wangari, or they
would come up in the streets and whisper in her ear. To openly criticize the Moi government could mean death.

Wangari spoke out against the government, and for some unexplainable reason she
was not assassinated. Njoya decided to preach a sermon on questioning the so-called
democracy in Kenya. He went home to die. Shortly, nine men came to his home and
attacked him with knives. As he protected himself, they cut off his fingers and almost dis-
emboweled him.

I was using my left hand to protect my heart. I had lost three fingers. I started to use this
hand, but I thought I don't want to waste my right hand, too, so I better use my legs [Lappé,
Hope's Edge, 191].

In the midst of the fight he yelled out, "Brother, I have forgiven you." Njoya asked
for forgiveness for hitting the man with his feet. All of a sudden the men stopped beating him and recognized that he was a priest, a good man. They bandaged up his wounds
and took him to the hospital. Timothy fainted before the whole ordeal was over but survived to tell his gruesome story.

Wangari explains that corrupt politicians have borrowed money from the World
Bank—and the World Bank no longer wants to loan or invest in a country that does not
always pay them back. They won't give any debt relief because they believe the money will
go into someone's personal bank account. This hurts the people in Kenya who need education, an infrastructure, and the ability to trade in the world market. Wangari faults the
United States for supporting dictators whom they know have huge bank accounts.

While rich nations were supporting our dictatorial leaders, people like me were being
thrown out of universities for speaking out, some became refugees or were sent to jail, some

even were killed. This is why I'm telling our people we must get out of this bus. It's the wrong bus and we must learn to elect the proper people in the government [Lappé, *Hope's Edge*, 189].

Career

Nyeri, Kenya, has been home to Wangari since her birth in 1940. When Wangari was a child, she thought that the whole world was contained in the Rift Valley. She could see two ridges and thought that the world ended at the top of both, until her mother took her on a trip to the top of a ridge. At that moment, she realized that there was more. "I discovered that there was something beyond. I was so happy to know that the whole world was not in that valley..." (Lappé, *Hope's Edge*, 192).

Wangari tells this story because for her, life has been climbing and reaching one ridge after another, one challenge after another. Instead of complaining about the mountain being too high or that the journey was too long, she just keeps walking and risking and reaching new worlds.

One of the first steps she took out of that valley was to attend St. Scholastica College in Atchison, Kansas. She was one of 300 fortunate Kenyans who were funded through a Kennedy foundation in the 1960s. Her own scholarship came through the Catholic Bishop of Nyeri. After earning a degree in Biology, she headed for the University of Pittsburgh where she obtained a master's degree in Biological Sciences. The percentage of women obtaining a degree in the sciences in the 1960s was very low. It was essentially an all-male field. During the 1960s through the 1970s, the graduation rate of women in Biology increased 12 percent.

In 1966 she was offered a research assistant position at the University of Nairobi and stayed there until 1982 (Maathai, *The Greenbelt Movement*, 86–89). In 1971 she obtained a Ph.D. in Anatomy at the same university. By 1976 she was named chair of the Department of Veterinary Anatomy and then Associate Professor in 1977. She left the academy to run for the Parliament in 1982 but was taken out of the race on a technicality (Breton, *Women Pioneers for the Environment*, 13). During her academic career she also worked as director of the Kenya Red Cross. And while she has spent that last 20-some years working to plant trees, she has also received invitations to teach at Connecticut College, Dartmouth College, and Yale University. In addition, other universities awarded her honorary doctorates in law, agriculture, and sciences.

Wangari has taken her tree-planting crusade to the world while serving on several United Nations committees such as the U.N. Commission on Global Governance and the U.N. Advisory Board on Disarmament. The world came to her doorstep with many prizes. And everywhere she served, she brought the plight of the Kenyan people to the table. Little by little, organization after organization, and business after business listened to her hopes and dreams and then offered resources to help her in her quest.

In 1992, Wangari ran for president but lost. Her goal was to unite people in an opposition party but it failed. She ran again in 1998.

> But during the campaign I also came to realize that in this country it is very difficult to get elected without money. I didn't have money. I realized that it doesn't matter how good you are, how honest you are and how pro-democratic you are, if you don't have money to give to the voters you won't get elected. So I lost [Anabarasan, "Wangari Muta Maathai," 50].

In 2002, with 98 percent of the vote, Wangari was finally elected to parliament on the Green Party ticket, and today she is the Assistant Minister for Environment and Natural Resources in Kenya ("Nobel Peace Prize to Maathai").

Personal Life

> "I lost a friend called a husband."
>
> (Lappé, *Hope's Edge*, 190)

Wangari was one of the very lucky people who studied abroad and obtained university degrees. Instead of staying in the United States, she went home to work.

Fortunate again, she was hired to teach micro- and developmental anatomy at the University of Nairobi, and obtained a Ph.D. But here she faced discrimination. It shocked her! She thought that everyone would be rewarded equally for hard work and productivity. The problem is that there are only so many slots at the top, and males saved those "cream" positions for themselves.

> I was teaching at the University of Nairobi in the 1970s, when I felt that the academic rights of women professors were not being respected because they were women. I became an activist at the university, insisting that I wanted my rights as an academic [Anbarascan, "Wangari Muta Maathai," 47].

In the United States she understood that there was a color problem and faced discrimination on many fronts. Returning home after a successful educational career, she found that she did not "fit" into the local standards of how a woman should speak, act, or perform.

> This time ... it was my gender that was the problem. I have since learnt that at the bottom of the pyramid there are very strict cultural and religious norms which govern the birth, life and death of women in society. These age-old traditions make the bottom quite heavy [Maathai, *The Bottom Is Heavy Too*, 9].

There is a saying that "you can never go home." And this is especially true for women who leave their families to become educated. When you return, you do not speak the same language. You do not have the same values. You have become "other" to norms that guide the rest of your family, your neighborhood, your ethnic group, and even your country. Wangari became an alien in her own country. "I never would have thought that all the things I had worked so hard for in school and at home would become a burden..." (Maathai, *The Bottom Is Heavy Too*, 9).

A women's group in Kenya charged her with being "a violator of the African tradition." She would not cower in the presence of males. Wangari had her own voice and she spoke up when others feared to move. But others think that women should have a master, a male. Her husband, who had fathered her three children, Waweru, Wanjira, and Muta, divorced her. She was charged with adultery with someone in Parliament. Wangari fought the divorce. "I told the judges that if they could reach that decision based on what they'd heard, they must be either incompetent or corrupt." She was sentenced to six months in jail for contempt but only served three days (Wallace, "Eco-Heroes," 12). She was "too educated, too strong, too successful, and too stubborn and too hard to control" (Sears, "Wangari Maathai," 55).

> African women in general need to know that it's okay for them to be the way they are as a strength, and to be liberated from fear and from silence. The worst problem for both men and women in Africa today actually is unspinning the cocoon of Western stereotypes, within which people are confined by the internationalization of Western culture's patronizing and exploitative conceptions of Africans [Sears, "Wangari Maathai," 1].

Wangari agrees:

> Our men think African women should be dependent and submissive, definitely not better than their husbands. There is no doubt that at first many people opposed me because I am a woman and resented the idea that I had strong opinions [Anabarasan, "Wangari Muta Maathai," 48].

And one of those men was her own husband, Mwangi, a member of Parliament.

Nobel Peace Prize

> "As for me, I've made a choice."
> (Slogan on Greenbelt Movement t-shirt)

In 2004, Wangari was awarded the Nobel Peace Prize, over a million dollars. Many have criticized the decision to give her the award because they can find no common link between her Green Belt Movement and peace efforts. These people do not understand the devastating effects of poverty upon a person's body, a person's mind, and their hopes for the future. Ole Danbolt Mjøs, chair of the Norwegian Nobel Committee, explained the committee's approach to the environment and peace:

> Maathai stands at the front of the fight to promote ecologically viable social, economic and cultural development in Kenya and in Africa.... Most people would probably agree that there are connections between peace on the one hand and an environment on the other in which scare resources such as oil, water, minerals or timber are quarreled over.... But where does tree-planting come in? When we analyze local conflicts, we tend to focus on their ethnic and religious aspects. But it is often the underlying ecological circumstances that bring the more readily visible factors to the flashpoint [http://www.nobel.no/eng_lect.2004a.html].

Wangari said it best immediately after she received the Nobel Peace Prize:

> [W]hat is important for us in the world is not only to bring peace.... And for them to recognize that the fight over natural resources is usually the source of conflict [Maathai, phone interview].

Mjøs makes a case for the environment being the basis for many conflicts around the world. He points to the problems in Darfur that can be traced back to desertification. Deforestation in the Philippines has promoted civil war. The Chiapas have revolted against the Mexican government because of deforestation and lack of good, tillable soil. Deforestation in the Amazonas, the Himalayas, and in Haiti has led to deplorable living conditions and civil unrest.

In giving this award to Wangari, the committee pays special tribute to the women of Africa who bear the greatest burdens of tilling the soil and providing for their families. To Wangari he said,

> You are the first woman from Africa to be honored with the Nobel Peace Prize.... You stand as an example and a source of inspiration to everyone in Africa who is fighting for sustainable development, democracy and peace. You are an outstanding role model for all women in Africa and the rest of the world. You bravely opposed the oppressive regime in Kenya. Your unique modes of action put the spotlight on political oppression both nationally and internationally [Danbolt Mjøs, "Nobel Peace Prize 2004 Presentation Speech"].

The committee recognized the personal risks that Wangari has taken during the past 30 years. They praised her for her courage and her mobilization of thousands of poor women. She has the unusual ability to speak a language that rallies both the world and the locals in her country. Her concern for the degradation of the environment led to a democratic revolt that is changing Kenya for the better. "Wangari makes you want to step into her arms and stay there, to be held like a beloved child. She is Mother Africa" (Wallace, *Eco-Heroes*, 2).

Bibliography

Anabarasan, Ethirajan. "Wangari Muta Maathai: Kenya's Green Militant." *The Unesco Courier*, December 1999: 46–50.

"Background Note: Kenya." U.S. Department of State Bureau of African Affairs. http://www. state.gov/r/pa/ei/bgn/2962.htm.

BBC News UK Edition. "Profile: Wangari Maathai." Available online at http://news.bbc.co. uk/1/hi/world/africa/3726084.stm.

Breton, Mary Joy. *Women Pioneers for the Environment*. Boston: Northeastern University Press, 1998.

Cuomo, Kerry Kennedy. *Speak Truth to Power: Human Rights Defenders Who Are Changing Our World*. New York: Power House Books, 2004.

Danbolt Mjøs, Ole. "Nobel Peace Prize 2004 Presentation Speech." Available online at http:// www.nobel.no/eng_lect.2004a.html.

Garriott, Gary. "Nobel Peace Prize winner Wangari Maathai." *China Daily News*, November 1, 2004. Available online at http://www.chinadaily.com.cn/english/doc/2004-10/19/content_383722. htm.

Government of Kenya. Ministry of Environment and Natural Resources Web site. http://www.environment.go.ke/assministers.html.

Green Belt Movement Web site. http://www.greenbeltmovement.org.

Lappé, Anna, and Frances Moore Lappé. "The Genius of Wangari Matthai." *International Herald Tribune*, October 14, 2004, op/ed page. Available online at http://iht.com/articles/2004/ 10/13/opinion/edlappe.html. Also available online from Common Dreams News Center at http://www.commondreams.org/views04/1014-32.htm.

_____. *Hope's Edge. The Next Diet for a Small Planet*. New York: Jeremy P. Tarcher/Putnam, 2002.

Maathai, Wangari. *The Bottom Is Heavy Too. Even with the Green Belt Movement*. The First Edinburgh Medal Address. Edinburgh: Edinburgh University Press, 1994.

_____. *The Green Belt Movement: Sharing the Approach and the Experience*. New York: Lantern Books, 2003.

_____. "Kenya's Green Belt Movement." *Unesco Courier*, March 1992, 23–26.

_____. "Nobel Peace Prize 2004 Lecture." Available online at http://nobel.no/eng_lect_2004b.html.

_____. Phone interview with Marika Griehsel after the announcement 2004 Nobel Peace Prize, October 8, 2004. Available online at http://nobelprize.org/peace/laureates/2004/maathai-telephone.html.

Mutiso, Clyde. "Wangari Maathai, Hero of the Week: Her Women's Army Defies an Iron Regime." *Time*, December 28, 1998. Available online at http://www.time.com/time/reports/environment/heroes/heroesgallery/0,2967,maathai,00.html.

"1991 Africa Prize Laureate Wangari Maathai, Founder of the Green Belt Movement." http://www.thp.org/prize/91/maathai.htm.

"Nobel Peace Prize to Maathai." Radio Netherlands, October 8, 2004. Available online at http://rnw.nl/hotspots/html/ken04008.html.

"The Right Livelihood Award. Roll of Honour. Wangar Maathai/Green Belt Movement (1984)." http://rightlivelihood.org/recip/maathai.htm.

Seabrook, Jeremy. *Pioneers of Change: Experiments in Creating a Humane Society*. Philadelphia: New Society, 1993.

Sears, Pricsilla. "Wangari Maathai: 'You Strike the Woman.'" *In Context: A Quarterly of Humane Sustainable Culture*, Spring 1991, 55. Available online at http://www.context.org/ICLIB/IC28/Sears.htm.

"10 Questions: Wangari Maathai." *Time Europe*, vol. 164, no. 15, October 18, 2004. Available online at http://www.time.com/time/europe/magazine/article/0,13005,901041018-713166,00.html.

Wallace, Aubrey. *Eco-Heroes. Twelve Tales of Environmental Victory*. San Francisco: Mercury House, 1993.

"Wangari Maathai—Biography." http://nobelprize.org/peace/laureates/2004/maathai-bio.html.

"Wangari Maathai—Curriculum Vitae." http://nobelprize.org/peace/laureates/2004/maathai-cv.html.

Appendix:
Nobel Peace Prize Winners
by Year, 1901–2004

Year	Recipient	Distinguished Service	Country	Life Span
1901	Jean Henry Dunant	Founder of the Red Cross, Geneva; initiator of the Geneva Convention	Switzerland	1828–1910
	Frédéric Passy	President and founder of the first peace society in France	France	1822–1912
1902	Élie Ducommun	Secretary of the Permanent International Peace Burea, Bern	Switzerland	1833–1906
	Charles Albert Gobat	Secretary General of the Inter-Parliamentary Union, Bern	Switzerland	1843–1914
1903	Sir William Randal Cremer	Member of Parliament and Secretary of the International Arbitration League	Great Britain	1838–1904
1904	Institut de Droit International	Institute of International Law, a scientific society founded in 1873	Belgium	1873–
1905	Baroness Bertha Sophie Felicita von Suttner	Writer and Honorary President of the Permanent International Peace Bureau	Austria	1843–1914
1906	Theodore Roosevelt	President of the U.S. who drew up the 1905 peace treaty between Russia and Japan	United States	1859–1919
1907	Ernesto Teodoro Moneto	President of the Lombard League of Peace	Italy	1833–1918
1908	Louis Renault	Professor of International Law, the Sorbonne, Paris	France	1843–1918
1909	Auguste Marie François Beernaert	Former prime minister, member of the International Court of Arbitration at The Hague	Belgium	1852–1924
	Paul Henribenjamin Balluet D'estournelles De Constant,	Member of the French Parliament; founder and president of the French parliamentary group	France	1852–1924

Year	Recipient	Distinguished Service	Country	Life Span
	De Rebecque	for international arbitration; founder of the Committee for the Defense of National Interests and International Conciliation.		
1910	Permanent International Peace Bureau		Switzerland	
1911	Tobias Michael Carel Asser	Cabinet Minister and initiator of the Conferences on International Private Law at the Hague	Netherlands	1838–1913
	Alfred Hermann Fried	Journalist and founder of the peace journal *Die Waffen Nieder*	Austria	1864–1921
1912	Reserved			
1913	Elihu Root	Former Secretary of State; initiator of several arbitration agreements	United States	1845–1937
	Henri La Fontaine	Member of the Belgian parliament; president of the Permanent International Peace Bureau.	Switzerland	1854–1943
1914	Reserved			
1915		The prize money for 1914 was allocated to the Nobel Institute's Special Fund.		
1915	Reserved			
1916		The prize money for 1915 was allocated to the Nobel Institute's Special Fund.		
1916	Reserved			
1917		The prize money for 1916 was allocated to the Nobel Institute's Special Fund.		
1917	The International Committee of the Red Cross	Founded in 1863	Switzerland	
1918	Reserved			
1919		The prize money for 1918 was allocated to the Nobel Institute's Special Fund.		
1919	Reserved			
1920		The prize for 1919 to Thomas Woodrow Wilson, president of the United States and the Founder of the League of Nations	United States	1856–1912
1920	Léon Victor Auguste	Former Minister of Culture, Minister of Justice and Prime	France	1851–1925

Year	Recipient	Distinguished Service	Country	Life Span
	Bourgeois	Minister, president of parliament, president of the Council of the League of Nations		
1921	Karl Hjalmar Branting	Prime minister, Swedish delegate to the Council of the League of Nations	Sweden	1860–1925
	Christian Lous Lange	Secretary General of the Inter-Parliamentary Union	Brussels	1869–1938
1922	Fridtjof Nansen	Explorer, scientist and humanitaria; Norway's delegate to the League of Nations. Initiator of the Nansen Passport (for refugees)	Norway	1861–1930
1923	Reserved			
1924		The prize money for 1923 was allocated to the Nobel Institute's Special Fund.		
1924	Reserved			
1925		The prize money for 1924 was allocated to the Nobel Institute's Special Fund.		
1925	Reserved			
1926	Sir (Joseph) Austen Chamberlain	Foreign Minister, a negotiator of the Locarno Treaty	Germany	1878–1929
	Charles Gates Dawes	Vice president of the United States; chair of the Allied Reparation Commission and originator of the Dawes Plan	United States	1865–1951
1926	Aristide Briand	Foreign Minister, a negotiator of the Locarno Treaty and the Briand-Kellogg Pact	France	1862–1932
	Gustav Stresemann	Former chancellor, Foreign Minister, a negotiator of the Locarno Treaty	Germany	1878–1929
1927	Ferdinand Edouard Buisson	Former professor at the Sorbonne, Paris; Founder and president of the League of Human Rights	France	1841–1932
	Ludwig Quidde	Historian, professor honoris causa, member of the Bavarian parliament; member of Germany's constituent assembly 1919; delegate to numerous peace conferences	Germany	1858–1941
1928	Reserved			
1929		The prize money for 1928 was		

Year	Recipient	Distinguished Service	Country	Life Span
		allocated to the Nobel Institute's Special Fund.		
1929	Reserved			
1930	The prize for 1929: Frank Billings Kellogg	Former secretary of state; negotiated the Briand-Kellogg Pact	United States	1856–1937
1930	Lars Olof Jonathan (Nathan) Söderblom	Archbishop, leader of the ecumenical movement.	Sweden	1866–1931
1931	Jane Addams	Sociologis; International President of the Women's International League for Peace and Freedom	United States	1860–1935
	Nicholas Murray Butler	President of Columbia University and promoter of the Briand-Kellogg Pact	United States	1862–1947
1932	Reserved			
1933		The prize money for 1932 was allocated to the Nobel Institute's Special Fund.		
1933	Reserved			
1934	Sir (Ralph) Norman Angell (Lane)	Write; member of the Executive Committee of the League of Nations and the National Peace Council; author of the book *The Great Illusion*, among others	Great Britain	1874–1967
1934	Arthur Henderson	Former foreign secretary; chair of the League of Nations Disarmament Conference	Great Britain	1863–1935
1935	Reserved			
1936	Carl von Ossietzky	Journalist, pacifist	Germany	1889–1938
1936	Carolos Saavedra Lamas	Foreign Minister, president of the League of Nations, arbitrator in the dispute between Paraguay and Bolivia in 1935	Argentina	1878–1959
1937	Viscount (Lord Edgar Algernon Robert Gascoyne Cecil) Cecil of Chelwood	Writer, former Lord Privy Seal, Founder and President of the International Peace Campaign	Great Britain	1864–1958
1938	The Nansen International Office for Refugees	An international aid organization established by Fridtjof Nansen in 1921	Geneva	Est. 1921
1939–1942	No prize money awarded	One-third of the money for this period was transferred to the Main Fund and two-thirds to the Nobel Institute's Special Fund.		

Year	Recipient	Distinguished Service	Country	Life Span
1943	Reserved			
1944		One-third of the money for 1943 was transferred to the Main Fund and two-thirds to the Nobel Institute's Special Fund.		
1944	Reserved			
1945	The International Committee of the Red Cross		Geneva	Founded in 1863
1945	Cordell Hull	Former secretary of state; one of the initiators of the United Nations	United States	1871–1955
1946	Emily Greene Balch	Former professor of History and Sociology; International President of the Women's International League for Peace and Freedom	United States	1867–1961
	John Raleigh Mott	Chair of the first International Missionary Council in 1910, Preside of the World Alliance of Young Men's Christian Associations	United States	1865–1955
1947	The Friends Service Council		London	Founded in 1647
	The American Friends Service Committee (the Quakers)		Washington	The society's first official meeting was held in 1672.
1948	Reserved			
1949		One-third of the prize money for 1948 was transferred to the Main Fund and two-thirds to the Nobel Institute's Special Fund.		
1949	Baron John Boyd Orr of Brechin	Physician, nutritionist, leading organizer and director general of the U.N. Food and Agricultural Organization, president of the National Peace Council and the World Union of Peace Organizations.	Great Britain	1880–1971
1950	Ralph Bunche	Professor at Harvard University, Cambridge, Massachusetts; director of the U.N. Division of Trusteeship, mediator in Palestine in 1948	United States	1904–1971
1951	Léon Jouhaux	President of the trade union CGT-Force ouvriére, president of the	France	1879–1954

Year	Recipient	Distinguished Service	Country	Life Span
		International Confederation of Free Trade Unions, vice president of the World Federation of Trade Unions, member of the ILO Council, delegate to the U.N.		
1952	Reserved			
1953	Albert Schweitzer	Physician and missionary, founder of the Lambarene Hospital in Gabon.	France (born in Kaysersberg, Alsace, then part of Germany)	1875–1965
1953	George Catlett Marshall	General, president of the American Red Cross, former secretary of state and of defense, delegate to the U.N., originator of the Marshall Plan	United States	1880–1959
1954	Reserved			
1955	The Office of the United Nations High Commissioner for Refugees	An international aid organization established by the U.N.	Switzerland	Est. in 1951
1955	Reserved			
1956	One-third of the prize money for 1955 was transferred to the Main Fund and two-thirds to the Nobel Institute's Special Fund.			
1956	Reserved			
1957	One-third of the prize money for 1956 was transferred to the Main Fund and two-thirds to the Nobel Institute's Special Fund.			
1957	Lester Bowles Pearson	Former foreign minister, president of the U.N. General Assembly	Canada	1897–1972
1958	Georges Pire	Dominican, head of the aid organization for refugess L'Europe du coeur au service due monde	Belgium	1910–1969
1959	Philip John Noel-Baker	Member of Parliament; campaigner for international cooperation and peace	Great Britain	1889–1982
1960	Reserved			

Year	Recipient	Distinguished Service	Country	Life Span
1961	Albert John Lutuli	President of the South African liberation movement and the African National Congress	South Africa (Born in Southern Rhodesia.)	1898–1967
1961	Dag Hjalmar Agne Carl Hammarskjöld	U.N. secretary-general (awarded the prize posthumously)	Sweden	1905–1961
1962	Reserved			
1963	Linus Carl Pauling	California Institute of Technology, Pasadena, California, campaigner especially for an end to nuclear weapons tests	United States	1901–1994
1963	The International Committee of the Red Cross		Geneva	Founded in 1863
	The League of Red Cross Societies		Geneva	
1964	Martin Luther King, Jr.	Leader of the Southern Christian Leadership Conference, campaigner for civil rights	United States	1929–1968
1965	United Nations Children's Fund (UNICEF)	An international aid organization	New York	Est. by the U.N. in 1946
1966	Reserved			
1967	One-third of the prize money for 1966 was transferred to the Main Fund and two-thirds to the Nobel Institute's Special Fund.			
1967	Reserved			
1968	One-third of the prize money for 1967 was transferred to the Main Fund and two-thirds to the Nobel Institute's Special Fund.			
1968	René Cassin	President of the European Court of Human Rights	France	1887–1976
1969	The International Labour Organization (ILO)			
1970	Norman Enest Borlaug	Led research at the International Maize and Wheat Improvement Center, Mexico City		

Year	Recipient	Distinguished Service	Country	Life Span
1971	Willy Brandt	Former Chancellor, initiator of West Germany's Ostpolitik, embodying a new attitude towards Eastern Europe and East Germany	West Germany	1913–1992
1972	Reserved			
1973	The prize money for 1972 was transferred to the Main Fund.			
1973	Henry A. Kissinger Le Duc Tho (declined the prize.)	Former secretary of state. Jointly negotiated the Vietnam peace accord in 1973	United States North Vietnam	1923–
1974	Seán MacBride	President of the International Peace Bureau, Geneva; U.N. Commissioner for Namibia.	Ireland	1904–1988
	Eisaku Sato	Former prime minister	Japan	1901–1975
1975	Andrei Sakharov	Campaigner for human rights.	Soviet Union	1921–1989
1976	Reserved			
1976	The prize for 1976 was divided evenly between			
	Betty Williams and	Co-founder of the Community of Peace People	Northern Ireland	1943–
	Mairead Corrigan.	Co-founder of the Community of Peace People	Northern Ireland	1944–
1977	Amnesty International	A worldwide organization for the protection of the rights of prisoners of conscience	London	
1978	Mohammad Anwar Al-Sadat	President of Egypt	Egypt	1918–1981
	Mehachem Begin	Prime minister; jointly negotiated peace between Egypt and Israel	Israel	1913–1992
1979	Mother Teresa	Leader of the Order of the Missionaries of Charity	India	1914–1997
1980	Adolfo Pérez Esquivel	Architect, campaigner for human rights	Argentina	1931–
1981	Office of the United Nations High Commissioner for Refugees	Geneva		
1982	Alva Myrdal	Former Minister, diplomat and delegate to U.N. disarmament conferences	Sweden	1902–1986
	Alfonso Garcí Robles	Diplomat and campaigner for disarmament	Mexico	1911–1991
1983	Lech Walesa	Founder of Solidarity, campaigner for human rights	Poland	1943–

Year	Recipient	Distinguished Service	Country	Life Span
1984	Desmond Mpilo Tutu	Bishop, former secretary general of the South African Council of Churches	South Africa	1931–
1985	International Physicians for the Prevention of Nuclear War		Boston	
1986	Elie Wiesel	Author, humanitarian	United States	1928–
1987	Oscar Arias Sánchez	President of Costa Rica, initiator of peace negotiations in Central America	Costa Rica	1941–
1988	The United Nations Peace-Keeping Forces			
1989	Tenzin Gyatso, the fourteenth Dalai	Religious and political leader of the Tibetan people		
1990	Mikhail Sergeyevich Gorbachev	President of the Soviet Union, helped to bring the Cold War to an end	Soviet Union	1931–
1991	Aung San Suu Kyi	Opposition leader, human rights advocate	Burma	1945–
1992	Rigoberta Menchú Tum	Campaigner for human rights, especially for indigenous peoples	Guatemala	1959–
1993	Nelson Mandela Frederik Willem de Klerk	Leader of the ANC> President of the Republic of South Africa	South Africa South Africa	1918– 1936–
1994	Yasser Arafat Shimon Peres Yitzhak Rabin	Chairman of the PLO Foreign minister of Israel Prime minister of Israel Awarded for their efforts to create peace in the Middle East	Palestine Israel Israel	1929–20xx 1923– 1922–1995
1995	Joseph Rotblat Pugwash Conferences on Science and World Affairs	For their efforts to diminish the part played by nuclear arms in international politics	England	1908–
1996	Carlos Filipe Ximenes Belo José Ramos-Horta	For their work towards a just and peaceful solution to the conflict in East Timor	East Timor East Timor	1948– 1949–
1997	International Campaign to Ban Landmines (ICBL) Jody Williams		United States	1950–

Year	Recipient	Distinguished Service	Country	Life Span
1998	John Hume	For their efforts to find a	N. Ireland	1944–
	David Trimble	peaceful solution to the conflict in Northern Ireland	N. Ireland	1944–
1999	Doctors Without Borders	In recognition of the organization's pioneering humanitarian work on several continents		
2000	Kim Dae Jung	For his work for democracy and human rights in South Korea and in East Asia in general and for peace and reconciliation with North Korea in particular		
2001	The United Nations (U.N.)			
	Kofi Annan	Secretary general of the U.N. For their work for a better organized and more peaceful world	Ghana	1938–
2002	Jimmy Carter	For his decades of untiring effort to find peaceful solutions to international conflicts	United States	1924–
2003	Shirin Ebadi	For her efforts for democracy and human rights, especially the rights of women and children in Iran and the Muslim world in general	Iran	1947–
2004	Wangari Maathai	For her contribution to sustainable development, democracy and peace	Africa	1940–
2005	International Atomic Energy Agency	For their efforts to prevent nuclear energy from being used for military purposes and to ensure that nuclear	Vienna, Austria	1957
	Mohamed ElBaradei	energy for peaceful purposes is used in the safest possible way.	Egypt	1942

Index